Redrawing the Lines

Redrawing the Lines: Analytic Philosophy, Deconstruction, and Literary Theory

Reed Way Dasenbrock
Editor

University of Minnesota Press, *Minneapolis*

Published by the University of Minnesota Press
2037 University Avenue Southeast, Minneapolis, MN 55414.
Printed in the United States of America.

Library of Congress Catalog Card Number 89-40293

ISBN 0-8166-1726-0   ISBN 0-8166-1727-9 (pbk.)

The University of Minnesota
is an equal-opportunity
educator and employer.

Contents

Minnesota

Acknowledgments

I wish to acknowledge, first of all, the help of all of the contributors to this collection of essays, for agreeing to contribute to the collection, for recommending other potential contributors, for being so responsible about deadlines, for responding to my editorial suggestions and queries with grace and patience, and for help with the bibliography, as well as, of course, for writing such excellent essays. I alone know how much both the introduction and the bibliography owe to the contributors' previous work on all these questions as well as to their work published here. Richard Rorty has been a help from the beginning, and I also thank Henry Staten for a helpful reading of my introduction; Jules Law, Sam Wheeler, Richard Shusterman, Steven Winspur, and Mike Fischer for sharing unpublished work with me; Henry Staten and Christopher Norris for sending me their contributions so far in advance of the deadline, which helped to get the whole project off the ground; and Charlie Altieri for his support of my work over the past few years. Tony Cascardi suggested writing an afterword and did so on a tight deadline. My thanks to everyone.

I would also like to thank Terry Cochran, my editor at the University of Minnesota Press, without whom this book would not exist. His advice and help have been invaluable. Eric Halpern, Sam Weber, Robert Con Davis, and Donald Davidson have also given useful advice. I also need to thank New Mexico State University for a sabbatical leave during which the bulk of my work on this book was completed. I would not have been able to complete the Annotated Bibliography without the help of the New Mexico State University Library's Interlibrary Loan Office; Sandra Valenzuela, Pat Martinez, and Fran Martinez have been extremely helpful on this project (and on many others as well). I would also like to thank my colleagues at New Mexico State, Harriet Linkin and Roger Cherry, for reading and commenting on my introduction. This project would have been unthinkable if it were not for years of conversation about Wittgenstein with Hugh Phibbs. I also thank Stanley Fish, who taught me much of what I know about speech-act theory, literary criticism, and the connections between the two.

Finally, my greatest debt is to my family. My part in this book is truly for my wife, Feroza, and my son, Homi.

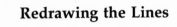

Redrawing the Lines

1

Redrawing the Lines:
An Introduction

Reed Way Dasenbrock

Periods of great vitality in literary criticism always seem to be periods in which criticism is in close working contact with philosophy. Plato and Aristotle are virtually as important in the history of literary criticism as they are in the history of philosophy, in both cases shaping the entire Western tradition, shaping even the reactions against them. More recently, the critical theory of romanticism was deeply imbued with the philosophy of its time, and Samuel Taylor Coleridge provides the point of access for that philosophical culture in English-language thought. In our century, the New Criticism was instigated by the work of T. E. Hulme, I. A. Richards, and T. S. Eliot, three critics educated at Cambridge and Harvard in early analytic philosophy.[1] Although most of the later critics thought of as the New Critics proper, such as Cleanth Brooks, John Crowe Ransom, and R. P. Blackmur, did not have Richards's or Eliot's philosophical training, the most precise and cogent theoretical formulation of New Critical tenets came from the collaboration of the critic W. K. Wimsatt and the aesthetician Monroe Beardsley. And of course the always more overtly philosophical and theoretical criticism of the Continent provides many more examples of such contact, from Heideggerian hermeneutics to the rise of structuralism.

Quite commonly, as in the case of the New Criticism, after an initial and fruitful period of contact, disciplinary frontiers get reestablished. Critics then begin to speak of the illegitimacy of borrowing ideas from other disciplines and to think of literary criticism as a freestanding discipline. Northrop Frye's *Anatomy of Criticism* provides one apposite example of this tendency, with his talk of literary criticism needing its own conceptual sources:

> The axioms and postulates of criticism, however, have to grow out of the art it deals with. The first thing the literary critic has to do is to read literature, to make an inductive survey of his own field and let his critical prin-

ciples shape themselves solely out of his knowledge of that field. Critical principles cannot be taken over ready-made from theology, philosophy, politics, science, or any combination of these. (6–7)

But once the literary critics have declared literary criticism a world unto itself, new winds of intellectual commerce start up, and new schools of criticism less intellectually isolated come into existence. These new schools, remembering the isolationism but forgetting the interaction that preceded it, always present themselves as theory-rich as opposed to their theory-poor predecessors. Hence, the proud complaint of Geoffrey Hartman at the beginning of a new cycle: "The separation of philosophy from literary studies has not worked to the benefit of either" (*Deconstruction and Criticism* ix). Here Hartman acts as if no one before him had ever connected the two disciplines.[2] But deconstruction, Hartman's new point of contact between philosophy and literary criticism, quickly enough became a new interpretive method practiced by literary critics without much grounding in the philosophical tradition from which it came.[3] So the cycle goes around again.

The last fifteen to twenty years have been extraordinarily vital ones in literary criticism, and again much of the stimulus has been provided by a close working relationship between philosophers and literary critics. But this most recent period of close contact has seen an interesting variant on the others: not just one but two different (and in some senses radically opposed) philosophical traditions have entered into commerce with literary criticism—deconstruction and analytic philosophy.

Of the two, the one that has attracted more attention is clearly deconstruction. Initially both hailed and reviled as the sharpest possible antagonist to ordinary modes of criticism, and now often criticized as less radical than it once seemed, deconstruction has been everywhere with us, inspiring debate and comment not only across a number of disciplines in the university but also in the popular media. Its impact has been largest, however, among literary critics, and certainly much of the enthusiasm for deconstruction came from "the assumption that 'deconstruction has deconstructed the boundaries between philosophy and literary criticism.' " (Staten, "Review of Culler and Norris" 876).[4] One important and insufficiently recognized consequence of the impact of deconstruction on English-language academic culture has been that it has established a proximate point of entry for the larger Continental philosophical tradition on which it depends.[5] Hegel, Nietzsche, Husserl, and Heidegger, to name four central figures, are now often cited and have been assimilated to an extent inconceivable even twenty years ago, when they were regarded as a group of justly forgotten, obscurantist, and totalitarian figures by most of the English-speaking world. Hegel was closely identified with Prussian Junkerism and Nietzsche and Heidegger with Nazism, Nietzsche as the supposed source of Nazi thinking and Heidegger for his actual collaboration with the Nazis at the beginning of the Third Reich (as well as for his silence on the subject for thirty years after the war). For these reasons and because of the difficulty of their thought, none of these philosophers (except Nietzsche, to a certain extent, as an influence on existentialism) had much currency in English-speaking culture as a whole. And they had little if any more currency in philosophy departments. Anglo-American philosophy saw itself as a radically different (and superior) kind of philosophy from the very loose and sloppy thinking indulged in on the Continent in which language seemed to have gone "on holiday" and given itself up to metaphysical nonsense.

There had been, of course, a very strong current of British Hegelianism in the late nineteenth century, but the revolution in English philosophy led by G. E. Moore and Bertrand Russell at the turn of the century killed off Hegelianism in England. Philosophy was to be analytic, not speculative, and concerned with mathematics and logic, not with metaphysical system-building in the grand sense. Subsequent analytic philosophers were inspired by the belief that analytic philosophy of language had revealed most famous issues of philosophy to be little more than linguistic muddles. As Peter Strawson put it looking back, "In the face of this refined examination of actual linguistic practice, a lot of traditional philosophical theorizing began to look extraordinarily crude, like an assemblage of huge, crude mistakes" (Magee 116). From this perspective, Continental philosophy looked like a continuation of these "huge, crude mistakes" with which serious philosophers need not concern themselves. Richard Rorty amusingly describes the attitudes inculcated during his education toward the tradition that has shaped deconstruction:

> During the same period, students of analytic philosophy were encouraged to keep their reading in literature well clear of their philosophical work and to avoid reading German philosophy between Immanuel Kant and Gottlob Frege. It was widely believed that reading Hegel rotted the brain. (Reading Friedrich Nietzsche and Heidegger was thought to have even worse effects — doing so might cause hair to sprout in unwonted places, turning one into a snarling fascist beast.) ("Deconstruction and Circumvention" 21)

Lest Rorty's description be taken as purely humorous, one might cite Marjorie Grene, a long-standing opponent of this cast of mind, who quotes Elizabeth Anscombe's description of contemporary Continental philosophy: "Of course everybody knows everything written on the continent is just gas" (37). This was the standard view of Continental philosophy held by Anglo-American philosophers, still held by many today, and for anyone still holding this view, the recent revival of interest in these "snarling fascist beasts" must be utterly bewildering. Moore and Russell had cleared the English-speaking world of their influence, but here they are again, though this time influencing misguided literary critics more than philosophers. So much the worse, one can imagine these philosophers saying, for literary criticism.

But at the same time that Continental philosophy, at least in the form of deconstruction, was winning a renewed hearing and proving itself influential for students of literature, so too was the philosophy that prided itself on its difference from the Continental tradition. Less noticed than deconstruction but nearly as pervasive has been the emergence of schools of criticism deeply indebted to Anglo-American philosophy of language. If Jacques Derrida is the key figure for literary critics learning from the Continental tradition, J. L. Austin is the equivalent figure for the Anglo-American, and Austin's work has been increasingly influential in literary theory.

Austin's influence can be seen most clearly in the reader-response school of criticism, particularly that of Stanley Fish. Austin's speech-act theory developed in *How to Do Things with Words* argued that what we did with words was primary, their truth or reference secondary. Comparably, Fish's emphasis was on what poems *did* as opposed to what they meant. These approaches might seem diametrically opposed given Austin's emphasis on the speaker and Fish's emphasis on the reader, but both replace questions of the relation of the word to the world with questions about relating the speaker/writer to the listener/reader. A concern with meaning is replaced by a concern with effects in a way that clearly links Fish's "affective stylistics" to speech-act theory.

Beyond Fish's reader-response criticism, other literary critics and theorists were listening to Anglo-American philosophy at the same time that deconstruction was beginning to have an impact. Richard Ohmann among others tried to apply Austin's work to literary texts more directly than Fish had; Mary Louise Pratt's ground-breaking *Towards a Speech Act Theory of Literature* (1977) also incorporated Paul Grice's related work on conversation and "conversational implicature." And slightly later Charles Altieri drew upon a range of Anglo-American philosophers, Wittgenstein, Austin, Grice, and Donald Davidson among others, in his *Act and Quality* (1981).

So in the years between 1965 and 1975, there was a renewal of contact between philosophy and literary criticism. But this renewal was somewhat paradoxical in that critics were attending to two different philosophical traditions that had little to do with each other and saw each other in extremely negative terms (when they paid any attention to each other at all). Continental philosophers did not reciprocate the horror with which they were regarded by Anglo-American philosophers as much as repay it with indifference. But given the increasing contact between each tradition and literary theory, this situation was not likely to last. Inevitably, these two philosophical traditions would come into contact with each other.

The moment of contact can be conveniently dated: 1977. In Montreal in 1971, Jacques Derrida had given a paper, "Signature événement contexte," that was largely a critique of Austin from a perspective close to that of his larger work, *Of Grammatology* (1967). When a translation of the paper on Austin appeared in the first issue of *Glyph* in 1977, Searle responded to Derrida's criticism of Austin; Derrida in turn responded to Searle's response in the next issue in a piece entitled "Limited Inc abc." Searle's piece was called "Reiterating the Differences," and certainly that was the initial effect of this exchange. At the beginning of his essay,

Searle explicitly invoked the model I have been using so far of two traditions of philosophy, one Continental and the other Anglo-American:

> It would be a mistake, I think, to regard Derrida's discussion of Austin as a confrontation between two prominent philosophical traditions. This is not so much because Derrida has failed to discuss the central theses in Austin's theory of language, but rather because he has misunderstood and misstated Austin's position at several crucial points, as I shall attempt to show, and thus the confrontation never quite takes place. (198)

As might be expected, Derrida in his response problematized Searle's assumption that he or Searle stood (or could be said to stand) for a larger philosophical tradition, but clearly the style and tone of "Limited Inc abc" were such a radical departure from any Anglo-American notion of philosophical argumentation that it seemed to confirm Searle's judgment. Searle and Derrida seemed like two ships in the night, passing in opposite directions and not even sharing a common language in which to exchange signals. (And this, of course, was grist for Derrida's mill, as his critique of Austin was precisely for Austin's privileging communicative success over communicative failure.) The Derrida-Searle exchange seemed a clear communicative failure, showing deep differences in philosophical method and philosophical positions between the two respective traditions.

The very first sentence of "Signature Event Context" questions something Searle wants to take for granted: "Is it certain that to the word *communication* corresponds a concept that is unique, univocal, rigorously controllable, and transmittable: in a word, communicable?" (172). For Searle, the general success of human communication, of speech acts, is axiomatic and goes without question. And Searle presents himself as a serious inquirer, wanting to get on with the job of understanding how—not why—ordinary language worked. For Derrida, Searle's stance already begs too many questions. Much more playful in style (although for a ["serious"?] reason), Derrida does not want to assume what Searle assumes to get to grips with his subject. Instead, Derrida wants to question every step Searle makes, not allowing him any tactical or provisional exclusions or assumptions. And although at times it is unclear whether Derrida has a different set of axiomatic assumptions about language or simply will not let Searle make any unquestioned assumptions, the exchange reveals a wide gulf between these two philosophers and their respective modes of inquiry.

Despite (or perhaps because of) its failure to produce any agreement, this exchange provoked a tremendous amount of interest among literary critics. And I think this was because the terms of this debate were so close to the terms of the debate already under way about deconstruction in literary criticism. As it began to be influential in American literary criticism in the mid-1970s, deconstruction quickly was attacked for its tendency to diverge radically from commonsense readings of a text. Deconstruction was widely presented—by critics and supporters alike—as a form of skepticism challenging Anglo-Saxon norms of common sense, and those critics opposing deconstruction from a commonsense perspective took on the role of Dr. Johnson refuting the skepticism of Berkeley and Hume by kicking a stone. In this context, Searle's position seemed to offer philosophical support for critics of deconstruction, which was particularly useful since deconstructive critics presented deconstruction as more "philosophical" than Anglo-American modes of criticism. For those convinced that the advocates of common sense had, as the Irish say of Dr. Johnson, kicked the stone but missed the point, Derrida's dazzling tour de force of (non)argument showed the intellectual superiority of deconstruction. Derrida had successfully deconstructed the philosophical support for Anglo-American criticism as he had the interpretive method. So literary critics paid a good deal of attention to this exchange—much more than did philosophers—because it was so congruent with debates already in progress in literary theory, and this reinforced both the sense that literary theory could benefit by attending to philosophy and the sense that these two philosophical traditions had little to do with each other. Paradoxically, the space separating literary theorists and philosophers seemed smaller than that separating different species of philosophers.

Yet that was only the first take, and the net result of the Derrida-Searle exchange has been rather different from what anyone might have expected in 1977. As the Annotated Bibliography to this volume should show, it sparked a wide-ranging discussion of the exchange and the issues at stake. At first, the discussion continued in the spirit of the initial exchange: there was a good deal of what one could call Searle-bashing, discussions of the exchange by partisans of deconstruction convinced that Derrida was utterly correct on all points, and a certain amount of Derrida-bashing from the other side. And the metaphor of two sides continued to be apposite, invoked by Searle- and Derrida-bashers alike. But all this discussion meant that more and more literary critics were reading philosophy of language in order to try to understand the context of the exchange, and in this process the work of other Anglo-American philosophers was brought into a widening discussion. Soon it began to be understood that the model advanced by Searle of two traditions in stark confrontation was not the only way to represent either the Derrida-Searle exchange or the recent history of philosophy. Shoshana Felman in Le Scandale du corps parlant (1980; trans. 1983) and Stanley Fish in "With the Compliments of the Author" (1982) revised our sense of the sides in the Derrida-Searle exchange by presenting a view of Austin as in some respects closer to Derrida than to Searle. Wittgenstein had already been invoked by Derrida-bashers such as M. H. Abrams and Charles Altieri as a commonsense philosopher of language who could be opposed to the skeptical position of Derrida. But later work, preeminently Henry Staten's Wittgenstein and Derrida (1984), argued for a reading of Wittgenstein, comparable to Felman's and Fish's Austin, as in substantial agreement with Derrida. (And Staten's work is continued, if on different lines, in the essays by Jules David Law and Steven Winspur in this collection.) Most of these arguments referred as I have so far to two traditions in the way Searle had; yet they also revised that picture substantially by successively capturing stars of the Anglo-American firmament for the other side. And this meant that once-sharp distinctions between Anglo-American and Continental philosophy began to erode.

Moreover, this was in keeping with other developments in philosophy: other analytically trained philosophers, in particular Richard Rorty and Stanley Cavell, were working in directions that helped to blunt any sense of two sharply opposed traditions. The work of Cavell, discussed in this collection by Michael Fischer, is important in this context both because of his repositioning of Wittgenstein in *The Claim of Reason* (1979) as less an opponent of skepticism than someone deeply responsive to its claims and because of his willingness in *The Claim of Reason*, *The Senses of Walden* (1972), and other works to discuss literary texts and to take their cognitive claims seriously.[6] The work of Rorty — discussed in this collection by Christopher Norris — is important because he has done more than anyone else to rewrite our sense of the recent history of philosophy. In *Philosophy and the Mirror of Nature* (1979), Rorty presented the work of Wittgenstein, Heidegger, and John Dewey as all parallel "deconstructions" of philosophy's traditional claim to privilege, to be the discipline that adjudicates the claims to knowledge advanced by the others. Philosophy had long presented itself as the epistemological foundation for all disciplines of knowledge, but these antifoundational philosophers argued that there was no such foundation to knowledge. Each discipline offers its own way of knowing, and philosophy should not place itself in a position of privilege vis-à-vis these ways of knowing. Rorty's alignment of figures from very different philosophical traditions as all turning on and questioning those traditions replaces Searle's distinction between two sharply opposed traditions with a distinction between those of each tradition who want to continue the old project of philosophy and those of each tradition who challenge the project. Derrida, though not extensively discussed in *Philosophy and the Mirror of Nature*, clearly belongs with Wittgenstein in the second category (as does Rorty himself). The total disagreement between Searle and Derrida may result less from their respective philosophical traditions than from the fact that Derrida — unlike Searle — is questioning traditional foundationalist claims of philosophy: "The weakness of Searle's treatment of Derrida is that he thinks of him as doing amateurish philosophy of language rather than as asking metaphilosophical questions about the value of such philosophy" (Rorty, "Deconstruction and Circumvention" 22). And Felman's and Fish's revisionist version of J. L. Austin (endorsed by Rorty[7]) may position him less as a deconstructionist *malgré lui* than as a philosopher sharing in the widespread questioning of "the idea of philosophy as a sort of universal science which can 'place' all other cultural activities" ("Deconstruction and Circumvention" 22).

Rorty's characterization of the recent history of philosophy does a good deal to bridge the gap between the two philosophical traditions.[8] It also does a good deal to bridge the gap between philosophy and literary theory: if philosophy is not the master discipline, then philosophers, like literary theorists, are simply people reading and interpreting texts and the philosophy-literature distinction is as factitious as any that separates analytic from deconstructive philosophers. And

Rorty both in *Philosophy and the Mirror of Nature* and in his essays (many of which are collected in *Consequences of Pragmatism*) has argued explicitly for a convergence of literature and philosophy:

> Pace Culler, I think that all of us—Derrideans and pragmatists alike—should try to work ourselves out of our jobs by conscientiously blurring the literature-philosophy distinction and promoting the idea of a seamless, undifferentiated "general text." . . . The only form of the philosophy-literature distinction which we need is one drawn in terms of the (transitory and relative) contrast between the familiar and the unfamiliar, rather than in terms of a deeper and more exciting contrast between the representational and the nonrepresentational, or the literal and the metaphorical. ("Deconstruction and Circumvention" 3)

So in the wake of all these redefinitions, the initial sense of sharp confrontation found in the Derrida-Searle exchange gave way quickly enough to a very different sense of convergence. Although Rorty has been criticized for the sometimes breezy way in which he groups together disparate intellectual phenomena, after his work absolute distinctions once customarily drawn between Anglo-American and Continental philosophy or between philosophy and literary theory no longer seem self-evident.

Yet this picture of converging traditions needs two further qualifications. First, ironically, if in keeping with the history I have just outlined, Rorty's (and Cavell's) work toward convergence has been much better received in literary circles than in philosophical ones. The interaction of the two traditions is still to a large extent taking place on the grounds of literary theory, in literary journals and with literary theorists as the interested spectators. I think it fair to say that a majority of analytically trained philosophers still do not quite understand what the fuss is about. They are aware of a tremendous interest in philosophy of language among literary critics, but are suspicious of it, thinking that literary critics cannot quite handle the terms and methods of analytic inquiry. Cavell himself—despite his interest in literature—offers an example of this when he writes that "the invocations of the name of philosophy in current literary debate are frequently not comprehensible to me as calls upon philosophy" ("Politics" 185). Moreover, most analytic philosophers retain their suspicion of the Continental tradition. They may have read some Derrida, but they do not quite see why they should be interested in him. And Rorty's call for philosophers to put themselves out of business is understandably received with even less enthusiasm, as the gains in such a move seem much less clear than the losses.

However, it is also fair to say, lest that account sound uncharitable, that analytic philosophers have shown much more interest in grappling with their Continental counterparts than vice versa, just as literary theorists oriented toward the Anglo-American tradition have been much more responsive to deconstruction than deconstructive critics have been to the Anglo-American tradition. Jacques Bouveresse's essay "Why I Am So Very unFrench" is an apposite document here, as testimony from a French analytic philosopher of the combination of hostility toward and ignorance of Anglo-American philosophy in France: "A French philosopher who openly displayed his sympathy for the analytic tradition at the time when I began to do so . . . could, even in the best of cases, never hope to be considered as anything but marginal or eccentric by the French philosophical milieu'' (11). Derrida himself has never betrayed an awareness of any philosopher in England or America other than Austin and Searle. Michel Foucault's vague references to "the speech act referred to by the English analysts'' in *The Archaeology of Knowledge* (83) indicates only the most minimal awareness of speech-act theory, and there is no French equivalent to Rorty, no one translating the arguments of Wittgenstein, Austin, Grice, Quine, and Davidson, to mention only a few names, as he has the arguments of Heidegger, Derrida, and others. To quote Bouveresse again: "Everything leads one to believe that the opposition between the analytic and continental traditions is gradually being transformed into a marked anachronism. But it is probable that France will for some time to come continue to make itself ridiculous by combating as a threat that which the philosophy of most other countries will have long ago integrated as a positive and essential contribution'' (14–15).

There is a comparable asymmetry among literary theorists in North America. Advocates of deconstruction seem much less informed about Anglo-American philosophy than those in the analytic camp are about deconstruction. Geoffrey Hartman can blithely argue for literary theory learning from philosophy in the passage already quoted from *Deconstruction and Criticism* without specifying what philosophy he had in mind as if philosophy and deconstruction were coterminous. Elsewhere, he has characterized the opposition between deconstruction and its critics in this way:

> There is, instead, a new isolationism masking under the name of Common Sense and characterizing what it opposes as Skywriting. The Skywriters march under the banner of Hegel and Continental Philosophy, while the Common Sense school is content with no philosophy, unless it be that of Locke and a homespun organicism. (*Criticism in the Wilderness* 255)

Perhaps because he feels that he will be in a stronger rhetorical position if he can identify deconstruction with philosophy itself, Hartman always presents deconstructive criticism as theory-rich and philosophical in contrast to the theory-poor, antiphilosophical opposition to deconstruction, ignoring completely that criticism's philosophical commitments. (And we will return to this sense of the relation between theory and philosophy later.) In the same vein, Edward Said's remarks contrasting the work of Derrida and Foucault to Anglo-American philosophy in *The World, the Text, and the Critic* (1983) are embarrassing in what they reveal about his awareness of contemporary Anglo-American philosophy:

> Thus, potentially at least, contemporary criticism exists to confront problems of the sort abandoned by philosophy when it became as insular and

scholastic as it became in the Anglo-American tradition. The problem of
language and of its unique and difficult being is central to this criticism.
(183)

It is difficult to imagine how anyone with the slightest knowledge of Anglo-
American philosophy could imply that it has failed to confront the problem of
language. The more common criticism is that it has done nothing else.

Those critics who do cite analytic philosophers are scarcely more satisfactory.
I have discussed elsewhere the inadequacies of Jonathan Culler's discussion of
Austin and Wittgenstein in *On Deconstruction* (1982). Even more peculiar is his
habit in the earlier *Structuralist Poetics* of quoting Wittgenstein frequently but
with the attribution only in the notes, as if it were taboo to mention his name in
the text. To cite one typical example:

> Structuralist discussions may seem to promote such a view by their failure
> to isolate and praise an author's 'conscious art', but the reason is simply
> that here, as in most other human activities of any complexity, the line be-
> tween the conscious and unconscious is highly variable, impossible to
> identify, and supremely uninteresting. '*When* do you know how to play
> chess? All the time? or just while you are making a move? And the *whole*
> of chess during each move?' (118)

Only if one recognizes this quotation from the *Philosophical Investigations* or
looks up the footnote, can one realize that Wittgenstein — not a "structuralist discussion" — is being quoted here. This appropriation of Wittgenstein is also a misunderstanding of him, for Wittgenstein — unlike Culler or the structuralists — is
supremely interested in the question Culler dismisses here, the line between the
conscious and the unconscious, and he asks these questions to raise the issue, not
to bury it. Similarly, Stanley Cavell has pointed out the eccentricity of Paul de
Man's use of Austin's terms "performative" and "constative" in *Allegories of
Reading* (1979): "So far as I understand his sense of what he wants the distinction to do, it contradicts Austin's" (192).[9] Against this dismal record, one can set
only the work of some of the contributors to this volume, Henry Staten's *Wittgenstein and Derrida* and Christopher Norris's *The Deconstructive Turn* and *The
Contest of Faculties* as examples of work by younger critics committed to deconstruction yet well informed about other philosophies of language and meaning.

Although I am not sure why this asymmetry exists, it seems to me admirable
that distinguished philosophers such as Rorty and Cavell or younger philosophers
such as Alexander Nehamas, Samuel Wheeler, and Richard Shusterman are willing to open themselves to new and challenging philosophical perspectives. But
however one takes this asymmetry, two points remain crucial here and have
helped to shape the collection of essays that follow. First, the interaction between
analytic philosophy and deconstruction has occupied literary theorists more than
philosophers and analytic more than deconstructive philosophers. Only now is
this interaction becoming of as much interest for philosophers as it has been for

literary theorists for a decade. Second, the interaction began in a confrontation that has gradually been replaced by moments and areas of convergence. And the result of these factors is that our map of the philosophical world is a more complex and variegated one than it might have been a generation ago, and our sense of the connection between philosophy and literary theory is also complex and variegated. For some, they have become virtually one discipline; for others, they have (or should have) little to do with each other.

Given this complex situation, the preceding narrative should be defined clearly as my own, the product of an American literary critic, educated in Canada, England, and the United States, interested in literary theory but not a "theorist," largely self-taught in philosophy, and more sympathetic to analytic philosophy than to deconstruction. Someone else writing in another place with different training might offer a different narrative with different points of emphasis. But I offer this sketch, even if it is not a definitive account, as a way to set a context for the essays collected in this volume, all of which are devoted to a critical examination of the interaction between analytic philosophy and deconstruction that has been taking place on the ground of literary theory. The contributors include both philosophers and literary theorists interested in this interaction and the related but partially independent interaction between literary theory and philosophy. Given the asymmetry I have described here, this also means that the contributors are primarily trained in analytic rather than Continental modes of inquiry. But given the shift from confrontation to convergence, the contributors are all interested less in bashing the other side, whoever that may be, than in moving beyond a sense of confrontation and of there being two sides. So the question is not who was right, but rather where do we go from here? What do the two traditions have in common? Where do they diverge? Are there really two traditions in the way we have assumed? Or is there another, more useful way of presenting the recent history of philosophy? Why has there been this turn toward philosophy on the part of literary theory? What consequences does this have for philosophy and for literary theory? What distinctions remain between the two aside from departmental addresses and footnoting conventions?

I do not think one set of answers to these questions emerges from the essays that follow. This is not an anthology committed in advance to a particular set of answers. If there is agreement, it is that these are important questions and that a conversation among philosophers and literary theorists of differing persuasions ought to continue. But it is as it should be that each contributor has a different turn to take in this conversation. There are, of course, some common points of reference in the conversation that follows: the Derrida-Searle exchange is one such common point; the invocation by Abrams, Altieri, and others of Wittgenstein as an alternative to deconstruction is another; Rorty's attempt to shut down the enterprise of foundational philosophy is a third. But each contributor has a distinct sense of what issues and philosophers are central in the interaction being depicted, and I hope this overlay of perspectives serves to orient readers to the history of the interaction to date and provides some direction for it.

Where it should go is, of course, the most important question. There are those, I expect, who think it should not go anywhere, and rather than going on to summarize the articles that follow, I would like to turn now to the various objections that might be made to this project of redrawing the lines that have fenced off deconstruction, analytic philosophy, and literary theory. By considering these objections, we can obtain a sharper sense of the project of the present collection. What follows will therefore be argumentative, in contrast to the narrative that has concerned us so far, but that should help to introduce the essays that follow, which tend to establish their own perspective by contesting other perspectives.

Two sets of people would obviously object to the project of deconstruction and analytic philosophy interacting with each other, namely, those who think deconstruction is right about everything and those who think analytic philosophy is right about everything — in the terms used earlier, unreconstructed Searle-bashers and unreconstructed Derrida-bashers. There are probably more of each category around than one might expect after a decade or so of convergence as well as confrontation, but these challenges internal to the discipline of philosophy are fairly fully answered, I think, by the essays in this collection.

Someone who thinks deconstruction has nothing to learn from analytic modes of philosophy might look at two different sets of essays in this collection to have this conviction challenged. Most obviously, one would look to Richard Shusterman's "Organic Unity: Analysis and Deconstruction," which exposes deconstruction's reliance on a notion of organic unity it claims to have deconstructed, and to Michael Fischer's "Stanley Cavell's Wittgenstein," which relates Cavell's response to skepticism to Derrida in a challenging way. These aspects of these essays suggest why we still need moments of confrontation and how we might use the resources of one way of doing philosophy to contest and challenge the less powerful aspects of the other. But the essays by Staten, Wheeler, Law, and Winspur may be more persuasive here to an advocate of deconstruction, for they establish common ground between Anglo-American and deconstructive philosophers in ways that should persuade anyone of the power of the analytic tradition. I am thinking here of Staten's use of Wittgensteinian language in his deconstruction of Putnam and Kripke in "The Secret Name of Cats: Deconstruction, Intentional Meaning, and the New Theory of Reference," Wheeler's use of Davidson to explicate de Man's views on metaphor in "Metaphor according to Davidson and de Man," Law's exposition of some points of agreement between Wittgenstein and Derrida, and Winspur's sketch of a Wittgensteinian theory in "Text Acts: Recasting Performatives with Wittgenstein and Derrida" that would build on Austin's speech-act theory in ways that answer Derrida's objections to Austin. So if one accepts the view advanced by Rorty and others that — despite obvious differences in modes of argumentation — the Anglo-American and Continental modes of philosophizing increasingly share a common perspective, these essays should help articulate that common ground.

But there is a counter to that claim, for it might be said that one of the things deconstruction aims to deconstruct is precisely the notion of argument I rely on here, that is, the notion of putting views more clearly, of a shareable terrain of exposition and argumentation. And here one encounters a fairly fundamental split among those who align themselves with the term ''deconstruction.''[10] On the one hand, early works by Derrida such as *Speech and Phenomena* and *Of Grammatology* seem to me to be carefully argued, even scholarly in their mode of procedure, and, likewise, explicators of deconstruction such as Culler and Norris argue that deconstruction is a ''rigorous'' way of working that can be argued for. On the other hand, later ''texts'' of Derrida such as *Glas* or ''Living On/Border Lines'' and work by various of his American disciples such as Geoffrey Hartman clearly dispense with and want to deconstruct any recognizable modes of argumentation. So we may need to make a distinction here between the side of deconstruction that prides itself on its ''rigor'' and the side that questions rigor and argumentation, ''deconstruction on the wild side'' as it has been called by Christopher Norris (*Deconstruction: Theory and Practice* 92–99). This distinction is close to that already made by Gasché and Staten between a philosophically informed deconstruction and deconstruction as it becomes an institutionalized interpretive method, and they use that distinction to differentiate between Derrida and some of his followers:

> Many deconstructionist critics have chosen simply to ignore the profoundly philosophical thrust of Derridean thought, and have consequently misconstrued what deconstruction consists of and what it seeks to achieve. From the perspective of what I establish here as to the nature of deconstruction, hardly any deconstructionist critic could lay claim to that title. (Gasché, *The Tain of the Mirror* 3)

But enough work by Derrida seems to fall on Norris's ''wild side'' that I do not think Derrida's more playful followers can entirely be blamed for ''deconstruction on the wild side.'' The more ludic side of deconstruction—whether authentic or spurious[11]—is basically ignored in the essays that follow, largely, I think, because no one quite knows how to address an argument to those who question argument. But rigorous deconstructors should be able to see a different kind of rigor in analytic philosophy and should see the advantages of the kind of patient argumentative exposition exemplified here by Wheeler's essay. As Henry Staten has put the case for the interaction of argumentative deconstruction and analytic philosophy, ''The great strength of contemporary American philosophy is in the logical analysis of arguments, and if deconstruction is to gain any recognition from philosophers in this country (as it has been slow to do), deconstructors will have to be willing to submit their arguments to such analysis'' (''Review'' 873).

This objection need not be answered the other way, for anyone committed to an analytic perspective does not need to be convinced of the need for exposition and argumentation. But there are certainly those on the analytic side as well as on the deconstructive side who feel that the two philosophical modes are so different that they can find no common ground. Anthony Appiah, for example, has recently attacked Christopher Norris's attempt in *The Deconstructive Turn*, later strengthened in *The Contest of Faculties*, to find common ground between deconstruction and analytic philosophy. His specific objections to Norris's treatment cannot concern us here, but more generally he thinks the whole project (and hence that of this volume as well) an impossibly flawed one. This perspective is really one with the ludic, antiargumentative deconstructors, for Appiah claims that the attempt to align the two philosophical modes produces "either a distortion of the analytic argument or a trivialization of [Norris's] own post-structuralist claims" (64). East is East and West is West, and never the twain shall meet.

Ironically, Appiah's piece in *Diacritics* immediately follows an excellent exposition by Shekhar Pradhan in "Minimalist Semantics: Davidson and Derrida on Meaning, Use, and Convention" of the similarities between Derrida's and Davidson's anticonventionalist views of language. And that contrast between the prescriptive declaration that there can be no common ground and the patient detailing of such common ground is instructive. Appiah's position is mistaken, I think, for two important reasons. His first mistake is that he holds what a deconstructive critic would call an essentialist vision of both traditions: deconstruction is one kind of thing, philosophical analysis another. But as we have seen by now, deconstruction is emphatically not just one kind of thing. Even if we restrict ourselves to the work of Derrida, the discussion of Husserl in *Speech and Phenomena* that Newton Garver called "a first-rate piece of analytical work in the philosophy of language" (ix) is very different from the play with Hegel in *Glas* celebrated by Geoffrey Hartman in *Saving the Text*. Analytic philosophy is an even more diffuse tradition, containing any number of conflicting positions and methods. Appiah's second mistake is to think that to want to find common ground between deconstruction and analytic philosophy is to want to obliterate all philosophical distinctions, to create a kind of intellectual mush. To find common ground is often to create new distinctions as well as to break down old ones. For example, Donald Davidson's critique of speech-act theory in "Communication and Convention" focuses on exactly the same issue Derrida is concerned with in "Signature Event Context," that is, the failure of speech-act theory to deal with the "non-serious." Davidson recalls Frege's use of the assertion sign to distinguish between pure assertions and other uses of language, but Davidson argues that natural language can never have such an assertion sign, such a clear distinction that obviates the need for interpretation. If an actor in a theater wanted to indicate to the audience that the theater was really on fire (as opposed to there being a fictional fire inside the play), such an assertion sign would be handy: "I really mean it this time, folks." But, as Davidson points out, "It should be obvious that the assertion sign would do no good, for the actor would have used it in the first place, when he was only acting" (270). Language does not come preinterpreted, with tokens that reliably tell us how it is to be taken. "There is no known, agreed upon, publicly recognizable convention for making assertions" (270).

Now, this is extremely close to Derrida in ways that obviously blunt any sense of a total opposition between Anglo-American and Continental philosophy. But this does not eliminate any distinction altogether, for both Derrida and Davidson are criticizing speech-act theory. A false global distinction between Anglo-American and Continental philosophy is replaced here by a local and provisional distinction between a conventionalist and an anticonventionalist view of language. So the answer to the analytic antideconstructionist is virtually the same as to the antianalytic deconstructionist: first, certain—if not all—modes of deconstruction involve argument and can be contested; second, those modes can be strengthened in places—if corrected in others—by analytic modes of argumentation and inquiry. Conversely, analytic arguments can be strengthened in places—if contested in others—by deconstructive arguments. For an example of successful contestation in this collection, I would point to Staten's deconstruction of Hirsch, Kripke, and Putnam; for an example of strengthening, I would point to Wheeler's essay, which infuses Davidson's position on metaphor with de Manian arguments as completely as it infuses de Man's position with Davidsonian arguments. Other essays, such as Richard Shusterman's, contain aspects of both.

As a whole, the essays in this volume suggest that the analytic and deconstructive refusal to engage is on each side a matter of an arbitrary—not an informed—refusal. It is, to put it simply, a matter of prejudice. The line that has been drawn defining the two traditions is an arbitrary one that will not stand up to sustained scrutiny. The Anglo-American tradition of course has deep Continental roots, in Frege, in logical positivism, and in the work of logicians like Tarski; and Wittgenstein—born in Austria but educated at Cambridge, teaching philosophy in English but writing mostly in German—perfectly embodies this connection. So our geographical shorthand terms ''Anglo-American'' and ''Continental'' are not adequate descriptive terms, nor are the methodological terms ''analytic philosophy'' and ''deconstruction.'' For as Rorty has shown, analytic philosophy self-deconstructed, with the work of Wittgenstein, Quine, Davidson, and others, and this is only one of the reasons why both analytic philosophy and deconstruction have only to gain from the interaction now under way between the two.

But what of literary theory in all this? The interaction of analytic philosophy and deconstruction was made easier by the interaction of each tradition with literary theory. But the discussion in the previous section could be taken as implying that now that the two philosophical traditions were well introduced, literary theory could disappear from the scene, its task as mediator well performed. Rorty's answer to this is clear enough. Literary theory and philosophy are just different names for the same thing and we should stop talking as if they are two different things: ''I take 'literary theory,' as the term is currently used in America, to be a species of philosophy, an attempt to weave together some texts traditionally labeled 'philosophical' with other texts not so labeled'' (''Philosophy without Principles'' 136). Certainly anyone reading this collection or much of the recent work cited in the Annotated Bibliography might think that Rorty was right, that the distinction between philosophy and literary theory is an outmoded disciplinary barrier that should disappear. Yet the barrier exists: philosophers teach in philosophy departments and literary theorists teach in literature departments, and only a few people—including Richard Rorty himself, Kenan Professor of Humanities at the University of Virginia—work in institutional situations that reflect the convergence Rorty is calling for.

I think this question of the relation between philosophy and literary theory is worth some reflection. Particularly since institutional and disciplinary frameworks do change—if at a glacial pace—we had better be clear about what relation between literary theory and philosophy we want, for we might get it. If philosophers decide that philosophy is not a separate disciplinary entity, philosophy departments will probably disappear. I am not at all sure, pace Rorty, that this would be a good idea, or that literary theory and philosophy have become different names for the same thing. Convergence is not the same as identity. And this is the important question addressed by Christopher Norris's essay in the collection, "Philosophy as *Not* Just a 'Kind of Writing': Derrida and the Claim of Reason." Norris takes direct aim at Rorty's stand on this question, arguing that Derrida's work does not sanction the obliteration of the philosophy-literature distinction in the way Rorty has claimed. There is an irony here in that it is Norris—the literary theorist—who is concerned with defending the continuing separateness of philosophy while Rorty—the philosopher—wants to abandon it. This demonstrates the powerful convergence of the two at the same time that Norris wants to maintain their separateness.

The question may be less the status of philosophy than the status of literary theory. After all, we have been doing philosophy for 2500 years; literary theory is the new kid on the block. Is it a form of philosophy in which philosophical amateurs in literature departments engage? Or is it a field with its own terrain and intelligibility? And what is its relationship to literary criticism, to the practice of reading and interpreting literary works? These questions have been posed by the convergence I have detailed between philosophy and literary theory, but they have also been posed from the other side, by two new positions within literary theory that would argue for the disengagement of literary theory from the abstract kind of thinking about language and meaning represented by philosophy of language, even for the end of theory itself. These positions perhaps represent a new cycle in that tendency of literary theory we have already noted, wherein after a period of interdisciplinary theory building, the call is sounded for critics to return home and stop "whoring after foreign gods." Both perspectives, that of the antitheorists or antifoundationalists and the new movement toward political and historical criticism now increasingly called the new historicism, would—I think—attack the concerns of this collection of essays as moving in the wrong direction. They would both argue—though for different reasons—that the kind of pure theorizing found in philosophy of language and increasingly in literary theory is not a good model for literary criticism. Criticism should separate itself from philosophy, and literary theory—if it continues to exist—should be firmly subordinate to "practice," to the practice of literary criticism.

Of the two objections, the one that is not addressed in the essays that follow—and that therefore needs to be looked at in more detail—is the antitheoretical objection. An antitheoretical account might well begin by criticizing the way this introduction began. I spoke of the advantages for literary theory deriving from a close proximity to philosophy, and one way of representing that relation would be to put philosophy as the more abstract field "above" literary theory, in just the way many literary theorists have sought to place theory above practice, informing it from on high. The way Geoffrey Hartman, in passages already quoted, congratulated his own critical approach for being "philosophical" is one example of this; another is Gasché's placing philosophical deconstructors above literary deconstructors like Hartman. Even Stanley Fish, in his critique of those who think that theory should direct practice, slips into the same metaphorical representation: "As soon as you descend from theoretical reasoning about your assumptions, you will once again inhabit them" (*Is There a Text in This Class?* 370). Certainly the influence of philosophy on literary theory has gone hand-in-hand with a way of seeing theory as governing critical practice and, usually, seeing philosophy (understood as deconstruction) as governing theory. There is, as Rorty has said, "a tendency to think that literature can take the place of philosophy by *mimicking* philosophy—by being, of all things, epistemological. Epistemology still looks classy to weak textualists" (*Consequences* 156).

This represents a return within literary theory to the model of philosophy as the mirror of nature presented by Rorty. And Rorty's philosophical heroes, Dewey, Heidegger, and Wittgenstein, are heroes precisely for abandoning this dream of philosophy as the master discipline, the mirror of nature. They argue that we should not look to philosophy as a special source of insight, as the way to get a more general view of our problems. Their position can be called antifoundationalism—to use Stanley Fish's term for this position ("Consequences" 112)—as it claims that there are no absolutely secure, context-free ways of knowing grounded in or secured by philosophy. And although both deconstruction and contemporary analytic philosophy are antifoundational in this way, antifoundationalism in literary theory argues that literary theorists should not look elsewhere, even to antifoundationalist philosophy, for a foundation for our particular way of knowing and working.

The most trenchant exposition of antifoundationalism in literary criticism has been Steven Knapp and Walter Benn Michaels's essay "Against Theory," which argues against theory as an autonomous, adjudicative realm in literary studies in a way closely parallel to (and influenced by) Rorty's argument against philosophy. The other major influence on their position is the work of Stanley Fish, particularly his claim advanced in *Is There a Text in This Class?* and elsewhere that theory has no consequences, that a change in theoretical beliefs should have no effect on critical practice. But Knapp and Michaels out-Rorty Rorty and out-Fish

Fish: Rorty calls for an end to philosophy's dream of mastery and Fish argues that theory has no consequences; in the same vein, Knapp and Michaels call for an end to theory's dream of mastery over practice, but they go on to argue for an end to theory itself. And from this hard antitheoretical position, surely the project of deconstruction and analytic philosophy finding common ground should be of no interest to literary critics per se. It should simply be considered a development in a neighboring country, not something to be slavishly or even carefully paid attention to. And this call for a pullback from theory and from engagement with the disciplines that have been interacting with theory has been widely sympathized with.

Obviously, I think this account of the (foreign) relations that should obtain between literary criticism and a neighboring state called philosophy is incorrect. Otherwise I would hardly have edited a collection of essays on philosophy and literary theory. But although there are flaws in the antitheoretical project, its attack on the previously generally accepted way of conceptualizing the theory-practice and the literary theory-philosophy relation helps us to see how those relations ought to be conceptualized, how theory and philosophy ought to interact. As Rorty points out in "Philosophy without Principles," that accepted way of thinking about the relation of theory and practice is vertical: either theory is above practice (Fish's heights of theoretical reasoning) or below it (as its foundation), but in either metaphor it is thought of as in a position of mastery. And I agree completely with Rorty's suggestion in this reply to Knapp and Michaels that they are right in wanting to replace this vertical model, but wrong in thinking that this requires an end to theory.

The first point to be made about the antitheoretical project is that it is caught up in a number of paradoxes. The first and most obvious one is that its attack against theory is itself a piece of theory. And this is true both in the weak sense of theory as a reflection of practice and in the stronger sense of theory as an attempt to regulate practice. The problem with theory, according to Knapp and Michaels, is that it tells us what to do, so we should stop doing it. But here, of course, Knapp and Michaels start doing theory, start telling us what to do. Related to this is a paradox in our reception of Rorty's antifoundationalist argument: philosophy should not try to stand above us and tell us how to think, Rorty tells us. But why do we listen to him? Precisely—if paradoxically—because he has the great philosophers on his side. So philosophy loses its place of privilege, but it loses it to (antiphilosophical) philosophers. In the antitheoretical argument, theory should lose its place of privilege, but if it does, it will lose it to the antitheoretical theoreticians.

The point to draw from this is not to follow an infinite regress in which the antitheoreticians lose their place of privilege to anti-antitheoreticians, but simply that the site of theory, the site of adjudication, is never and never can be empty. We cannot shut down the business of influencing what others in the field do: we can try to opt out of it, but that can be the most influential move of all. Theory in the sense of directive reflection, the sense developed by Knapp and Michaels, is ineradicable. Every field looks somewhere for direction, and the only choice we have is where to look.

So we could reformulate the argument of "Against Theory" as the less paradoxical claim that we have simply been looking in the wrong direction, that the abstract speculations on meaning and language found in philosophy of language are not that helpful for criticism. But the next paradox is that the antitheoretical argument in general and Knapp and Michaels in particular look as clearly to philosophy as anyone else. They cite Searle, Grice, and Davidson; their argument depends quite directly on Rorty's work; and behind Rorty's work lies the work of Wittgenstein and the American pragmatists, without whom "antifoundationalism" would obviously be impossible. So the work of Knapp and Michaels might have been cited earlier as a perfect example of the way theoretical arguments have been bolstered in recent years by borrowings from analytic philosophy of language.[12]

I would not want to argue, therefore, with the criticism made by Knapp and Michaels of the "vertical" way of thinking about the practice-theory and literary theory-philosophy relation. But their own work exemplifies another way of thinking about the relation between literary theory and philosophy. I would have us do as they do, borrow freely from philosophy in the service of a theoretical argument, rather than do as they say, namely, shut down the theoretical project altogether and write no more articles like "Against Theory." But that does not require placing philosophy in a place of privilege. The central point to grasp is that no one knows in advance where good ideas are going to come from, either in terms of an individual's work or in terms of the discipline as a whole. Good interpretation or good criticism does not get made according to a formula, like Diet Coke.[13] So one cannot say in advance to a practical critic, "Go and read this work of theory and it will give you a theory to use." It does not work that way. Nor can one say to a theoretician, "Go and read philosophy of language, for there you will find the theory of theories." But precisely because there is no way of legislating where ideas come from, neither should one say, "Don't look that way for direction for you won't find anything." Those sorts of directives are utterly dysfunctional.

A more general way of putting this is to say that there can be antifoundationalists, but antifoundationalism is a contradiction in terms. What we can say is that the project of finding a ground for all human knowledge has not been successful, and therefore we recommend that it be abandoned. But if we say that it cannot exist, we have turned back into closet foundationalists. The central gesture of foundational philosophy is to make the general claim, "This is the way things are." What the work of Wittgenstein, Derrida, and others has shown is that all such claims made to date are untrue because they are based on a particular philosophical practice, are part of a given form of life. We have not escaped those particularities and the betting is that we never will. But to say absolutely that we never will is to fall back into the error we are trying to avoid.[14] And I think there is a sense in which Fish and Knapp and Michaels have made a new foundationalism out of antifoundationalism. By making the general claim that no general claim can validly be made, they are still doing theory, still doing philosophy, still making general foundational claims.

So if I can generalize about the problems of generalization, there are two ways of thinking about theory. The first way would see it as developing out of particular cases of practice but then necessarily ordering and informing subsequent practice. Once a theory is arrived at, it is "proved" by showing how many cases it can fit. And the aim of the theoretical enterprise is to build a system in the old philosophical sense. It was precisely this use of theory that was objected to, correctly, by the antifoundationalists. And given Derrida's complete agreement with the Wittgensteinian position sketched earlier, it is more than a little ironic that so many readings by critics influenced by Derrida have this predictable, premeasured feel to them, and that deconstructive critics have been among the worst offenders in claiming a vertical position of privilege for theory, still finding — as Rorty says — epistemology classy. The other way of thinking about theory would suggest that there is no automatic, already given relationship in force between reading a specific text and mulling over a general question that crops up again and again. Nonetheless, such general questions are interesting and worth spending time on, just as the antitheoreticians do. All of us reflect on what we do in addition to doing whatever we do, and theory is a term that covers that activity of reflection as well as the activity of theory building.

Faced with this divided situation, with a plethora of systems and theories and widespread doubt about such systems, one may choose to emphasize either the impulse toward systems or the doubts about them. But in either case, one is still within the realm of theory, that of reflecting about our practices, that of positing, testing, and questioning answers to general questions; and one's position can be sustained by reference to comparable issues and struggles in philosophy. And it is not as an unquestioned authority that theorists should turn to philosophers, but as one neighbor to another, sharing problems and resources. It is in that spirit that the conversation between philosophers and literary theorists in this volume is maintained, I think, and I hope that this interchange can serve as a model for such conversation in the future. Those antitheoretical theoreticians calling for an end to theory are like the people who drive Toyotas but call for import restrictions: they think others should be prevented from doing what they themselves do and like to do. My sense, in contrast, is that the trade imbalance is not that substantial, that philosophers are learning from literary theory as well as vice versa, and that free trade in these matters will benefit us all.

The other position that might object to a continued interaction between theory and philosophy of language is the growing Marxist and historicist current in literary studies. This perspective can take antitheoretical form and argue that what are important in the understanding of any text are local, contextual, and therefore necessarily provisional factors, and therefore one cannot get to a general theory of meaning.[15] Although this position is of course a theoretical position, since it makes a general claim about all interpretation, certainly a critic concerned with contextual, historical factors is going to be less interested in philosophy in the same way that a logician is going to be less interested in literary theory than an aesthetician. The two disciplines share a border, but not everyone lives near that border.

But there is another way of putting the "new historicist" case that is less appealing. This is implicitly addressed in Charles Altieri's essay in this collection, "Judgment and Justice under Postmodern Conditions; or, How Lyotard Helps Us Read Rawls as a Postmodern Thinker," so all I need to do here is quickly sketch a context for that essay. Many newly historicist critics would present themselves not as antitheoreticians but as applied theoreticians, using the insights of recent theory but returning from the "prison house" of theory to the real, historical world. But the theory they would apply is remarkably single-minded and univocal. Thus Edward Said attacks the work of Derrida for its solipsistic textualism and criticizes the quest for a single theory as an idealist flight from the world, but his practical criticism is deeply indebted to Derrida. Likewise for the young new historicists: they have returned to the world with only one side of the recent theoretical discussion in their baggage, generally a combination of Derrida, Foucault, and the poststructuralist Marxism of Althusser and others. In other words, they claim to have moved from theory to a politicized criticism, but they do not seem to have moved too far.

This is the context in which the essay by Altieri in this collection is important. Altieri's point, put simply, is that there is a gap between theory politicized and an adequate political theory. Many of the same tensions already detailed within philosophy of language are replicated within political philosophy. Jean-François Lyotard comes out of much the same milieu as Derrida; John Rawls is in important respects a characteristically Anglo-American philosopher. And the opposition Altieri establishes between them parallels other moments of confrontation between Continental and Anglo-American thought. So I see Altieri's essay as a challenge to the recent wave of "political theory": if you want a political theory, you had better know political theory. Other people have reflected on the relation between power and language besides Marx, Nietzsche, Foucault, and Derrida, and a genuinely political theory (as opposed to simply theory politicized) is going to have to engage these other theoretical approaches to politics. One cannot liquidate all theoretical disputes simply by announcing a politicization of theory.

So while the recent politicization of criticism and the rise of antitheoretical theory both have important consequences for literary studies—most of them, in my opinion, positive—they will not do away with the ongoing interaction between philosophy and literary theory as much as lead that interaction onto new terrain. And this perfectly illustrates how the interaction of literary theory and philosophy does not privilege any particular site of interaction. What I would want to privilege, however, is simply intellectually adventurous work, work that tests and redraws disciplinary lines. I would hope that we can avoid returning to the intellectual isolationism that both in literary theory and in philosophy ineluctably seems to follow periods of interdisciplinary exploration. We need to keep the promising dialogue reflected in the essays collected here vigorous and alive.

Notes

1. Hulme is customarily linked to Bergson and Eliot to Bradley rather than to analytic philosophers, but in an important series of papers, Richard Shusterman has been persuasively arguing for the closeness of Hulme's and Eliot's critical formulations to the philosophical work of Russell and Moore.

2. Richard Shusterman, citing this passage, refers to the myth "propagated by deconstructionist literary theorists . . . that before deconstruction's fortuitous arrival, philosophy and literary studies suffered from a huge and deplorable gap" ("Deconstruction and Analysis" 311).

3. This has been a point made by a number of critics of "Yale school deconstruction," including Gasché and Staten.

4. Staten's point, however, is that this assumption "must not become an excuse for not doing the work that is necessary for anyone who pretends to comment interestingly on philosophy" (876).

5. This claim only apparently contradicts the point made in note 3 that American deconstructionists do not fully grasp the philosophical context of deconstruction. First, whether these critics grasp Continental philosophy or not, they think they do, so their discussions of Hegel, Nietzsche, etc., have certainly made these figures more prominent—if perhaps no better understood—in American cultural discourse. (Cf. Hartman's invocation of Hegel in *Criticism in the Wilderness* and *Saving the Text*.) Second, the gap between American and Continental deconstruction has been pointed out often enough (by Gasché, Staten, etc.) that noting this gap paradoxically becomes a new way for that philosophical tradition to achieve currency. Here I can only posit—not explore in detail—the indebtedness of Derrida to the Continental philosophical tradition; for book-length studies of this issue, see Staten, *Wittgenstein and Derrida*, and Gasché, *The Tain of the Mirror*. Staten's book treats both Continental and analytic traditions, Gasché's only the Continental tradition.

6. Cavell has also deplored the gaps between Continental and Anglo-American philosophy and between philosophy and literary studies: "I was more and more galled by the mutual shunning of the continental and the Anglo-American traditions of philosophizing, and I was finding more and more oppressive the mutual indifference of philosophy and literature to one another" ("Politics" 184). However, he has characterized the current interaction in considerably less positive terms than I have here; in "The Division of Talent," he cites some of the work I would see as connecting philosophy and literature as instead showing "the antagonism of literary and philosophical studies" (522).

7. "Stanley Fish seems to me right in reading *How to Do Things with Words* as saying (about language, if not about philosophy) pretty much what Derrida himself wants to say" ("Deconstruction and Circumvention" 21).

8. Rorty himself has said, however, that "we should not fuss about 'building bridges' between analytic and Continental philosophy. . . . If we put aside wistful talk of bridge-building and joining forces, we can see the analytic-Continental split as both permanent and harmless" (*Consequences of Pragmatism* 225–26). This statement is a little startling, given the amount of just such bridge building Rorty has done. But I think he is suggesting that seeing, say, Heidegger and Wittgenstein as comparable antifoundational philosophers does not cancel the differences in method and style that separate the respective traditions in which they worked. And it is less important to try to cancel those kinds of tradition-specific differences than it is to examine the whole discipline.

9. In the same essay (187–91), Cavell also takes exception to Stanley Fish's appropriation of Austin's term "ordinary language." I think Cavell is right here in pointing out a gap between Austin's use of the term "ordinary" and Fish's (in essays in *Is There a Text in This Class?* such as "How Ordinary Is Ordinary Language?" [97–111] and "How to Do Things with Austin and Searle: Speech-Act Theory and Literary Criticism" [197–245]), but this does not deny Fish's deep indebtedness to Austin's work.

10. Derrida himself has recently expressed some disenchantment with the term. The following parenthesis follows his use of the word deconstruction in his "The Time of a Thesis: Punctuations": "(I use this word for the sake of rapid convenience, though it is a word I have never liked and one whose fortune has disagreeably surprised me)" (44).

11. Richard Shusterman has acutely pointed out some problems with these claims made by Gasché: "Thus Hartman's playful writings are occasionally branded as fraudulent corruptions of deconstruction, despite Hartman's patriarchal status in the movement and his prolonged propinquity to the Derridean presence. Yet the whole idea of the privileging distinctions of essential/marginal, pure/derivative, serious/non-serious seems embarrassingly out of line with the dominant deconstructionist principle of reversing and undoing these privileging hierarchies" ("Deconstruction and Analysis" 316). Christopher Norris's "Methodological Postscript" to *The Deconstructive Turn* (163–73) criticizes Gasché along similar lines.

12. It should be noted, however, that the work of Knapp and Michaels is one of Stanley Cavell's examples in "The Division of Talent" of the antagonism of literary theory to philosophical inquiry. Specifically, Cavell finds Knapp and Michael's call to abandon theory—correctly, I think—to be vastly different in spirit from Wittgenstein's struggle with philosophy, which it superficially resembles.

13. Also relevant here is the antimethodological argument of Paul Feyerabend's *Against Method*, another important source for the antitheoretical position.

14. My argument here relies upon Jules David Law's excellent dissection of the "new pragmatism": "For the pragmatist to designate certain questions as essentialist, and therefore illusory or incoherent, is to work against his own pragmatism. If there are no inherent properties, but only contingent, assigned ones, then there are no cultural activities which are *inherently* antipragmatic, and thus no activities which might *not* still play a part in a pragmatic culture" (328).

15. This is basically the position of Edward Said, who is something of an antitheoretical theorist, although on different lines from Fish, Knapp, and Michaels.

Works Cited

Information on many of the works mentioned in passing can be found in the Annotated Bibliography.

Appiah, Anthony. "Deconstruction and the Philosophy of Language." *Diacritics* 16, No. 1 (Spring 1986): 49–64.

Bouveresse, Jacques. "Why I Am So Very unFrench." In *Philosophy in France Today*. Ed. Alan Montefiore. Cambridge: Cambridge UP, 1983. 9–33.

Cavell, Stanley. "The Division of Talent." *Critical Inquiry* 11, No. 4 (June 1985): 519–38.

———. "Politics as Opposed to What?" 1982. Rpt. in *The Politics of Interpretation*. Ed. W. J. T. Mitchell. Chicago: U of Chicago P, 1983. 181–202.

Culler, Jonathan. *Structuralist Poetics: Structuralism, Linguistics, and the Study of Literature*. Ithaca, N.Y.: Cornell UP, 1975.

Dasenbrock, Reed Way. "Coming to an Understanding of Understanding: Deconstruction, Ordinary Language Philosophy and Contemporary Critical Theory." *Missouri Review* 7, No. 3 (1984): 234–45.

Davidson, Donald. "Communication and Convention." 1982. In *Inquiries into Truth and Interpretation*. Oxford: Oxford UP, 1984. 265–80.

Derrida, Jacques. "Signature Event Context." Trans. Samuel Weber and Jeffrey Mehlman. *Glyph* 1 (1977): 172–97.

———. "The Time of a Thesis: Punctuations." Trans. Kathleen McLaughlin. In *Philosophy in France Today*. Ed. Alan Montefiore. Cambridge: Cambridge UP, 1983. 34–50.

Fish, Stanley. "Consequences." In *Against Theory: Literary Studies and the New Pragmatism*. Ed. W. J. T. Mitchell. Chicago: U of Chicago P, 1985.

_____. *Is There a Text in This Class? The Authority of Interpretive Communities*. Cambridge, Mass.: Harvard UP, 1980.

Foucault, Michel. *The Archaeology of Knowledge*. Trans. A. M. Sheridan Smith. New York: Harper & Row, 1972.

Frye, Northrop. *Anatomy of Criticism: Four Essays*. Princeton, N.J.: Princeton UP, 1957.

Garver, Newton. Introduction to Jacques Derrida, *Speech and Phenomena and Other Essays on Husserl's Theory of Signs*. Evanston, Ill.: Northwestern UP, 1973. ix–xxix.

Gasché, Rodolphe. "Deconstruction as Criticism." *Glyph* 6 (1979): 177–216.

_____. *The Tain of the Mirror: Derrida and the Philosophy of Reflection*. Cambridge, Mass.: Harvard UP, 1986.

_____. "Unscrambling Positions: On Gerald Graff's Critique of Deconstruction." *MLN* 96, No. 5 (December 1981): 1015–34.

Grene, Marjorie. *Philosophy in and out of Europe*. Berkeley: U of California P, 1976.

Hartman, Geoffrey. *Criticism in the Wilderness: The Study of Literature Today*. New Haven, Conn.: Yale UP, 1980.

_____. "Preface." *Deconstruction and Criticism*. New York: Seabury, 1979.

_____. *Saving the Text: Literature/Derrida/Philosophy*. Baltimore: Johns Hopkins UP, 1981.

Knapp, Steven, and Walter Benn Michaels. "Against Theory." 1982. In *Against Theory: Literary Studies and the New Pragmatism*. Ed. W. J. T. Mitchell. Chicago: U of Chicago P, 1985. 11–30.

_____. "Against Theory 2: Hermeneutics and Deconstruction." *Critical Inquiry* 14, No. 1 (Autumn 1987): 49–68.

Law, Jules David. "Uncertain Grounds: Wittgenstein's *On Certainty* and the New Literary Pragmatism." *New Literary History* 19, No. 2 (Winter 1988): 319–36.

Magee, Bryan. *Modern British Philosophy*. New York: St. Martin's Press, 1971.

Norris, Christopher. *The Contest of Faculties: Philosophy and Theory after Deconstruction*. London: Methuen, 1985.

_____. *Deconstruction: Theory and Practice*. London: Methuen, 1982.

_____. *The Deconstructive Turn: Essays in the Rhetoric of Philosophy*. London: Methuen, 1983.

Ohmann, Richard. "Speech Acts and the Definition of Literature." *Philosophy and Rhetoric* 4 (Winter 1971): 1–19.

Rorty, Richard. *Consequences of Pragmatism: Essays 1972–1980*. Minneapolis: University of Minnesota Press, 1982.

_____. "Deconstruction and Circumvention." *Critical Inquiry* 11, No. 1 (September 1984): 1–21.

_____. "Philosophy without Principles." In *Against Theory: Literary Studies and the New Pragmatism*. Ed. W. J. T. Mitchell. Chicago: U of Chicago P, 1985. 132–38.

Said, Edward. *The World, the Text, and the Critic*. Cambridge, Mass.: Harvard UP, 1983.

Searle, John R. "Reiterating the Differences: A Reply to Derrida." *Glyph* 1 (1977): 198–208.

Shusterman, Richard. "Deconstruction and Analysis: Confrontation and Convergence." *British Journal of Aesthetics* 26, No. 4 (Autumn 1986): 311–27.

_____. "Eliot and Logical Atomism." *ELH* 49 (1982): 164–78.

_____. "Remembering Hulme: A Neglected Philosopher-Critic-Poet." *Journal of the History of Ideas* (1985): 559–76.

_____. *T. S. Eliot and the Philosophy of Criticism*. New York: Columbia University Press, 1988.

Staten, Henry. "Review of Jonathan Culler, *On Deconstruction* and Christopher Norris, *Deconstruction: Theory and Practice*." *MLN* 100, No. 4 (September 1985): 871–77.

_____. *Wittgenstein and Derrida*. Lincoln: U of Nebraska P, 1984.

2

The Secret Name of Cats: Deconstruction, Intentional Meaning, and the New Theory of Reference

Henry Staten

> *But above and beyond there's still one name left over,*
> *And that is the name that you never will guess;*
> *The name that no human research can discover,*
> *But THE CAT HIMSELF KNOWS, and will never confess.*

> —T. S. Eliot, "The Naming of Cats"

I

What are literary theorists to do with philosophy? For that matter, what *have* literary theorists to do with philosophy? Is philosophy something to be "used," borrowed from at the theorist's convenience? What are the theorist's responsibilities to the *rigor* specific to philosophical discourse? It is sometimes said that literary theory is a branch of philosophy. Yet despite the developments of recent years, despite the enormous interest of theorists in such deconstructive philosophers as Heidegger, Derrida, and Wittgenstein, it is questionable whether the line between these two disciplines is any less distinct than it has ever been. In the United States, almost all the excitement about the deconstruction of this boundary has come from literary theorists; the notion seems to have an appeal for them that it entirely lacks for American philosophers. Why should this be so? Is it anything more than the incorrigible dilettantism of literary people that makes the idea so appealing? Surely there is more to it than that (though there is that too); there is something profoundly intriguing, something for which the historical moment seems to be right, in the confluence of discourses that is in the air.

The other side of the questions I have asked so far is: What have philosophers, especially analytic philosophers, to do with literary criticism? What is their responsibility to the questions of language and style elaborated by literary theorists and deconstructive philosophers? Why do they find so little appeal in the possibility of the opening out of their discourse? Is it their incorrigible professionalism, their addiction to technical problems posable and disposable in technical languages? Again, this is only part of the answer, though an important part; but it does not explain, for example, Stanley Cavell's problems with a Paul de Man or his justified irritation at the "philosophical impatience" of others who leap ill-prepared into the fray. [1]

Perhaps more fundamental than the questions posed so far would be to ask what it means to write like a philosopher, or as a philosopher, and what it means to write like or as a literary theorist. The objection comes to mind immediately that there is no one way, or even any manageable small number of ways, in which philosophers or literary theorists write. And yet there it is: it's almost always clear enough whether one is writing as the one or the other. Richard Rorty, for example, writes very much in the style, the language, of contemporary Anglo-American philosophy; and Rorty is a particularly interesting case, since he wants very much to bridge the gap between languages, and sometimes talks as though the gap did not exist. [2] So, given that the gap *does* exist—what does it mean to write as a philosopher, or as a literary theorist? There is an obvious answer, and an irrefutable one so far as it goes: it means to have received one's professional training in a philosophy department or in a department of literature. This is not a trivial answer, either—but it only pushes the question back further, because now the question becomes how these departments got that way. There is a distinctive ethos of the philosophy department that is not that of the department of literature, and it is not purely accidental that each is as it is.

I do not propose here to explain how the ethos of each has developed, or even what it is. In this essay I propose only to look at a few texts, philosophical and literary-theoretical, that have become intertwined in recent discussion, and to further the investigation of the larger problems I have raised by some close local investigation. I want to look at what *one* literary theorist, E. D. Hirsch, has done with "philosophy," and at the style of approach to questions of language that characterizes two analytic philosophers who have influenced Hirsch, Hilary Putnam and Saul Kripke.

Hirsch is worth focusing on in this context because his critical project has from the outset drawn upon the fund of concepts associated with the analytic tradition of philosophy, a fairly rare thing among contemporary critics. Most recently, Hirsch has been influenced by the "new theory of reference" of Kripke and Putnam, a remarkable new development in realist metaphysics that is well worth the attention of literary theorists. It is true that the phenomenologist Husserl has been Hirsch's greatest influence, but not the later "transcendental" Husserl; rather, the Husserl of the *Logical Investigations*, who is still quite close to the problematics of analytic philosophy. (At the period of the *Investigations*, Husserl was in dialogue with Frege, and crucially involved with the problems arising from the distinction between meaning and reference.)

With the aid of first Frege and Husserl, and more recently Kripke and Putnam, Hirsch has consistently attempted to build a bulwark against those types of interpretations that challenge the fixity and objectivity of meaning. He has been one of the most outspoken, and probably the most philosophically sophisticated, American opponents of deconstructive modes of reading.

But how accurately has Hirsch read the philosophers whose work he has adapted to his project? It would be ironic if this apostle of the ethical responsibility of the reader should turn out to be himself a careless reader, no more dependable (and perhaps a good deal less dependable) than those he has attacked for their "cognitive atheism." A loose appropriation of philosophical concepts would, of course, simply mark Hirsch's practice as typical of the literary critic. But it would also raise questions about the degree to which an allegiance to truth, objectivity, and the intent of the author can do anything to guarantee more accurate reading. It may be that such allegiance turns out to be a fifth wheel, one that is not attached to the drive mechanism.

But what of our philosophers? They, of course, are admirably rigorous—but at what price? They have studied their Wittgenstein, yet their work continues to show that obsessive fascination with *essence*, with the truth of the object, that has characterized the philosophy of language at least since Aristotle. Of course the problematic of reference is interestingly, in some ways fundamentally, transformed in their hands; but still, there is no place in their work for the productive or constitutive force of language that is recognized by deconstructive philosophers such as Derrida and Wittgenstein.

II

I will begin by giving a brief account of the "new theory of reference." This theory was developed as a criticism of and alternative to the traditional theory of meaning that has held sway, in one form or another, since ancient times.[3] In its most familiar form, the traditional theory says that to know what a word means is to have a concept present in one's mind. Putnam and Kripke have challenged the adequacy of this account as an explanation of how proper names and natural-kind terms function. The crucial point in the traditional account, the point that Kripke and Putnam refute, is the idea that the "concept," in the case of a referring term, "fixes the reference" by defining a set of properties that tell us what that thing is that is referred to.

For example, according to the traditional theory, when we call something a "lemon" what we do is match the properties belonging to our concept (or "intension," as the defining conjunction of properties is called) with the observed properties of the object.[4] But, Putnam objects, this "intension" cannot determine the reference or "extension" (that is, the set of things included in the range of applicability of a term) of the word "lemon," because there may be abnormal lemons that do not have yellow peel, tart taste, or whatever other properties are included in the intension, and yet they would still be lemons ("Semantics"

103–5). The general problem is that the properties of things can change, or may have been mistakenly attributed in the first place, and that such contingencies do not in fact affect the use of referring terms in the way that they should if it were true, as the traditional theory holds, that the intension (or concept) determines extension (the thing or set of things referred to).

The traditional theory attempts to fix the *reference* of a term by fixing its *description*, but this makes too rigid the applicability of the name, which is then restricted to the terms of the description. Such a restriction implies that the qualities attributed to the thing by its description *necessarily* belong to that thing, and this yields ludicrous results.[5] For we have to acknowledge the possibility of finding out new facts about the things we name, which could revise our concept of the thing yet which would still be facts about that very thing (or kind of thing).

A second objection to the traditional theory, made by Kripke, concerns the way language functions to express counterfactual situations. For example, "We use the term 'Aristotle' in such a way that, in thinking of a counterfactual situation in which Aristotle didn't go into any of the fields and do any of the achievements we commonly attribute to him still we would say this was a situation in which *Aristotle* did not do these things" (*Naming* 62). The point is that, if it were true that intension determines extension, we *could not* strip "Aristotle" of all his defining attributes and still be referring to "Aristotle." Yet we do exactly that when we suppose that "Aristotle" did not do any of the things commonly attributed to him, and it is an important property of our language that we can make such suppositions. Kripke frames these considerations in the language of a formal model called "possible worlds semantics," which translates the preceding considerations by saying that "in some possible world Aristotle did none of the things which he actually did in this actual world." This is another way of saying "Aristotle *might not* have done any of the things he actually did"; which means that all the properties we can use to identify Aristotle are *contingent*, and that therefore Aristotle's being Aristotle is independent of his having been Alexander's teacher, and so forth.

The alternate account offered by Putnam and Kripke is that a name is initially bestowed upon a *this*, a something manifest in some way to the namer, and that the name refers to the thing as it were directly, without having to go through an identifying description. Future uses of the term to name the thing or other members of its kind may well be based on a description, but there is nothing necessary about the description. Thus, for example, someone who was the first in his tribe to see a bear might describe it for others as a biped (because he only saw it standing on its hind legs), yet the term "bear" (or his tribe's equivalent for "bear") would refer to animals of the kind he saw, whatever their actual characteristics might turn out to be. Thus Kripke says (in that science fiction modality that is such a peculiar feature of the style of contemporary American philosophy) that cats might have turned out to be strange demons planted by a magician, in which case it would not have been true that cats are animals—and yet cats would still have been cats; the word "cat" would still have picked out the very same entities as before, even though the intension previously associated with the name turned out to be quite false. "The original concept of cat is: *that kind of thing*, where the kind can be identified by paradigmatic instances" (*Naming* 122).

Once the paradigmatic identification has been made, it is transmitted to future users by a "causal chain": my uses of "Aristotle" or "bear" do not refer by virtue of my concept of these entities, but because my use of the terms is related to others' use of them in a chain that goes back to those who made the original reference.

There is thus an initial "baptism" of an object or natural kind, and the name that is bestowed is a "rigid designator" that refers to the real, underlying essence of what is referred to, even though that essence is not as yet known. The name is then passed down by a historical chain of transmission, and eventually the community may come to know the real nature of the thing referred to. Regardless of how the entity might change in any of its externally knowable manifestations, regardless of how deceptive my perceptions of it or my ideas about it might be, through the contingent deformations of its appearance in its passage through history or any number of possible worlds, the name "X" still picks it out as that very X that was baptized once and for all as *this X* upon the initial bestowal of its name.

Nothing could be more indicative of the distance between the linguistic sensibility of the contemporary literary theorist and that of the philosopher than Kripke's choice of the term "rigid designator," which, from the point of view of Derrida's critique of philosophy, betrays such linguistic naïveté. It is almost as though the term were a joke inspired by Derrida's equation of *logos* with *phallos*. On the other hand, it is doubtful that the logician Kripke could even take seriously the charge of phallogocentrism. But we might ask: whatever the case may be with a strictly *logical* discourse, can a *philosophical* discourse, especially one that makes claims about terms drawn from ordinary language, insulate itself as a *technical language* from the linguistic forces that swirl all about it? For example, as in the present case, from the types of linguistic forces analyzable from a Freudian standpoint?

We will return to other questions raised by the "new theory of reference," but for the moment this account will serve as a preparation for our examination of Hirsch's recent work.

III

Hirsch, sensing the power of the idea of rigid designation, has alertly seized upon it to fortify his theory of intentional meanings. In two recent articles, he has extended the notion of rigid designation to "embrace the meaning-reference of language use generally" ("Meaning" 220). Hirsch's purpose is to overcome the limitations of his own earlier theory of intentional meaning, which, he says, failed to take account of the fact that "many texts were authored with intentions of futurity" ("Past Intentions" 83), intentions of communication with future

readers who live under changed conditions and necessarily will associate different specific realities with the words of the old texts they read. For example,
Hirsch points out that the Constitutional requirement of "equality" was at one
time interpreted as allowing "separate but equal" treatment for blacks. In 1954,
"separate but equal" was struck down, Hirsch claims, because "laws have intentions of futurity, and we now know more about the realities of our present
social arrangements. We now believe that separate facilities are inherently
unequal" (86). According to Hirsch, "referential intent remains fixed to whatever the referred-to reality will turn out to be" (87), and so "equal" is quite
legitimately, in accord with the *referential intention* of the framers of the Constitution, reinterpreted in light of prevailing circumstances.

Now, legal interpretation is as radically problematic as is literary interpretation, and the objections to Hirsch's quick fix will be obvious to anyone who has
attended to the ongoing debate on the subject. But such objections would not
necessarily be relevant, since Hirsch is here *stipulating* how he will take the
sense of Constitutional terms and referential language in general. Hirsch has
always granted that there are other ways to approach meaning and his argument
has always been conditional: "*If* we wish to have determinate meaning and communal agreement based on such meaning, *then* here is how we must proceed."

Hirsch concludes that there is an essential component of "allegory" in all referential language that aims at continued truthfulness in the future. All literature
that continues to be interesting to us over the ages is "allegorical" in this sense;
it relates truths about essential or underlying human realities while clothing these
truths in terms that literally refer to gods or animals or to fictional humans or to
historical situations that may, in themselves, have ceased to exist or simply hold
no continued interest for us. The gods of Homer and the questions of warriors'
honor and the division of spoils give way to modern circumstances, but the reference of the *Iliad* to certain truths of human experience does not alter; the *Iliad*
continues as a "rigid designator" of these truths. Correspondingly, "scientific
names like 'electrons' are allegorical indexicals that rigidly refer to realities irrespective of the concepts that represent them provisionally" ("Past Intentions"
94); that is why Bohr accepted Schrödinger's revision of Bohr's account of the
nature of electrons.

Hirsch moves very fast here, and there is a superficial plausibility to his analogies that conceals a multitude of differences between the cases he brings together. At the level of generality of Hirsch's account, the following two cases
seem parallel:

Allegorical name	Reference
Homeric gods -------------	Unchanging real nature of human experience
Electron --------------------	Unchanging real nature of electrons

Hirsch reasons that just as concepts about human life change, so do concepts
about electrons, yet in both cases the reference of the *name* continues to be to a
reality that endures regardless of the changing concepts. He homogenizes the

picture thus: "All stories (and all laws) which carry future reference must necessarily be allegorical, must refer to something beyond what can be literally presented or known" ("Past Intentions" 92).

But Hirsch's account is questionable as it concerns both literary and scientific "reference," if we consider the strict terms of the account he has generalized. The new theory of reference rejects the notion that reference is determined by a concept (intension), by a set of characteristics definitive of the nature of the thing meant. Reference is, initially, the relationship between a name and a *this*; subsequently, in its use by persons who may not know firsthand what *this* is referred to by some name, the name is used to refer to whatever was referred to by those who originally "baptized" the entity or natural kind in question. There may be considerable variation in the concept of the X in question held by the original and subsequent users of the name, but the name refers to the same X whatever its real nature may turn out to be. There is nothing in this account that says the nature of X lies "beyond what *can* be literally presented or known," only that this nature may *in fact* not be known at some given time. When water was first named, humans did not know its chemical composition, but when in our own time we say that water is H_2O we do not speak allegorically; chemical composition is "literally presented or known" when the proper tests are performed. It is crucial to note that in the case of "natural kinds," there are in fact *two* names, one of which we can if we like call allegorical ("water") and the other of which, the scientific name ("H_2O") *might* in fact tell us what the X in question really *is*.[6]

Let us now turn to the case of literature and see if we can flesh out Hirsch's exceedingly vague suggestions. Are Homer's gods really allegorical namings of unknown natures, as "electron" may be said to have been in Bohr's time? Take the scene in Book XIV of the *Iliad* in which Aphrodite's magic girdle makes Zeus himself forgetful with passion for Hera. We say, "Ah, yes, that's how love is, all right—it clouds our eyes to the facts. As Freud says, it's an 'overestimation of the love object.' " The scene does not name a something whose nature remains to be discovered—for nothing we can "discover" about love that would tell us what it *really is* could replace Homer's accounts in the way Schrödinger's picture of the electron replaced Bohr's. Homer does not offer a hypothesis about love, as Bohr offered a hypothesis about electrons—if he did, then some libido theory or theory of brain physiology would tell us what he "really" was referring to. In literature as in "experience" in general, what you see is what you get, and what you get is an enactment of the phenomena involved, not a "naming" of a hidden, rigidly designated, ultimately inaccessible *entity*. If we speak of the "mysterious nature" of human existence, this is not like the "mysterious nature" of, say, a quark, and we must not let the apparent analogy that is given in the language mislead us. The feeling that a "human experience" has a "real nature" that can be rigidly referred to is a remarkable effect of the compulsion our thing language exercises upon us, the compulsion Wittgenstein was so concerned to exorcise in his later work.

The preceding examples of Hirsch's notion of rigid designation are taken from the Bateson Lecture, but this "reifying" tendency in Hirsch's analysis is even more obvious in the 1984 article, where his chief examples of revisable reference are to things like "memorials" and "Japanese cars." It is difficult to see how we are to make the jump from the following remarks on Shakespeare's sonnet 55 to any interesting question about the "reference" of poems to truths of human experience:

> If Shakespeare's future reader could not understand what was referred to by "monuments" and "masonry," his rhyme would not continue to be "powerful." Yet Shakespeare asserts that particular monuments will *not* endure. So he must have assumed that replacements for the decaying monuments of his own day will come into existence in the distant world of the reader, making the rhyme as applicable to that future world as it is to his own and, thus, still a powerful rhyme. ("Meaning" 208)

Again, however, a closer look at Hirsch's example shows the disanalogy with "rigid designation." In the transition from Elizabethan monuments to those that exist today, the concept of a monument has not changed: all that has happened is that the extension has acquired new members. Furthermore, there is no "real nature" in question here at all, since what makes an object a memorial is simply that it be *used* as one.

The most persistent problem with Hirsch's attempted adaptation of rigid designation is that he uses the notions of "name" and "concept" loosely, according to convenience. In the Bateson Lecture he tries to expand the sense of "naming" to make it fit what the *Iliad* does; in the 1984 article, realizing that mere naming will not serve his purpose, Hirsch decides to make *concepts* rigidly designate.

Thus, whereas in the Bateson Lecture he had shown a willingness to move beyond the limits of a "mentalistic conception of meaning" ("Past Intentions" 87), in the 1984 article Hirsch actually moves back toward a position on intentional meaning that is not essentially different from that of *Validity in Interpretation*, and his references to Kripke are now hedged about with strong qualifications. Hirsch now explicitly dissents from "Kripke's hostility to mental content" ("Meaning" 221) and once again associates meaning with "mental objects" (219). More important, Hirsch now affirms that what keeps literary works transhistorically valid is the fact that their original meaning is an "exemplification of a broad . . . concept" (217) that can find application to new exemplifications in later times. This is the old "type idea" notion that Hirsch had argued in *Validity in Interpretation*, and it is difficult to see how his new version of it actually does go beyond his former analysis. It is true that Hirsch now emphasizes the element of "futurity"—the idea that new things, not the ones actually referred to by the historical author, may be subsumed under his referential intention if they are exemplifications of the same concept that was exemplified by the original instances. But Hirsch's emphasis on futurity of intention here is a rhetorical embellishment rather than a substantive emendation of his earlier theory, for, as before, it is here merely a case of subsumption of new particulars ("our present-day monuments") under a class concept ("monuments"). It is true that Hirsch tantalizes us with the claim that, in his new account, "the provisionality of speech sanctions a degree of adjustment in the original *concepts*" ("Meaning" 223), thus expanding the province of intentional *meaning* to include elements of applications that Hirsch would formerly have considered as belonging to *significance*. But there is no real revision of the original concept involved in Hirsch's account, only a sliding between a narrow concept and a broader concept that, as Husserl would say, has been implicitly "co-intended" with the narrower one.

For example, I may say "Jack's Toyota" and accept the correction "Jack's Datsun." Hirsch comments that I can accept the adjustment "*because my first, inaccurate content is close enough to the updated content to belong to the same meaning*" (Hirsch's emphasis), for when I said "Toyota" I "also intended to refer to that thing in the world which is Jack's new Japanese car" ("Meaning" 220). Here we see clearly how Hirsch blurs the concept of rigid designation to make it fit his own notion of intentional, conceptual meaning. Hirsch says the intention was to refer to "that thing in the world," Jack's car — and this sounds like "rigid designation"; but he sneaks in the concept "Japanese car," as the "broad concept" that can subsume *both* "Toyota" and "Datsun." It is really the latter move that is consistent with Hirsch's repeated insistence that "the identity of meaning in different applications is preserved only when the application is an instance subsumed by the original intention-concept" (214), but the glancing tribute to rigid designation keeps verbally alive the pretended alliance with Kripke. Hirsch wants to have his cake and eat it too: he wants to keep the idea of *revisability* of the "intention-concept" (214) as a consequence of the impact of the world upon the referential intention (an idea loosely derived from Kripke), and this gives his new theory its apparent new scope for "futurity"; but in fact he describes no such genuine revisability, reiterating instead the notion of new exemplifications of a type-concept. In order to fuzz over the problems with his account he loosely runs together the different concepts that Kripke keeps distinct. Thus he argues that "a concept is by its nature both an 'internal' generality and an 'external' array of things embraced by the generality; it is both an 'intension' and an 'extension' " (210). But this is not a new synthesis; it is merely a restatement of the view rejected by the new theory of reference, the view that intension determines extension.

IV

But if the change in Hirsch's theory is not precisely that it now allows for a genuine "revisability" in the "intention-concept," there is nevertheless a change, and it turns out to be something quite surprising. For in the Bateson Lecture Hirsch confesses that his earlier theory was strictly "mentalistic" and, being restricted to "mental objects," was unable to account for reference "to reality" ("Past Intentions" 87). This, I say, is surprising, because Hirsch's earlier account, being Husserlian, had not, before Hirsch's confession, seemed to be at all inadequately cognizant of the reference to reality. But Hirsch's characterization of Husserl's theory as merely "mentalistic" forces a rereading of the classic essay of 1960 entitled "Objective Interpretation" in which Hirsch set forth his adaptation of Husserl to hermeneutics, and what emerges is that Hirsch has all along been working with a fundamentally mistaken interpretation of Husserl. For it is as clear as any such thing can be that Husserl's theory in the *Logical Investigations*, Hirsch's main source, is anything but "mentalistic"—is, in every aspect of its intention, aimed at reference to *the thing itself*. For Husserl, the notion of a meaning intention is defined by its relation to the notion of *fulfillment*, that is, to the "filling-in" of a mere signification by the *intuition* of the thing signified, say, for example, by the sense intuition (perception) of an object. "Talk about recognizing objects, and talk about fulfilling a meaning-intention . . . expresses the same fact" (*Logical Investigations* 695); "the fulfilling act has a *superiority* which the mere intention lacks" (720); "signitive intentions are in themselves 'empty,' . . . they 'are in *need* of fullness.' . . . A signitive intention merely points to its object, an intuitive intention gives it 'presence' " (728); "where a presentative intention has achieved its last fulfillment, the genuine *adaequatio rei et intellectus* has been brought about" (762).

I have multiplied the quotations from the *Sixth Investigation* because Hirsch is not the only one to have a mistaken impression of the bearing of Husserl's ideas; even professional philosophers often miss this realist emphasis of Husserl's. It is true that Husserl's later work can be misinterpreted on this point even by careful students, but this is not the case with the *Investigations*.

Now, it is not obvious in Hirsch's account of 1960 that he had so fundamentally misread Husserl. Hirsch duly recites Husserl's example of the perception of a box that remains the identical unchanging object of my changing perspectives on it, and comments that "an object for the mind remains the same even though what is 'going on in the mind' is not the same"—this "mental object is self-identical over against a plurality of mental acts" ("Objective Interpretation" 217–18).[7] He then goes on to describe "verbal meaning" as a self-identical object on the analogy of the box. In this account the only sign that Hirsch is not saying what Husserl is saying is his use of the term "mental object" where one would expect "intentional object," but everything else is in order, so it looks like a terminological variant. But it was not for nothing that Husserl devoted a section of the *Fifth Investigation*, entitled "Avoidance of Verbally Tempting Misunderstandings," to the critique of the notion of the "immanent" or "mental" object, which, he concludes, "is in truth not really immanent or mental" (557–60). Hirsch has apparently been snared by this verbal temptation, as we see in the Bateson Lecture remarks about Husserl's "mentalism" and again in the 1984 piece in which he describes Husserl's "intentional objects" as "objects-for-the-mind" ("Meaning" 203). And indeed, in a passage of the 1960 article that one might have been inclined to overlook, the confusion is perfectly explicit: Hirsch tells us that the "intentional object" is "the object as perceived by me" and distinguishes it from "the object which exists independently of my perceptual act" (218). It thus appears that Hirsch has all these years been working with an erroneous notion of "intention," since for Husserl intention is precisely reference to a *transcendent*, not mental, object. Husserl declares unequivocally that "*the intentional object of a presentation is the same as its actual object . . . and . . . it is absurd to distinguish between them*" (595; Husserl's emphasis).

Hirsch does not, therefore, require Kripke at all in order to secure the reference to reality, which was right there all along in Husserl. On the other hand, Hirsch's "mentalism" now is seen to lack the rigorous foundation Hirsch purports to find in the *Logical Investigations*, for Hirsch's "mental object" turns out to contain psychologistic remnants. It is in fact a curious hybrid, belonging to the mental space of an individual yet transcending the transient psychological acts of that individual; shareable "under linguistic conventions" by others, yet containing invisible boundaries within itself that limit the operation of those conventions according to the "intention" that originally shaped the verbal meaning ("Objective Interpretation" 225–26). Despite Hirsch's claim to the contrary it is clear that his use of "intention" drifts away from the phenomenological and back to a psychologistic sense.[8]

V

In one sense it may seem strikingly inappropriate for Hirsch to have looked for allies in Kripke and Putnam, who work within the strongly antimentalist tradition of analytic philosophy; Putnam, for example, declares emphatically, "Cut the pie any way you like, 'meanings' just ain't in the *head!*" ("Meaning and Reference" 124). The antimentalism of the New Theorists is implied by their criticisms of the notion that intension determines extension. If there is no set of defining characteristics that necessarily picks out the object referred to by a name, it follows that there is no concept we can have in mind that will determine the relation of reference. Reference therefore is not dependent upon intention; "it is only the sociolinguistic state of the collective linguistic body to which the speaker belongs that fixes the extension" (127). Although intention does not drop entirely out of the picture (*Naming* 96), it has here a severely circumscribed role, and reference becomes primarily a question of the way language is used by the whole community.

But Putnam and Kripke reject intention only in relation to the problem of *reference*. The questions of intentional meaning that Hirsch is concerned with reach far beyond the problem of reference in the strict sense. That is why Hirsch's adaptation of Putnam's and Kripke's work is so questionable; but it is also why their antipsychologism may not be directly relevant here. Despite their differences, Hirsch and the New Theorists remain allies in resisting the descent into mere language that characterizes much poststructuralist theorizing. Their strategies are fundamentally different, yet both approaches are founded in a commitment to boundaries of sense that remain anchored in some way outside of language.

It is true that the "outside" of language is conceived in a sophisticated post-Kantian way by Putnam, who has elaborated a complex strategy of what he calls "internal realism" that rejects the correspondence theory of truth. Putnam, like many analytic philosophers influenced by Wittgenstein or Quine, disavows the idea that there is any unique relation of reference between words and "mind-independent or discourse-independent 'states of affairs' " (*Reason* 50). Signs do correspond to objects, but only "within the conceptual schemes" of the language users of a particular language community. "Objects do not exist independently of conceptual schemes. We cut up the world into objects when we introduce one or another scheme of description. Since the objects *and* the signs are alike *internal* to the scheme of description, it is possible to say what matches what" (52).

So does not Putnam's denial that there exist "discourse-independent 'states of affairs' " contradict my assertion that he anchors sense in something transcendent to language? The issue is not so simple. There is discourse and then there is discourse: a discourse of the phenomenal surface and one of the essential subsurface. "Internal realism" denies that the essential subsurface is inhabited by "discourse-independent" objects, yet it is inhabited by objects that are more stable, more fixable in relation to the language that picks them out, than are the "objects" that are suggested by the undisciplined language of the phenomenal surface. We say "cat" or "water" or "heat," and these phenomena play certain roles in our lives; but hidden from the ignorant eye is the internal structure (itself constituted at another level of our discourse), what the name aims at beyond our "concept" of the thing.

I do not wish to defend the theory of meaning that these writers reject. It is basically the theory that Wittgenstein rejected before them, and indeed Putnam sometimes uses Wittgenstein's own arguments. But there is something else in Wittgenstein's account that is lost in those of Kripke and Putnam, the investigation of a "concept" in a Wittgensteinian sense, a sense quite different from the "mentalist" sense rejected by the New Theorists. For Wittgenstein, a "concept" is not an "intension," a mental object, but the topography of a word's uses. A Wittgensteinian "concept" cannot be summed up by specifying a conjunction or cluster of properties;[9] all we can do is *survey* the variety of our uses of a word, and in this way call attention to some aspect or other of the diversity of these uses.

But then there is no special privilege to the concept of "reference" that would call for its being reified as a very special sort of relation between certain words and the essence of things. "Reference" has, like other words, a varied array of uses, and to understand reference is to understand the complex ways in which the concept of reference is woven into these contexts. We could say that reference is deeply rooted in its contexts. We cannot pluck it up for easy inspection like a carrot, as Kripke and Putnam would like to do; it is more like a tree that when uprooted brings with it a considerable chunk of the meadow.

There is no place in the arguments for rigid designation and for the determination of reference by causal chains for the vague, shifting topography of the word's use as the use is intertwined with our experience. If the word "cat" refers to *this kind of thing*, and "kind" is to be cashed in only in terms of internal structure, then the role that cats play in our lives is not relevant to the reference of the word "cat."

But there is more to the concept "cat" than any conjunction or cluster of properties—"cat" has a certain "physiognomy" (not just a "stereotype" in Putnam's sense), a certain role in our lives—and if cats turned out to be robots, or demons, this entire role would be altered, and our lives and our language with it. Perhaps we would find them somewhat revolting; cat haters would be vindicated, and former cat lovers would perceive in cats the sinister quality that some cat haters now ascribe to them. When we saw one it would elicit a creepy feeling, and we might now say something like "There's one of those cat things." Perhaps eventually they would generally be called "cat things." This does not mean I want to say that "cats are animals" is analytic—only that it is part of the form of life within which cats play a role that cats are understood to be animals, and that this whole form of life would be fundamentally altered if they were not. Reference is not just a matter of internal structure, it involves the whole *scene of reference*.

For Wittgenstein, the "concept" in this sense, as the entanglement of the name in the diversity of its contexts of usage, its "grammar," is the object of the philosophical investigation of meaning. But Kripke and Putnam, although they are deeply influenced by Wittgenstein, approach their investigation of language drawn by the logico-objective *telos* that is the traditional lure of philosophy. For them, the grammar of ordinary language converges upon the nodal points identified as real being by science, which Kripke says, "attempts, by investigating basic structural traits, to find the nature, and thus the essence (in the philosophical sense) of the kind" (*Naming* 138).

It is clear that the new theory of reference breaks, in a profound way, with certain themes that have been central to classical theory of language. I have already mentioned its antipsychologism. It also seems to imply a radical break with the Aristotelian *eidos* concerning which Heidegger has written so much. For the Greeks, essence is rooted in the visible manifestation of entity; the new theory of reference is a theory of essential nature that responds to the modern scientific postulation of hidden essences. Furthermore, as we have seen, Putnam makes very strong arguments against taking science as dealing with "facts" that are not interest-dependent; he is as skeptical as Rorty concerning the fact-value dichotomy. Nevertheless, as value-laden and interest-determined, as "internal" to our conceptual scheme as the discoveries of science may be, there is constituted, within and by our language and forms of life, a privileged instance of language use that inhabits the other uses as their *telos* or normative instance: that use of language that is associated with the search for the *essential nature* (*Reason* 104).

It thus appears that in some supremely occulted way, the new theory of reference continues to be driven by the urge for presence of which Heidegger and Derrida speak. Being becomes more and more rarefied, and is detached from the self-presence of a knowing subject, since the subject here becomes only a link in a chain, a member of a *knowing community*. Yet is not the self-presence of consciousness entirely recuperated within the transparency and univocity of terms that refer in all possible worlds to one and the same essence? Is not the knowing community a kind of *transcendental subject* who is not susceptible to the lapses of awareness of an empirical consciousness or group of such consciousness? The "sociolinguistic state of the collective linguistic body" is nothing other than the residue or deposit in language of a series of conscious mental acts by which this "state" has been constituted, a deposit that can always be reactualized as new empirical acts of cognitive consciousness. Thus the antipsychologism of the New Theorists is a strategy by which the ideal survival and ascendancy of certain privileged moments of consciousness may be conceived. It is the classical elision of the empirical individual in order, as Derrida says, for "a relationship with presence in general to be instituted" (*Speech and Phenomena* 54).[10]

Kripke and Putnam, like analytic philosophers in general, approach the question of language fundamentally in terms of the relation between words and objects, and in so doing they pierce through that shifting phenomenal surface of language that so preoccupies Wittgenstein and Derrida. We could say that the issue is the relation between *two languages*, one that says "water" and one that says "H$_2$O." The latter seems to express clearly what the former only stammers at trying to express. Actually, we need to mention a third language in order to keep clear the relation between these two: the language that would refer to a discourse-independent thing, the thing-in-itself, the ineffable "X" that lies beyond language. Let us call this the X language, in order to mark the fact that the privileged language, the language of essential nature, refers to realities-for-us. We thus distinguish three languages:

The phenolanguage	Words that name appearances
The ontolanguage	Words that name essential realities-for-us
The X language	The nonexistent metaphysical language, words that would name things-in-themselves

The phenolanguage speaks without knowing the essential nature of what it names; for example, it says "heat," on the basis of our sensations of heat, without knowing what heat really is. Let us keep the phenoname and the ontoname distinct in this way: we will use HEAT as the signifier of the ontolanguage, to mean "the external phenomenon itself (as given within the conceptual scheme of science) which happens to be (but need not have been) the cause of the sensation of heat in humans"; and "heat" (in quotation marks) as the phenoword, which means—what? Well, whatever the phenoword means, which, I will argue, is not anything that can be simply stated. The phenoword does not mean just one thing; it has a variety of uses, what Wittgenstein calls a "grammar," and it is questionable whether this grammar has any unique anchor of reference that it "rigidly designates."

Now, if one does not consistently observe the difference between these two names, HEAT and "heat," there arises an ambiguity as to the relation between the ontolanguage and the phenolanguage, and it may be that some of Kripke's most spectacular effects depend upon this ambiguity. Kripke informs us that "the term 'heat' doesn't *mean* 'whatever gives people these sensations,' " because "people might not have been sensitive to heat, and yet the heat still have existed in the world" (*Naming* 131), and it is conceivable that Martians could get the heat sensation from ice and the cold sensation from fire ("Identity" 95). Nevertheless, because heat is in fact the motion of molecules, "still, heat would be heat, and cold would be cold" (96–97). The term "heat" is a rigid designator, and therefore, since heat is in fact the motion of molecules, "it is going to be *necessary* that heat is the motion of molecules" (97). On the other hand, it is only a "contingent fact" that we humans are sensitive to heat in the particular way we are.

Now, within the context of discussion that Kripke assumes, there are certain points, in fact his main points, that we must ignore here. Kripke is arguing against other theories of reference and making points about how to deal with modality in possible-worlds models of formal semantics. Within the context of those discussions Kripke's arguments have a force that I do not question here. Nor am I arguing the *converse* of what Kripke asserts—I am not claiming that "heat" *does* mean "whatever gives people these sensations." To say that would be to replace a real essence with a subjective essence; but the phenolanguage does not know any *one* thing that would count as *the heat sensation*. Consider:

Drinking a cup of scalding-hot coffee.
Feeling the July sun beating down on one's head (and think of how different this is in Houston from what it is in the desert).
Touching a glowing ember.
Feeling the forehead of someone who has an extremely high fever.
Running (say, on a cool day) until one is sweating profusely.

For a "grammatical" investigation in Wittgenstein's sense the *differences* among contexts of language use are the object of interest, not the factor upon which they might all be made to converge. So what I am trying to do is to bring out a certain implication of Kripke's method, its relation not to competing theories but to the phenolanguage that is the common point of departure for *all* theories. Using our conventional notation for the pheno-and ontolanguages, we can see that Kripke's claim is ambiguous as between "HEAT is the motion of molecules" and " 'Heat' is the motion of molecules." He uses a single signifier that says both at the same time, and this makes his claim not only one about transworld identity in possible-worlds semantics but *also*, in a confused and question-begging way, about ordinary language. There is nothing controversial or new about "HEAT is the motion of molecules," which translates without residue into "the phenomenon that causes the heat sensation in humans is the motion of molecules," which reduces further to "the motion of molecules is the motion of molecules" (and, as Kripke would want to add, is *necessarily* the motion of molecules). But then this is either a restatement of a scientific discovery or a tautology that states the old familiar philosophical notion (ridiculed by Wittgenstein as nonsense) that a thing is identical with itself. The identity of HEAT and molecular motion may be ''necessary'' in Kripke's sense, but that of ''heat'' and molecular motion would appear to be, not contingent, but a fact about one use, among others, of the word ''heat.'' The fact that Kripke does not distinguish HEAT from ''heat'' is not a simple oversight, for what is at issue in this nondistinction is precisely the role of the signifier ''heat.'' The question is whether ''heat'' really is HEAT.

On Kripke's account, the signifier as given in ordinary language, prior to knowledge of the essential nature, already in some way aims at the ontoword. The word is initially solicited by some manifestation of the thing—an appearance, an initial something that calls our attention to it. This manifestation as yet only hints at the essential nature. We give a name on the basis of this manifestation, but this name is to the real name, the secret name, as a poker chip is to money. It is provisional, a marker that holds a certain uncertain place open for the moment. When I know more, I will be able to cash in the provisional name for a more truthful name, a name that manifests knowledge (not necessarily *my* knowledge, but that of my community)—I will be able to say ''molecular motion'' or ''H_2O,'' and this will be the coming to light of what lay darkly in the phenolanguage.

I do not want to say that this picture is *wrong*. It is a picture, and it expresses an attitude toward language and sanctions a particular philosophical use of language, a particular philosophical style. So our question still concerns philosophical styles and how to read them. I want to counterpoint the style of investigation of the New Theorists with another conception of language and another style of investigation, a descriptive investigation to which Kripke and Putnam pay minimal attention. They do use apt examples from ordinary usage to support their arguments, but compared to philosophers who are really devoted to the descriptive enterprise (Wittgenstein, Bouwsma, Cavell) they have no ears for the full (not just philosophical) nuance of language. Their remarks concerning rigid designation make perfectly good sense understood as comments describing the grammar of the ontolanguage, but, in their move toward nailing down (even provisionally) what a being essentially is, *do they preserve the relation of their language to the language in which we ordinarily speak?* When they speak of ''reference,'' they are really only interested in REFERENCE, yet the jump from one to the other goes unnoticed, and they seem to be claiming to tell the truth about the former by purifying it into the latter. Unlike the logical positivists, they have no program for the construction of an ideal language, yet in their investigation of reference they insist on piercing through the phenolanguage to what Derrida in his reading of Husserl calls the ''logico-objective core of language.''

The same points that apply to Kripke on ''heat'' apply to Putnam on ''water'' (*Reason* 21–25). Putnam says that there is no possible world in which water is not H_2O, but if we drop the disputed term ''water'' all he is saying is that there is no possible world in which H_2O is not H_2O. As to whether "water" could not be H_2O, Putnam's arguments do, I think, prove the point he is arguing, namely, that "mental state," even *collective* mental state, does not determine reference. But these arguments do *not* show that water (that is, "water") is necessarily H_2O (though we can say, trivially, that WATER necessarily is), unless we accept as a stipulation the idea that reference is determined in some unique way by an essential nature.

If instead of beginning with the end point—with the selfsame something that is prejudged as the referent—we begin by trying to understand the use of the word "water," things turn out rather differently. For "water" even on this earth does not in its ordinary uses "refer" to one substance named H_2O; even in its most "literal" use, it refers indiscriminately to H_2O along with whatever else might happen to be in it. Seawater is as much water as fresh water is, and yet it is undrinkable and will not sustain human life; in fact, since there is a lot more seawater than fresh we could plausibly argue that it is the *real* water. Pure H_2O is, in ordinary usage, a special case—it comes in bottles and is labeled "distilled water." There is drinking water, irrigation water, hard water, soft water, ice water, boiling water, "white water," deep water, water in the desert, water to a drowning man—all kinds of water. (Keep in mind that what we are doing in reminding ourselves of all these different kinds of water is reminding ourselves of the variety of contexts in which we use the word "water.") Now, of course today we know all this water has "something in common"—it is, in some proportion, H_2O. Yet what proportion? Both Kool-Aid and coffee are mostly water—for that matter, so are our bodies—but we do not ordinarily count these as "water." Really brackish water can, I suppose, have a lower proportion than coffee does of H_2O to its total volume, yet we still call it water. For scientific purposes a cup of coffee is just one form of impure water.[11]

Putnam argues that Twin Earth water, which has a different chemical composition than Earth water, simply is not water, but we could imagine friendly relations established between Earth and Twin Earth, such that a joint semantic congress agreed that Twin Earth water was water too, and we need not even give it a special label like "Twin Earth Water," any more than we have a special name for Mexican water—only, we would warn our friends who are about to visit Twin Earth, "Don't drink the water."

Of course one may still feel like saying that, call it what we like, Twin Earth water *still is not water*, but now all we are doing is expressing our adherence to a certain way of talking, even as someone might say, "Call rock and roll 'music' if you like, but for all that it still isn't music." And there can certainly be strong reasons for these avowals of adherence—reasons that, if well argued, might convince other people to use the words the same way. But it will not be the case that "the reference was fixed" by a selfsame something out there; it is *we* who fix a reference—if and when we do, and for the most part we do *not*, at least, not one single essential reference, but references in abundance, varying as the occasion requires.

VI

At the same time, we cannot evade the fact that there is a major enterprise called "science" whose movement is precisely toward the real essence. Nor is this enterprise isolated or anomalous in human life—the search for the real essence is rooted in the most everyday kinds of practical discriminations. Will this fruit nourish me or kill me if I eat it? Is this the right kind of rock to make arrowheads out of? Is this man dependable or deceptive? The question is whether this project has a transcendental privilege such that it can define the essence of reference in the phenolanguage.

The question comes to a peculiarly sharp focus on the question of the signifier "light," because here it becomes a question of the condition of possibility of the language game concerning the essence itself. When Kripke urges us to believe that there would still have been light in a dark universe, a universe in which human beings, those very beings whose word this is, were *blind*, one hardly knows what to think. The tension between ontoword and phenoword is almost unbearable here. Grant the metaphysical point that streams of photons would have existed—grant it "grammatically," that is, grant that it belongs to the grammar of the ontolanguage that we would say this. *But what does it mean to say that this would still have been light?*

Kripke anchors his analysis on the notion that the thing rigidly designated is to be, in all possible worlds, that very thing that *we* mean in *our language* when we use the word that names it (*Naming* 77). But our language is the phenolanguage, and the phenolanguage is only the beginning, a *point d'appuie* for the further movement by which the husk of the phenoword will eventually be shed as the real reference that had gestated within it comes to maturity. Once this happens, a circle closes—the real reference, discovered at the *end* of the process that began with our naive use of the word ("heat" or "light"), links up with what was already there *before* we came on the scene with our words.[12]

Yet none of this is statable, or even conceivable, except in terms of the language of philosophy. Although science may come to know the essence of water and cats and heat and light, we can only know this, say this, because we have at hand the concepts of "knowing" and "essence," which belong to the language of philosophy. But the concepts of "knowing" and "essence" have been constituted by metaphors of light and vision, the *eidos* and *eidenai* of the Greeks. Is this accidental? How can we meaningfully even pose this question? How can we "know" whether the "essence" of "essence" and "know" *could have* been constituted in *other words* by beings differently constituted than we are— whether, under the invisible light of some other sun, a race of intelligent bats might not have constituted a language of sonorous or ultrasonorous essence? What we do know is that, whether we conceive such a development in some "possible world" as that of another race or of our own race under a different conceivable evolutionary turn (but would this still be *our* race? Where does the rigid designation of "*Homo sapiens*" find its boundaries?), the language spoken would be *another* language—not ours. (Or let us say that I rigidly designate our language as *this* one here, of which "light" and "heat" are samples.)

Within the closed circle of the language of essence, there is an automatic response to the question I have raised. Language is a ladder to be kicked away once we reach the essence, and just as we kick away "heat" once we mentally view HEAT, we can kick away images of light and vision, knowing what *eidos* and *eidenai really refer to*.

We know as well what the deconstructive response to this move would be—that it begs the question, that it has merely *aufgehoben* the image of vision, that *in fact* this image of pure knowledge of a transcendental essence remains dependent upon the language it seeks to deny or transcend.

We arrive, then, at a standoff. We do not know how to adjudicate these counterclaims. Our language reaches this far and no further.

The most difficult thing is to rest content with the reach of our language—not to seek to go beyond what it can say, but merely to note what it is that we do say, or what has been said. This is what makes the style of "textual" philosophers like Derrida and the later Wittgenstein fundamentally different from other philosophers, and brings them close to literary critics. They never speak of the thing itself, but comment on the language they find about them (ordinary language in the case of Wittgenstein, the things philosophers have said in the case of Derrida). Of course the method and the results in the two cases are very different, but I want to press the shared *difference from* the philosopher's traditional enterprise. Like literary critics, as Socrates says, they do not rely as they should on their own voices discoursing on truth but let another voice, like the voice of a flute, be their medium (*Theaetetus* 347d). Following the Pied Piper of language, a grammatical or deconstructive investigation misses the essential nature, fails to move toward the *Grenzbegriff* of reason. The true philosopher resists this temptation.

Notes

1. Cavell's remarks on de Man appear in "The Politics of Interpretation" (41–48). These remarks, which pit Cavell's own style of linguistic virtuosity against that of de Man, deserve close study by students of deconstruction. The remark about "philosophical impatience" concerns the essay "Against Theory" by Steven Knapp and Walter Ben Michaels; Cavell makes it in "The Division of Talent" (524).

2. See my critique of Rorty's reading of Derrida, "Rorty's Circumvention of Derrida," and Rorty's reply, "The Higher Nominalism in a Nutshell."

3. An excellent survey of the issues raised by the new theory of reference is that of Stephen P. Schwartz in his introduction to a volume of essays edited by him, *Naming, Necessity, and Natural Kinds*, which contains key articles by Kripke and Putnam I shall draw on later in this essay.

4. I omit discussion of the "cluster theory" of names in the interests of space. See Schwartz (15, 19) for discussion. However, Schwartz's remark, following Kripke, that Wittgenstein held a "cluster theory," is erroneous. According to the cluster theory, Schwartz says, there must be "enough" features from the "cluster" of properties associated with the term. The "cluster theory" interpretation regularizes Wittgenstein's remarks, but his remarks contain no such regularization, and emphasize precisely the irregular character of the phenomenon: "Have I decided how much must be proved false for me to give up my propositions as false? . . . Is it not the case that I have a whole

series of props in readiness, and am ready to lean on one if another should be taken from under me and vice versa?'' (*Philosophical Investigations*, remark 79). I take these remarks to point up precisely the impossibility of weighing the set of features to find out how much is "enough" to warrant the use of a name (see also remark 82). There is certainly nothing in Wittgenstein's remarks that can accurately be construed in terms of John Searle's idea of a "logical sum" (quoted by Kripke, *Naming and Necessity* 61).

5. As Putnam points out, "There are no *analytic* truths of the form *every lemon has P*" ("Semantics" 105).

6. With the proviso, of course, that scientific theories are revisable, and that it could conceivably turn out, upon future discoveries, that water is *not* H_2O. But this ordinary sort of scientific modesty is compatible with scientific *realism* and is not to be confused with the skeptical view that treats scientific "truths" as *merely* allegorical in the sense that they have the same, or a similar, epistemological status as poems and ideological constructs. To say that water *might not* be H_2O still, on the realist view, leaves open the possibility (indeed, the probability) that water *is* indeed H_2O. The skeptical view would be that water *cannot* in fact be H_2O, that "H_2O" is just our inescapably mythic way of conceiving water. Hirsch comes close to such a skeptical point of view when he speaks of scientific language as "allegorical." He seems to differ from the skeptics only in his sense of a truth-seeking *intention* that, however, seems inevitably to founder in the alleged inability of language ever to speak the intended truth. But the new theory of reference does not support such a view of scientific names.

7. However, even though the box is Husserl's example, cited at a crucial moment in the *Fifth Investigation* (565–66), Hirsch credits someone else with having "suggested" the example to him (217n). This, along with the further considerations I will raise, makes one wonder how carefully Hirsch studied the *Investigations*.

8. Hirsch claims that for Husserl "any particular verbal utterance, written or spoken, is historically determined," fixed "once and for all by the character of the speaker's intention" ("Objective Interpretation" 219). Hirsch cites the *Logical Investigations* in support of his claim (2nd German edition, vol. 2, 91; cited by Hirsch in "Objective Interpretation" 219n), but the place cited clearly does not support his claim—quite the contrary. Husserl is here (section 28, *First Investigation*) dealing with the problem of "essentially occasional expressions" (what we now call "indexicals"), which seem to fluctuate in meaning from speaker to speaker. *These* expressions may perhaps be said, in Hirsch's terms, to be "historically determined," or, as Husserl says, to be influenced by "chance circumstances of speaking" (I cite Findlay's translation, 320). But that is exactly why they present a problem for Husserl—they are "subjectively defective" (322) and seem to pose a challenge to the *fixity* of objective meanings that do *not* vary with the circumstances of utterance. As it turns out, Husserl argues that "ideally speaking" (though not in fact) such "subjective expressions" could be replaced by fixed, objective ones (321) with meanings that "themselves do not alter" (322). Husserl's view of meanings as "ideal unities" demands that meanings stay the same "whenever anyone uses the same expression" (322). This does *not* mean, as Hirsch takes it to, that the meaning is "historically" fixed, but rather than the meaning is impervious to the historical circumstances of utterance.

9. See note 4, this chapter.

10. See also Henry Staten, *Wittgenstein and Derrida* 57–61, 150–51.

11. Putnam does say that "what the essential nature is . . . depends both on the natural kind and on the context" and thus that "iced tea may be 'water' in one context but not in another" (*Reason* 103), but this kind of consideration does not play a significant role in his arguments. When Putnam makes the case for water's being H_2O, he privileges the context of scientific investigation over any other. Interestingly, when he makes the preceding remark he does so in order to contrast "iced tea" with *gold*, whose essential nature, he argues, is *not* dependent on context: "For gold what counts is ultimate composition, since this has been thought since the ancient Greeks to determine the lawful behavior of the substance." Kripke too lays considerable emphasis on gold to exemplify the search for the real essence: "In the case of gold," he says, "men applied tremendous effort to the task" (*Naming* 139). He then adds (possibly ironically, but the context suggests not) that this demonstrates

man's "natural scientific curiosity." Nothing better illustrates the flattening of the differences among language games (which, remember, involve at the same time the words and the things named, in the way that these things are woven into our forms of life) than this context-free invocation of the essence of gold. Gold is the figure of the proper itself—it is the *etymon*, the incarnation of the genuine. It is the measure of value, yet it has a hidden nature. It appeals to the eye, yet this appeal can be duplicated by what is not gold, so the split between appearance and reality becomes urgent. Gold is *precious*, and the essence of the precious is different from the essence of what is not precious. Water is not like gold, although in some circumstances it becomes precious—so precious that we would trade gold for it. But the nature of water, insofar as we are *practically* interested in this nature, is not hidden in the same way. If we view things only from the scientific perspective, it may seem as though the nature of water *is* hidden in the same way. Both gold and water have an atomic and molecular structure, and this seems to be their true nature. But men have powerful motives for trying to falsify gold, and as powerful for investigating whether what they see is the real thing—motives that do not usually attach to water. Gold is thus the prototype of the scientifically investigatable nature (but not for scientific reasons); and when we consider the role it played in alchemy, out of which chemistry grew, we could argue that there is even a historical sense in which the scientific pursuit of real essence is linked to gold.

12. Although, if we accept Putnam's "internalism" what was there before we came along would have to have been there in a way that is difficult to state—it would have to have been there as that which was capable of manifesting itself as that very thing-for-us that it in fact becomes once we interrogate it. The questions that arise at this point are not unlike those that arise concerning the constitution and mode of being of geometrical objectivities in Husserl's *Origin of Geometry*.

Works Cited

Cavell, Stanley. "The Division of Talent." *Critical Inquiry* 11, No. 4 (June 1985): 519–38.

———. "The Politics of Interpretation." In *Themes Out of School: Effects and Causes*. San Francisco: North Point, 1984. 27–59.

Derrida, Jacques. *Speech and Phenomena and Other Essays on Husserl's Theory of Signs*. Trans. David B. Allison. Evanston, Ill.: Northwestern UP, 1973.

Hirsch, E. D. "Meaning and Significance Reinterpreted." *Critical Inquiry* 11, No. 2 (December 1984): 202–25.

———. "Objective Interpretation." 1960. In *Validity in Interpretation*. New Haven, Conn.: Yale UP, 1967. 209–44.

———. "Old and New in Hermeneutics." 1975. In *The Aims of Interpretation*. Chicago: U of Chicago P, 1976. 17–35.

———. "Past Intentions and Present Meanings." *Essays in Criticism* 33, No. 2 (April 1983): 79–98.

Husserl, Edmund. *Logical Investigations*. 2 vols. Trans. J. N. Findlay. New York: Humanities, 1970.

———. *The Origin of Geometry*. Trans. David Carr. In Jacques Derrida, *Edmund Husserl's Origin of Geometry: An Introduction*. Stony Brook, N.Y.: Nicholas Hays, 1978. 155–80.

Knapp, Steven, and Walter Benn Michaels. "Against Theory." *Critical Inquiry* 8, No. 4 (Summer 1982): 723–42.

Kripke, Saul. "Identity and Necessity." In Schwartz. 66–101.

———. *Naming and Necessity*. Cambridge, Mass.: Harvard UP, 1972.

Putnam, Hilary. "Is Semantics Possible?" In Schwartz. 102–18.

———. "Meaning and Reference." In Schwartz. 119–32.

———. *Meaning and the Moral Sciences*. Boston: Routledge & Kegan Paul, 1978.

———. *Reason, Truth, and History*. Cambridge: Cambridge UP, 1981.

Rorty, Richard. "The Higher Nominalism in a Nutshell: A Reply to Henry Staten." *Critical Inquiry* 12, No. 2 (Winter 1986): 461–66.

Schwartz, Stephen P., ed. *Naming, Necessity, and Natural Kinds*. Ithaca, N.Y.: Cornell UP, 1977.

Staten, Henry. "Rorty's Circumvention of Derrida." *Critical Inquiry* 12, No. 2 (Winter 1986): 453–61.

———. *Wittgenstein and Derrida*. Lincoln: U of Nebraska P, 1984.

Wellek, Rene, and Austin Warren. *Theory of Literature*. 1949. New York: Harcourt Brace, 1956.

Wittgenstein, Ludwig. *Philosophical Investigations*. 1953. Trans. G. E. M. Anscombe. New York: Macmillan, 1958.

3

Stanley Cavell's Wittgenstein

Michael Fischer

Most critics agree that Wittgenstein can contribute something to contemporary literary theory, especially to the controversy still surrounding deconstruction. Many find in Wittgenstein the most powerful answer to Derrida. These critics picture Wittgenstein dissolving the doubts raised by deconstruction and bringing literary theory peace, much as he presumably brought philosophy peace in the *Investigations* by undoing those problems that called philosophy itself into question (*Investigations*, remark 133). I want here to examine this view of Wittgenstein en route to introducing yet another way of understanding him and his relevance to contemporary criticism. That way grows out of the writings of Stanley Cavell. I use Cavell not to bury or to praise deconstruction, but to raise new questions about it.

Wittgenstein's therapeutic powers have been most persuasively championed by M. H. Abrams and Charles Altieri.[1] For both Abrams and Altieri, Wittgenstein is an especially potent antidote to Derrida because the two philosophers have much in common. Both oppose any metaphysical grounding of human values, meanings, and cultural practices. By "metaphysical grounding," Abrams means some absolute, extralinguistic or supraconventional foundation — what Derrida would call a transcendental signified — sanctioning the correctness of an interpretation. As Altieri similarly puts it in "Wittgenstein on Consciousness and Language: A Challenge to Derridean Literary Theory," Wittgenstein shares with Derrida "a fundamental opposition to traditional essentialist forms of philosophy" and "subordinate[s] a logic of reference to a rhetoric of significations or speech acts" (1398).

Both Abrams and Altieri think that from this common starting point — opposition to metaphysical absolutes — Derrida and Wittgenstein diverge. Abrams calls Derrida "an absolutist without absolutes," and Altieri also sees him as ironically trapped in the metaphysical reasoning he wants to deconstruct. In this reading, absolutes, although dead, remain necessary for Derrida—necessary to the objectivity of interpretation. In Abrams's words, "[Derrida] shares the presupposition of the [metaphysical] views he deconstructs that to be determinately understandable, language requires an absolute foundation, and that, since there is no such ground, there is no stop to the play of undecidable meanings" ("How to Do Things" 570). Without absolutes, in other words, interpretation is unstable, uncertain, and arbitrary. From Derrida's point of view (as represented by Abrams and Altieri), although we admittedly act as if we know what a given statement says, we do so out of habit or fear (among many other possibilities): we are accustomed to taking the particular statement that way; we may get in trouble if we do not. Derrida thus realizes that in practice we put a stop to the otherwise endless play of undecidable meanings. But he questions the legitimacy of our interpretive decisions. Lacking the support of nature, reason, or some other transcendental signified, these decisions seem to him groundless or, what becomes the same thing, authorized only by custom and convenience.

According to Altieri and Abrams, Wittgenstein takes a different tack. Although the *Investigations* says very little about literary criticism, Altieri and Abrams extrapolate from it as well as from the work of other ordinary-language philosophers (especially J. L. Austin) a way of salvaging the cognitive claims of interpretation while conceding its lack of metaphysical grounding. For Wittgenstein, in this reading, interpretation admittedly rests on criteria that are flexible, diverse, subtle, approximate, and institutionally (as opposed to metaphysically) based. Moreover, when we construe the meaning of a text, such seemingly subjective qualities as tact, imagination, and temperament do come into play. But Wittgenstein helps us resist Derrida's conclusion that interpretation is therefore arbitrary. From Wittgenstein's point of view, although we cannot be absolutely sure about the meaning of a text, we can be sure enough. As Abrams puts it,

> Language is a highly complex conventional practice that requires no ontological or epistemological absolute or foundation in order to do its work; furthermore, . . . we have convincing evidence that as speakers or auditors, writers or readers, we share the regularities of this practice in a way that makes possible determinacy of communication and also makes it possible to utter assertions that can not only be understood determinately, but adjudged validly to be true or false. Such understanding can never be absolutely certain, nor can the asserted truths be absolute truths; understanding can at best be an adequate or practical assurance, and the truths practically certain within the limits of a given frame of reference. That is simply our human condition. But we should not let what Derrida calls our human "nostalgia" for absolute certainties blind us to the fact that, as an inherited and shared practice, and despite the attested failures in some attempts at communication, language in fact can work, can work determinately, and can work wonderfully well—in literature as in other modes of discourse. ("Construing" 162)

Instead of satisfying Derrida's metaphysical longing for absolutes, Wittgenstein thus sets it aside by attending to our practical ways of settling meaning. In Altieri's phrase, there is no center—but there need not be one. Instead of plunging us in an abyss, the fall from metaphysics reaches bedrock in what we humans do. We thus "arrive at a perspective on origins that voids the whole problem" ("Wittgenstein" 1418).

For Abrams and Altieri, the problem, again, is Derrida's insatiable desire for absolutes, a holdover from the metaphysical thinking that he claims to deconstruct. Both Altieri and Abrams read this desire as a misapplied demand for certainty that can leave the literary critic feeling understandably vulnerable and apologetic. But in their view this defensiveness gives way to confidence when we realize that interpretive criteria, though admittedly soft by scientific standards, nevertheless are shared. In Abrams's opinion, these criteria have withstood centuries of debate about literature—and they continue to hold up well: "In the last analysis, we can only appeal to our linguistic tact, as supported by the agreement of readers who share that tact." But because these readers include just about everyone, or everyone whose opinion we care about, their sharing our view of interpretive competence sufficiently validates it. "Such an appeal," Abrams concedes, "has no probative weight for a reader [like the deconstructionist] who has opted out of playing the game of language according to its constitutive regularities; nor is the application of our inherited practice verifiable by any proof outside its sustainedly coherent working" ("How to Do Things" 587). Still, the near universality of our criteria shows that they are stable enough for us to be assured (though never absolutely certain) of their value.

Altieri makes much the same point in *Act and Quality,* although he emphasizes less the constancy of interpretive criteria than our sharing them here and now:

> It is the grammatical competence which education in a culture produces that enables us to establish criteria for appropriateness and then to rely on practical considerations for defining degrees of probable relevance in hypotheses about meanings. . . . Within these procedural frameworks, Derrida's ontological skepticism is not so much refuted as revealed to be irrelevant for the rough grounds that sustain human communication. It may well be the case that we have no absolutely secure grounds for *truth,* but the more important question is whether we need these grounds for coherent discourse, even on the self-reflective levels within which philosophical analysis takes place. (40)

In literary criticism as in everyday language, from this point of view, we do not need these "absolutely secure grounds for truth," however much Derrida might inappropriately seek them. Probabilistic grounds are all we have to go on and all we need.

"All we need" reintroduces those practical considerations that both Abrams and Altieri emphasize. Even without metaphysical sanctions, language works well enough to allow one person to warn another to get out of the way of an onrushing bus, to use one of Abrams's examples. Derrida's relentlessly questioning the meaning of a statement thus seems impractical and perhaps dangerous, a luxury that not even apparently idle literary critics can afford. Altieri asks us to "imagine how long one could function in a human community, which is founded on probabilities, not certainties, if each time he received this message ["I will come next week"] he didn't bother to pick the person up, because, after all, he doesn't see it as *exhaustively determinable* and is not sure of all the person's motives" (*Act and Quality* 227–28). Abrams similarly pictures Derrida's skepticism as stymieing the everyday activities of criticism and eventually blocking "access to the inexhaustible variety of literature as determinably meaningful texts by, for, and about human beings" ("How to Do Things" 588). The costly impracticality of Derrida's skepticism reflects its remoteness from what Abrams calls "our ordinary realm of experience in speaking, hearing, reading, and understanding language" ("The Deconstructive Angel" 431), its residing in a "purely logical universe," to use Altieri's phrase (*Act and Quality* 225) where a text is absolutely clear or indeterminate. For Abrams and Altieri, Derrida's questioning thus illustrates what Wittgenstein calls "the confusions which occupy us . . . when language is like an engine idling, not when it is doing work" (*Investigations*, remark 132)—the work of asking for help, warning a friend, and teaching a literary text.

This view of Wittgenstein's pertinence to recent theory appeals to me very much, but I want here to focus on some of its loose ends. This account has difficulty explaining why Derrida is such an absolutist blindly in quest of certainty. Abrams mentions Derrida's nostalgia, Altieri hints at his lack of trust, and, along similar lines, a more recent commentator, James Guetti, alludes darkly to "some powerful compulsion" (I, 77) driving deconstruction. Guetti continues:

> At times any of us may be drawn to the illusory originality of such "theorizing," in our reluctance to accept any sort of "given." The groundlessness of language, the idea that language itself is the ground, at such times seems nothing but a threat and a challenge. We come to a wall, as it were, and then, instead of describing what it looks like, continue to beat on it as if it were a door. (I, 83)

I want to know why we do this. Guetti's explanation sounds condescending to me ("we all make mistakes and do silly things," he seems to be telling the deconstructionist); Altieri and Abrams's account is more sympathetic but still vague. All three of these critics have a hard time appreciating deconstruction, despite the generosity they want to show it. Conceding that "some of [Derrida's] characteristic modes of verbal and rhetorical play are very infectious," Abrams compares deconstructive criticism to epideictic rhetoric or "display oratory" in which the critic, instead of trying "to tell us anything we don't know already about his ostensible subject," (merely?) attempts "to display his own invention, verbal and rhetorical skills, and aplomb for the admiration and delight of his audience" ("Construing" 173, 170). Altieri values Derrida's doubt "for applying a kind of pressure on familiar realities that can make us aware of how our ordinary activities are in fact anchored and how we characteristically determine meanings and values'' ("Wittgenstein on Consciousness'' 1398). This is a little like saying sickness makes us appreciate health.

Wittgenstein's capacity for accepting ordinary criteria, for giving up Derrida's vain desire for absolute certainty, also needs analyzing. In Derrida's all-or-nothing world, according to the reading that I have been discussing, the glass (for some unexplained reason) is always empty; for Wittgenstein, it is half full, or full enough to slake our real thirst (as opposed to our gluttonous metaphysical cravings) and to let us carry on with the day-to-day, practical activities of criticism. Critics who take such a view of Wittgenstein tend to idealize him, as Guetti does when he discusses Derrida's fatal "appetite'' for absolutes: "Either Wittgenstein did not have such an appetite, such an urge to account for and dismiss all at once—and that is hard to imagine of any human being—or he was heroically capable of controlling it'' (I, 78). Guetti opts for the latter possibility, going on to praise how in Wittgenstein "descriptive attention to the specific ways words work in our use of them is *never* sacrificed to anything else'' (78, my emphasis), especially not to the "relentless abstractions'' that preoccupy the deconstructionist. I want to know whether there is any way of accounting for Wittgenstein's apparent forgoing of both metaphysics and skepticism—any way short of canonizing him.

The questions I have been asking of this reading of Wittgenstein and Derrida are prompted by a question Cavell asks of the ordinary-language critique of skepticism. Put very briefly, this critique faults the skeptic for obsessively, or inexplicably, seeking certainty. J. L. Austin (in "Other Minds'') offers a version of this argument when he objects that the skeptic is "prone to argue that because I *sometimes* don't know or can't discover, I *never* can'' (quoted in *Claim* 133). Austin here indicts the skeptic's impatience with "sometimes'' and the rough ground of human experience, where birds (to use one of Austin's illustrations) will not sit still long enough for us to identify them conclusively but where we can nevertheless be reasonably sure that X is a woodpecker and not a goldfinch. The similarity between this response to skepticism and the critique of Derrida that I have been reviewing derives from Abrams and Altieri's indebtedness to Austin as well as to Wittgenstein, which I noted earlier. (Abrams's "How to Do Things with Texts'' obviously alludes to Austin.) While acknowledging differences between Austin and Wittgenstein, both Abrams and Altieri emphasize that the two philosophers share an appreciation for ordinary language and everyday experience—an appreciation they find missing in skepticism. Although also influenced by Austin (*The Claim of Reason* is in part dedicated to him), Cavell is less willing to conflate him with Wittgenstein as antiskeptical philosophers. "Compared with Wittgenstein,'' Cavell notes in "The Politics of Interpretation,'' "Austin has no account of [the] emptiness'' into which skepticism drifts (37). Put differently, Austin seems more intent than Wittgenstein on preventing skepticism "from getting off the ground'' (''Politics'' 33)—more inclined to blunt the skeptic's questioning than to probe its motivation.

Austin's example here leads Cavell to ask why the skeptic sets the sights of knowledge too high—why he is drawn ''to just *this* form of self-defeat'' (''In Quest'' 216–17), why he apparently turns an everyday difficulty (making sure X is a woodpecker) into an epistemological impossibility:

> To suppose [as the ordinary-language philosopher supposes] the philosopher has done the foolishly self-defeating thing of raising standards (here, standards of certainty) so high that *of course* no human knowledge can attain them, is to treat him as though he had set his heart, say, on having human beings rise ten feet in the air without external prompting, or defined ''getting into the air'' as ''getting ten feet into the air,'' and then, finding the world high jump record to reach short of eight feet, realized with a shock that no human being can really even get off the ground, and said as consolation to all jumpers, ''You jump high enough for practical purposes.'' (*Claim* 221–22)

In Cavell's account, the quest for certainty itself needs explaining, lest it seem gratuitous or perverse, something the skeptic is only ''prone to argue'' and everyone else is entitled, even encouraged, to forget.

Cavell suggests that ''skepticism's 'doubt' is motivated not by (not even where it is expressed as) a (misguided) intellectual scrupulousness but by a (displaced) denial, by a self-consuming disappointment that seeks world-consuming revenge'' (*Disowning Knowledge* 5–6). According to Abrams and Altieri, as I have been saying, skepticism's ''doubt'' is expressed as intellectual scrupulousness in Derrida and other recent theorists for whom the context and intent of a statement must be ''exhaustively determinable,'' ''totally present,'' and ''immediately transparent to itself and to others'' for the statement to be determinate (quoted in Altieri, *Act and Quality* 225). Cavell's own example of declared intellectual scrupulousness is Othello, who illustrates ''the murderous lengths to which narcissism [defined here as ''a kind of denial of an existence shared with others''] must go in order to maintain its picture of itself as skepticism, in order to maintain its stand of ignorance, its fear or avoidance of knowing, under the color of a claim to certainty'' (*Themes* 61). By Othello's ''stand of ignorance,'' Cavell in part means Othello's professed uncertainty about Desdemona's virtue, his suspicion that she is a whore. ''A claim to certainty,'' that is, a commitment to intellectual scrupulousness, presumably fuels Othello's doubt: he wants to be absolutely sure that Desdemona is chaste. He will have ''ocular proof.'' When the evidence (the handkerchief, for instance) apparently suggests Desdemona's guilt, or at least fails to demonstrate her innocence, Othello accordingly convicts her in the play's final scene.

I say ''professed uncertainty'' because in Cavell's view Othello in fact knows that Desdemona is innocent but tries to avoid that knowledge (hence Cavell's putting ''doubt'' in quotation marks in the passage I started out discussing). Ignorance (of Desdemona's fidelity) is a stand he wants, maybe even has, to take; similarly, his commitment to certainty, instead of justifying or motivating his actions, belatedly tries to excuse them. Although Othello knows the falsity of Iago's suspicions, he has a use for them. In Cavell's words, "However far he believes Iago's tidings, he cannot just believe them; somewhere he also *knows* them to be false" (*Claim* 488).

But where? How does Cavell know this? Othello's own actions betray him. His urgent latching on to Iago's version of things smacks of desperation, not dispassionate inquiry. Cavell derives this desperation not from Othello's failure with Desdemona (his impotence, say, or her frigidity) but from his success, his eliciting her desire. He is surprised, Cavell says, "that she is flesh and blood" (*Claim* 491), the one thing this romantic hero does not want to see about himself (for if she is flesh and blood, then he must be, since they are one). In Cavell's words, "He cannot forgive Desdemona for existing, for being separate from him, outside, beyond command" (*Claim* 491), for contesting his pure image of himself, for finding him out or making him face his own sexuality and mortality. His anxiously arrived at doubts about her faithfulness thus cover or evade an even more terrible certainty: Desdemona exists, is flesh and blood, separate, and in need. So is he.

Instead of confronting his own humanity, Othello thus tries to change the subject. He would rather make Desdemona's love "an intellectual difficulty, a riddle" (*Claim* 493) than acknowledge what it says about him. What Othello lacked was not knowledge, no matter how hard he tried to maintain his stand of ignorance or how often he pledged his allegiance to certainty. "He knew everything," Cavell writes, "but he could not yield to what he knew, be commanded by it. He found out too much for his mind, not too little. Their [Desdemona and Othello's] differences from one another—the one everything the other is not— form an emblem of human separation, which can be accepted, and granted, or not" (*Claim* 496). Othello's "self-consuming disappointment"—his denial of his own mortality—thus encourages his "(misguided) intellectual scrupulousness" and leads him to kill Desdemona, his "world-consuming revenge."

This reading of Othello's declared commitment to certainty and proof returns us to Wittgenstein and Derrida. For Cavell, philosophical expressions of skepticism "intellectualize" problems also worked out in literature. More specifically, skepticism in philosophy appears as tragedy in literature. Cavell leaves open any question of priority here, preferring to say that what philosophy (for instance, Wittgenstein) interprets as other-minds or external-world skepticism, literature (here Shakespeare) analyzes as tragedy and even melodrama. In Cavell's words, "Both skepticism and tragedy conclude with the condition of human separation, with a discovering that I am I; and the fact that the alternative to my acknowledgment of the other is not my ignorance of him but my avoidance of him, call it my denial of him. Acknowledgment is to be studied, is what is studied, in the avoidances that tragedy studies" (*Claim* 389).

Derrida's stated dedication to certainty links him to Othello. Cavell notes that skepticism tends to "soberize, or respectify, or scientize itself, claiming, for example, greater precision or accuracy or intellectual scrupulousness than, for practical purposes, we are forced to practice in our ordinary lives" ("In Quest" 197). Along these lines, Derrida and the critics he has influenced represent themselves as unusually tough-minded, uncompromising, suspicious, and rigorous.[2] They see themselves as seeking a tighter connection with texts than everyday academic life demands, as consequently staring harder at the text and otherwise paying more careful attention to it than we ordinarily do—hence the often stated commitment of these critics to close, good, or slow reading.

Altieri and Abrams, as I have suggested, take deconstructive critics at their word but go on to find their intellectual fastidiousness misguided. From this point of view, recent theorists (for some unexplained reason) expect too much.[3] Their commitment to certainty is admirable but out of place in literary criticism and everyday life, where we have to be content with half-truths, probabilities, inferences, educated guesses, and some degree of indeterminacy.

Likening Derrida to Cavell's Othello, as I have begun to do, puts Derrida's call for conclusive proof in a much different light.[4] In Cavell's terms, the resemblance suggests that Derrida's doubt about literary meaning, though expressed as a (misguided) intellectual scrupulousness, is nevertheless motivated by a (displaced) denial, a self-consuming disappointment that seeks world-consuming revenge (a revenge that leaves nothing outside the text?). I mean this statement to be provocative. I would like it to provoke questions like these: What might Derrida deny or avoid under the guise of seeking certainty? What might he be disappointed in? Instead of expecting too much from literature and language, is he recoiling from their lucidity, their considerable power to reveal us?

I want here to raise these questions, not to answer them. But I feel obligated at least to suggest what thinking about them will entail. Take the deconstructionist's stated commitment to close, or slow, reading. Such apparently careful attention to the text (say in an essay by Paul de Man or J. Hillis Miller) resembles the hyberbolic concentration at work in external-world skepticism, where, Cavell says, "the philosopher is as it were looking for a *response* from the object, perhaps a shining" (*Disowning Knowledge* 8). The literary critic's excruciatingly detailed interrogation of the text at first looks like a strained attempt really to know it and not just glance at it as most of us presumably do. But staring at the text, though apparently aiming at penetrating it, may be evading an uncomfortably close connection that has already been made—much as staring at people, Cavell notes, "shows a specific response to the claim they make upon us, a specific form of acknowledgment; for example, rejection" (*Must We Mean* 331). Our problem as critics accordingly may not be making the text present but acknowledging its presence—not establishing a more certain view of the text (say by reading it more closely or slowly) but facing up to what is already clear (say by acting on it).[5]

This response to deconstruction is inspired not only by Cavell's reading of *Othello* but also by his more general suggestion that in skepticism "we first deprive words of their communal possession and then magically and fearfully attempt by ourselves to overcome this deprivation of ourselves by ourselves" ("In Quest" 197). "Deprives" suggests not that our ties to others are initially frayed, as the skeptic would have us suppose, but that if anything they can feel too tight. Among these ties to others, I am implicitly including literature, putting literary works on a par with shouts, gestures, embraces, and jokes, in short, with "all the whirl of organism Wittgenstein calls 'forms of life' " (*Must We Mean* 52). From Cavell's point of view, our attunement with others—"our sharing routes of interest and feeling, modes of response, senses of humor and of significance and of fulfillment, of what is outrageous, of what is similar to what else, what a rebuke, what forgiveness, of when an utterance is an assertion, when an appeal, when an explanation" (52)—all of this goes even more deeply than Abrams and Altieri imply. Human relationships still depend on choice, risk, and effort, but we choose to let ourselves be known, we risk acknowledging our expressions as us, and we struggle against our fear of exposure, our terror of being found out.

The inability, or unwillingness, to notice something because it is before one's eyes and our wanting to *understand* something that is already in plain view are of course two of the problems taken up by Wittgenstein in the *Investigations*. Wittgenstein (refracted through *Othello*) plays a crucial role in formulating the questions that Cavell asks of skepticism and that I have been trying to direct toward recent literary theory. Using Wittgenstein to raise questions, not to answer them, becomes in Cavell one way of countering the idealization of Wittgenstein that I objected to earlier. In this reading, familiar phrases in Wittgenstein become complex tasks, not talismans for warding off skeptical doubt.

Here is just one example, chosen because it bears on the critique of deconstruction made by Abrams and Altieri: "What *we* do is to bring words back from their metaphysical to their everyday use" (*Investigations*, remark 116). Cavell resists the temptation to read this as a boast. "We" here is opposed not to "metaphysicians" or "skeptics" but to that side of ourselves that allows words to stray, or drift. Philosophical problems (e.g., the problem of other minds) and their often desperate solutions (e.g., "I can only *believe* that someone else is in pain, but I *know* it if I am" [remark 303]) arise when words (such as "know" and "believe") stray. Turned in circles by these problems, we feel lost ("A philosophical problem has the form: 'I don't know my way about' " [remark 123]).

As Abrams and Altieri point out, in responding to these problems, Wittgenstein does counsel bringing words back, or home, to the language games in which they are ordinarily used. But instead of voiding philosophical problems, as Altieri would have it, bringing words back constantly treats these problems as everyday temptations. In Cavell's words, "Wittgenstein's form of philosophical problem does not speak of *a* middle of a journey, but of many journeys, many middles, of repeated losses and recoveries of oneself" ("Wittgenstein" 7). Noting the "incessant turnings [of the *Investigations*] upon itself," Cavell finds

in Wittgenstein an "acceptance of a repetition that includes endless specific suc-
cumbings to the conditions of skepticism and endless specific recoveries from it"
(*Disowning Knowledge* 39). Instead of answering skeptical doubts or always
mastering them, Wittgenstein undoes them, "repeatedly, unmelodramatically,
uneventfully" ("Wittgenstein" 40).

Some recent writers on Wittgenstein, influenced by Derrida, have noted the
twists and turns in the *Investigations* that Cavell is alluding to here.[6] But for these
writers, repetition in Wittgenstein smacks of unintended failure or deliberate
irony. Endlessly having to bring words home suggests that Wittgenstein himself
is paradoxically lost, like "a blind man feeling his way with his stick . . . constrained by the accidental [as opposed to the essential or ontological] at every
turn," as Henry Staten describes it (94). Cavell, too, sees Wittgenstein stumbling as he traverses the admittedly uneven ground of our life together. (One
moral of Cavell's treatment of skepticism is that we learn "to live with stumbling" ["In Quest" 184], say in our reading one another.) But for Cavell, instead
of annulling Wittgenstein's progress, repetition and stumbling characterize it.
The result is neither irony (Wittgenstein slipping and sliding and getting nowhere) nor some final victory over skepticism (Wittgenstein making philosophical problems disappear once and for all) but everyday, purposive activity, analogous in its pedestrian but goal-directed endlessness to constructing or keeping
up a house.[7] (Interested in bringing words home, Wittgenstein, like Thoreau,
makes building a crucial trope for his own writing, not just a source of illustrations.) This is how Cavell understands Wittgenstein's claim in the *Investigations*
to give philosophy peace (remark 133). It is not that philosophy ever ends, or
never ends, but "that in each case it brings itself to an end" ("Wittgenstein"
39), time after time after time.

Cavell speaks of Wittgenstein seeking conversion and discipleship from his
readers and consequently being leery of understanding not accompanied by inner
change.[8] As a response to Wittgenstein, "belief is not enough" (*Must We Mean*
71–72): for one thing, it is not clear what there is to believe (as Wittgenstein puts
it in the *Investigations*, "If one tried to advance *theses* in philosophy, it would
never be possible to debate them, because everyone would agree to them"
[remark 128]). This commitment to inner growth and ceaseless self-scrutiny can
seem narcissistic or self-indulgent. But Cavell uses Wittgenstein to explore our
mutual attunement, or, what is the same thing, to counter our murderous evasions
of the existence we share with others. As I have been speculating, these evasions
may take the form of smothering a person, or a text, with seemingly scrupulous
questions.

Notes

1. I should also mention Walter Glannon, who argues that Wittgenstein is at odds with deconstructive theory despite superficial similarities (270), and Anthony Close, who uses Abrams's "basically Wittgensteinian and Austinian" approach to underwrite a "traditionalist" critique of Foucault
and Derrida.

2. Apologists for deconstruction like Jonathan Culler and Christopher Norris routinely laud its rigor. See Norris's *Deconstructive Turn* for a typical affirmation of "deconstructionist rigor" (6–7).

3. For a similar complaint about recent theorists, see Gombrich 689–90.

4. In comparing Derrida to Othello, I am tacitly aligning deconstruction with skepticism. I realize that this is a move that has been challenged but will only note here that I am extending the willingness of friends as well as foes of deconstruction to link it to skepticism. On the differences between deconstruction and skepticism, see Cascardi; on their similarities, see Goodheart, Cantor, Altieri, *Act and Quality*, Abrams, "Construing" 130, and Norris, *Deconstruction* xii.

5. Among the many questions raised, or begged, by this analysis, one is particularly important: what is my alternative to the slow or close reading favored by deconstructionists? In thinking that such an alternative exists, I have been helped by Peter Rabinowitz's argument in "Against Close Reading."

6. I have in mind Norris, *The Deconstructive Turn* 34–58, and Staten. Norris makes much of Wittgenstein's alleged wariness of metaphor and the power of figurative language to subvert Wittgenstein's supposedly antiskeptical, logocentric intentions. Cavell's Wittgenstein is much more hospitable to metaphor and not at all bent on refuting skepticism. See *Themes*, where Cavell argues that Wittgenstein's "call for the return to the everyday," instead of being threatened by figurative language, "requires its own ironies, hints, jokes, parables, and silences" (231). For further discussion of Staten, see Fischer.

7. In *Themes* Cavell accordingly notes that "irony is as much [Wittgenstein's] enemy as his aspiration" (196). Cavell's "Wittgenstein" highlights the importance of building to the *Investigations* as well as to *Walden*.

8. Cavell has often questioned whether Wittgenstein's aims and methods can be institutionalized. Cavell's willingness to pursue these aspirations in his own work may explain his long-standing quarrel with academic philosophy as well as his need to write many of his themes out of school.

Works Cited

Abrams, M. H. "Construing and Deconstructing." In *Romanticism and Contemporary Criticism*. Ed. Morris Eaves and Michael Fischer. Ithaca, N.Y.: Cornell UP, 1986. 127–82.

———. "The Deconstructive Angel." *Critical Inquiry* 3 (1977): 425–38.

———. "How to Do Things with Texts." *Partisan Review* 46 (1979): 566–88.

Altieri, Charles. *Act and Quality*. Amherst: U of Massachusetts P, 1981.

———. "Wittgenstein on Consciousness and Language: A Challenge to Derridean Theory." *MLN* 91 (1976): 1397–1423.

Cantor, Jay. "On Stanley Cavell." *Raritan* 1 (1981): 48–67.

Cascardi, A. J. "Skepticism and Deconstruction." *Philosophy and Literature* 8 (1984): 1–14.

Cavell, Stanley. *The Claim of Reason*. Oxford: Oxford UP, 1979.

———. *Disowning Knowledge in Six Plays of Shakespeare*. Cambridge: Cambridge UP, 1987.

———. "In Quest of the Ordinary: Themes of Recovery." In *Romanticism and Contemporary Criticism*. Ed. Morris Eaves and Michael Fischer. Ithaca, N.Y.: Cornell UP, 1986. 183–240.

———. *Must We Mean What We Say?* 1969; rpt. Cambridge: Cambridge UP, 1979.

———. "The Politics of Interpretation." In *Themes Out of School*. 27–59.

———. *Themes Out of School*. San Francisco: North Point, 1984.

———. "Wittgenstein as a Philosopher of Culture." Unpublished paper.

Close, Anthony. "Centering the De-Centers: Foucault and *Las Meninas*." *Philosophy and Literature* 11 (1987): 21–36.

Culler, Jonathan. *On Deconstruction*. Ithaca, N.Y.: Cornell UP, 1982.

Fischer, Michael. Review of Henry Staten's *Wittgenstein and Derrida*. *Philosophy and Literature* 10 (1986): 93–97.

Glannon, Walter. "What Literary Theory Misses in Wittgenstein." *Philosophy and Literature* 10 (1986): 263–72.

Gombrich, E. H. " 'They Were All Human Beings—So Much Is Plain': Reflections on Cultural Relativism in the Humanities." *Critical Inquiry* 13 (1987): 686–99.

Goodheart, Eugene. *The Skeptic Disposition in Contemporary Criticism*. Princeton, N.J.: Princeton UP, 1984.

Guetti, James. "Wittgenstein and Literary Theory I." *Raritan* 4, No. 2 (1984): 67–84.

———. "Wittgenstein and Literary Theory II." *Raritan* 4, No. 3 (1984): 66–84.

Norris, Christopher. *Deconstruction: Theory and Practice*. London and New York: Methuen, 1982.

———. *The Deconstructive Turn*. London and New York: Methuen, 1983.

Rabinowitz, Peter. "Against Close Reading." Lecture, Hamilton College, October 25, 1986.

Staten, Henry. *Wittgenstein and Derrida*. Lincoln: U of Nebraska P, 1984.

Wittgenstein, Ludwig. *Philosophical Investigations*. 3rd ed. Trans. G. E. M. Anscombe. New York: Macmillan, 1958.

4

Judgment and Justice under Postmodern Conditions; or, How Lyotard Helps Us Read Rawls as a Postmodern Thinker

Charles Altieri

We have lived long enough with the complex of critical ideas developed by the poststructural revolution of the seventies that we no longer have much passion for debate. Indeed, in literary criticism, at least, abstract debate is almost impossible—in part because the master theorists like Derrida and Foucault have now become so assimilated into a range of perspectives that there are too many variants for any theoretical argument to address cogently, and in part because the new ways of reading have so pervaded critical practice that it is extremely difficult to isolate the relevant underlying assumptions. But there may be a substantial price for such freedom, since we now have considerable trouble managing to create the distance necessary if we are to exercise on ourselves the same critical scrutiny we try to impose on the authors and the social orders we study. How do we make judgments about the social values of our practices when the practices themselves seem so adamantly suspicious of all moral generalizations and so insistent on self-interest and wills to power as the only realistic motives attributable to (other) human agents? And how can criticism clearly distinguish its version of those attitudes from quite similar stances that are basic to the bourgeois values most of the new criticism is eager to condemn? There too a demystified materialism makes all traditional ideals suspect, requires seeking other, hidden motives beneath a person's overt claims, and breeds a suspicion of all abstraction so that one's self-interest need not be justified by any publicly shareable criteria—after all, what categories could possibly hold authority in a marketplace defined as the site for maximizing individual benefits?

My moral in offering such reflections is obvious: even though we can no longer debate the incommensurable epistemological principles informing our critical commitments, we may be able to find common grounds for assessing the ethical values that critical positions inculcate and the self-representations they allow us to give to our actions as we pursue those commitments. For here the relevant theater does not require our engaging in the kinds of foundational arguments that have become suspect. The basic questions are pragmatic—at stake is the degree to which we can subscribe to or respect particular ways of taking responsibility for values and of spelling out their possible social consequences. So it should be possible to locate representative positions and to elaborate significant comparisons with those who do not accept the stances that are now becoming increasingly naturalized. The work will not be easy and cannot be definitive. Nonetheless I think we will find it very instructive to concentrate on one particular contrast—between the recent work on justice done by Jean-François Lyotard, arguably the poststructuralist philosopher who has most broadly and least ideologically faced the important ethical issues, and by John Rawls, a philosopher working out of the Anglo-American analytic tradition. I shall argue that Lyotard provides a compelling case against the basic assumptions of most analytic work in ethics, but as he tries to address the problems he exposes he ends up revealing fundamental limitations in poststructural modes of thinking. Then we can see that Rawls actually provides a political ethics that responds better to Lyotard's version of the postmodern condition than do Lyotard's own positive claims.

Lyotard succintly sets the historical and the conceptual stage in the summary passage of his *Postmodern Condition*:

> We no longer have recourse to the grand narratives—we can resort neither to the dialectic of Spirit nor even to the emancipation of humanity as a validation for postmodern scientific discourse. But as we have just seen, the little narrative remains the quintessential form of imaginative invention, most particularly in science. In addition, the principle of consensus as a criterion of validation seems to be inadequate. It has two formulations. In the first, consensus is an agreement between men, defined as knowing intellects and free wills, and is obtained through dialogue. This is the form elaborated by Habermas, but his conception is based on the narrative of emancipation. In the second, consensus is a component of the system, which manipulates it in order to maintain and improve its performance. It is the object of administrative procedures in Luhmann's sense. In this case, its only validity is as an instrument to be used toward achieving the real goal, which is what legitimates the system—power. (60–61)

Then he proceeds to argue that the only possible alternative to these disguised impositions of someone's will to power is to replace those failed theories, even those on the left, by establishing models of judging "without criteria." Such models will make it possible to separate the "discourse of justice" from "the discourse of truth" and therefore will cast justice as the liberating of minorites from the "terror" that always follows the authority of the "Idea" (*Just Gaming* 16, 98, 92).[1]

A pre-postmodern thinker would find much here that seems melodramatic, or that tempts one to read against this text. Clearly it takes a version of grand narrative to announce the demise of grand narratives; it takes monumental ignorance of science to think that it has given up its commitments to general principles of rationality and even of progress; and it takes sublime gall to assume either that there ever was some simple principle of consensus making validation possible in social life or that the force of Habermas's position depends on his narrative of emancipation. And yet there is something undeniably right and undeniably challenging in this account of how the political and moral theater has changed in the past two decades. While human beings have probably never agreed on political ends, they have perhaps never had so many available ways to justify disagreement or even to find it impossible to understand what could possibly produce agreement. And while science may still hold to its particular version of rationality, this diversity of political perspectives makes it increasingly difficult to imagine that rationality having any relation to a social order composed of historical practices over which agents have very little control. There has always been skepticism, but there has rarely been such widespread skepticism about the "authority of the 'idea' " itself or about the nature of the agents who must make judgments in terms of such ideas. As we break ideas down into the narratives that produce them, we also break the integrated self down into the various language practices that afford it its positions for desiring and rationalizing certain ends. And as we then grow increasingly suspicious of abstract efforts to adjudicate those differences, the authority of any adjudicating discipline (the dream of philosophy) gives way to warring sociological accounts of how ideas actually pursue and distribute power.

As much as one might resent Lyotard's tone and his methods, it is difficult to deny that he is persuasive in his insistence that we have entered an age that is irrecuperably post-enlightenment, and therefore postmodern. We find ourselves relegating to the distant past the faith that all "progressive" modes of social thinking could agree on a version of the emancipation story in which a single set of methods could dispel superstition and establish a shared criterion by which competing ethical positions could adjudicate their differences. Now those differences have overwhelmed the categories that had contained them. And now it seems to me necessary that any plausible theory of general social bonds derive not from general categories but from what can be predicated of those incommensurable libidinal and economic interests manipulating the very ideals of consensus and rationality. Thus while the noble project of a Habermas may continue to tempt us, perspectives like Lyotard's force us to face the difficulties involved in positing a single teleology of speech behavior, in preferring a story of liberated rationality to other possible teleologies, and in imposing certain models of the good that have made it impossible to hear the needs and desires of groups committed to other versions of political judgment.

However, while such changes may be inevitable, it is by no means clear that they are as desirable as thinkers like Lyotard make them out to be, nor is it clear that the kinds of solutions proposed by Lyotard, or even by less radical and melodramatic postmodern thinkers like Rorty, adequately address the problems that call them into being. It may be that the more Enlightenment values seem to fail because of their false universalism, the more we need to return to the other side of the Enlightenment coin by once again worrying about how agents can constitute public identities for themselves under conditions of social reciprocity. Such ambitions may also be able to negotiate the incommensurable differences characterizing the contemporary polis. In fact, if we set these ideals in opposition to Lyotard, we may be able to locate the basic limitations in his way of facing the issues. And on that basis we may be able to tease out what remains problematic in the fundamental assumptions about the needs and powers of human agents and the nature of political structures governing most poststructural thought.

To do that to Lyotard is why Rawls shall appear on the scene. Yet I am equally interested in what Lyotard will do for our appreciation of Rawls. Although Rawls's *Theory of Justice* has for the past decade been the central work in American political and economic theory, it is almost never taken up by poststructuralist philosophy and by literary theory, even in its recent political phase. The reasons are not hard to envision: Rawls is quite clearly a rationalist bound to the most dangerous of Enlightenment illusions (i.e., that diverse agents could agree on a contractual model of the state); his reliance on Kant is not likely to charm thinkers devoted to Nietzsche; and the issues he concentrates on smack of the empirical interests that still make French philosophers treat utilitarianism as vulgar social science. Yet once we begin to read Rawls in the light of self-consciously postmodern thematics, I think we begin to see how thoroughly and intensely this classical bourgeois thinker has in fact confronted precisely those issues that must now engage poststructural theory. While Rawls's aims involve the restoration of consensus, his version of a Kantian model of agency provides him the means to address a political and ethical order torn between incommensurable versions of the good. Rawls offers accounts of political judgment and of political identity that build the social order not on what agents share but on what they must make of their irreconcilable differences. Rather than conceive difference as derived from identity, Rawls begins with the primacy of difference, then tries to construct a reflective theater in which the differences can be negotiated and a complex model of hypothetical identifications elaborated. I do not think even these devices will ensure the desired consensus, but they can at the very least force the competing positions to make their interests clear so that observers can see how interests might overlap or can judge the delusions that emerge as the agents adapt those interests to a Rawlsian calculus.

I

Lyotard's version of political judgment has its origin in aesthetics, for it is there that he first worked out the limitations of discursive representation and postulated a psychology enabling him to emphasize immediate libidinal energies unrecuperable by reflection. Thus the Bergsonian distinctions between discourse and the visible explored in *Discours, Figure* provide the conceptual framework for the map of the psyche defined by *Economie Libidinale*. Then armed with his vision of agency Lyotard could turn to the historical analogues modulating the aesthetic into the political:

> Modern aesthetics is an aesthetics of the sublime, though a nostalgic one. It allows the unrepresentable to be put forward only as the missing contents; but the form, because of its recognizable consistency, continues to offer the reader or viewer matter for solace and pleasure. . . . The Postmodern would be that in which, in the modern, puts forward the unrepresentable in presentation itself; that which denies itself the solace of good forms, the consensus of a taste which would make it possible to share collectively the nostalgia for the unattainable, that which searches for new presentations, not in order to enjoy them but in order to impart a stronger sense of the unrepresentable. . . . It must be clear that it is our business not to supply reality but to invent allusions to the conceivable which cannot be presented. (*Postmodern Condition* 81)

In many respects this is Derrida historicized, since the sublime is the force of difference that pervades both the object of representation and the formal framework of presentation. But Derrida historicized is a very different animal from Derrida imitated. For Lyotard "the fact that the unrepresentable exists" (*Postmodern Condition* 78) imposes two eminently political tasks—locating in society the fundamental energies that continually undo representation and testing theory's own capacity to employ the gulf between the conceivable and the presentable in order to show how the collapse of master narratives might provide the framework necessary for making these unrepresentable forces active within political life. Such tasks free the concept of an "other of representation" from the romantic discourses on which it is based, while at the same time projecting concrete historical implications for the modes of the sublime that the model generated. Locating what is not represented within presentations is not a mystical endeavor; we need only attend to the ways in which certain groups or speech communities lack the power to establish their own versions of their interests and actions. Then the metaphysics of difference becomes the politics of the *différend*, acutely aware of how the power to regulate conflicts imposes "the idiom of one of the parties while the injustice suffered by the other is not signified in that idiom" (*Le Différend* sec. 10). The *différend* is what the prevailing idiom cannot represent, so the task of the conceivable is to begin restoring a voice to that other of representation. For there to be a politics we must be willing to judge—otherwise one only complies with or evades the tyranny of established models of representation; yet if we are also to heed that voice of the other we must insist on judging "without criteria" (*Just Gaming* 16). Once we posit the need for criteria we inevitably rely on the descriptive and deductive models that result in imposing inappropriate demands on those who are "different" and whose ways resist our representational structures. Moreover, in judging without criteria we stand outside the entire domain of representations and displacements. There cannot be descriptive claims that justify such choices on the basis of either need or plausible consequences. Instead, we rely on the conceivable by basing our sense of justice on a pure prescription obliging us to preserve the independence and purity of the various language games or genres of discourse that enter the social sphere.

The grammar of the *différend* and its implications for undoing the anthropocentric dimension even of philosophers like Wittgenstein receives its richest treatment in Lyotard's recent *Le Différend*. However, because there he has such grand ambitions and bases them on far-ranging concrete analysis, I find it much more useful to concentrate on *Au Juste*, his work most directly and concisely devoted to the philosophical construction of a distinct political position.[2] In the formulating of that position he shows both why criteria for justice are not available and why one must nonetheless make judgments rather than simply watching or tolerating existing states of affairs.

The case against criteria relies on three basic claims. First, the very idea of criteria assumes that one derives one's sense of prescriptive judgments from descriptive or empirical ones: how we characterize certain features of experience will lead us to certain normative conclusions. But, as Kant knew, one cannot derive an imperative from a description. Descriptions tell us what is, but prescriptions define what we project as ends for what is. More important, prescriptives arrive with the force of an obligation that no description can carry. The point is a familiar one in deontological ethics, but Lyotard gives it a distinctive analysis in terms of the positions that allow narrative theory to connect language games to specific psychological structures:

> This passage from the true to the just raises a problem, because if one were to ground it, it would mean that a prescriptive statement would constitute an obligation only if the one who receives it, that is the addressee of the statement, is able to put himself in the position of the sender of the statement, that is, of its utterer, in order to work out all over again the theoretical discourse that legitimates, in the eyes of this sender, the command that he is issuing. (*Just Gaming* 23)

Lyotard needs his intricate syntax here because he wants us to see that the ideal of description is really an ideal of putting the one who states the imperative in the position where she could also understand the grounds for the utterance. Then every obligation we accept could be traced to its originating condition. But this demand for proof, and for the pyschological flexibility to see how observations generate imperatives, denies the very core of what Levinas shows is fundamental to Jewish culture—the sense that the prescriptive is uttered from a subject position that the auditor cannot share but must heed as absolute obligation. And once we grasp that, we realize that this condition of being obliged to what we cannot observationally replicate also occupies a central place in secular culture, for example, in what Lyotard claims is the pagan structure of relations between sender and addressee. Rather than imagine the narrator as capable of sharing some originating condition, the pagan insists that the narrator comes to stories as their mediator, as first an addressee defined in large part by the terms of the story that she is given. As Bernard Williams argues, although in very different ways, there can be no question of deriving an obligation because it is the story that creates what must count as the moral world within which the agent can improvise.

The next two claims about the relation of description to prescription follow from this grammatical positioning of the subject and the object of obligation. The second claim insists that we can no longer accept the Kantian model of moral autonomy. For an ethical agent to be autonomous it must be possible for the subject who states the law to see herself as the same person as the subject who obeys the law (*Just Gaming* 30–31). Autonomy entails casting the self as both the subject and object of the imperative, both the one who chooses the conditions that bind and the one who then sees itself fulfilled by accepting the obligation. How else can freedom be reconciled with rational objectivity? Such autonomy, however, can have no role in pagan or Jewish language games of prescription because "every narrator presents himself as having first been a narratee" (32). Heteronomy or otherness to the law is the condition of there being a law at all because the obligation comes in the form of being given the command or the story, which then makes demands by defining the position the agent must play within it. The author position is not primary, not the locus of freedom, but is instead subordinated to the other positions defined by the narrative triangle, the poles of reference and of the addressee. Caught in such heteronomy, it becomes plausible to think "There are gods" (or an unconscious) so that "human beings are not the authors of what they tell": "They have a thousand things to do, and they must constantly match wits with the fate they have been given, as well as with the fate they are being given in being made the addressee of any given speech act, such as an an oracle or a dream" (36). This variety then provides the third reason why there can be no criteria for prescriptives because there is obviously a range of incommensurable ways that cultures or language games correlate the claims of the stories that provide identity and the facts within which identity must be played out. As *Le Différend* makes clear, the domain of politics exists because there are no universal imperatives and no means for deriving them by interpreting facts, since the facts must be construed within the narrative positions that are privileged by the various phrase regimes and genres of discourse.

Yet one must judge, and one must do so in the name of ideals of justice. Anything less condemns us to the struggle of warring opinions, each fueled by a will to power and each irreducible because given by the histories that enclose us within them. Lyotard's task then is to elaborate a model of judgment that can admit the lack of criteria yet still have sufficient universalizing force not simply to determine a field for will but to allow us to "to discriminate" and thus "decide between opinions" by "distinguishing what is just and what is not just" (87–88). Such a model could sustain a pagan politics devoted to preserving the multiplicity of local narratives, and it could resist the deconstructive tendency to treat that multiplicity as displacements of some absent yet haunting figural center. But to elaborate the model will take considerable intellectual legerdemain since the project runs counter to the basic Western ways of defining judgment.

Lyotard faces his difficulties directly by engaging Kant, the thinker most influential in shaping philosophical notions of judgment. Lyotard cannot accept Kant's commitment to autonomy or his vision of the idea as defining a universal community shared by all agents to the degree that they are rationally rather than empirically determined in their actions. (In fact, he seems unable even to "conceive" the sense of a distinctive level of rational agency that transforms the individual and gives her access to a domain in which true freedom allies the person to the supersensible.)[3] Yet he still finds in Kant's way of handling judgment two crucial principles that lead in his contrary direction. Kant shows that for there to be morality at all there must be a radical gap between description and prescription, and he then postulates as the *telos* of those prescriptions what he calls "transcendental ideas." For Lyotard that teleology is perfectly suited to his postmodern condition:

> In this manner of instruction, though I start from a description, I do not draw prescriptions from it because one cannot derive prescriptions from descriptions. I start with a description, and what one can do with a description — and that is why I was using the Kantian term of "Idea" a little while ago — is to extend or maximize as much as possible what one believes to be contained in the description. There is, then, a language game that bears upon the description of the French intelligentsia today, especially as a result of the fact that the great narratives that it used to dedicate itself to, no longer claim its allegiance or even concern. And the idea that emerges is that there is a multiplicity of small narratives. And from that "one ought to be pagan" means "one must maximize as much as possible the multiplication of small narratives." This "ought" belongs to the game of dialectics in the Kantian sense, in which there is the use of the concept that is not a use of knowledge but a use of the Idea. . . . Now this "ought" does not signal that a field of prescriptions is opening up; it marks a transit point from a descriptive game whose goal is knowledge of the given, to a descriptive game (by Ideas) of the exploration of the possible. The transit point is marked by the prescriptive. (*Just Gaming* 59)

In Kant a transcendental idea is one that requires our postulating certain properties that can have no referent in the phenomenal world — for example, ideas of a freedom that gives us access to the supersensible or of a teleological force within nature that explains its harmony with the imagination. But the ideas themselves depend on following out the commitment to unity and the principles of syllogistic thinking basic to reason, constraints far too limiting for Lyotard. From his perspective it is necessary to realize that this emphasis on rationality is determined by a single master story. Therefore one must seek instead to see how the transcendental idea can be a quality of various stories, which then can create forms of judgment not bound to specific criteria and yet still capable of establishing an "ought" maximizing the prescriptive force of the game. Lyotard finds the necessary principle in the specific way Kant derives imperatives. One understands why lying must be forbidden or why we must treat the other as an end in itself simply from the sense of how the specific ideal posited within the language game can be most fully realized. While this nondescriptive "Idea" may not have a determinate content that can be derived from experience or tested against it, it still has regulatory power. For the idea is both transcendental and projective. As transcendental it comes as pure obligation so that there is no question of putting oneself in the subject position and giving a rationale for its authorship: one does not rationalize the imperative to be fair that comes with certain games, nor need one justify the feeling of rebellion that comes when certain forces of terror make it impossible to express the feelings of obligation that come to one's particular social group (69–70). Yet these obligations cannot be said to "determine" the will "the way a cause determines an effect" but only in "the way a teleological idea regulates a conduct" (84). That is, the prescription defines a transit point at the horizon of a given game or practice where one realizes what its maximum force or claim might be. The imperatives local to the game then project ideal consequences without quite determining what they are, in the same way that Kant's aesthetic idea suggests an ideal state of agreement for an audience without specifying what that agreement must consist in (91).

II

Lyotard makes the reader do a great deal of work in order to get even this grasp of his argument. Is the result worth the labor? The quest certainly is, since there is no more pressing challenge to political philosophy than to establish normative models compatible with the diverse local positions that we must take as givens within the polity because there is no higher principle for combining interests or imposing shared criteria. Yet there remain crucial problems in Lyotard's formulation that make him for me less useful as an independent thinker than as a measure of what Rawls provides for the same tasks. I think I can support this position by developing three general arguments: that Lyotard's version of the transcendental is even more difficult than Kant's to reconcile with the empirical order that it must eventually effect; that his obsession with terror as the contrast to justice and his refusal to flesh out the obligations of the subject position which are stressed by autonomy theories make it impossible for even a modified version of his principles to help adjudicate actual political conflicts; and that Lyotard's vision of diverse "pure" language games in need of a single regulating principle invites deconstructive analyses showing how political commitments cannot be derived from the regulative ideals that he tries to posit.

All of these problems come to the surface in the passages where Lyotard states the practical import of his arguments:

> If a narrative has the value of a prescriptive, that is, if it claims to prescribe or if it appears to legitimate prescriptions or if a denotative discourse presenting itself as scientific contains or implies prescriptions as well, some-

thing that happens frequently in the case of "experts" in modern capitalist society, then, in such cases one can say the game is impure, and it is clear that, at that moment its effects must be regulated by the Idea of justice. Here the Idea of justice will consist in preserving the purity of each game, that is, for example, in ensuring that the discourse of truth be considered as a "specific" language game, that narration be played by its "specific" rules. To the extent that these language games are accompanied by pre-scriptions of the type "Repeat me" or "Carry me out" or "Implement me," then the idea of justice must regulate these obligations.

It is by means of plurality that it regulates them; it says, "Careful! There is *pleonexia* here, there is excess, there is abuse." . . . The person . . . is not abiding by the pragmatics "proper to the game played." (96–97)

And then the justice of multiplicity: it is assured, paradoxically enough, by a prescriptive of universal value. It prescribes the observance of the sin-gular justice of each game such as it has just been situated: formalism of the rules and imagination in the moves. . . .

JLT: Here you are talking like the great prescriber himself . . . [Lyotard's ellipses] (laughter). (*Au Juste* 100)

I find it less easy than JLT (Jean-Loup Thébaud) to let laughter absolve or displace the difficulties in these claims. As stated, Lyotard's "Idea" seems to me incapable of addressing many real-world problems and all too capable in its ab-stract piety of using its resistance to terror as an excuse for dismissing those ac-tions that are necessary for moving from procedural to distributive justice. The incapacity should be clear if we ask whether it can suffice to cast justice as the principle that reminds society of the limits of the language games people are en-gaged in. Such marking of limits is a crucial component of justice—this we see clearly in Plato's *Republic*. But imagine if Plato had been content to say that jus-tice consists in pointing out to each segment of society and each source of ener-gies within the pysche that they ought not exceed their own limits. That would beg the question, since each domain would have its own version of the appropri-ate limits. So it is difficult to be satisfied with an idea of justice that cannot in itself produce an independent procedure for determining what the limits are to each game and how one adjudicates between competing claims. Justice requires not only a regulating principle but also a coordinating principle that can both specify how practices and desires might fit together and establish measures for negotiating those situations when the fit becomes problematic.

In Lyotard's scheme every attempt to postulate that coordinating principle will be suspect because it must necessarily propose criteria that give it authority over the other games. What will sustain that authority? This is where Kant had trouble because he located the authority in a rationality whose principles could be clari-fied only by isolating it from the heteronomous ways of the empirical order. Lyo-tard's situation is far more problematic because he refuses any supplementary discourse providing alternative terms for identity or allowing any comparative judgments. This leaves the idea of justice floating free, bound only by the unlikely assumptions that the limits of language games are visible and that the desire to maintain those limits will emerge at the horizon of our practices. With this ideal idea, and with the refusal of all determinants that might define the idea's actual place within experience, there emerges a strange and disturbing double bind that is also increasingly prevalent in academic discourse about "power." On the one hand, there is no way to distinguish when one is responding to the demands of justice and when one is in bad faith and thus is in fact determined by forces that one does not take responsibility for. Would even Lyotard buy a used car from someone who says, "Here I feel a prescription to oppose a given thing, and I think that it is a just one. This is where I feel that I am indeed playing the game of the just" (*Just Gaming* 69)? Why should anyone trust such feelings? Yet because such feelings appear direct and unmediated by either ideology or the will to power, the advocate of them finds it all too easy to condemn anyone projecting measures of justice that rely on more abstract and mediated frameworks. That person is not respecting the purported integrity of language games and is willing to impose power on those with different commitments.

I shall argue that the major value of Rawls's theory of justice is its establishing various levels of interests so that it becomes possible at least to decide in particular cases what criteria might hold and how some adjudication among different claims might take place. But I do not think the full force of that accomplishment will emerge until we also take up the more complex conceptual problems that derive from Lyotard's two fundamental poststructuralist commitments—to the concept of "terror" as his fundamental definition of the injustice that the idea of justice must oppose, and to the necessity of treating questions of human agency within a rhetorical or narratological framework that insists on treating the first-person subject as simply one of several positions constituted within the social forms that the language games constitute.

By making terror one's measure of injustice one then necessarily characterizes justice as liberation from oppression, a stance that again evades the question of distributive justice and makes no demands for collective judgments. Lyotard's concerns are by no means trivial: there are tyrannical structures imposing power and principle on those who have competing interests. Yet the rhetoric of terror seems to me to obscure what we can expect from the concept of justice. When talk of terror is really appropriate—as in South Africa—the situation has usually degenerated to a point where all of the adjudicatory mechanisms that are associated with the idea of justice have lost their authority. And when differences become this absolute it will not suffice to return to old limits: blacks in South Africa "ought" not let the whites keep all they have gained within the practices they controlled. In other situations, however, using terror as one's contrastive principle blinds us to the fact that in most cases problems of justice are less questions of imposing one incompatible ideology on another than of resolving different emphases within overall principles that the agents do or can share, at least provisionally. By immediately invoking cries of terror we ignore the entire domain of negotiation in order to fix secure limits that may be in no one's interest because greater goods might be available if both sides could compromise. Moreover, such invocations have the melodramatic effect of casting the "other" in such disputes as a monster with whom negotiation is impossible. That, I hasten to add, is precisely why the closing remarks of *Au Juste* leave Lyotard in the role of grand prescriber, for the only plausible stance against terrorism is counterterrorism. Thus in the name of justice one denies all the reciprocity with the other that must be the precondition of any adjudication. If, on the other hand, we treat injustice as a form of blindness we have a heuristic framework in which the discourse of justice can be cast as in everyone's possible interest.

Lyotard's melodramatic preempting of social processes (which I think goes a long way toward explaining his popularity in literary circles) has even more serious consequences when we try to flesh out the question of what kind of agent or agent roles we can rely on when we make attributions about judgments and justice. When one is so abstract as to subsume agents under language games and all forms of justice under a single opposition, theological models like Levinas's provide especially tempting versions of judgment. If the person is clearly positioned within absolute limits, it makes perfect sense to emphasize the role of addressee over the role of authoring one's value claims. Identity is primarily a matter of heeding obligations, and judgment then becomes largely a matter of understanding the limits that accrue from those obligations. There are few roles for self-consciousness to play, since there is no opportunity to posit alternative terms for one's identity and little call for the adaptations that a more negotiation-based model of social interaction would entail. At stake, after all, is one's relation to God, or to analogous absolutes. But while it is certainly possible to acclimatize ourselves to the picture of social life Lyotard presents, it seems to me worth asking whether that life is necessary or desirable, or even whether the fact that some people "choose" it (or are obligated by it) forces us to shape our models of justice in terms consistent with those preferences.

There are two ways in which we can formulate those doubts about Lyotard's treatment of the subject position in making judgments—one negative and one positive. The negative one is rather complex but leads neatly into the intricacies of the subject role in political judgment. Lyotard can privilege the position of addressee over that of the subject because he has so substantial a sense of the language games or stories as defining the relevant values. Under such conditions it makes perfect sense to underplay subjective preferences or conflicts. The stories and language games provide both the necessary focus and the desired authority for engaging in the appropriate specific practice. One can even go on to show how such frameworks create general political principles since they can play the formal role of establishing maximal conditions that carry the force of nondeterminant but regulatory ideas of justice: knowing that I am a pagan makes me aware both of the limits this entails and of the horizon where other language games must be allowed their claims on the real or, conversely, feeling my tribal identifications as an oppressed *différend* provides the impulse to revolution in the name of justice.

The case seems a tight one. But I think there is a crucial gap between the "I" positioned by the story as bound to certain obligations and the "I" who develops the regulatory idea by maximizing the terms of the specific practice. The former can subsume judgment under received categories or immediate impulses, while it is difficult to imagine the latter coming to a sense of what to maximize without reflecting on the nature of the obligation and its relation to other possible claims on the agent. Lyotard is quite good at rendering the immediacy available to the tribal agent who judges without criteria:

> This is where the *Critique of Judgment* becomes of interest to me. I propose that we overlook that it is a critique of the feeling of pleasure and pain, and consider it exclusively as a critique of feeling, and I further propose to translate feeling by the simple assertion: *I am for, I am against, yes, no*. Assent granted or denied. I think that it is this sort of feeling that is put into play by any political judgment. (*Just Gaming* 80–81)

But how do we envision the maximizing of such assertions as somehow engaging a form of justice? One can all too easily imagine the obvious political maximizing of this immediacy. It entails the dream world cultivated by Madison Avenue—the impulsive is the good, and power consists in the ability to exercise that to the maximum degree. This obviously would not satisfy Lyotard (even as an example of a pure language game), since he wants the maximizing to be regulatory. But the regulatory is incompatible with the immediate—there only force regulates, not idea. Regulation is a matter of the symbolic, and the symbolic requires accounting not only for the conditions in which the "I" makes direct assertions of its own interests but also for its generalizing about those interests by including itself as a member of a group. The person must decide what it belongs to and how that belonging not only creates feelings but defines some of them as important enough to extend into the political sphere. This maximizing "I" has feelings it attributes not simply to the moment (Hegel's nefarious "here and now") but to its status as a "Jew" or "black" or "worker." So the "I" whose feelings generate an immediate yes or no cannot be the same "I" as the "I" who makes the kind of identifications out of which maximizings are made or, for that matter, limits stipulated and confirmed.

To have a political domain at all Lyotard must modify the radically empiricist subject of *Economie Libidinale* so that it not only wills but wills *as* a certain kind of person. That "as," however, is by no means an innocent one. It involves the subject's not merely expressing but also deliberately accepting the identity and the affiliations afforded by a genealogical narrative or entailed by a prescriptive. Such identifications need not derive from elaborate deliberative processes. But they do imply that the agent will take certain responsibilities if pressed, especially when the person has available the options afforded by a complex society. Once there are options, there is selection; and when the selection becomes the basis for political prescriptions, however free of universals, there are obvious claims on the person that cannot be satisfied by resorting to the role of addressee. Many things address us, but few are chosen.

Ironically this gulf between subject roles leads directly into the positive way Lyotard's treatment of agency projects beyond his own interpretations. For he makes a powerful case that for there to be a politics at all there must be some form of maximizing connected to the stories that bind agents to certain fealties. This means that any model of agency we imagine making such judgments must also be one that seeks and uses predicates tying it to other agents. The self-interested calculator will not do as an account of human motives. There are always identifications, projections, and an awareness of the consequences of our affiliations. But if all this is true one cannot understand the subject simply in terms of how it is positioned as addressee in some story or language game. We are no longer speaking only of feelings for or against. The chooser accepts a position where certain feelings will prevail over others. So even if one cannot in most cases speak of the agent as authoring the actual position by creating its specific terms, our theory must be able to handle the authorial role of letting certain prescriptives prevail and acknowledging a hierarchy of affiliations that in their turn carry continuing obligations.[4]

As we shall see, these demands on theory make it necessary to incorporate first-person principles that warrant a modified version of autonomy. In fact, Lyotard's own model provides a very useful way of understanding how that version of autonomy can take hold because the more one denies that prescriptives depend on descriptions, the more one puts the agent in the position of both subject and object determining the very conditions that will dictate moral choices. The lack of public criteria puts the burden of responsibility entirely on the one who assumes the role of addressee. To deny personal responsibility in such cases is to remind us of how often in the past versions of Lyotard's call for undivided obligation to language games that can be kept pure have become the stuff that terror is made on. The minimum condition for dispelling terror is probably the need for each agent to have to take explicit personal responsibility for the voices to which it accedes so that the person accounts for the consequences of those loyalties.

Lyotard is not unaware of these problems. However, the specific path he takes for handling his doubts turns out to provide the third and most compelling general argument that sets off by contrast what Rawls has accomplished. Again there are two closely related ways to put the case—one involving the forms of evasion Lyotard allows himself, the other the fact that such evasions play directly into the hands of the deconstructive stances that most of him seems to want to subordinate to the project of defending specific political values. Consider first the ways in which Lyotard's choice of the dialogue form enables him to stage his own ambivalence on these issues. Lyotard is as conscious as Baudrillard that with any political statement one's assertions betray an underlying set of interests contaminating the descriptive by the prescriptive, proposition by the ruses of rhetoric. This indeed is why he seeks a mode of judgment that does not claim to be independent of prejudices. And this is why he chooses the dialogue form as the vehicle for dealing with the issues because that form carries the need to let another voice mark his own ruses and provoke him to responses that he does not entirely control. But having posited what Plato knew was not a bad formal equivalent to a minimally just social order, Lyotard is constantly tempted to let the play of dialogue take the place of discursive argument, especially since he distrusts all efforts to rationalize a position. On that level the final laughter is a superb index of the difficulties that arise when someone bound to his sense of the incommensurable tries to propose general principles. But where does the laughter leave us? For critics like Geoff Bennington we are left with an elegant deconstructive gesture. Lyotard's text demonstrates that there can be no thematized model of judgment and justice that does not collapse into what Bennington calls a "third justice . . . unjust both to the idea and the constituted multiplicity." ("August: Double Justice" 70). The regulative principle, then, is not of a particular justice but of an irreducible tension between the idea and the multiplicity of local movements it is called upon to sanction. The justice of this third justice then takes the form of playing the movement between the poles "to the limit and precipitating its own dissolution, signaled in the final laughter" (70).

However, once the deconstructive turn is made, one must decide whether Lyotard is its hero or its victim and hence whether any politics at all can emerge from his model of justice. For the latter, more comprehensive deconstruction one need go no further than Sam Weber's brilliant "Afterword" to *Just Gaming*. Weber too is struck by the laughter, but for him it is a lot more uneasy than the laughter Bennington hears. For it is in the surrender to laughter that Lyotard gives up his game and in effect yields to the irreducible dichotomy between idea and multiplicity that only deconstruction can simultaneously expose and reweave. Lyotard's final gesture in effect reveals that "to safeguard the incommensurability of each game, there must be an authority capable of determining the rules that constitute each game as such" ("Afterword" 102). At the core of a defense of plurality one requires a logic of identity (103), and in order to regulate the intricacy of language games one needs to attempt to step outside particular games to posit a comprehensive one that sets the rules for all the others. Centers die hard. Yet die they must. So Weber makes Lyotard serve the same role for Nietzsche that I shall ask him to play with respect to Rawls: we see in this text the materials for appreciating why a Nietzschean agonistics insists that "the game is necessarily *ambivalent* from the start" (106), with the figure of otherness always already inscribed within it (108). Ideally this agonistic sense of the game will underwrite a more dynamic politics pervaded by the constant play of differences. But in the end Weber opts for a position where the play of differences remains too intricate for any actionable ethics or politics: "So perhaps there remains nothing for us to do but to judge, to play, to cut to the heart of the matter, to try to arrest the machine in motion, at least for a moment, for a twinking of an eye, just long enough for a fitful start, judging as always . . . de justesse" (120).[5]

III

For Rawls, acting "de justesse" is little more than an aristocrat's way of avoiding the social need to replace the cultivation of style with principles that everyone can invoke. Like the part of Lyotard trying to escape the performative world of deconstruction, Rawls seeks a social philosophy capable of developing a model of judgment that can negotiate competing and "incommensurable" visions of the good without subordinating them to any encompassing metatheory.[6] And like Lyotard he seeks a model of identification that can locate regulatory ideas capable of defining limits and suggesting maximizing possibilities within political practices. But such parallels serve primarily to define several important differences. First and perhaps most important is Rawls's desire as an analytic philosopher to narrow the field of inquiry so that he can avoid the temptations to rhetoric that accompany abstract oppositions like the one between justice and terror; then within that narrowed field he hopes to locate historical and practical motifs enabling him to construct a version of human agency that need not subsume judgment under any one tribal identification.

Rawls's means for narrowing the field is to isolate the "circumstances of justice . . . under which human cooperation is both possible and necessary" (*Theory of Justice* 127–28). When goods are extremely scarce, it is foolish to imagine that concerns about justice will govern any large group. The crucial question becomes one of survival, and terror is much more than a metaphor referring to the imposition of one language game on another. Conversely, in the unlikely situation where everyone is satisfied there is no need to adjudicate the distribution of goods. So it only makes sense to imagine justice as a plausible motive when there are social conditions of "moderate scarcity" (128) allowing the political resolution of problems. Once we accept that limit, we gain the crucial benefit that we can then also give individuals reasonable motives for acting in accord with justice. When there are compelling demands for survival, seeking justice is at best a prudential step that one takes in the hope of mollifying an antagonist. But as soon as the pressures lessen, it becomes possible to concern oneself with the symbolic as well as with the real. In addition to concerns for preserving life, people can devote themselves to determining the kind of person that various courses of action would make them. Here the theory of justice becomes necessary so that we can distinguish between situations where the agents are satisfied simply to resolve conflicts (or circumscribe language games) and those where an effort is made to resolve them so that the agents can characterize their actions as just or fair, even if their views of the good are incommensurable with those of others involved in the adjudication.

From the perspective I am taking justice is possible only where there is the desire for justice. This may seem circular. But the circle is by no means vicious. Rather, it locates justice as an element of the symbolic order woven into other concepts; it requires a psychology as well as a politics; and it indicates the stakes involved in having an elaborate and articulate social theater within which competing versions of justice can present themselves. If we are to represent ourselves or our social plans as just, we must position ourselves within a cultural grammar that enables us to treat actions as earning certain attributions from the society. And then the discourse of justice can be considered a complex language game in its own right, so that it can be played by those from very different speech communities.

This is all from a Rawlsian perspective. Lyotard obviously disagrees — both with what Rawls claims about justice and with what he posits as the criteria for assessing those claims. So before we even start our comparison we find ourselves facing the problem of incommensurable views. All the rest may be terror. There can be no compelling argument that brings both thinkers under a single set of criteria. But perhaps we do not need compelling arguments on such matters, especially when what is at stake is a concept that makes its appeal primarily to a symbolic order in which the crucial determinant is not veridical description or deductive coherence but simply the possibility of regulative ideas capable of taking on social force. If there are no compelling arguments for shared criteria, there can be no compelling arguments against them (since that too requires criteria). What we lose in certainty we gain in the modes of flexibility that characterize the realm of the plausible, where the only test of claims is to continue this effort to try out contrasting cases, examining each for how it can appeal to the audience's practical sense of coherence and of compatibility with experience.

Traditionally, the effort to define justice led to the positing of a principle that could provide a hierarchy capable of adjudicating between competing claims about the good. Philosophy had to secure a site where conflicting wills to power could be suspended and judgment could conform itself to an established calculus. For Plato, and somewhat differently for Kant, that requirement could be met only by showing that the mind had access to a priori principles of reason that could then be applied to particular cases. So long as there is only one "reason" this model prevailed, but by the nineteenth century, with its increasingly diverse social constituents, the interpersonal site had to be established on far more procedural and empirical grounds. Thus various forms of utilitarianism emerged, all sharing the belief that we could replace the deduction of principles by establishing concrete practical measures that translate the competing claims into a single calculus. This calculus would then make it possible to rank order the choices in terms of the ways they could probably satisfy some collective set of interests. But just as there proved more than one reason, there proves more than one way to order social interests, so the effort to assess utility tends either to cover up what remain incommensurable versions of the good or to rely on measurements so abstract that they seriously oversimplify the nature of the human agents involved. Moreover, the commitment to overall calculations makes it very difficult to establish a truly distributive justice. If one must average the overall benefits, one has no protection against letting the increasing welfare of an already well-off majority justify continuing suffering on the part of the disadvantaged.[7] Therefore Rawls wants a measure of justice at once more abstract and more concrete — more abstract in its insistence on rules that bind individuals to keep certain considerations paramount even if utility suggests greater overall payoffs, and more concrete in the sense that the rules hold not because they serve specific material interests per se but because they are central to the identities sought by the agents making the judgments. Only on the basis of such individual obligations can one introduce qualitative concerns that are not easily measured by empirical calculi.[8]

Rawls's means for creating this new measure is elegantly simple. In the place of positing a single shared theory of the good, he tries to develop an essentially dramatistic test for letting the competing stances play out their differences in a site abstract enough to provide the distance necessary for justice without denying the desires that each empirical individual has for distinct goods. Rather than deny the desires, he tries to postulate a mode of judgment that can be abstracted from them so that it can locate the common site not in a calculus so much as in a shareable commitment to a framework for working out what would establish the agents as just. This project requires two fundamental steps. First Rawls must show how we can adapt ourselves to the task of agreeing on what justice involves; then he postulates a practical strategy for making and assessing judgments.

In rejecting a single calculus for measuring social goods Rawls puts himself in a very difficult position. In effect, he has renounced empiricism for the Wittgensteinian principle that we can understand one concept only in terms of its grammatical coherence or fit with related notions that the culture promulgates. In our fragmented culture this is not promising grounds for a workable collective model. Nonetheless Rawls proposes a complicated process of triangulation that he thinks can isolate the level of investment in which agreement may be possible. If we are to establish "a coherent framework of deliberation" ("Social Unity" 168), we must seek "a reflective equilibrium" between the concerns that engage individuals in moral issues and the actual abstract principles that shape public decision making (*Theory of Justice* 20–21). Such balancing retains the authority of the individual. There is no higher synthetic reason obliging individuals to accept a definition of justice that does not correlate with their considered judgments. Yet the very process of seeking a reflective equilibrium leads one out of any one "pure" language game to the site where for Lyotard one prescribes the limits to each. Now, however, there is no question of bad faith. The seeking of an equilibrium is fundamental to the very idea of justice because one must be able to see oneself as able to stand in at least partial judgment on one's own interests. Yet rather than treat standing outside a given language game as a betrayal, one can regard it as a sign of the flexibility that cultural grammars offer agents in certain societies. If agents can seek the distance and disinterest basic to the concept of fairness, it is at least possible that there are available identities that are not exhausted by attributions such as pagan or Jew. What matters is the capacity to enter a reflective theater where certain performances earn one predicates that can bind pagan and Jew within a single set of concerns. Weber's discovery that language games are woven into each other becomes the basis for testing the kinds of persons our actions allow us to become.

This theater need not deny differences. It only circumscribes those differences relative to particular functions and particular aspects of identity engaged by the ideal of justice. In order to show how within that set of concerns limited agreement becomes possible even though there is no one shared consequentialist calculus Rawls returns to Kant via Plato: if you want to know what justice can be you must dwell on what makes an individual person just; then try to imagine how a collective of such individuals might form a public contract establishing a state bound to rules of fairness that can regulate competing ideals of the good. Rather than pursue prescriptive or descriptive practices, philosophy must turn hypothetical. Relying on the coordinates defining reflective equilibrium, it composes a fictional site that Rawls calls ''the original position'' agents must assume in order to develop a social contract to which they could all fully subscribe without a Hobbesian sense of compromise. The fundamental obligation is that each assume a veil of ignorance as the strategy for handling the incommensurable demands that stem from their different, heteronomous positions. Under the veil no one knows what his own individual attributes are and no one knows which of the lives possible in the society might be assigned to him. By maintaining the general knowledge available to society but suspending all the affiliations that give one a specific concept of the good for oneself, this position literally constitutes the agent in a site where the primary identification is with the possibility of justice:

> Among the essential features of this situation is that no one knows his place in society, his class position or social status, nor does anyone know his fortune in the distribution of natural assets and abilities, his intelligence, strength and the like. I shall even assume that the parties do not know their conceptions of the good or their special psychological propensities. The principles of justice are chosen behind a veil of ignorance. This ensures that no one is advantaged or disadvantaged in the choice of principles by the outcome of natural chance or the contingency of social circumstances. Since all are similarly situated and no one is able to design principles to favor his particular condition, the principles of justice are the result of a fair agreement or bargain. For given the circumstances of the original position, the symmetry of everyone's relations to each other, this initial situation is fair between individuals as moral persons, that is, as rational beings with their own ends and capable, I shall assume, of a sense of justice. (12)

Rawls will then use this hypothetical model to defend and elaborate the two basic principles on which he assumes his hypothetical actors will agree:

> First Principle: Each person is to have an equal right to the most extensive total system of equal basic liberties compatible with a similar system of liberty for all. Second Principle: Social and economic inequalities are to be arranged so that they are both: (a) to the greatest benefit of the least advan-

taged, consistent with the just savings principle, and (b) attached to offices
and positions open to all under conditions of fair equality of opportunity.
All social primary goods—liberty and opportunity, income and wealth,
and the bases of self-respect—are to be distributed equally unless an unequal distribution of any or all of these goods is to the advantage of the
least favored. (302–3)

Even this degree of concreteness, however, makes the difficulty of Rawls's
enterprise all too apparent. Each of these specific claims has been shown to
harbor serious problems. And those problems in turn reflect back upon the
method because they show that Rawls's own use of the veil of ignorance is by no
means successful in bracketing his own version of the good.[9] For in order to
secure the role he gives to the position of the least advantaged, Rawls must make
some very questionable moves that do not seem necessary within the reflective
equilibrium he establishes. For example, he denies that the agents under the veil
of ignorance could know the probabilities of ending up in the position of the least
advantaged. Having done that, he is justified in basing all his calculations on the
most cautious of measures because when crucial information about probabilities
is lacking it is wise to rely on maximin strategies that prefer the set of options
with the least risk. If one cannot calculate the odds of turning out least advantaged, the least risk consists in making sure that every distribution of goods benefits that position. But if the worst outcome could be given a low probability—
itself perhaps a measure of a just society—then one might be justified in using
other less cautious calculi that make it worth taking risks in the chance of much
greater gains.

But once we have raised the worries about inescapable self-interests, what alternatives are we to propose? If we turn back to Lyotard's principles we have no
way to alter the distribution of goods, and if we adapt classical utilitarianism we
cannot approximate this degree of clarifying the interests that underlie proposals
about disinterested measures. So it seems worth the effort to see how Rawls
might be modified, the better to address Lyotard, if not his free-market American
opponents. Perhaps it is an unnecessary feature of Rawls's model to insist on a
Kantian suspending of all interests when we assume the veil of ignorance. Perhaps the important thing is how even making the gesture demonstrates that we
can suspend some interests and can, for the sake of argument, understand interests that are not our own. And perhaps one can show that it is precisely because
we cannot fully distance ourselves from our own interests that the veil of ignorance proves so important. For it requires our casting the effort to suspend interests in a way that exposes to clear view what we in fact fail to suspend.

The best way to begin such modifications is to notice that Rawls does not rely
on the rather sentimental psychology that shapes the work of anti-Hobbes contract theorists. We do not seek or enter such contracts out of benevolence—benevolence is not the only alternative to the rational maximizer of economic
theory. The original position precludes any need for benevolence because it lit-

erally puts the agent in the position of the other. One is not careful of the rights of others for their sake but because under the veil of ignorance one has to imagine the possibility of actually occupying that life (*Theory of Justice* 148). So if there is any benevolence it consists in agreeing to the original position in the first place. Yet that decision too is probably best understood as the pursuit of a version of rational self-interest—both because it makes a secure state possible and because it affords an entire domain of cultural representations enabling society to establish terms for self-respect and mutual obligation.

But once we make these concessions to empiricism we must deal with competing models of self-interest—one stressing the rational attempt to realize preferences, the other concerned with the heteronomous ways self-interest distorts our judgments and conceals its own unjustifiable givenness in its ways of manipulating abstractions. Here Anglo-American philosophical traditions diverge entirely from the modes of thinking Nietzsche, Freud, and Marx fostered on the Continent. Yet while Rawls is not exactly Nietzsche, I think his hypothetical model for discussing principles of justice provides a limited enough version of those rational self-interests that it can accommodate many features of the Continental perspective. For example, one can use Rawls without committing oneself to the belief that persons have the self-control sufficient to bind them in practice to what they conclude under the veil of ignorance. In fact, it is because self-interests lead individuals to distort the veil of ignorance that we need the kind of dramatic method that may make those distortions visible and negotiable. Rawlsian theater provides incentives by giving people overt public identities to live up to, and it imposes substantial pressure on the range of casuistry one is allowed before one simply can no longer claim to have a concern for justice. In addition, the ideal of a hypothetical veil of ignorance requires participants to isolate the specific elements and consequences of their versions of the good in a way that clearly reveals how their specific interests continue to shape their efforts at generalization. There is no hiding of those overriding concerns under more specific and more controllable contexts, and there is no way to control the neutral background against which stand out those particular affiliations that we in fact cannot bracket. Thus while no individual is likely to achieve the distance necessary for disinterestedly distributing social advantages, there is a good chance that an audience can do a decent job of filtering out most of the distortions and insisting upon the necessary conceptual coherence. They too will have distorting interests, but conditions of visibility created by the hypothetical circumstances will at least increase the likelihood that we can recognize the differences at stake and be able to appreciate the struggle that others go through in order to resist such influences.

IV

Assume now that we could choose a political ethics. It seems to me that even with its shortcomings a Rawlsian approach is far preferable to its competitors in terms of the range of interests it addresses and the possibilities of socially useful adjudications it allows. Rawls has forcefully made the comparative case against the utilitarianism that he conceives as his major antagonist. I shall try here to make the appropriate case against the Lyotardian atomism that I think is central to the most influential versions of postmodern social thinking (in literary studies this means central to both both Fishian and Foucauldian understandings of the consequences of an antifoundational emphasis on the social construction of reality). For this task I shall concentrate on the three general areas where I think we see most clearly how the example of Lyotard sets off by contrast the achievement of Rawls—the status of reflective argument, the ways in which social identities can be constructed and defined, and the models of agency that dictate how autonomy and heteronomy must be understood.

Let us start with the first and most abstract of these. Perhaps the saddest irony in *Au Juste* (substantially modified in *Le Différend*, at the cost of suspending the political focus) is that this thinker so acutely aware of the dangers inherent in master narratives nonetheless remains completely committed to the authority of generalized abstraction. If terms must be defined differentially, then the opposition to terror will have to account for all senses of justice. If there are prescriptive and descriptive language games, then there can be no mixing. And if some language games are incommensurable, then there ought be a purity for each that makes them all incommensurable. But why should someone believe these claims, or accept them as an account of Wittgenstein? And what conditions would make the claims either useful or inescapable? There is no attempt to question the authority of the pure play of ideas, no effort to establish the kind of reflective equilibrium giving each participant a sense of the theater that can bring into focus the terms allowing for adjudication, and no way to see how the ideas might be held up against actual and possible social circumstances.

To give him his due, Lyotard does not ignore these concerns—he repeatedly insists that the illusion that one can sanction adjudication in terms of general principles does more to perpetuate injustice than to reduce it. Since Lyotard does not seem to take that as a claim that admits empirical assessment, he leaves us only the test of the dramatic situation such beliefs create for the speaker as he tries to sustain the dialogue form that must be the basis for all social relations. However, the actual terms of dialogue leave us a long way from politics. Such fluid relations remain the domain of the ruse, where the only response must be the long-term adjustments individuals make to each other. More important, the emphasis on dialogue makes it possible, perhaps necessary, for the author to avoid taking explicit responsibility for crucial features of the speech act involving what one decides to publish for a larger audience. If we are dealing with art it is reasonable to suppress immediate social interests. But in politics such decisions leave us confronting that last laugh with considerable anxiety and/or suspicion, wondering how it creates an illocutionary register for the entire discourse. Even if one defends that gesture on familiar textualist grounds, the problem remains that the writing does not take responsibility for its own need to register the contradictions that the laughter implies between the universal prescription and the individual speech act. How does the author understand the force of that contradiction and how does its presence indicate the kinds of responsibilities one can and cannot take for one's own discourse? From my perspective there is no way to escape the fact that in relying on that laugh Lyotard forces his discourse out of the dialogical and tribal into a public theater where it becomes necessary to address the contradiction. Yet Lyotard's model of judgment has no way to handle contradiction except by the gestures of deconstructive play. And then there is no distinction between justice and "de justesse," which means there is no politics aside from a performative haptics.

Rawls too is flawed in his philosophical politics. But in his case the clarity with which the flaws emerge becomes part of the achievement because it demonstrates one basic value of his methodological concerns. Instead of an immense indeterminate gap between pure abstraction and an acute personal sense of irony, Rawls must insist that conditions "not justified by definition or the analysis of concepts" put an extraordinary burden on clarifying looser but equally demanding models of "reasonableness" (131). This indeed is what it means to bring philosophy to the domain of politics, where charm must at least be tempered by that most un-French of virtues, a direct earnestness, and earnestness must submit itself to a public tribunal capable of making demands on those interested desires.

In order to flesh out the values this tribunal affords, we must shift to the two more concrete contrastive areas I have proposed. For the best way to understand the destructive effects of misplaced abstractness is to focus on its tendency to postulate extremely reductive models of society and of agency. What utilitarianism does in order to guarantee a single measure of the good, Lyotard does in order to insist that there can be only incommensurable language games. In Lyotard's case this produces the sad spectacle of a remarkable flexibility of intelligence devoted to defending a remarkable limitation on personal identifications. As is even more stunning in Le Différend, the ingenious eye for differences among phrase regimes and genres never allows itself to concentrate on how these elements might be purposively and distinctively woven together or even give access to one another. That sense of differences then has the enormous consequence of reinforcing the atomistic and heteronomous models of psychic life first developed in Economie Libidinale. By Le Différend, in fact, Lyotard is so committed to heteronomy of "pulsions" that he rejects the idea of personal identity as a way of imposing continuity among speech situations because he thinks that such attributions distort the ways in which the psyche is actually organized by language.

For Rawls, on the other hand, the diversity of language games opens up the possibility that agents can participate in a shared rhetorical theater for making and testing binding claims about justice. This in turn substantially alters what one can say about the relation between descriptions and prescriptions, and that makes plausible the complex model of identification on which the entire project of the veil of ignorance is based. Insofar as the determinants of a value claim must be either prescriptions or descriptions, the terms of one practice preclude the other.

But as soon as one turns to hypotheticals and posits a theatrical framework for them, the ontological boundaries dissolve into practices for testing how certain decisions involve connecting projected selves to projected consequences. These projected selves must be seen as originating in prescriptions: desire and social history create the framework of values. But once we grant the possibility of deliberation, and once we realize that even on Lyotard's account there is no reason why empirical selves are bound to only one set of prescriptions, we see that hypotheticals can work out descriptions of the various desires the agent brings so that one can elaborate probabilities and possible payoffs.

At stake in these projections is more than the abstract question of the limits of language games. The limits of language games are the limits of selves, of how identifications can be made and identities pursued. Therefore, by showing how certain descriptions take hold in the limited prescriptive context of the original position, Rawls teases out an interpersonal framework in which it makes sense to shift from the private context of making prudent choices to the public context of seeking justified ones. Justification depends on accepting some agreed upon obligations—either to perform certain deeds that one is commanded to do in the position of addressee or to meet certain explanatory criteria for deeds one claims to author. Lyotard's challenge is to show how that authoring could reach beyond the conditions of obligation and still have terms that can be negotiated in order to claim the identity of just person from some community. Justification can take place only where there is provisional identification within those communal terms. Rawls acknowledges those difficulties. But he goes on to show that in acknowledging them we put ourselves in a position where we can then try to negotiate the difficulties. For the fact of incommensurable differences provides strong incentives to abstract ourselves from our empirical desires sufficiently to attempt understanding the other, to assume that others will find themselves in the same dilemma because universals are lacking, to try to find shareable interests, even in hypothetical spheres, and to test strategies like game-theoretical procedures that might be sufficiently impersonal to secure provisional agreement.

In order to show how we can respond to such incentives Rawls tries to redefine Kant's case for the self's ability to seek identifications not bound to its empirical commitments. If one desires justice, or at least the self-representation of one who desires justice, this necessarily positions the self as at least interested in exploring identities that are not "immediate," not given with one's specific cultural affiliations but definable by the ways in which one aligns with principles.[10] In Kant that alignment is simply a function of binding the will to the categorical nature of reason—one simply enters the world of rational beings. In Rawls, rationality itself must be defined in social terms, another reason why the hypothetical testing of possible criteria is so important. There is still a second nature made available by moral reason, but now that second nature is startlingly literal. The identity one seeks as a moral being depends on one's effort to suspend the imperatives of one's prereflective orientations so that one can take responsibility for one's principles, and eventually for one's actions, before communities that will not accept the claim that one is obligated to assume certain positions. Even Lyotard requires such distance if his agents are to understand what distinguishes their language games. Rawls adds that the very idea of seeking justice suggests that we can assume the kinds of identities for which it makes sense to speak of justification. In attempting to act on that assumption we enter a second nature. For we enter a distinctive language game where we can seek the approval of communities who do not care whether we are pagans or Jews because they can confer a much more flexible range of possible identities that also promise a deeper set of affiliations with cultural traditions.

Rawls's last and, to me, most important difference from Lyotard consists in his extending this work on identification into a plausible model of human agency based on the ideal of autonomy and the attendant obligations that entails. For Lyotard the central fact of moral life is that one finds oneself an addressee who cannot author one's position (*Just Gaming* 30–31). One is condemned to heteronomy and must learn to value the limitations and permissions this involves. For Rawls, on the other hand, the use of hypotheticals restores the possibility of our provisionally occupying both the subject and the object position with respect to the imperatives we generate as rules for determining justice. So in this sphere at least there are plausible neo-Kantian grounds for establishing a distinction between autonomy and heteronomy. Where Kant had to base autonomy on a reason capable of ruling the empirical self, Rawls derives it from the ability to manipulate hypotheticals, then bind oneself to the identifications they make available. In this framework we need not overcome the empirical self by sublime struggle; we simply evade it by testing what we can author once we suspend enough of our empirical identities to be able to imagine obligations that stem from positions one can share with others. Then the binding that makes the self the object of the law stems not from reason per se but from aligning oneself with that public self:

> Kant held . . . that a person is acting autonomously when the principles of his action are chosen by him as the most adequate possible expression of his nature as a free and equal rational being. The principles he acts upon are not adopted because of his social position or natural endowments, or in view of the particular kind of society in which he lives or the specific things that he happens to want. To act on such principles is to act heteronomously. Now the veil of ignorance deprives the persons in the original position of the knowledge that would enable them to choose heteronomous principles. The parties arrive at their choice together as free and equal rational persons knowing only that those circumstances obtain which give rise to the need for principles of justice. (*Theory of Justice* 252)

This is tepid Kant because it refuses to acknowledge his quite mystical sense of how true moral rationality creates an identity that aligns us with the supersensible. But tepid Kant can be vital postmodernity because it affords a view of rationality that comes down to very practical and plausible investments in those possible identities made available to us through reflection. Once we can occupy the original position, or, more cynically, once we want to take responsibility for representing ourselves as capable of occupying that position, then we do have a clear distinction between those identities conferred upon us by history and those for which we can claim authorship—not because we invent them but because we take responsibility for the principles shaping them. If one is only the addressee of the law, one must assume that all expression is confined to acting out the determining force of a particular nature (253). But although there is no escaping that nature, there may also be no necessity of worshipping it as an absolute. If we allow ourselves to take seriously the cultural dream of just action and the terms for it which reflective equilibrium recovers, we must at least explore the possibility of bracketing that nature so that we can make judgments and then test the degree to which those judgments alter our ways of acting.

Such actions are not "free" in the sense that they originate in some spiritual realm. But as we try to live in accord with certain hypothetical possibilities we may be able to give expression to modes of behavior that are potential within our own psyches and within our own cultural traditions, although rarely realized in the marketplace. These potential identities are as public as any tribal obligations. They get their claims upon us from the symbolic order sustained by cultural traditions, and they require our accepting certain determinate communal criteria. But once we derive the identifications from Rawlsian reflection, we can conceive those social bonds as states we will rather than repressions we suffer. By positing a social self that can will its own obligations Rawls makes the lack of shareable empirical conditions and descriptions the precondition for appreciating another very different realm where objectivity becomes possible on the basis of agreement to rely on certain definitions of the natures in question. In science such stipulation makes research possible; in ethics it creates the necessary preconditions for a just society.

We cannot be sure we do not delude ourselves in casting ourselves as free to make such identifications. But neither can we afford to let abstract Lyotardian grounds persuade us to dismiss the possibility that it makes sense to seek a distinctive moral identity. If there is to be a genuine postmodern philosophical and artistic culture, it must at least try to resist the various forms of self-congratulatory and self-interested despairs that constitute the popular heritage of modernism. Yet when we turn to the loudest proponents of a distinctive postmodern condition we find them still bound to the Nietzschean ontology that I think shapes that cultural modernism. There must be immanent will, and then if there is to be any affirmative moment or workable politics it must base its will on accepting the forces that determine it, if only to make that "fatality" a pretext for sublime Baudrillardian ecstasies. However, these versions of Nietzsche's eternal return cannot take us beyond a politics of "de justesse" which confine the will's objectifying of its generating conditions to a melodramatic metaphysical theater. Radical immanence ironically needs the consolation of abstract metaphysics, and postmodernity repeats modernism's efforts to preserve the escape from social despair once provided by religion.

Rawls matters because he defines a different theater and hence a different way of determining the forces that threaten to determine us. If one cannot escape the empirical self, one can try to bracket it and to find in such hypotheticals other aspects of our nature that can then effect practical judgment to the degree that they focus or intensify commitments to justice that are already part of the social fabric we inherit. Such experiments require replacing the consolations of metaphysical theater, however ironic or pataphysical, by the demands of a publicly constructed tribunal for which we take responsibility as its authors and its addressees, since the condition of going on stage is being able to become authors identified with their characters. The play we see will rarely warrant rave reviews because the parts are much more difficult to play than Rawls seems to think. But in this theater there is no more valuable lesson than that difficulty, because the constant pressure of our incommensurable differences reminds us that this is the only show in town we cannot afford to let close down. Only within its confines can we correlate the fundamental public need of postmodernity—the need for shareable norms within an increasingly diverse society—with the central private need defined by modernism—the need to be able to establish expressive identities capable of resisting intellectual climates that try to reduce everything to race, epoch, and milieu.[11]

Notes

1. For other good philosophical attempts to describe the priority of differences and the political importance of resisting the categorical work of reason that follow from poststructural thinking see Vincent Descombes, "An Essay in Philosophical Observation," and John Rajchman, "Lacan and the Ethics of Modernity." For a defense of my negative claims with respect to recent efforts to draw ethical conclusions from this work by literary critics like J. Hillis Miller and Robert Scholes, see the introduction to my forthcoming book, *Thinking through Literature: Essays in the Pragmatics of Aesthetic Idealism.* And for a very useful measure of the task Lyotard has set himself we can turn for our contrasts to Jean Baudrillard. By insisting that all of contemporary reality be seen in terms of simulacra Baudrillard leaves no possible politics and only the most indulgent of ethics, so I suspect that he is the basic contemporary antagonist (Marx is the main antagonist) provoking Lyotard to seek a workable political extension of poststructural sensibility that can ask itself "comment l'idée de justice peut s'y mêler sans s'y perdre." (I quote from the cover of *Au Juste.*) This contrast is important to me because an earlier, too lengthy version of this essay tried to show how Baudrillard and Lyotard expose limitations of the postmodern political project at two extremes—one collapsing everything into an oppressive sameness of symptom against which there are only ludicrously melodramatic cures, the other so collapsing sameness into difference that there is not sufficient foundation for a political order, with the effect of licensing only slightly less melodramatic deconstructive strategies for dealing with the differences as they proliferate and divide within themselves.

Now I have only this margin in which to support my point about Baudrillard. So I ask my readers whether they can imagine a more oppressive master narrative than Baudrillard's tale of the black social magic that transforms a sign-referent model of reality into the impenetrable play of simulacra. On the one hand nothing can escape it, since there is always a perspective from which a sign defines rather than indicates the object. On the other hand there is very little incentive to escape because the narrative serves virtually as a mythic context allowing its author an imaginary substitute for the real in which every element of the world can be resignified with a new emotional import, won not in the domain of politics but only in the domain of rhetoric. I came to this realization listening to a Baudrillardian talk by Arthur Croker in which an elaborate litany of the evils of the contemporary world invoked an even more elaborate rhetorical elegance. There was a time when despair bred silence. In allowing myself such complaints, however, I play into Baudrillard's considerably better developed ironic sensibility (which is well described in Meaghan Morris's essay in Frankovitz [ed.], *Seduced and Abandoned: The Baudrillard Scene*). For his more recent work realizes that the only possible response to a world in which all political gestures, even terrorism, become mere counters in the imaginary's efforts to find a condition that will seduce it is to internalize the fascination of simulacra within his own rhetoric. Thus we first find Baudrillard trying out the possibility "aller plus loin, trop loin dans le même sens—destruction du sens par simulation, hypersimulation, hypertélie. Nier sa propre fin par hyperfinalité . . . n'est-ce pas aussi le secret obscène du cancer" (*Simulacres et simulation* 233). Hyperreality requires hype, and all hope for ends must turn into a sense that we inhabit "l'ère des événements sans conséquences (et des théories sans conséquences)" (236). In his more recent work it seems that even this degree of will must be suspended for a more radical relation to the hyperreal that we must project beyond the simulacra. Now what matters is the ecstasy afforded by identifying with the fatal object in its pure banality and chance: "Why should we think that people want to disavow their quotidien lives in order to search for an alternative? On the contrary they want to make a destiny of it: to redouble it in the appearances of the contrary, to engage themselves within those appearances to the point of ecstasy, to ratify monotony by a grander monotony. Surbanality is the equivalent of fatality" (my translation from (*Les Stratégies fatales* 263). With such politics to contend with one can forgive Lyotard a great deal.

2. I should note some of the major differences in terminology between the two texts because I shall use that of *Au Juste* while hoping that I honor the qualifications that Lyotard makes later. The main differences are in aim and in the way language communities are handled. Where *Au Juste* imagines accepting the dialogue form as also directly accepting the role of being discursive about political ideals, *Le Différend* returns to the work of the reflexive philosopher "examining cases of the differend and researching the rules of the genres of discourse which occasion these cases" and seeking a metalanguage that can describe these cases without hoping to provide a logic for them (12). Under this grammatical eye Lyotard gives up the idea of the language game as too anthropocentric—it implies a purposive player—in order to break utterances down into the phrase regimes and genres that do the work of establishing and organizing differences. Finally *Le Différend* renounces the uneasy self-consciousness which keeps questions about rhetoric, the ruse, and laughter central to the dialogue form of *Au Juste* for a no less self-conscious insistence on straightforward assertion.

I cannot resist concluding this picture of differences with signs of how they stay the same. The following is Geoff Bennington's poststructuralist response to the different tone of *Le Différend*: "The willfully unmodish sobriety of that style, its declared desire for self-effacement before 'thought,' will no doubt scandalize those who hasten to misrecognize 'logocentrism.' But more interestingly, that style gives rise to a tone . . . which Lyotard describes as 'sententious' [13], and which 'should be disregarded.' Why should it be disregarded? What is at stake in a sententious tone? Sententiousness might, after all, be a good name for a certain undecidability of description and prescription" ("August: Double Justice" 70–71).

3. Lyotard wants a transcendental Kant without a transcendental subject. That is why he is most comfortable with the third *Critique*, where nature takes on the attributes of subject. But this project makes it difficult to understand or to apply his interpretations. In Kant one can have concepts that are not empirically determinable because the rational agent is not exhausted by her phenomenal activities. There is thus another entire realm of transcendental forces that can be attributed to real agents. Lyotard must attribute these forces to language games or discourse genres, where it is much more difficult to imagine actual agencies that then realize the transcendental horizon of the mental activity.

4. Lyotard and those who use him are likely to respond that ideals like mine evade the degree to which we are in fact determined by what we cannot author. But two responses are possible. One can borrow from the Kant-Lyotard ontology in order to argue that the model of public responsibility makes no claims that we are free of empirical determinants. It insists only that we take the kind of responsibility for a prescriptive that is compatible with a political sense of standing by one's word as one's own commitment to certain performances. Our taking of responsibility need not establish a

cause but need only afford a retrospective account fitting the deed to the reason and assuming the obligations that follow from the rationale. My second response would have to acknowledge that this model will not work in all cases, but it at least avoids the serious problem Lyotard has in stating where the imperatives can come that put one in the position of addressee. The demand for responsibility requires that one make visible as much of one's loyalties as possible. And that enables us to see how one's interests can be negotiated in conjunction with competing social positions. The saddest feature of those general cultural structures that Lyotard sets against the dream of rationality is the way they tend in practice to exile competing value frames from the society they want to keep pure.

    5. The ellipses are Weber's. I find it instructive that Bennington also picks up the play between "justice" and "de justesse" (whose English equivalents I elaborate for quite conventional humanistic purposes in my *Act and Quality*). For acting "de justesse" is ultimately the dream of the dandy flaunting his adaptive wit that makes all general commitments mere vulgar abstractions when the mind can be so fine as to adapt in the twinking of an eye. So there is no better model for radical chic. Baudrillard, one might note, inspires just the opposite critical reaction in the academy. Although he insists that his own texts are hype, his followers tend not to deconstruct the work but to take the claims more literally than the master, even when, as in the case of Jameson, these claims make it rather difficult to maintain an oppositional idealism.

    6. The best place to see this commitment in Rawls is "Social Unity and Primary Goods," which is also the most definitive Rawlsian statement on the nature of the moral agent who wants to make such judgments. On incommensurability see 179, and for a summary of his project see 160–61. I should add that in what follows I take some liberties with Rawls. First, I need in a very short space to mark out a consistent path among signs that lead in more than one direction. Rawls seems to me to want both an independent model of judgment that could judge his specific ideas about justice in comparison with other theories about justice and a model that clearly demonstrates the superiority of his own specific model of justice (see *Theory of Justice* 15). However, the more one reads in the criticism he has spawned, the more it seems necessary to try to separate his ideas about judgments of justice from the theories of the good that shape his conclusions. Only that will help us make the range of decisions this critical discourse has made necessary, and only the possibility of treating Rawls the contractarian liberal as one of the players within the theater that Rawls the theorist of judgment constructs will fully address the suspicion of universals that Lyotard claims is the postmodern condition. Therefore I stress the methodological features of the argument, and on a few occasions I even allow that purpose to warrant my silently making slight modifications in Rawls's formulations. For example, I shall soon refer to Rawls's construction of "a reflective equilibrium" that he claims balances moral intuitions and public principles. Because I distrust all talk of intuitions, I transform that into an equilibrium between the specific terms that constitute a person's individual moral concerns and the public discourse that tries to establish principles for resolving disputes. The difference is small, but my modification preserves the sense that even the subjective concerns are part of a public fabric with no authority derived from anything that introspection might be said to discover. My rationale for such acts is, first, that for our purposes Rawls is less a monument to be contemplated than a process of thinking to be used, and, second, that by subjecting his work to different pressures than it usually receives one locates points where slight changes might substantially strengthen the stance.

    7. For these critiques see *Theory of Justice* (secs. 5, 6, 27–30), and both the introduction and several of the essays in Sen and Williams. It is no small testimony to Rawls that his utilitarian opponents have come to sound very different from their predecessors as they try to claim that the position can handle his objections.

    8. I think we require these demands on individuals because no empirical model of people's best interests will plausibly require seeking anything more than a minimal or prudential model of justice that keeps the peace so that the fruits of injustice can be enjoyed. In my "From Expressivist Aesthetics to Expressivist Ethics" I make the case by recalling Gyges' ring. Here I want only to point how empty the standard liberal defense of civil liberties is when based on the empirical ground that what I protect for another may in the long run protect me. In fact, most law-abiding people have a very low probability of ever having the same rights abused because they will never have to exercise

them. Certainly the odds of their being the victims of crime are greater than the odds of their being victims of real tyranny. This is no reason not to defend civil liberties, but it is a reason to begin defending them on the grounds that they conform to ideals of justice that are in my interest not because I may be prosecuted but because it matters to me that I live in a society that is willing to defend those most likely to have their rights abused.

9. In logical terms we are faced with a problem of the regress involved in having people suspend their empirical interests, since the suspending too would be shaped by the way one interprets the nature and implications of that act. Rawls wants a theory of distributive justice based on procedural grounds alone, and this seems to me insufficient. Yet the effort to enforce the regress from stating empirical interests to having to cast one's position as impersonally as possible can make considerable practical differences in social adjudication because the one trying to suspend empirical interests, or better bound by a method to suspend empirical interests, is at least publicly obligated to different procedures than the one simply free to pursue versions of the good that do not involve identities in the symbolic order. We see both poles emerging in the concrete assessments of Rawls collected in Blocker and Smith. On the one hand there are several good illustrations of Rawls's biases that affect how he casts the original position; on the other there is the constant effort by the opponents, even a Marxist opponent, to say that while Marxists must point out the ahistorical features of Rawls and his willingness to accept class divisions, they would do well to attempt to integrate Rawlsian measures (see especially 428–29). That collection also shows the critical force of the Rawslsian theater because he forces the right to baldly deny social bonds and the left to admit that it cannot provide a theory of justice under present social conditions. Thus while he may not persuade, he does clarify stakes—and he makes that clarity crucial because he connects it with the various ways we can represent ourselves in the symbolic order.

10. If the Lyotardian argues that the desire for such identities is given within liberal bourgeois culture, he must take the further step of showing why that is either an illusion or something to be rejected on other grounds—for the possibility of such identifications is conceded and one cannot go back to the necessity of narrower obligations.

11. At times it seems as if Lyotard's sense that he has rejected master narratives leads him to recapitulate nineteenth-century determinism—in his psychology as well as in his politics—differing only in the fact that he cannot overtly celebrate himself or science for the accomplishment. Now that I mention this I see that similar charges could be leveled against Deleuze and perhaps all who share Nietzsche's twin fascinations with science and with the immanent will.

Works Cited

Altieri, Charles. *Act and Quality*. Amherst: U of Massachusetts P, 1981.

_____. "From Expressivist Aesthetics to Expressivist Ethics." In Anthony Cascardi, ed., *Literature and the Question of Philosophy*. Baltimore: Johns Hopkins UP, 1987. 132–66.

Barry, Brian. *The Liberal Theory of Justice*. Oxford: Clarendon Press, 1973.

Baudrillard, Jean. *Simulacres et simulation*. Paris: Editions Galilée, 1981.

_____. *Les Stratégies fatales*. Paris: Bernard Grasset, 1983.

Bennington, Geoff. "August: Double Justice." In Lewis, ed. 64–73.

Blocker, H. Gene, and Elizabeth H. Smith, eds. *John Rawls' Theory of Justice: An Introduction*. Athens: Ohio UP, 1980.

Descombes, Vincent. "An Essay in Philosophical Observation." In Alan Montefiore, ed. *Philosophy in France Today*. Cambridge: Cambridge UP, 1983. 67–81.

Foster, Hal. *Recodings*. Port Townsend: Bay Press, 1985.

Frankovitz, André, ed. *Seduced and Abandoned: The Baudrillard Scene*. New York: Semiotext(e), 1984.

Lewis, Philip, ed. *Special Lyotard Issue*. Diacritics 14 (Fall 1984).

Lyotard, Jean-François. *Le Différend*. Paris: Les Editions De Minuit, 1983.

———. *The Postmodern Condition*. Trans. Geoff Bennington and Brian Massumi. Minneapolis: U of Minnesota P, 1984.

———, and Jean-Loup Thébaud. *Au Juste*. Paris: Christian Bourgois Éditeur, 1979.

———. *Just Gaming*. Trans. Wlad Godzich. Minneapolis: U of Minnesota P, 1985.

Rajchman, John. "Lacan and the Ethics of Modernity." *Representations* 15 (1986): 42–56.

Rawls, John. "Social Unity and Primary Goods." In Sen and Williams, eds. 159–85.

———. *A Theory of Justice*. Cambridge: Belknap Press, 1971.

Sen, Amartya, and Bernard Williams, eds. *Utilitarianism and Beyond*. Cambridge: Cambridge UP, 1982.

Weber, Sam. "Afterword." In *Just Gaming*. 101–20.

5

Organic Unity:
Analysis and Deconstruction
Richard Shusterman

I

One of the more striking and shocking features of postmodernist theory is its
fierce attack on the notion of organic unity, surely one of the most central and
seminal notions in the history of Western thought. Dating back to the Greeks
(and perhaps even implicit in their very idea of cosmos), the notion of organic
unity has found significant application in a host of philosophical enterprises:
ethics and political theory, philosophy of mind, aesthetics, cosmology, and, of
course, the philosophy of biology with whose central concept of organism it is
clearly and etymologically connected. Moreover, one could argue that just as organic unity provides one of the two classical theories of art (the other being *mi-
mesis*), so it furnishes one of the two most fundamental models of truth and
knowledge—that of a systematic unity or coherence of belief. Here again, the
other major (and perhaps traditionally more dominant) epistemological model is
that of representational correspondence to the real. It is intriguing that for all
their apparent differences, aesthetics and epistemology strikingly share the same
basic alternative strategies: representation or unity.

Since representational theories of knowledge are currently in embarrassed de-
cline and disarray, and since mimetic theories of art have long been discredited
by developments in twentieth-century art and criticism, it would be nice to find
reassurance in organic unity. Certainly most forms of twentieth-century Anglo-
American aesthetics and literary theory seem to have sought their ultimate principles and justification in such a notion, whether it located that unity in aesthetic
experience or the actual work of art. This deep dependence on the idea of unity
as a foundation or explanation of aesthetic value is perhaps most evident in the
work of Moore, Dewey, Richards, Osborne, Beardsley, and the New Critics.[1]

But, no less than representation, organic unity has recently come under an intense attack in which the whole idea of unity is radically challenged. The powerful phalanx of this attack is formed by poststructuralist thinkers in the Continental (and particularly French) tradition. Foucault, of course, provides a general and wide-ranging case against what he sees as the repressive structures of unity and continuity in our thinking (see esp. 4–38); and Macherey, from his Marxist standpoint, lashes out more specifically against the "organicist" presumption governing traditional aesthetics: "The postulated unity of the work which, more or less explicitly has always haunted the enterprise of criticism, must now be denounced. . . . Rather than that sufficiency, that ideal consistency, we must stress that determinate insufficiency, that actual incompleteness which actually shapes the work" (78–79). But probably the most radical and rigorous attempts to discredit and overthrow the notion of organic unity in aesthetic theory come from deconstruction.

One of Derrida's central themes is to challenge and dismantle the traditional idea of structure as a totalized and complete organic whole, limiting the field of "free play." This field, through the inescapable medium of language, must always be "a field of infinite substitutions"; and through its infinite play of substitutions "excludes totalization" and overruns all putatively fixed limits of structural closure ("Structure, Sign, and Play" 260).[2] Such a vision of unlimitable freedom and substitution clearly conflicts with our most familiar (originally Aristotelian) understanding of organic unity as a complete whole having a definite "beginning, middle, and end," and having parts so integrally connected "that if any one of them is displaced or removed, the whole will be disjointed and disturbed."[3]

In Paul de Man (and after him in Culler and Norris), the attack on organic unity is aimed more directly at Anglo-American aesthetics as represented by the New Criticism, whose organicistic celebration of semantic richness in the unity of a text is said to end up by revealing "a plurality of significations that can be radically opposed to each other." But this, according to de Man, "explodes" the very idea of any organic unity in poetry, of any unity analogous to "the coherence of the natural world." "This unitarian criticism finally becomes a criticism of ambiguity, an ironic reflection on the absence of unity it had postulated" (de Man, "Form and Intent" 28).[4] De Man's argument obviously begs two very crucial and dubious premises (which for him are perhaps ultimately the same): viz., that organic unity can never embrace any radical oppositions, and that the unities or coherences of "the natural world" (which de Man equates with "the organic world") involve no similar oppositions or conflicting forces. Yet a whole skein of thinkers stretching back to Heraclitus insist on the possibility that such unity not only contains but is sustained and enhanced by the tension of the opposites it embraces;[5] and modern science seems to reveal that radical opposition inhabits the unities of nature right down to the positive and negative charges of the atom. De Man's unwarranted and unconvincing assumptions are never argued for. They appeal to a univocal, monolithic concept of organic unity that is never articulated, and their problematic character points to the need for a more critical and rigorous analysis of this concept.

This essay will make a start toward providing such an analysis by clarifying some (but surely not all) of the very different senses and levels in which the notion of organic unity is used. Although I would like to hope that dispelling the clouds of confusion that shroud this notion will aid in its vindication, clearer exposure may instead simply expose more blemishes. Indeed, the very elucidation of its plurality of senses might be seized by some as evidence that this concept itself lacks the unity it names and is thus uselessly ambiguous and self-divided. But this charge falsely assumes that serviceable notions must be univocal and that to endorse organic unity at all we need to endorse all of its senses. Neither assumption is convincing.

In relating my analyses to the contemporary critique of organic unity, I shall confine myself to deconstruction. For it provides not only the most penetrating indictment of this notion in aesthetics but also the most powerful challenge and alternative to the analytic philosophy of language on which much of the Anglo-American aesthetics of unity rests. Indeed, the notion of organic unity provides a peculiarly fruitful focus for mapping the oppositional relations in which deconstruction and analysis are most deeply interlocked.[6] For although deconstruction opposes organic unity in aesthetics, we shall find that beneath this aesthetic surface, at a much deeper logical level, it is itself fundamentally committed and inextricably wedded to one central (originally Hegelian) sense of the principle of organic unity. Moreover, its attack on aesthetic organicism relies precisely and essentially on this organic principle. Conversely, analytic philosophy, while advocating some form of organic unity as an aesthetic principle, vigorously denies the more radical logical principle of organic unity that forms the crucial foundation of deconstruction's assault not only on aesthetic unity but on the very possibility of reference and individuation — the foundational core of the analytic project.

To chart these oppositional reversals we need first to distinguish the various senses of organic unity; and surely the best place to begin is with its tripartite analysis by G. E. Moore, who together with Russell created analytic philosophy in the beginning of this century and who in fact led Russell in their common revolt against the then prevailing Hegelian idealism.[7]

II

Moore's treatment of organic unity is complex because complexly motivated. This notion, which he often refers to by the term "organic whole," plays a central role in his two major philosophical projects of defending realism and the objectivity of intrinsic value. In the former it is a demon of idealist thinking that must be exorcised, whereas in the latter it plays a very positive role in explaining how the intrinsic value of something can be dependent on its parts (themselves of possibly negligible value) but still not be reducible to mere causal, instrumental, means-end value or to the sum of the values of its constituent parts. This organic principle where wholes can have intrinsic value even if their necessary constitutive parts have none greatly widens the range of possible intrinsic goods and hence the opportunities of realizing the good life. It is thus crucial to Moore's ethics. Moore sought to resolve the conflicting valencies that organic unity had for his ontological and ethical projects by clearly distinguishing different senses of the notion to which the conflicting valencies could then be allocated. We therefore see him move from a virulent blanket rejection of organic unity in "The Refutation of Idealism" to the more careful and balanced tripartite analysis in *Principia Ethica*.[8]

For Moore's realism, organic unity is an inimical principle to be savaged, since it supplies his idealist opponents with a weapon for denying the force of the distinction between "a sensation or idea and . . . its object," a distinction crucial to Moore's argument that there is some real object beyond or distinct from what is perceived. According to Moore, although idealists would in some sense grant that green and the sensation of green can be distinguished, they would counter that "the things distinguished form an " 'organic unity' . . . [such that] each would not be what it is *apart from its relation to the other.*" Hence to consider them as "separable" or independent from each other is an "illegitimate abstraction," and thus any apparent distinction between them cannot be used to argue for the reality of green or green objects outside our ideational experiencing of green. Moore describes the principle of organic unity as asserting "that whenever you try to assert *anything whatever* of that which is a *part* of an organic whole, what you assert can only be true of the whole"; and he roundly condemns it as absurdly implying (given the premise of true universal substitutivity entailing identity) that the whole is absolutely identical with the part while at the same time presuming them somehow distinct by contrasting them ("Refutation" 14–15). This summary rejection of organic unity is accompanied by a viciously derisive denunciation of its Hegelian source:

> The principle of organic unities . . . is mainly used to defend the practice of holding both of two contradictory propositions, wherever this may seem convenient. In this, as in other matters, Hegel's main service to philosophy has consisted in giving a name to and erecting into a principle, a type of fallacy to which experience had shown philosophers, along with the rest of mankind to be addicted. No wonder that he has followers and admirers. ("Refutation" 16)

It is striking but not surprising that deconstruction has been similarly criticized for simultaneously denying and employing distinctions that it seeks to undermine but to which it is inescapably tied. For Hegel's view of organic unity is the prototype, if not the explicit source, of deconstruction's principle of *différance* and its doctrine that binary oppositions not only conceal but rely on some underlying complicity. Hegel sees whole and parts as united in their oppositional contrast and requiring and defining one another in order to be what they are, a view that reflects his idea of the Absolute as revealing "the identity of identity and nonidentity; opposition and difference are both in it'' (*Differenz* 77).[9] But for Moore's critique of Hegelian unity to shed greater light on the current debate between analysis and deconstruction, we must pursue its elaboration in *Principia Ethica* through the contrasting context of the types of organic unity that he and analytic philosophy can endorse.

In the opening chapter of this epoch-making book (which not only served as the Bloomsbury Bible but effectively restructured moral philosophy by placing metaethics at its core), Moore distinguishes between three senses of "organic unity" or "organic whole." The first is where the parts of a whole are so related "that the continued existence of one [part] is a necessary condition for the continued existence of the other [parts]; while the continued existence of the latter is also a necessary condition for the continued existence of the former" (*Principia Ethica* 31). This conception is more than the mere assertion that an organic whole could not exist precisely as it does, if its parts were not precisely what they were. For that will hold for any whole rather than mark a specifically organic one. It seems a trivial logical truth that any change of a whole's parts must change to some extent that whole, which then, *ex hypothesi*, would have different parts and thus be a different whole. (This argument, however, was enough for Moore's teacher McTaggart to maintain that all wholes are organic wholes, and from this to conclude that the universe must ultimately be one necessary monistic whole, all of whose so-called different, independent parts are actually intrinsically internally related.)[10]

What Moore's first sense of organic unity instead asserts is that not simply the whole but its constituent parts could not survive the destruction of other parts. And again this is more than simply the assertion (with which it may easily be confused) that the constituent parts could not survive as parts of that same whole; for this again follows trivially from the fact that the whole would no longer be the same whole since some of its parts would be absent or different. Moore is not speaking of the continued existence of the part *qua* part of that whole, but of the part's continued existence *simpliciter*. In such an organic whole the constituent parts (or at least some of them) have "a relation of mutual causal dependence on one another" (*Principia Ethica* 32), the sort of relation once thought (before recent advances in medical technology) to exist between the various vital organs of the body. One's heart would not simply stop being a part of the same body if one's lungs and liver were removed; it would soon stop existing altogether. This particular conception of organic unity, familiar from antiquity, has been standardly associated with living organisms and Moore so introduces it. But he remained skeptical whether "this relation of mutual causal dependence was only exhibited by living things and hence was sufficient to define their peculiarity" (32). For surely it seems that there are parts of some mechanical systems or constituents of certain engineering structures that have this reciprocal dependence and could not survive the destruction of one another in the whole they unite to form.

But if this relation of parts constitutes a legitimate form of organic unity, then the influential romantic tradition (disseminating from Schelling and Coleridge) that sharply contrasts between organic and mechanical unity is simply incorrect. Moreover, such a dichotomy seems remote from the ultimate source of the notion, for the original Greek sense and root of "organic" (*organikos, organon*) relates to tools and thus connotes initially the instrumental rather than the specifically "living." One is therefore not compelled to reject organic unity, simply because one wants (like Valéry and de Man) to conceive of the text as lifeless machine or mechanical language.[11]

Although Moore recognizes this first, "causal" sense of organic unity as meaningful and valid, it is not the sense he finds so indispensably useful to his ethics and aesthetics. The crucial organic phenomenon is rather that a whole can have emergent properties that are not reducible or even proportionate to the properties of its constituent parts. Moore typically expresses this principle of holistic organicist emergence in terms of value: that an organic whole "has an intrinsic value different in amount from the sum of the values of its parts"; indeed, that "*the value of such a whole bears no regular proportion to the sum of the values of its parts*" (36, 27). But since he clearly recognizes that there is no difference in value without difference in properties (35), this sense or organic unity can be more generally regarded as a unity where the properties of the whole are different from the sum of the properties of its individual parts and not reducible to them. This sense differs from the first by allowing no inference from the existence of one part to the existence of the others without which that part could not exist. Here the organic relation is not a matter of the parts' reciprocal dependence for their existence but of the whole's dependence on the parts for its qualities and value. Of course this second organic unity applies to living organisms in which the bodily system as a whole has special properties and value absent from its special parts (even when these parts might be capable of independent existence). But such unity was often thought to be especially characteristic of works of art (which would not ordinarily be organic in the first sense), and Moore thus illustrates it aesthetically: "All the parts of a picture do not have that relation of mutual causal dependence, which certain parts of the body have, and yet the existence of those which do not have it may be absolutely essential to the value of the whole" (32). But again, such unity can easily be found outside the living and the aesthetic, as any salad or sandwich maker knows.

These two eminently intelligible notions of organic unity are then contrasted with the Hegelian one condemned in "The Refutation of Idealism." That suspect unity claims to be one where "just as the whole would not be what it is but for the existence of its parts, so that parts would not be what they are but for the existence of the whole." Therefore, "any particular part could not exist unless the others existed too" (*Principia Ethica* 33). However, this is not the mere causal dependence of the first sense. It is rather a more logical dependence, where the very essence or identity of the part involves the whole to which it is related, so that without the whole it would not strictly be the same part. The idea is that when a thing forms a part of such a whole it possesses predicates it would otherwise not possess. At the very least it has the predicate of being part of that whole. But advocates of organic unity think it also acquires more substantial emergent properties through its participation in the whole. A hand when part of an organically whole human being has powers and properties different from that hand as a detached member. Things with different properties cannot be identical, so the hand as an organic part must be essentially different from that same hand cut off from the whole. Its different identity clearly seems due to or constituted by the whole to which it belongs. Since the whole allegedly forms part of its part's identity, that part cannot be what it is and loses its very "meaning or significance apart from its whole." Hence such "parts are inconceivable except as parts of that whole" (34, 36).

Moore repudiates this form of organic unity as both confused and self-contradictory. It confuses emergent properties belonging properly only to the whole with intrinsic defining properties of the part itself. Second, it asserts, in effect, that any part of such a whole necessarily has that whole as part of that part itself; but this is inconsistent with the part's being a distinguishable part of that whole. The first point is that for a part to display an emergent property or value in conjunction with the whole's other parts but not to display it by itself in isolation means that it itself (i.e., the part) does not really have this property as part of its identity. For to display a property only as part of a whole, only together with other parts, is not to have the property at all but rather to be part of that (i.e., the whole) which does have it. This idea that the emergent properties and values belong in truth to the organic wholes as wholes alone and not properly to the parts whose conjunction in the whole produce them is the crucial point for Moore, and one he effectively uses in questions of ethical valuation in *Principia Ethica*. But it is easy enough to apply in aesthetics. We may, for example, point to a part of an artistic whole (say, a line in the picture of a face) and assert that this part is a silly or sly smile but would not be one if not for the arrangement of the other lines of the face. But the silliness or slyness of the smile is a property of the whole face, not just of the single line; even though we may just point to that line, a single part of the whole, in order to focus perception so that this emergent expressive property of the whole is better grasped. [12] Moore makes this point non-aesthetically in arguing against investing the human arm with the emergent properties it displays when connected with the living body:

> We may easily come to say that *as* a part of the body, it [the arm] has great value, whereas *by itself* it would have none; and thus its whole "meaning" lies in its relation to the body. But in fact the value in question does not belong to *it* at all. To have value merely as a part is equivalent to having no value at all, but merely being part of that which has it. Owing, however, to neglect of this distinction, the assertion that a part has value, *as a part*, which it would not otherwise have, easily leads to the assumption that it is also different, as a part, from what it would otherwise be; for it is, in fact,

true that two things which have a different value must also differ in other respects. (*Principia Ethica* 35)

There is still the further charge of self-contradiction. At the same time that this organicism asserts that there is a part (*P*), which helps to form a whole (*W*) and is therefore logically distinguishable from *W*, it denies that *P* has any such independent or indistinguishable nature of its own, but rather that its very identity involves the whole (*W*) and its system of interrelations of which it is a part. Thus, while *P* is originally identified as being distinct from *W*, as being a mere part of *W*, it is then contradictorily taken as analytically including *W* as part of itself, since it itself is constituted by the whole set of *W*'s interrelations of parts. As Moore argues, "The mere assertion that *it* is a part of the whole involves that it should itself be distinct from that which we assert of it. Otherwise we contradict ourselves since we assert that, not *it*, but something else—namely it together with that which we assert of it—has the predicate which we assert of it" (33). In other words, the radical notion of organic unity requires that any individual part we distinguish as contributing to form the whole cannot be so distinguished. It cannot be the same part in itself and as part of the whole, because as part of the whole it has different essential or constitutive properties (viz., those of its emergent interrelations and value with the other parts in the whole). Thus we are led to the contradiction that *P* is and is not part of the whole, *W*; or alternatively that *P* is not *P* (since it is not the same thing when it is part of the whole and when it is isolated). As Moore sums it up, "The assumption that one and the same thing, because it is a part of a more valuable whole at one time than at another, therefore has more intrinsic value at one time than at another, has encouraged the self-contradictory belief that one and the same thing may be two different things, and that only in one of its forms is it truly what it is" (35).

III

Moore's analysis and critique of organic unity is undoubtedly powerful, resting as it does on such deeply entrenched principles as the laws of identity and contradiction and the reality of self-identical particulars or logically independent individuals. But it is not immune to criticism. In the first place, his tripartite analysis does not exhaust the senses of organic unity that have been influential in intellectual history. What is most clearly lacking in Moore is any awareness of the temporal, vitalistic, developmental sense of organic unity, which was very important in romantic aesthetics (see Benziger). For many romantic thinkers, an organic whole was not simply something more than the sum of its parts, but was a dynamic unity whose parts developed and unfolded into the whole they formed by some process of natural (organic) growth or necessity. It is surely preoccupation with this special romantic notion of organic unity, distinctively contrasted to merely mechanical or static unity, which misleads (romantically inspired) thinkers like de Man to presume that all organic unity is vitalistic and developmental on the model of living organisms.

There may be good reason why Moore's account of organic unity ignores temporality and vitalistic development. For to admit such fluidity to his account might suggest that what his commonsense understanding grasps firmly as the particular, logically independent, and stable parts of a whole are not fixedly given in the nature of things. And if what counts as a part can change with time, if parts can simply be differently constituted by different temporal interpretations of an array into parts and wholes, then the whole idea of the logically durable self-identity of parts becomes more problematic while the Moorean commonsense argument from contradiction that relies on it becomes much less compelling. From a Hegelian perspective, one might say that in ignoring the temporal aspect and the formative play of the mind in its shifting interpretive constitution of what the parts and whole are, Moore locks himself into the secure but philosophically jejune level of commonsense understanding. This level naively thinks the objects, parts, and wholes with which it deals are firm, nonmental realities, while the Hegelian and deconstructionist will instead regard them as but the flexible abstractions and constructed products of the activity of mind or language's play of differences (see *The Phenomenology of Mind* 171–78). *Hegel*

We shall soon go further into the likely debate between deconstructionist and analytic philosophy concerning the validity of Moore's refutation of the radical Hegelian sense of organic unity, a dizzyingly deep debate having crucial and far-reaching consequences for philosophy of language and metaphysics. But to appreciate more fully deconstruction and analysis's dramatic dance of reversals around this notion, we should first see how the deconstructionist attack on (the analytically endorsed) *aesthetics* of organic unity relies precisely on the radical logical sense of this notion that Moore and analysis have put into question. The best way to show this is by showing how their critique of aesthetic organicism relies on the notion of *différance*, and by showing how *différance* is essentially a version or corollary or application of the older notion of radical organic unity. Let us start from the second point.

Derrida's concept of *différance* is based on the Saussurian structuralist idea that "in the linguistic system there are only differences, *without positive terms*" (Saussure 120).[13] For example, the identity of any particular phoneme is not constituted by any positive essence, any real distinctive acoustic sound (for it is realizable in a multitude of qualitatively different sounds), but instead by its differential relations with other phonemes in the system. Building on Saussure and recognizing further that all the objects and concepts of our world are linguistically mediated and constituted, Derrida asserts that all the objects, elements, or categories of discourse are also differentially constituted and do not rest on foundationally real, positive essences beyond the differential network of language. They "do not have as their cause a subject or substance, a thing in general, that is somewhere present and itself escapes the play of differences" ("Différance" 141); and he warns against the metaphysical response to supply such positive el-

ements, "to respond with a definition of essence, of quiddity, to reconstitute a
system of essential predicates" (*Positions* 58). *Différance*, then, is "a structure
and a movement . . . of . . . the systematic play of difference, of traces of differences, of the spacing by which elements relate to one another . . . without
which the 'full' terms could not signify, could not function" (*Positions* 27). In
other words, since any thing or element depends for its individuation and meaning on its differential interrelations with other elements, what any thing is, is essentially a function of what it is not. Since it is thus constituted by its differential
relations with elements that, as different, are neither simply present in it nor necessarily simultaneously or contiguously present with it (and here the deferring
sense of *différance* is displayed), any thing or element is never fully present in
itself nor constituted simply by (or for) itself. The

> . . . play of differences involves syntheses and referrals that prevent there
> from being in any moment or in any way a simple element that is present in
> and of itself and refers only to itself . . . , no element can function . . .
> without relating to another element which itself is not simply present. This
> linkage means that each "element" . . . is constituted with reference to the
> trace in it of the other elements of the sequence or system. . . . Nothing,
> either in the elements or in the system, is simply present or absent. There
> are only everywhere, differences and traces of traces. (*Positions* 26)

The essential sameness of *différance* and the radical concept of organic unity
should now appear obvious, especially if we take the notion of whole as representing the (perhaps not fully totalizable) system or structure of linguistic differences. For, as we saw, this organic principle asserts that any part or element "can
have no meaning or significance apart from its whole," that no individual part
can be a self-identical, self-sufficient, "distinct object of thought," since all
"the parts would not be what they are but for the existence of the whole," "are
inconceivable except as parts of that whole," as each part derives its meaning
from its relations to the whole's other parts (*Principia Ethica* 33, 34, 36). Now
since any object that we ordinarily conceive as a whole can itself be seen as part
of a larger whole, structure, or system in which it is a part (at the very least in the
minimal, vague sense that it is part of the world) we can apply this principle of
organic unity or difference to any object. From this logical principle of organic
unity or *différance*, it then follows that what any object is, is essentially a function of what it is not; it is essentially constituted by its differential relations with
other objects from which it is distinguished but without whose associative, relational distinctions it could not be or be distinguished as what it is.

As indicated earlier, and as Moore clearly recognized, this idea that every
thing is constituted by what it is not can be traced back to Hegel, that philosopher
of the whole most repudiated by analytic thinkers: "Everything that exists stands
in correlation, and this correlation is the veritable nature of every existence. The
existent thing in this way has no being of its own, but only in something else"
(*Hegel's Logic* 191). It is also salient and pervasive in the thought of Nietzsche

(another Teutonic protodeconstructor and analytic anathema), where it forms the logical core of his central doctrines of the will to power and the eternal recurrence:

> Things that have a constitution in themselves—a dogmatic idea with which one must break absolutely. . . . In the actual world . . . everything is bound to and conditioned by everything else. . . . No things remain but only dynamic quanta, in relations of tension to all other dynamic quanta: their essence lies in their relation to all other quanta. (*The Will to Power* pars. 559, 584, 635)[14]

It is time to see how this organicistic logic of *différance* is deployed in contemporary deconstructions of organic unity as an aesthetic notion. We find it as the structuring logical foundation for the two major arguments aimed at undermining the coherence of the traditional idea of a work of art's unity. As is characteristic of deconstructive arguments, both start with the assumptions of aesthetic unity but then work through them to reveal an aporia or internal contradiction within the very idea of such unity that necessarily violates it.

The first argument concerns the sense of wholeness and integrity contained in the idea of a work's organic unity. We regard the work as a distinct integral whole, composed of the parts belonging to it and complete in itself as a whole constituted by those and only those parts. But such unity, it is argued, is constituted only on the basis of distinguishing and excluding something outside it, elements not part or constitutive of the unified whole. If we hold with Aristotle that an organically unified work must have a beginning, middle, and end (or even just a beginning and end), we must recognize that it cannot have them without having something before the beginning and beyond its end in order to mark them and shape or frame the work they try to enclose. Thus, what is alleged to be outside, apart from, or irrelevant to the self-sufficient work as whole, becomes essential to it and constitutive of it. What seems to lie outside the work and beyond it is as much a part of what makes the work (and is as essential to it) as the constitutive parts inside the work. The whole distinction between inside and outside the work, on which the notion of integral unity rests, becomes problematized when what lies outside the work becomes internal or essential to it. The very possibility of a work's integrity as an organic unity composed only of its parts is voided when it is seen to be as much constituted by what is not its parts but rather frames them. Its unity of parts, constituted by what is foreign and contrastively opposed to this unity, is thus fundamentally and ineluctably self-divided rather than unified.

This general line of argument is employed by Culler, who notes that "the 'organic unity' of works of art is the product of framing," which relies on "the distinction between inside and outside [that] evades precise formulation," a distinction between an external background or supplementary frame and the unified totality of the work this frames. But then "this marginal supplement" or outside is therefore "essential, constituting, enshrining," for "framing is what creates the aesthetic object.'' Although outside the work's intrinsic structure, ''the frame is what gives us an object that can have an intrinsic content or structure.'' So, for Culler, the external or marginal to the work ''becomes central by virtue of its very marginality'' (*On Deconstruction* 195–99). Culler's dialectical argument of the frame (which he nicely elaborates both in terms of criticism as a framing discourse of literature and in terms of the framing metalinguistic devices in the work itself) is taken from Derrida's analysis of the frame as *parergon*. In their formulations it may seem somewhat more complex than the first general form of organicistic argument I outlined above, but this is only because the frame itself, as they see it, is not clearly identified with the outside of the work. Rather, in Derrida's words, ''it is a *parergon*, a composite of inside and outside, but a composite which is not an amalgam or half-and-half but an outside which is called inside the inside to constitute it as inside'' (''The Parergon'' 26). Nonetheless, we have here the same essential argument. For it is the frame's being outside that makes it be summoned and drawn into the inside to make the inside an inside, just as it is the excluded external nonparts in the logical principle of organic unity that are ineluctably reinscribed as essential and constitutive of the internal parts.

The second basic argument against the work of art as an organic whole concerns not the work's distinction from what is outside it, but rather distinction within the work itself. To constitute the work as an organic unity of parts we need to distinguish some coherent order or structure (invariably somehow privileging or hierarchical) of parts in the whole. We therefore typically speak of what is central as opposed to marginal in a work; and analytic aestheticians often distinguish the work's ''hard core of essential features'' from ''the surrounding penumbra of inessential ones'' (Harrison 125), or in Goodman's terms its ''constitutive'' from its ''contingent'' properties (*Languages of Art* 115–20, 209–10).[15] We are all familiar with the conventions of literary competence, by which we disregard some features of the text as ancillary, inessential, or accidental in order to concentrate on what really counts in the text. Apparently insignificant words or punctuation, the text's visual shape and color,[16] the homonymic meanings or alternative uses of its words, distant associations that they might raise in other fields but are plainly out of place in the literary context—all these we standardly dismiss as being beside the point and as obstructing, if we focus on them, the real meaning and unity of the work. But, the deconstructors ask, if these irrelevant aspects belong to the text and its words, what justification is there for branding them irrelevant or inessential vis-à-vis some contrasting essence of the text? For by the logical principle of organicism, the essential properties or meanings could neither be nor be distinguished as essential if not for the so-called irrelevant and inessential ones that frame them. And if the inessential is thus revealed as essential to the essential, this would undermine the privileging structure of parts and meanings that constitutes the work as an organic unity. It would suggest, moreover, that the inessential (as essential) deserves our attention as critics and appreciators; but such attention would seem to disrupt the psychologically experienced unity of the work. Organic unity is thus undone both objectively and subjectively.

This argument, saliently reflected in Derrida's logic of marginality or supplementarity and in deconstruction's interpretive practice of focusing on textual "irrelevancies," is set out most clearly in Culler. "Interpretation generally relies on distinctions between the central and the marginal, the essential and the inessential: to interpret is to discover what is central to a text or group of texts." But since marginality is not something ontologically given but a product of interpretational framing, "what has been relegated to the margins or set aside by previous interpreters may be important for precisely those reasons." Yet the fact that we can "reverse a hierarchy to show that . . . [the] marginal is in fact central" does not lead "to the identification of a new center . . . , but to a subversion of the distinctions between essential and inessential, inside and outside. What is a center if the marginal can become central?" (*On Deconstruction* 140). Moreover, building on de Man's suggested reversal of the traditional "ethos of explication" by attempting "a reading that would no longer blindly submit to the teleology of controlled meaning" ("Foreword" ix–x), Culler repudiates "our inclination to use notions of unity and thematic coherence to exclude possibilities" of meaning that would pose a problem for a coherent interpretation of the text "because they would disrupt the focus or continuity" of such a reading (*On Deconstruction* 246–47).

This further twist of the argument is important, since a defender of organic unity might concede the point that the marginal or inessential is logically essential for framing, but then go on to argue that we must not confuse such essentiality with aesthetic centrality or worthiness for aesthetic attention. In rejoinder, Culler would first point out that our standard of judging what in a text is central or appropriate for aesthetic appreciation is the criterion of its fit or contribution to the postulated unity of the work. But this, he would then insist, is precisely to beg the question that the text is unified. We cannot appeal to the text's disputed organic unity to prove that unity. We especially have no right to posit as a metaphysical axiom of organicistic reification that literary works are organic unities by virtue of some special ontological status, irrespective of the intentional acts of authors and interpreters. De Man's critique of New Criticism's reification of the autonomous literary work and its organic form is compellingly correct here. The postulated unity of a text (like the text's meaning) is at best an interpretive structure, hermeneutically and contextually constructed, not a foundational and unchanging given.

But without foundational unity, there remains, I think, pragmatic justification for postulating unity in the work as a strategy of reading and an interpretive criterion of relevance and centrality. For rich and coherent unity and the satisfactions it affords are what we primarily seek in reading literary texts. Culler is quick to reject this aim as reflecting a narrowly formalist hedonism, as falsely relegating literary works to the realm of play and pleasure, devoid of the cognitive rigor and seriousness that close reading involves. Defensively reacting to the apparent hedonistic, ludic excesses of some older deconstructors like Barthes and Hartman, he and Christopher Norris eschew the interpretive aim of "enriching elucidations'' and "refuse to make aesthetic richness an end" (*On Deconstruction* 221–40), positing instead deconstruction's "demonstrable rigour" and the "knowledge and feelings of mastery" its decentering readings afford as the privileged, overriding aim of criticism (*The Deconstructive Turn* 7).[17] But, if the pleasure of aesthetic richness provides its own immediate justification, Norris and Culler's indictment of it lacks any similarly compelling power. Their attitude instead reflects not only the puritanical prejudice of a Protestant work ethic (directed at the dismembering of "seductively" pleasurable verbal icons) but the presumption of a false dichotomy between reading for pleasure and reading for understanding.[18] The basic human need to perceive and experience satisfying unities in the disordered flux of experience is what motivates our interest in art, whose works not only afford such satisfactions in themselves but can lead to a more satisfyingly integrated experience of the world.

Culler would try to dismiss this basic presumptive bias for unity as merely a cultural "convention" of literary competence, and therefore arbitrary and dispensable. But such a move falsely assumes that all our cultural conventions are indeed superficially arbitrary, an assumption based on an uncritical acceptance of the natural/conventional distinction. As I have shown elsewhere, there are no clear lines to be drawn between natural and culturally informed or "conventional" human interests and practices. Many of our so-called conventions are so deeply entrenched that we naturally live and perform them as part of the fabric and bedrock of our form of life and sense of self. Doing without them, if indeed feasible, would be doing most poorly, alienating ourselves from what constitutes our very forms of thinking, action, and experience.[19] With respect to our conventional aesthetic prejudice toward unity, Culler is honest enough to admit that "the critical writings that most vigorously proclaim their celebration of heterogeneity are likely to reveal, under exegetical scrutiny, their reliance on notions of organic unity that are not easy to banish" (*On Deconstruction* 200). This indeed is precisely what I have shown in Derrida and Culler's own celebration of the philosophical heterogeneity of *différance*.

There is a further and far from narrowly aesthetic justification of the interpretive presumption of a work's unity. It is the Heideggerian-Gadamerian idea that interpretive understanding is the working out of a foreunderstanding based on "the fore-conception of completion," the presumption "that only what constitutes a unity of meaning is intelligible" (Gadamer 261). We always expect a text or utterance we encounter to issue in some coherent whole when it is worked out and understood. Thus when it seems incoherent, either in itself or in its relation to our views on what it concerns, we need to interpret it so that some "unified meaning can be realized" (261). We typically do this either by interpreting the text as more coherent (with itself or with our beliefs) or by interpreting its incoherencies within a coherent explanatory account (e.g., its author's different spatiotemporal or psychological context), in other words, within a larger coherent totality of meaning. Even de Man, for all his critique of organic unity as natural and reified, still recognized its hermeneutic reality: the undeniable "intent at to-

tality of the interpretative process," "the necessary presence of a totalizing principle as the guiding impulse of the critical process" ("Form and Intent" 31–32).

However, this principle of interpretive holism, the idea that intelligibility
somehow relies on some idea of unity, has recently been denounced by Derrida as
the pervasive, baneful burden of "the axiomatic structure of metaphysics, insofar as *metaphysics itself* desires, or dreams, or imagines its own unity": "Since
Aristotle, and at least up until Bergson, 'it' (metaphysics) has constantly repeated and assumed that to think and to say must mean to think and to say something that would be a *one*, one *matter*" ("Interpreting Signatures" 256–57). In
terms of analytic philosophy this assumption has been expressed in the idea that
all intelligible thought and language relies on "individuating reference" and that
anything we can refer to (hence speak about) must be self-identical. As the once
popular dictum put it, "no entity without identity." To what extent is this assumption of unity and identity really necessary, valid, or even possible? Are there
"ones" we can really refer to and distinguish as independent from others; and
must we at least presume that there are? We are thus led back to organic unity at
its most fundamental and challenging stratum—as a principle of logic, metaphysics, and philosophy of language, a principle that perhaps most sharply divides
analysis and deconstruction yet binds them in an unavoidable and perhaps interminable agon of confrontation.

IV

We should recall that Moore's analytic critique of organic unity attacks it first for
mistaking the emergent relational properties that belong properly only to the
whole for defining properties of a given part, and second for self-contradictorily
holding that a part (as a part) is both logically distinct from the whole (and other
parts in the whole) and yet essentially includes them all as part of its own nature.
The potency of both these criticisms clearly depends on the assumption that we
can really talk about a part and its intrinsic nature. Yet precisely this assumption
is what radical organic unity is challenging when it asserts that everything (hence
any part) lacks any intrinsic features of its own but is constituted solely through
its interrelations with, and differences from, everything else—relations that (as
Nietzsche and Hegel would urge) are not foundationally fixed but the product of
(possibly changing) interpretation. Any identification of part depends on what
other parts it is interpreted as being related to and distinguished from; there are
no parts, like no facts, without interpretation. But if there is no identity apart
from interpretation, we can dismiss the charge that the part's identity is misde-
scribed or self-contradictorily construed. Parts simply become different parts by
being differently interpreted in terms of different interrelations. Moore's logic-
chopping argument has lost its blade.

To this differential, interpretive account of identity the analyst might respond
in two related ways.[20] He could argue that the whole notion of differences or
interrelations presupposes that there are entities differentiated or interrelated, and

that we cannot speak of an entity without identity. Difference relies conceptually on identity, as much as identity seems to presuppose the idea of difference. The inseparability of these notions seems to be James's pragmatist point in listing "the same or different" as *one* of our most important commonsense concepts (*Pragmatism* 76). But the deconstructor (or pragmatist) could cogently reply that this need not entail foundational self-identical substances, since sufficient identity for differentiation is provided in the idea of "identity according to a particular interpretation." Similarly, the analytic argument that we need real particulars to serve as individual referents without which we could not think or talk about anything can be answered by the idea that such referents on which our thought and speech are structured can simply be individuals according to some interpretation.

The analyst might then press further by questioning more specifically the basic differential terms or Nietzschean "dynamic quanta" that are seen as entering into the interrelational intepretations that constitute all objects. What are these interpretational elements? If they are basic atoms, then some things that enter into the interpretational constitution of objects are not themselves so constituted. If instead these basic elements are themselves the product of interpreting still more basic elements in *their* interrelations, then we can and should ask the same question about those. Recursively applying this analytic strategy (the essential strategy of logical atomism), we must then either end in atomic elements of some sort or instead "never end" in an infinite regress or circle of interpretations, where ultimately there is nothing beyond interpretations to interpret. This is not simply a question of the independent world collapsing into the texts that represent it (a position also embraced by pragmatists like Goodman and Rorty). Here the very idea of text itself dissolves into interpretations without any independent "interpretation-free" text or object that they are interpretations of. Derrida would hardly flinch at such consequences, and he would certainly repudiate the analytic argument (with its reductive quest for basics and its bugaboos of circularity and infinite regress) as a paradigm symptom of that ontotheological metaphysics which has so long enthralled our thought. In responding to Searle, he warned against the analytic "enterprise of returning 'strategically,' in idealization, to an origin or to a 'priority' seen as simple, intact, normal, pure, standard, self-identical [as] not just *one* metaphysical gesture among others; it is the metaphysical exigency, the most constant, profound, and potent procedure" ("Limited Inc abc" 236).

The ontological roots of traditional analysis are surely clear.[21] What is far from clear, however, is whether deconstruction, in its very critique of analysis, is not itself ensnared by a metaphysics that it desperately seeks to avoid. For the notion of organic unity that underlies its critique seems to reflect a potent and pervasive metaphysical gesture of its own. The deconstructive idea that everything is a product of its interrelations and differences from other things, that there are no independent terms with positive or intrinsic essences, rests at bottom on the idea that all these interrelated and differential terms are indeed inexorably and ineluctably interconnected. This idea of the world as an organic totality or system of terms, and its use to undermine the existence of independent substances, is clearly present in Hegel and Nietzsche, where it could hardly loom more explicitly as a metaphysical thesis. To recall, in Hegel: "Everything that exists stands in correlation, and this correlation is the veritable nature of every existence. The existent thing in this way has no being of its own, but only in something else." (*Hegel's Logic* 191). Similarly with Nietzsche, who is probably closer to Derrida: "In the actual world . . . everything is bound to and conditioned by everything else. . . . No things remain but only dynamic quanta, in relations of tension to all other dynamic quanta: their essence lies in relation to all other quanta. . . . Every atom affects the whole of being" (*The Will to Power* 584, 634).

This view of the world as a totality of organically interrelated and reciprocally relationally defined elements, a world whose apparently independent individual objects are simply interpretive constructs of such internal systemic relations, is this not a metaphysical view? And why should we accept it as a true one? Derrida himself has recently condemned the idea of "a totality of beings" as a dangerous metaphysical idea, one from which he would like to extricate Nietzsche (and ultimately, if unknowingly, himself) ("Interpreting Signatures" 258–61).[22] One likely way to effect this escape would be to regard Nietzschean cosmological organicism not as a foundational metaphysical view but simply as one more interpretive perspective on the world, or, in Goodman's pluralist, pragmatist terms, one more "world-version" or constructed "world."[23] The problem, then, is that mere perspectival status seems to rob organic unity of its power to refute the "positivist" or "atomist" perspective, which sees the world as having some real and logically independent things with positive natures (which need not be eternal essences) of their own. As merely another perspective on the world, why should this organic, differential, holistic view of the world be preferred or privileged? What does it have to offer? It surely does not provide a view either congenial to or practical for our entrenched logocentric ways of speaking, thinking, and acting; and its advocates quite openly and happily admit this. Is it then offered more on aesthetic than on pragmatic grounds? There is, we should stress, nothing wrong with assessing ontological perspectives aesthetically; and perhaps nothing ultimately divides their aesthetic and pragmatic justification. Certainly Quine's ontological minimalism was simultaneously linked both to pragmatism and a taste for desert landscapes.[24]

Although we saw it primarily employed to undermine the aesthetic satisfaction of the alleged unities of artworks, the ontological perspective implied by the deconstructive notion of organic unity or *différance* might seem to offer some other sort of aesthetic satisfaction: a peculiarly metaphysical aesthetic gratification. For it presents the chaotic and unfathomable congeries of our world as ultimately (or at least best construable as) an organic whole of essentially interrelated elements that have no life or meaning apart from their interconnections and that can be differently arranged, shaped, and manipulated by intervening interpretation. We can therefore look through the shattered and disjointed fragments of our post-

modern wasteland and see them all as one vast sum and unity of essentially interrelated objects. Moreover, apart from the satisfying, reassuring consolation of
this comprehensive unity of essential interrelations, there is the comforting
promise that any disturbing fact or object in the world can simply be transfigured
or deconstructed by reinterpretation of the differential elements into more pleas-
ing interpretive constructions.

This unity will strike many (the analyst, the pragmatist, and the common man)
as too remote and metaphysical to be of much real comfort. It seems an unsa-
tisfying substitute for the loss of the positive, substantive, or traditionally entrenched unities we are accustomed to regarding as the individual objects or
beautiful artworks of our ordinary world, things which deconstructive organic
unity asks us to question and abandon. But if our faith in those unities has already
been lost, if, as marginalized intellectuals in the humanities, we have become
disenchanted with both the ideology of facts and the facts themselves, and even
with the works of art through which we hoped to change or escape the facts, then
the principle of organic unity offers some solace of unification. For not only is
everything essentially connected but all facts dissolve into interpretations.

Pragmatism, to my mind the best mediator and option between analysis and
deconstruction, can also see things as being in some sense (or having been at
some time) interpretations, but interpretations so inextricably entrenched in our
actual thinking that they have the status of fact or reality. However, it does not
rush from the unavailability of foundational facts to the totalizing conclusion of
hermeneutics and deconstruction that all understanding is interpretation (or misinterpretation), that in the free and fluid play of intelligible experience there is
nothing to distinguish them, no priority or hierarchy. For this would be giving up
a frequently valuable distinction (functional or pragmatic, not ontological) between understanding and interpretation, between what we grasp without requiring further elucidation and what needs to be interpreted for us to handle it
satisfactorily.[25] Because reality for the pragmatist is basically what has "coer-
civeness, in the long run, over thought" (James, *Collected Essays* 18), and truth
is roughly "whatever proves itself to be good in the way of belief" and "expe-
dient in the way of our thinking," "in the long run and on the whole" (James,
Pragmatism 36, 98), there is little doubt that pragmatism will be closer than deconstruction to the worldview of common sense, with its particular objects and
independent things having characters of their own. But it may not want to move
from this way of seeing and using the world to a fundamental metaphysical inference regarding what there ultimately is. It will want to leave that ontological
question an open one, or perhaps better yet simply leave it as a bootless non-
question.

Derrida no doubt would deny the charge that his version of organic unity or
différance is caught up with the metaphysics of totality. For does he not explicitly
repudiate the idea of totality? But it is hard to see how we can make sense of the
systematic differential production of meaning without presupposing the idea of at
least a provisional (and possibly ever-expanding) totality of interrelated terms.

He himself in maintaining that language excludes totalization characterizes its differential field as "a field of infinite substitutions in the closure of a finite ensemble" ("Structure, Sign, and Play" 160). Moreover, even forgoing the question of totality, the very presumption that *all* the elements or objects in our languaged world are essentially differentially interconnected and reciprocally constitutive of each other (however untotaled or untotalizable they may be) clearly seems in itself to constitute a metaphysical perspective predisposed to cosmic unity and coherence. To break the web of *différance* all we need is one independent entity, one positive term with its own intrinsic character, not a universe totally shot through with such entities.

Confronting traditional analytic philosophy with deconstruction on the deepest ontological level we are confronted with a choice: Russell and (early) Wittgenstein's atomistic metaphysics of basic, independent, unified, and self-identical (though perhaps never actually identifiable) entities forming the structure of facts through their external relations, versus the Hegelian-Nietzschean deconstructive picture in which there are no such separate individual entities or unities but only because there is a much vaster differential unity of all there is, an all-embracing unity whose internal differential relations constitute what the analyst takes as individual things. What the pragmatist sees on this ontological level (where she is reluctant to tread) is neither: not a world of autonomous atoms nor one solely of integrated interrelations and their essentially connected, reciprocally constituted terms. What she instead sees (on an ontological level where she feels more comfortable) is rather "a world imperfectly unified still," largely "the common-sense world, in which we find things partly joined and partly disjoined" (James, *Pragmatism* 72). And what does the pragmatist want with respect to organic unity? James provides a handy declaration that suggests an answer while it weaves some themes and catchwords of analysis and deconstruction. "Provided you grant *some* separation among things, some tremor of independence, some free play of parts on one another, some real novelty and chance, however minute, she is amply satisfied, and will allow you any amount, however great, of real union" (71).

I should note in conclusion that I do not expect (or desire) any real union between analytic philosophy and deconstruction with respect to organic unity, apart from their continued union in opposition. But I shall be amply satisfied to have shown how and where they are partly joined and partly disjoined on this issue, and in doing so to have promoted a deeper, more tolerant, and more fruitful dialogue between these two powerful philosophies from which contemporary pragmatism has greatly learned. It is perhaps not too much to hope that they might learn something from pragmatism.

Notes

1. See, e.g., G. E. Moore, *Principia Ethica* 26–30, 189–208. I shall later be discussing this work's analysis of organic unity in considerable detail. Harold Osborne treats organic unity as the defining characteristic of beauty and works of art: "A work of art is an organic whole of interlocking

organic wholes'' (203). I. A. Richards in defining the aesthetic experience (with which he identifies the work of art or literature) defines it in terms of its distinctive unity and completeness (43, 142–43, 184–87). Monroe Beardsley's organicism is evident in his definition of the aesthetic experience as a complete and coherently unified experience and in his insistence that unity and completeness are two of the three objective canons of aesthetic criticism (464–66, 527–30). Apart from Richards's and Beardsley's connection with New Criticism, Cleanth Brooks's ''The Heresy of Paraphrase'' can provide an example of New Criticism's commitment to the idea of a richly complex unity of parts all of which help constitute the poem as a well-wrought whole. For Brooks this essential unity that informs the good poem is a matter of ''imaginative'' rather than strictly logical coherences,'' ''of balancing and harmonizing connotations, attitudes, and messages . . . [which] unites the like with the unlike'' in a polyphonic ''achieved harmony'' (195, 202). Finally, Dewey's organicism (clearly adumbrating Beardsley's) pervades his treatment of aesthetic experience as one of ''internal integration and fulfillment reached through ordered and organized movement'', where the work of art ''is a unity of interrelated parts,'' whose ''different elements and specific qualities . . . blend and fuse in a way in which physical things cannot emulate'' (38, 92–93, 192).

2. In what follows we shall be examining in more detail Derrida's other (and more explicit) attacks on organic unity as an aesthetic idea and as a metaphysical presumption. That he himself does not escape but rather deeply relies on this metaphysical presumption in the very strategy of deconstruction is an issue this essay will later consider.

3. See Aristotle's *Poetics*, VII-VIII (Butcher 35). Plato to some extent adumbrated this idea of organic unity in his *Phaedrus* where he says that ''every discourse ought to be a living creature, having a body of its own and a head and feet; there should be a middle, beginning and end adapted to each other and to the whole.'' (Jowett, Vol. 3 172–73).

4. Elsewhere, in asserting that ''deconstruction always has for its target to reveal the existence of hidden articulations and fragmentations within assumedly monadic totalities,'' de Man falsely suggests that a totality needs to be monadic to be satisfyingly unified (*Allegories of Reading* 249). It is indeed far from clear how, logically, any real textual totality *could* be truly monadic, i.e., unarticulated or individuated into elements (different characters, words, lines) that form the totality. Norris follows de Man's critique of New Criticism's ''formalist'' organicism in *Deconstruction: Theory and Practice* (13–17, 102–4), and Culler's attack on the aesthetic idea of organic unity, as expounded in his *On Deconstruction: Theory and Criticism after Structuralism*, will be given detailed attention later in this essay.

5. Heraclitus clearly advocates a unity embracing difference and conflict when he states, ''Opposition unites. From what draws apart results the most beautiful harmony. All things take place by strife.'' (See fragment 46 in M. Nahm 91.) Moreover, Coleridge, who introduced the term ''organic unity'' into English criticism, spoke of its expression in the imagination of poetic genius as a ''unity that . . . reveals itself in the balance or reconciliation of opposite or discordant qualities; of sameness with difference'' (174).

6. I have elsewhere explored some other points of deep opposition as well as of surprising convergence between deconstruction and analytic aesthetics. See my ''Analytic Aesthetics, Literary Theory, and Deconstruction'' and ''Deconstruction and Analysis: Confrontation and Convergence.''

7. For Russell's own admission of Moore's leadership in their analytic revolt, see Russell (xviii).

8. Both these works were first published in the same month, October 1903; so the conflicting valencies and applications of organic unity must have been very clear in Moore's mind.

9. For the dialectical logic of part and whole, see *Hegel's Logic* (191–92).

10. See McTaggart, *The Nature of Existence*, chapter 20.

11. See de Man, ''The Purloined Ribbon'' 42–45.

12. I have elaborated and defended this point in my ''Osborne and Moore on Organic Unity'' 352–59.

13. I am well aware that Derrida might protest that *différance* cannot in any way be based on this (or any) Saussurian notion, since one of Derrida's aims is precisely to undermine the whole Saussurian project of explaining language as a closed and totalizable differential system. I am also aware

that Derrida would dispute my talk of the "concept of *différance*," since he repeatedly insists that it is "neither a word nor a concept" (see Jacques Derrida, "Différance," in *Margins of Philosophy*, and also *Positions* 39–40). With respect to this second point, I would reply with Rorty that authorial fiat cannot immunize a term against concepthood, "that all that it takes for something to be a concept is a place in a language-game," and that *différance* clearly has such a place (indeed a central and almost ritualistic place) in the language game(s) of deconstruction (see Rorty, "Deconstruction and Circumvention" 18). As to the first point, it is not only possible but (given deconstruction's avowed strategy of inhabiting and dismantling positions from within) perhaps necessary for it to build on concepts of theories it seeks to subvert. Moreover, as my ensuing discussion will try to bring out, it is not at all clear that the strategy of *différance* can be effective against analytic philosophy and aesthetic unity without an appeal to some sort of totalizing move regarding objects as differential relations.

14. Nehamas has recently suggested the ways in which Nietzsche's organicistic dissolution of things into differential relations within a whole can be connected with doctrines of the will to power and the eternal recurrence.

15. The theorizing of Harrison and Goodman reflects the discourse and practice of traditional criticism that characteristically seeks not simply what is in the work but what is its central and most formative dimension, in Helen Gardner's words "a work's centre, the source of its life in all its parts" (23). Even radically organicist (but nondeconstructionist) theorists like Strawson and Cleanth Brooks who insist that all the work's parts are necessary for its identity, never assert that they are all equally important; and they certainly would deny (what deconstructors challengingly suggest) that all the possible meanings of the work's parts are part of the work, and may be essential to it. For a more detailed account of the differing conceptions of work-identity in analytic aesthetics, see R. Shusterman. *The Object of Literary Criticism* 110–47.

16. I have elsewhere argued that in a great many literary works, particularly poetry, the visual features of the written or printed text are aesthetically very relevant and often essential. The false but widely held view that poetry is sound and sense but never sight is largely the product of an ancient philosophical bias for the phonocentric and the spiritual as nonmaterial, coupled with a misguided metaphysical superstition that sees the oral as somehow less material than the written. On this issue, see my "The Anomalous Nature of Literature" 317–29; "Aesthetic Blindness to Textual Visuality" 87–96; and "Ingarden, Inscription, and Literary Ontology" 103–19.

17. Also see Jonathan Culler, *Roland Barthes* (98–100), *On Deconstruction* (132n, 225), and Norris, *Deconstruction: Theory and Practice*, 92–108, and *The Deconstructive Turn* 6–7.

18. I have exposed this false dichotomy in my "Eliot on Reading: Pleasure, Games and Wisdom" 1–20. Marxian critics of art sometimes fall victim to another false and stultifying dichotomy: appreciative enjoyment of art's unity and perfection versus critical appropriation of art in terms of the unreality of such unity and perfection in the real world. I discuss this in detail, along with the first dichotomy, in *T. S. Eliot and the Philosophy of Criticism*, chapter 6.

19. See my "Convention: Variations on a Theme" 36–55. The common confusion of the conventional with the superficial is nourished by the conflation of two different senses of "arbitrary": contingent or not ontologically necessary versus capricious, haphazard, unreasoned, and easily reversible.

20. There is also a third and two-tiered objection that might be brought here. It would maintain that organic unity's dissolution of substantial identity into a network of interrelations is not only contrary to what our language implies about the world (as ontologically structured in terms of substance and attributes) but would make any reasonably stable or shared individuating reference and hence any effective language impossible. Nehamas provides, I think, a very simple and effective reply to the first part of this objection, when he defends Nietzsche against Danto's charge that Nietzsche relies on the very language he is undermining by refuting its ontological implications. It is "not that our language is wrong but that we are wrong in taking it too seriously," wrong in inferring ontological commitments from it, in seeing it as "metaphysically loaded" (*Nietzsche: Life as Literature* 96). The objection's second aspect seems answerable by recognizing that the shared normative regularities nec-

essary for effective individuating reference and speech need not be based on any unchanging ontological referent outside a culture's social practices, and can admit of some change or divergence without necessarily incurring a breakdown of communication. The shared "referents" or objects of our
language could be traditionally shared and pragmatically constituted "unities" or "individuals"
rather than foundational substances. Further discussion of this issue of referential identity and language will soon follow.

21. They are also clearly recognized by analytic philosophy's sympathetic exponents and histo-
rians. See, for example, J. O. Urmson, *Philosophical Analysis: Its Development between the Two
World Wars* 45–47.

22. Derrida's specific target is Heidegger's interpretation of Nietzsche, one that recognizes and
emphasizes this totalization. It should be mentioned, however, that this interpretation is not merely
Heidegger's, but is present, in Nehamas and more importantly finds clear evidence in Nietzsche's
text. Nietzsche's notion of organic unity and in particular Nehamas's application of it are criticized in
greater detail in my "Nietzsche and Nehamas on Organic Unity."

23. See Goodman, *Ways of Worldmaking* 1–22, 91–140. Since for pragmatists like Goodman we
cannot speak meaningfully of *the* world apart from all world versions, we can speak more simply of
different worlds rather than different acceptable versions of the world. Such talk of worlds rather than
world interpretations does not throw us back to foundational metaphysics, because we are left with a
plurality of worlds, all of which are in some sense humanly constructed and none of which enjoys
unique and final philosophical privileging as *the* real world.

24. See W. V. Quine, *From a Logical Point of View* 4, 16–19, 20, 46.

25. For elaboration of this point, see *T. S. Eliot and the Philosophy of Criticism*.

Works Cited

Beardsley, Monroe C. *Aesthetics*. New York: Harcourt, Brace, 1958.

Benziger, James. "Organic Unity: Leibniz to Coleridge." *PMLA* 66 (1951): 24–48.

Brooks, Cleanth. "The Heresy of Paraphrase." In *The Well Wrought Urn*. 1947. New York: Harcourt
Brace, 1956. 192–214.

Butcher, S. H. *Aristotle's Theory of Poetry and Fine Art*. London: Macmillan, 1911.

Coleridge, Samuel Taylor. *Biographia Literaria*. 1817. London: Dent, 1965.

Culler, Jonathan. *On Deconstruction: Theory and Criticism after Structuralism*. Ithaca, N.Y.: Cornell
UP, 1982.

_____. *Roland Barthes*. New York: Oxford UP, 1983.

de Man, Paul. *Allegories of Reading*. New Haven, Conn.: Yale UP, 1979.

_____. "Foreword." In Carol Jacobs, *The Dissimulating Harmony*. Baltimore: Johns Hopkins UP,
1978. vi–xiii.

_____. "Form and Intent in American New Criticism." In *Blindness and Insight*. 2nd ed. Minne-
apolis: U of Minnesota P, 1983. 20–35.

_____. "The Purloined Ribbon." *Glyph* 1 (1977): 28–49.

Derrida, Jacques. "Différance." In *Speech and Phenomena and Other Essays on Husserl's Theory of
Signs*. Trans. David B. Allison. Evanston, Ill.: Northwestern UP, 1973. 129–160.

_____. "Interpreting Signatures (Nietzsche/Heidegger): Two Questions." *Philosophy and Litera-
ture* 10 (1986): 256–261.

_____. "Limited Inc abc." *Glyph* 2 (1977): 162–254.

_____. *Margins of Philosophy*. Trans. Alan Bass. Chicago: U of Chicago P, 1982.

_____. "The Parergon." *October* 9 (1979): 3–40.

_____. *Positions*. Trans. Alan Bass. London: Athlone, 1980.

_____. "Structure, Sign, and Play in the Discourse of the Human Sciences." In *The Structuralist
Controversy*. Ed. Richard Macksey and Eugenio Donato. Baltimore: Johns Hopkins UP, 1972.
247–72.

Dewey, John. *Art as Experience*. 1934. New York: Perigree, 1980.

Foucault, Michel. *The Archaeology of Knowledge*. Trans. A. M. Sheridan Smith. New York: Harper & Row, 1976.

Gadamer, Hans-Georg. *Truth and Method*. Trans. Garrett Barden and John Cumming. 1975. New York: Crossroad, 1982.

Gardner, Helen. *The Business of Criticism*. Oxford: Oxford UP, 1970.

Goodman, Nelson. *Languages of Art*. Indianapolis: Bobbs-Merrill, 1968.

_____. *Ways of Worldmaking*. Indianapolis: Hackett, 1978.

Harrison, Andrew. "Works of Art and Other Cultural Objects." *Proceedings of the Aristotelian Society* 68 (1967–68): 125.

Hegel, G. W. F. *Differenz des Fichte'schen und Schelling'schen Sustems der Philosophie*. Ed. Georg Lasson. Leipzig, 1923.

_____. *Hegel's Logic*. Trans. William Wallace. 1873. Oxford: Oxford UP, 1975.

_____. *The Phenomenology of Mind*. Trans. J. B. Baillie. 1910. New York: Harper & Row, 1967.

James, William. *Collected Essays and Reviews*. New York: Longmans, 1920.

_____. *Pragmatism and Other Essays*. New York: Simon & Schuster, 1963.

Jowett, Benjamin, ed. & trans. *The Dialogues of Plato*. 1892. Oxford: Clarendon, 1953. 3 vols.

Macherey, Pierre. *A Theory of Literary Production*. Trans. Geoffrey Wall. London: Routledge & Kegan Paul, 1970.

McTaggart, John McTaggart Ellis. *The Nature of Existence*. Cambridge: Cambridge UP, 1921.

Moore, G. E. *Principia Ethica*. 1903. Cambridge: Cambridge UP, 1959.

_____. "The Refutation of Idealism." 1903. Rpt. in *Philosophical Studies*. London: Routledge & Kegan Paul, 1922. 1–30.

Nahm, Milton, ed. & trans. *Selections from Early Greek Philosophy*. New York: Crofts, 1934.

Nehamas, Alexander. *Nietzsche: Life as Literature*. Cambridge, Mass.: Harvard UP, 1985.

Nietzsche, Friedrich. *The Will to Power*. Trans. Walter Kaufmann and R. J. Hollingdale. New York: Vintage, 1968.

Norris, Christopher. *Deconstruction: Theory and Practice*. London: Methuen, 1982.

_____. *The Deconstructive Turn*. London: Methuen, 1983.

Osborne, Harold. *The Theory of Beauty*. London: Routledge & Kegan Paul, 1952.

Quine, W. V. *From a Logical Point of View*. New York: Harper & Row, 1961.

Richards, I. A. *Principles of Literary Criticism*. 1923. London: Routledge & Kegan Paul, 1976.

Rorty, Richard. "Deconstruction and Circumvention." *Critical Inquiry* 11 (1984): 1-23.

Russell, Bertrand. *The Principles of Mathematics*. 1903. 2nd ed. New York: Norton, 1948.

Saussure, Ferdinand de. *Course in General Linguistics*. Trans. Wade Baskin. London: Peter Owen, 1960.

Shusterman, Richard. "Aesthetic Blindness to Textual Visuality." *Journal of Aesthetics and Art Criticism* 41 (1982): 87–96.

_____. "Analytic Aesthetics, Literary Theory, and Deconstruction." *Monist* 69 (1986): 22–38.

_____. "The Anomalous Nature of Literature." *British Journal of Aesthetics* 18 (1978): 317–29.

_____. "Convention: Variations on a Theme." *Philosophical Investigations* 9 (1986): 36–55.

_____. "Deconstruction and Analysis: Confrontation and Convergence." *British Journal of Aesthetics* 26 (1986): 311–27.

_____. "T. S. Eliot on Reading: Pleasure, Games and Wisdom." *Philosophy and Literature* 11 (1987): 1–20.

_____. "Ingarden, Inscription, and Literary Ontology." *Journal of the British Society for Phenomenology* 18 (1987): 103–19.

_____. "Nietzsche and Nehamas on Organic Unity." *Southern Journal of Philosophy* 26 (1988): 379–92.

_____. *The Object of Literary Criticism*. Amsterdam: Rodopi, 1984.

_____. "Osborne and Moore on Organic Unity." *British Journal of Aesthetics* 23 (1983): 352–59.

_____. *T. S. Eliot and the Philosophy of Criticism*. New York: Columbia UP, 1988.

Urmson, J. O. *Philosophical Analysis: Its Development between the Two World Wars*. Oxford: Oxford UP, 1956.

6

Metaphor according to
Davidson and de Man
Samuel C. Wheeler III

I. Introduction

This essay discusses Donald Davidson's account of metaphor in the light of the thinking of Paul de Man and interprets de Man's thinking on metaphor by means of Davidson's conceptual framework.[1] The hypothesis is that to a helpful extent, de Man's discussions of figuration can be understood as supporting and supported by a Davidsonian account of meaning, truth, and reference. De Man and Davidson share a thesis about language that shapes much of their thought. They both hold, putting it crudely, that every level of representation is essentially language-like. Words are explicated by words, not by reference to magic, self-interpreting representations such as thoughts. Although there are differences between Davidson's view and the kind of view that infuses de Man's accounts, they agree about the relation between language and meaning. They both hold that linguistic meaning is not reducible to non-language-like meaning bearers. Other parallels and resemblances follow from this one. Both Davidson and de Man, for instance, treat the metaphorical as a matter of the force with which a sentence is uttered.

Some of the differences between Davidson and de Man can be understood as arising from their different starting places and traditions. On the one hand, de Man's thought starts from literary concerns, and the problem of figuration and the rhetorical is the central core from which his accounts develop. On the other hand, Davidson arrives at such issues having started from traditional analytic philosophical concerns about the theory of meaning and reference.

The main doctrinal difference, I argue, is one where Davidson can learn from de Man. Briefly, Davidson cannot have a notion of truth that will sort out the literally true from the literally false in a determinate way that will systematically keep metaphorical assertions from being true as meant. By Davidsonian principles, the notion of truth-value ultimately turns out to be quite indeterminate in any areas except the most monolithically controlled, even though the formulation of truth-conditions may be precise. Thus the way is open to treating the literal as a limiting case of the metaphorical.

On the other hand, de Man's arguments on figuration are clarified and strengthened by arguments from Davidson and his tradition. Consider, for instance, Davidson's demonstration that no "rhetorical force marker" can be conventional. This analytic philosopher's way of describing the uncontrollable disseminating power of figuration supplements Derrida's and de Man's metaphors in a convincing way.

I treat Davidson's theory of language as the underlying ground for de Man's view. Proceeding to de Man by means of Davidson is my way of making de Man clear to myself and to people with roughly my background of training. What counts as "making it clear" is a question of what texts and modes of discussion are familiar. The more we read in other genres the wider our notion of "the clear" can become. Thus, a translation into analyticese does not suggest that the patterns of discussion and argument that define the genre of analytic philosophy are the only correct standards. I think those patterns *do* produce depth and illumination. New modes of argument give startling and valuable views of problems originally formulated and discussed otherwise. In addition to helping analytic philosphers read de Man, this essay may show some ways analytic philosophy can be useful to literary thinkers.

II. Davidson's Theory of Meaning

The Davidsonian insight that determines the rest of his theory is that any level of meaning must be language-like. Davidson is an antireductionist about words and their meaning: all meaning carriers are like words in being subject to interpretation. "Being subject to interpretation" means that nothing intrinsic to the term determines that it must refer to a given object.

Davidson thus denies the most fundamental element of the standard theory of meaning that has come down to us form the time of Plato, at least. The dream of the standard theory of meaning depended on there being a level of representation by completely present tokens whose very self-revealing nature determined what they referred to. Such tokens or presences might be thought tokens (the "ideas" of Berkeley et al.) or Forms or meanings, for instance. I call a system of such representations the "magic language." Quine's deconstructive arguments have shown that a "magic language" that allows meaning to be fixed by the very natures of the signifiers is incoherent with the following three theses: (1) that essentialism is false; (2) that reference is a function of intrinsic features of concepts available to the user; and (3) that necessity is linguistic, if anything (see Wheeler, "The Extension of Deconstruction"). Such a "magic language" would be required by any "foundational" theory of meaning, that is, by any theory that demands that interpretation end. Davidson has extended and purified these deconstructions to eliminate Quine's residual essentialist suppositions about observation (see esp. "On the Very Idea of a Conceptual Scheme).

If words carry meaning in as fundamental and irreducible a way as there is, then the meaning of some word is a contribution to truth-conditions given by some other word or by some formula whose interpretation is as problematic and subject to vagaries as the word whose meaning is being given. If words are as basic as meaning bearers get, then their meaning and truth-value are derived from a single kind of phenomenon—persons in a culture using words. The same data determine both meaning and truth. This entails an indeterminacy avoided by traditional theories of meaning, which have interpretation-free tokens. For Davidson, the total data both for determining meaning and for determining truth-value are what is said and when. That is, speech behavior in concrete situations gives all there is to get both of what terms mean and what sentences are true.[2]

So an account of meaning can be nothing more than a truth-definition, a finite set of biconditionals about the contributions of individual words to the truth-conditions of sentences.[3] Such a set has as consequences all sentences like " 'The sea is gong-ridden' is true if and only if the sea is gong-ridden.'' So neither literal nor figurative uses of language have senses associated with them, if those senses are supposed to be non-language-like meanings. Davidson does not understand "meaning" and "truth-conditions" in a way that requires that word meaning be given in some more fundamental terms, such as Quinean stimulus conditions or Carnapian protocol sentences. Truth-conditional semantics does not describe the truth-values of predications of semantically primitive predicates in more helpful or basic terms.

The dispositions of speakers are affected by beliefs, desires, and other propositional attitudes. The interanimation of sentences based on such propositional attitudes generate *evidence* for a given matching of words to words, but neither the pattern of connection nor the propositional attitudes are the meaning, which is *arrived at* on the basis of the evidence. In the same way, a scientific theory does not mean the data that confirm it.

III. The Metaphorical and Literal according to Davidsonism

A. Exposition

A view of meaning such as Davidson's will have some prima facie difficulties with the traditional notion of metaphor as transfer of meaning. The usual explications of metaphor presuppose the existence of a non-language-like meaning that lies behind speech. Without that kind of meaning, two kinds of difficulties seem to arise.

First, Davidson's semantics seems to say too little. In a way, Davidson's prima facie problem in accounting for metaphor is that his *semantics* leaves metaphor untouched.

Second, there seems to be a difficulty in ever saying what a metaphor really means, with Davidson's semantics. The meaning of a metaphor can no longer be encoded in the magic language of thought in which figuration is somehow impossible, so that the real message of a metaphor is transparent when the meaning of the thought-sentence is understood. On Davidson's account, language is always interpreted in language. So whatever allowed figural understandings in the interpreted language will also allow such understandings in our interpreting language. Without the magic language, there is no unturnable, metaphor-free discourse. Thus there is always the possibility of understanding the explication as a trope. The fond dream of a metaphor-free language in which the meaning of a metaphor can be given is the idle dream of a purely descriptive magic language of thought, the language in which the very tokens require that they be taken in exactly one way.

Davidson's exposition in "What Metaphors Mean" is primarily negative, and his own account is only cautiously sketched. He shows that accounts of metaphor as compressed simile and as synonymous with a simile fail to meet conditions of adequacy for an account of metaphor. All accounts that use the etymological metaphor of another meaning coming across, whether a meaning of another word or a meaning from a special poetic realm of meaning for metaphorical language, fail to be adequate. In particular, accounts that take the literal and metaphorical to be senses of words, so that a sentence that can be taken literally or figuratively is ambiguous, are criticized.

I find most of these arguments against other views utterly convincing. I will briefly sketch two points where the de Manian improvement suggested below differs from Davidson's view.

First, Davidson believes that an account of metaphor must explain why metaphors cannot be paraphrased. This rules out as too simple any theory of metaphorical meaning that takes a metaphor to be a compressed simile or synonymous with a simile, since then the metaphor would have a perfectly good literal paraphrase. If Yeats's "gong-tormented sea"[4] is short for "the sea that is like something tormented as if by a gong" (a sort of doubly imbedded metaphor), then it would have a perfectly clear literal paraphrase. Similarly, any simple "transfer" is ruled out.

Davidson's grounds for holding that metaphors are not paraphrasable is the radical one that a metaphor does not *say* anything different from its literal meaning. What makes an utterance a metaphor is not a matter of saying something ineffable, or saying anything at all. In "What Metaphors Mean," Davidson says that "paraphrase, whether possible or not, is appropriate to what is *said*: we try, in paraphrase, to say it another way. But if I am right, a metaphor doesn't say anything beyond its literal meaning" (246).

Second, Davidson holds that there is a difference in kind between applying a term literally to a new and unfamiliar case and applying the term metaphorically. This condition marks the crucial place where Davidson and I disagree on what should be said and why. In "What Metaphors Mean," Davidson uses the example of a Saturnian learning our language (251). In accord with his general conception of meaning and language, and his rejection of all three dogmas of empiricism, Davidson notes that there is no real difference between learning the language and learning what the world is like. Learning what "cat" means cannot be separated from learning what things are cats.

The Saturnian has learned to use and understand the term "floor" on Earth, so that he is able to apply "floor" to new and different floors. On his voyage home, taking Davidson along, he hears Davidson characterize the Earth below as a floor, and takes this to be yet another item in the extension of "floor." Davidson, however, was alluding to Dante's "small round floor that makes us passionate," a metaphorical rather than a literal use.

To see more clearly what will be at issue here, suppose that it is the Saturnian who characterizes the Earth as a floor. According to Davidson, he has spoken incorrectly and made a mistake. He is objectively wrong about what is a floor and what is not. Dante, on the other hand, although he has said something false, has not made a mistake, since he was speaking metaphorically. That is, the very same utterance, with the very same meaning, is false on both literal and metaphorical understandings, but only constitutes a mistake as uttered literally.

For Davidson, the metaphorical differs from the literal in the forces with which metaphorical and literal utterances are written or said, rather than differing in meaning. The purposes for which one produces a sentence with some truth-conditions vary, because words are versatile and malleable tools. That is, a sentence has given truth-conditions and so a given truth-value, but that sentence can be uttered for a number of reasons, and can function in a number of different speech acts. A person has made a mistake if something goes wrong with the intended purpose of utterance, while a sentence uttered for a purpose is true or false independently of its intended purpose. The truth-conditions of a sentence are what make the various things that can be done with it (including asserting what is the case) possible. "Force" is (roughly) the intention with which the sentence is produced. "Metaphorical" describes how an utterance is meant, not what it means. So, metaphors are not a class of sentences or phrases.

For Davidson, a literal utterance is the plain assertion of the truth-conditions as obtaining. To speak of an utterance as "literally false" is to say that if it were an assertion that the truth-conditions obtain, it would be a mistake. According to Davidson, the metaphorical use intends other purposes than telling it as it is. Metaphorical utterances are false, but not thereby defective, any more than are commands that are not yet obeyed.

The Davidsonian placement of the metaphorical in force rather than in semantics is virtually required by any theory of meaning that holds that there are no carriers of meaning more fundamental than words or wordlike phenomena. There are no other distinctions available, given that there is no magic language of thought in which metaphor is impossible and in which the pure meaning shines through from the very nature of the thought token.

Davidson proposes that the distinction between the metaphorical and the literal is one of *force* rather than meaning because there is nothing to meaning (in the sense of "sense") but words, and words do not distinguish the metaphorical from the literal. That is, without the idea of a perfectly expository language that could not be taken metaphorically, the "interpretation" of a metaphor is itself subject to both metaphorical and literal interpretation, because the interpreting language is just a language. Also, such interpretation gives such trivialities as that "my love is a rose" is true if and only if my love is a rose. When I explain what I mean by "gong-tormented sea" according to Davidsonian semantics, it turns out that "this sea is gong-tormented" is true if and only if this sea is gong-tormented. There is nothing in the terms to explain what metaphors do, so it must be a matter of use and the intention with which a sentence is uttered.

I thoroughly agree, both with Davidson's semantics and with his appeal to use as what is crucial to the metaphorical. I also agree that a very important part of what some metaphors do is other than conveying information. As Rorty points out in "Hesse and Davidson on Metaphor," the fragment "that dolphin-torn, that gong-tormented sea" is not valued for telling us about gongs or the sea.

B. Some Preliminary Difficulties

The main difference between the account I will suggest and Davidson's account concerns whether metaphorical remarks are ever true in a way that differs from the way they are sometimes literally true. This in turn rests on whether metaphorical use is really different in kind from ordinary application of a predicate to a new case. That again in turn depends on whether metaphor is regarded as central or marginal to the philosophy of language.

A fuller argument against parts of Davidson's account of metaphor is given in Section V, which joins features of Davidson's and de Man's accounts of metaphor. For the moment, let me state one kind of difficulty.

The account on which metaphors are never true assertions either presupposes a non-Davidsonian notion of truth-conditions, or begs the question of whether metaphorical utterances might be intended as true assertions. The literal and metaphorical meanings of "He was burned up" are identical. The utterance is true iff he was burned up. Now, Davidson would say that this sentence is false, on occasions where the person is angry but not incinerated. But what are the grounds for saying that it is really false? Davidson must hold that incineration is the literal meaning of "burned up," and that a surfeit of heat under the collar is always insufficient for incineration.

But an alternative account is that being really burned up sometimes involves combination with oxygen and sometimes not. Unless Davidson has in mind an account of meaning in which meaning is given by privileged webs of belief, he has no more basis for claiming that all cases of being burned up are oxidations than to claim that all plates are crockery, or that all pain is a sensation. It is no objection, either, that you can be burned up one way and not the other, since you can have your armor plate but not have a dinner plate.

So, the appeal to "literal truth" and to the literal falsity of metaphorical utterances begs the question. If metaphorical remarks are sometimes true assertions, then the truth-conditions of those remarks *do* obtain.

The key problem here is that the notion of literal truth is quite obscure and indeterminate on a Davidsonian (or Derridean) conception of language. Although the truth-conditions of "Fred is burned up" are quite clear, the truth-value may not be. "Fred is burned up" is true if and only if Fred is burned up, but the question of the truth or literal falsity of a metaphor is whether Fred is actually burned up.

Since there are no tokens that determine sets by their very essence, that is, no senses expressed that determine by their very nature what objects fall under them, there are only patterns of what people say, and when, to fix extensions of terms and thus the truth-values of sentences. As Davidson notices, such truth-*values* can be indeterminate, since patterns of what people in a culture say, and when, can be mapped onto totalized linguistic systems in numerous ways, with different ascriptions of truth and error to particular sentences on various mapping schemes. Not all contents of assertions will be either true or not true, except relative to some arbitrary choices.[5]

A related problem is Davidson's account of the death of metaphors. Metaphors die slowly, and whether they are alive or dead is sometimes indeterminate. "Indeterminate" here does not mean that we cannot tell whether the metaphor is still alive and so false, by Davidson's lights, but that there is no fact of the matter. Metaphor slides insensibly over into the literal, but it is difficult to imagine that falsity could slide insensibly over into truth.

In a subsequent section, I will show what a Davidsonian account would look like that avoided this kind of difficulty.

IV. de Man's Discussions of Metaphor: Rousseau's Language Learner

A. Preliminary Remarks and Cautions

De Man discusses many of the philosophical questions about metaphor in the chapter of *Allegories of Reading* on Rousseau, entitled "Metaphor (Second Discourse)." This section will be a translation of de Man's discussions into terms that connect with analytic philosophy and Davidson's discussions of metaphor. I do not pretend to carry "de Man's authentic view" over into the new terminology. The supposition that there is a common thought, or set of problems, that can be expressed indifferently in one group of predicates or another is contrary to the thinking of both Davidson and de Man. The terms in which de Man and Davidson think of language are mutually alien, with no simple term-to-term equivalences.

Yet, there is the deep similarity that both these thinkers deny the standard logocentric view of the relation of thought and language. The logocentric supposition is that thought takes place in a "magic language," a way of representing that cannot be mistaken, by means of terms whose very nature reveals what they are terms for. Such self-interpreting terms would be Hume's ideas of the contents of our intentions with respect to the use of language according to Carnap.

Two further cautions remain. First, the rhetoric of de Man's text makes some parts of "de Man's account" questionable, since important theses are given as expositions of other thinkers or in texts where it is not clear whether the author is speaking "in his own voice." Given the views I will ascribe to de Man, though, "in his own voice" is always problematic.

Second, part of giving a philosophical account in "analytic philosophy" terms is giving genre-appropriate arguments or argument sketches for the theses being translated. In the translation to follow, I will supply such arguments. But since there is more than one way to supply arguments, the thesis that these will be "de Man's arguments" would take long defense.

So, the translation to be proposed as the thought of Paul de Man will be surrounded by indeterminacy on even the best account. We have, in fact, a good case of Indeterminacy of Translation in Quine's sense or Indeterminacy of Radical Interpretation in Davidson's sense. There is just no fact of the matter as to what exactly de Man means in "our terms," unless there are magic terms that both de Man's and Davidson's language express. Apart from such a magic language, there will be no way of saying exactly what de Man said except in de Man's words, or words that have the textual and theoretical connections his have.

B. de Man's Account of Metaphor and Meaning

I will present de Man's account as a theory of the nature of language, while commenting on his commentary on Rousseau. I will supplement his discussion of Rousseau with some remarks derived from his article "The Epistemology of Metaphor."

According to de Man, Rousseau says two apparently incompatible things about the relation between naming and conceptualization. In the *Discourse on the Origin of Inequality (Second Discourse)*, Rousseau takes naming to be the primitive linguistic act, whereas predicating is an articulation, a division into categories, of the named objects. Since predication or, in de Man's words in *Allegories of Reading*, "conceptualization, conceived as an exchange or substitution of properties on the basis of resemblance, corresponds exactly to the classical definition of metaphor" (146), this account seems to make nomination literal and to divide language into the literal and figurative.

In the *Essay on the Origin of Languages*, on the other hand, language is supposed to start with an expression of passion, specifically through the use of a general term. ("Start" here should be taken logically, not temporally. De Man reads this narrative as an allegory of linguistic dependencies.) De Man's reading attempts to make these two doctrines constitute parts of a single view.

In the *Essay* (246–47), Rousseau takes the first general term to be an expression of fear, when a person applies a term more or less translated as "giant" to a fellow human. In *Allegories*, de Man surprisingly, not to say bafflingly, calls this application metaphorical and metalinguistic (152–53).

As a first approximation, this utterance of "giant" is metaphorical because an outer item, the man, is called by a term proper to an inner item, the fear, thus meeting the conditions for carrying across meaning. But for de Man, figuration is essentially a matter of rhetorical force. He even speaks of the fear felt at the approach of another human as a "figural state" because that fear is a *hypothesis* of future harm rather than a known fact. Propositional attitudes, or "passions," are to be thought of as different rhetorical forces with which propositional contents can be entertained or uttered. Rhetorical force will turn out to distinguish the literal from the metaphorical for de Man in a way precisely analogous to Davidson's account.

De Man calls such deviations of force "figural," the notion being that there is a turning from a direct ascription of a description to reality. Something other is meant *by* the representation. De Man identifies the rhetorical explicitly with the figural. Meaning is a feature of speech acts, primarily, for de Man, so a turning of meaning is a turning of a speech act. A troping is a use of a representation for something other than direct reporting of what is the case. Something untroped, purely and literally true, would be an assertion that is literally and strictly the case, with no admixture of representing what is not the case.[6] So, "giant" is a metaphor, even in this narrative in which such a word is being uttered for the first time in a stimulus situation.

For de Man, then, rhetoric begins at home, in the interiority of the person who has the various attitudes toward contents of sentences. A person in relation to her own representations is in a rhetorical situation. Since on de Man's view the representations themselves have a dubious rhetorical standing, the special status of a person in relation to her own utterances begins to be erased. That is, the representations themselves already have rhetorical histories, due to their use of general terms. These contaminated histories raise the same questions about their relation to some originating intention that the utterance has to its originating intention.[7]

There are other important features of this case: de Man says that this metaphor "disfigures." This is de Man's paradoxical term for the change that takes place when a figural state is put into words. The figural state, when put into words, can be taken literally, so the metaphorical expression, *qua* expression, falsifies something. The idea seems to be that a "literal" reading is the prima facie force of whatever is put in a declarative sentence.

To put this in other terms: as an utterance, "giant" cannot carry a "rhetorical force marker," a sign that would say how it was intended. As Davidson has argued in "Moods and Performances" and "Communication and Convention," a rhetorical force marker, a token that could be attached to an utterance to fix its rhetorical force, would, in virtue of being a mark at all, allow being used with different rhetorical force. This permanent possibility that rhetorical force can be misunderstood relative to the "intentions of the speaker," or could be indeterminate at a deeper level of analysis, is a main source of the instability, indeterminacy, and unreliability of language, according to de Man.

This point is crucial to de Man's whole conception of language. Suppose we have a sincere assertion marker, like "Hey, I really mean that . . . " Now, when I say "Hey, I really mean that you're my type," we do not know whether I am kidding. Iteration does not help either: "Hey, I really mean that I really mean that you're my type" can still be used to lie or to give an example in a philosophy paper. Force cannot be put into words, because words, by being words, are detached from any necessary connection with an intention. As soon as intention is expressed, it must be expressed in something that need not carry that intention.[8]

On my reading of de Man, his talk about "meaning" being misrepresented, or language being deceptive about what we really mean, is a necessity of exposition that does not commit him to holding seriously that there are intentions that are epistemologically more reliable than language.[9] De Man needs the old logocentric notion of "intention" to describe the indeterminacy of language, but that old notion is then abandoned and replaced by an abyss. At ground level, there are no intentions apart from language and no language without ulterior rhetorical force, that is, undirected by intention. This pattern of mutual presupposition points up a kind of groundlessness and is repeated in the discussion of Rousseau on the relative priority of denomination and predication.

This is not to say that consciousness is nothing but language, but rather that there is no separating out the conscious intention behind language from the language. There is no such thing as the pure intention informing the pure language.[10]

The "falsification" in the metaphorical use of a term, then, is twofold. First, the inner state, a passion, is ascribed to the external world—the object is characterized by something representing the passion. I argue later that this misnaming is really to be understood along Davidsonian lines, as an utterance produced for purposes other than saying how things strictly are. Second, by being put into words, the representation loses its privileged tie to a particular rhetorical force, that of a hypothesis, and is turned into what can legitimately be read as an assertion of what is the case.

The nature of rhetoric also can explain why de Man calls metaphor "metalinguistic." If the rhetorical force with which something is thought is something like the intention with which a sentence is said, then saying something sarcastically or ironically presupposes a consciousness of and a representation of the sentence said. So the rhetorical use of language requires that the user have a metalanguage in which sentences of the object language can be represented.

How much of language is affected by this kind of dislocation and disfigurement? Here we need to turn to the passage from the *Second Discourse* (155–57) that de Man discusses in *Allegories of Reading*. This is the passage where, apparently, acts of denomination are the primitive linguistic operations, rather than the kind of general term that expresses passions. Rousseau's picture there seems to be that objects are first named, and then, on the basis of resemblances among named objects, a general term is applied that labels distinct things the same. Distinct objects are all called by the same name "tree," so that a transfer of meaning from one case to the next takes place. That is, "conceptualization, conceived as an exchange or substitution of properties on the basis of resemblance, corresponds exactly to the classical definition of metaphor" (146). This is metaphor, since, when a new entity is to be labeled "tree," it is called by a term previously applied to something else. So, for Rousseau, the use of predicates, what de Man calls "conceptualization," is essentially metaphorical. The crucial argument for de Man shows how this process is always able to be analyzed as a turning of rhetorical force.

De Man accepts Rousseau's narrative of conceptualization, but does not suppose that "natural resemblance" will fix the language into a system. For de Man, there are multiple "natural" bases in "resemblance," so that the metaphors that constitute the predicate "system" will not be a system.[11]

De Man resists the usual interpretation of this passage as contrasting the literal, denominative stage of language with the conceptual, figural stage. Rousseau says that denomination depends on noticing difference, so that individuals are given distinct names only when they are noticed to be distinct. But "different" is a concept, which would have to have been applied to new pairs on the basis of the metaphorical extension described earlier and explicated in detail in the remainder of the present section. So Rousseau takes denomination to presuppose conceptualization.

De Man's reading thus both makes denomination presuppose conceptualization *and* makes conceptualization presuppose denomination. It also makes metaphor, the calling of something by the name of something else, part of every use of language whatsoever. Given that a metaphorical utterance introduces a new rhetorical indeterminacy into a figural, rhetorical situation where there had not been *that* indeterminacy (although perhaps other indeterminacies already), language itself turns out to be intrinsically unreliable. Metaphor corrupts any "direct" naming of what is the case, and metaphor, calling something by some improper name, is required by any conceptualization, which in turn is required by any language whatsoever.

Figural displacement is fundamental to language in two ways, according to de Man. First, language is figural in the sense that it involves disfiguration, the misrepresentation of the force of a propositional content. The gap between an intended force at a particular level and the liberation from any necessary connection with that force when the utterance is produced makes every level of representation subject to misrepresentation.

Second, de Man holds that all predication is calling one thing by a term that is not by nature appropriate to it. Here is the crucial point at which the assimilation of all metaphor to rhetoric needs to be made: this characterization, which is used to label predication as metaphorical, sounds like the typical definition of metaphor as calling one thing by another's name, as de Man notes. So de Man seems to have two notions of figure going, the figural as intending a different rhetorical force, and the figural as using a name for an object to which it does not properly apply. The first is his general conception of figure, whereas the second is used to describe metaphor, a special case of figure. De Man needs some account of how the second notion is really a special case of the first, in order to maintain the identification of the rhetorical with the figural.

How is meaning some other referent than what is said a matter of rhetorical force? How does de Man assimilate the account of conceptual extension as metaphorical to the rhetorical analysis of saying something other than what is meant? Surprisingly, the account turns out to be Davidsonian.

Conceptualization is said to be calling one thing by another's name. Consider the situation in other terms: when Charles is discovered and said to be a frog, and Albert and Bertha are familiar frogs, the term "frog" at that point has the set (Albert, Bertha) as its extension (barring the "natural division" of things, which would make Charles *already* in the extension of the term).[12] So, when Charles is said to be a member of that set, to be a "frog," the remark is not strictly true, and is not strictly "meant." The speaker or thinker does not seriously believe that Charles is identical to Bertha or to Albert.

The rhetorical force involved in the predication is then exactly like the force Davidson ascribes to metaphor: the sentence is not asserted as true, but to point up something. It is recognized as not literally true, but said for some other point. In this case, the point is to bring out a felt resemblance or to illuminate Charles by calling him an element of the set (Bertha, Albert).

When one *says* or thinks "Charles is a frog" the utterance is now freed from any special attachment to the complex metaphorical intention. This "disfiguring" amounts to a kind of literalization, so that Charles is said to *be* a frog. Then the "extension" is "in effect" the set (Albert, Bertha, Charles), and the feeling that there is something about Doris that makes it appropriate to call her a frog sets the narrative on another cycle. (Given that every frog is thus labeled, none of the predications are "really and strictly true" by some Platonic standard of "true.")

In short, Rousseau's narrative as transcribed by de Man and read here pictures ordinary predication as involving exactly the kind of rhetorical force, the intention that the utterance not be understood as strictly a description of how the object really is, that Davidson takes to be characteristic of metaphorical utterance. In both cases, there is a turning that is to be understood in rhetorical terms, that is, in terms of how sentences are used rather than what they mean.

So, de Man and Davidson agree that metaphorical remarks are never strictly true, as meant. The difference is really that de Man holds that, given the exigencies of extending predicates to new cases, there are no strictly true predications, in the required sense of "strictly true." So the only point of doctrine separating de Man from Davidson is that Davidson's account of metaphor holds that there is a kind of application of terms, the regular literal assertion, where this turning does not apply, where the new candidate is *already*, by its nature or by the nature of the thought, in the set of objects to which the term applies. This is a difference the last section suggests Davidson should dispense with.

An inspiration for de Man here is Nietzsche's "On Truth and Lies in the Extramoral Sense." Nietzsche points out that there is no such thing as "really" proper application of a term to an object, since words are nothing like their referents. So *all* predication is metaphorical, in the sense that one thing is called something else. Fear is called "fear," which is nothing like it. I read the Nietzsche passage here as an especially vivid way of saying that there is no magic language, so that there are no anchors in the nature of things to keep a term stably connected with its referent.

The main difficulty in accepting de Man's idea is his use of the notion of unreliability. Nietzsche's idea, after all, seems to be little more than an excited response to the arbitrariness of the signifier, or a descendant of Berkeley's thought that an idea can only resemble another idea.

"Unreliability" must be understood in a way that is not really grounded on anything *reliable*, since there is no possibility of a language or representation system without these "defects." In the same way, for Rousseau, on de Man's reading, there is no possibility of a pure language of denomination. This part of de Man's thinking may annoy the philosopher, since "unreliable" seems to suppose a standard or reliability that something logically could meet. The objection would go: "Nothing could be 'reliable' by de Man's standards of telling it like it is, so it's just hyperbolic to say that there is anything fundamentally defective about language."

But there *could be* a kind of representation that yields a reliable, determinate language, namely, the magic, self-interpreting language of thought that makes intention clear and that can be the background of determination by which to anchor interpretation, translation, and meaning. The remarks about unreliability are ways of saying that there is no such magic language, and that these slippages relative to that dream are forgotten consequences of that absence.

"Unreliability" and "indeterminacy" for de Man are expressed in his Wittgenstein-like suspicion that accounts of the world will never be complete, that there is no "system," in a strict sense, to practices. This view depends on the arbitrariness of the signifier, as well as on considerations of rhetoric. A view of language and the world that supposed natural connections between words and things, as Aristotle does for the magic words of nousing, would derive systematicity from that of the world. A system without such ties, which recognized the "arbitrariness of the sign," might try to achieve system by convention, by somehow fixing what means what. But then the rhetorical observation that there can be no force markers in words eliminates the possibility of a conventional determination of how things are meant (see Davidson's "Communication and Convention").

So, the indeterminacy, for de Man, has two sides. First, the determinacy produced by a natural connection between word and referent is unavailable. Second, the determinacy that might be established by a fixed set of conventions, rules of language for extending terms, is unmanned by the unconventionality of force.

That this is de Man's view, and not just ascribed to Rousseau, is borne out by other de Man texts, especially "The Epistemology of Metaphor." In this text, de Man observes that, in the empiricist tradition, the extension of general terms is difficult to control by means of the natures of the entities they refer to, since we have access only to the ideas of them. Control of extensions of general terms by definitions will not achieve stability because of simple ideas, whose extensions are irremediably subject to troping.

The project of getting our ideas to correspond to real kinds in nature, or even to be a fixed arbitrary collection of ideas, is undermined by the possibility of meaning things otherwise, or troping. In the case of Locke's condemnation of arbitrary ideas that do not correspond to real natures, de Man says in "The Epistemology of Metaphor" that "the condemnation, by Locke's own argument, now takes all language for its target, for at no point in the course of the demonstration can the empirical entity be sheltered from tropological defiguration" (21). The basic idea on which de Man's analyses turn is that the ideas of the empiricist tradition always threatened to function as words, since there was no necessary connection between features of the idea and the nature that gave rise to it. So ideas could not be trusted to correspond to the same things in nature. The wordlike nature of thought-terms tended to subliminally undermine the magic of the language of thought.

Ideas as words had features that could connect them with each other in virtue of their accidental properties rather than in virtue of the underlying realities they represented. The language that expressed these ideas was subject to the same difficulties, so philosophers nervously sensed that their derogatory remarks about the unreliability of language would also apply to ideas. So, the distinction between legitimate representation and misleading tropological representation cannot be made a distinction of kind. Given the contingency of the connection between idea and thing, there will be no reliable basis for grouping ideas according to their corresponding underlying realities. "In each case, it turns out to be impossible to maintain a clear line of distinction between rhetoric, abstraction, symbol, and all other forms of language. In each case, the resulting undecidability is due to the asymmetry of the binary model that opposes the figural to the proper meaning of the figure" ("Epistemology" 28).

De Man's reading unpacks an aporia in the tradition's notion of the thought and its relation to reality: the thought was supposed to consist of magic words that would reveal by their very nature what they were true of, much like Aristotle's *nous* words. But the tradition needed to find something we could actually be said to think in, and "ideas," which were basically sensory particulars like Aristotelian phantasms, seemed to be the only candidates. But the ideas that were the only appropriate candidates for the tokens of such a language turned out to be irremediably wordlike. They were not magic, but had characters unconnected with the real natures of their referents. Those characters supported tropic, inappropriate connections and thus allowed misinterpretation. (If the child's idea of gold, by its nature, leads him to apply ''gold'' to a flower, the misapplication of the idea is formally the misinterpretation of a word.)

De Man believes that the wordlike features the philosophers found threatening are always in any thought; that is, that thought is wordlike. Thus the permanent possibility of troping, and the indistinguishability of the trope from the straight, means that the instability and indeterminacy feared by the tradition are actual.

V. Davidson with de Man

In this final section I show two things. First, I show that Davidson's account of metaphor could be amended by the addition of de Man's insights to repair exactly the difficulties we found with Davidson's account. (The amendment here is symmetrical, since I take this whole essay to indicate some of the ways Davidsonian considerations can supplement the argument and exposition of de Man's account.) Second, I argue that the main amendment, to the conception of predication, is really already implicit in Davidson's thinking.

A. Amended Davidsonism

The most easily stated difference between the accounts of Davidson and de Man concerns the truth-status of metaphorical utterances. For Davidson, they are always false, as meant, except accidentally. For de Man, metaphorical remarks are as true as any predication ever is.

Amended Davidsonism takes up Davidson's suggestion on pages 248–49 of ''What Metaphors Mean'': ''When we read, for example, that 'the Spirit of God moved upon the face of the waters' . . . 'face' applies to ordinary faces and to waters in addition [but] all sense of metaphor evaporates. If we are to think of words in metaphors as directly going about their business of applying to what they properly do apply to, there is no difference between metaphor and the introduction of a new term into our vocabulary: to make a metaphor is to murder it.''

To summarize in advance: amended Davidsonism questions the notion ''properly apply to'' and the existence of a ''sense of metaphor'' that distinguishes the metaphors from the literal assertions. Metaphorical uses of sentences are sometimes true assertions — applications of the very same terms in the very same senses as literal uses. But although waters have faces, they do not therefore have noses.

On the amended account, the literal and the metaphorical would be separated as follows: a sincere, ''literal'' assertion is intended to be automatically interpreted, making the routine connections to other predications and taking all the routine evidence and consequences to be relevant to the predication. The metaphorical assertion is proposed as true, but those automatic routines of interpretation are intended not to be followed. The metaphorical assertion intends that a routine group of connections and generalizations be suspended. The metaphorical assertion is a claim that the predicate really applies to the case, but that some other predicates that are often connected with it do not apply in this case.

"Interpretation" as it is used here is not just the simple application of Davidsonian truth-definition clauses so that sentences of the interpreted language can be understood in terms of the interpreting language. "Interpretation" is here "understanding the other as rational." The broad notion of Davidsonian interpretation, so understood, holistically tries to maximize agreement with the other.[13] Given a prima facie strange remark, such interpretation can attribute error to the other on certain topics, decide that the other is using words differently, or reinterpret the rhetorical force with which the remark is made. All such judgments are evaluated holistically, without any guarantee that there will be a single optimal solution.

One important device for treating the other as rational by our lights is that of reading the rhetorical force of the other's remark as other than assertive. This is the strategy Davidson holds to be correct for all interpretation of metaphorical remarks. But strategies of radical interpretation other than making the force non-assertive sometimes enter into the interpretation of metaphorical remarks. Let me begin by characterizing interpretation.

To simplify a great deal,[14] the "interpretation" of another's ascription of a predicate always involves ascribing beliefs to that other. When I hear Fred say, "There is a dog," my decision that by "dog" he means "dog" is my ascription of an ill-defined array of my beliefs to the other. For instance, I ascribe the belief that dogs are animals, that no dogs are Saxons, that my friend Pam has a dog named Jeff, and so forth.

The interpretation strategy to be followed in understanding someone's remark as a literal assertion ascribes all or most of the interpreter's "important" general beliefs involving the terms in the sentence to the other person being interpreted. The rhetorical force of a literal assertion that a predicate applies to some new case includes the intention that all "important" general beliefs are applied to the case.

In a metaphorical ascription of a predicate to a new case, the intention is that some important general beliefs not be ascribed to the speaker, that the adjustment be elsewhere in the maximizing of agreement. When the metaphor is familiar, some adjustment may already have been made, and there may be different sets of generalizations more or less in place in the theory of the other. When a person is (metaphorically) crushed, I might believe that a shopping trip would be therapeutic, a change from my beliefs about those crushed by boulders rather than by life itself. Such a metaphorical use, with its own generalizations, begins to rate its own entry in the dictionary.

That is, if the metaphor is taken as a true assertion, the modified beliefs and the adjustments in surrounding theory ascribed to the speaker are adopted by the interpreter. Where a metaphorical remark is taken to be a true assertion, the interpreter of a metaphor may maximize agreement by suspending or dropping some of her own general beliefs, and adding others. If the crushing metaphor was new to her, and the remark about the crushed person seemed true, the interpreter would qualify her own beliefs about the physical damage crushing entails in order to understand the remark that I am crushed.

A new metaphorical application of a term X supposes that there are more kinds of X's than we thought. There are not different "senses" of "fly," with or without the flapping of wings, which apply to birds and airplanes, respectively. These are just two *kinds* of flying, and were proposed as such on the first extension of the term to flying machines. This extension of the understanding of a term by an interpreter is like realizing that "some dinosaurs were protected by plates" is not a remark about an early use of crockery. "Plate" as it occurs in "tectonic plate" or "armor plate" may be taken to be metaphorical by the naive. It is not "really" metaphorical, though, since most people already believe that there are many kinds of plates, and that different things are true of tectonic plates and dinner plates.

All such plates share a certain flat configuration, but the necessary and sufficient conditions for meeting that configuration (i.e., for being some kind of plate) are only specified by the condition of being a plate. So "plate" is unparaphrasable in the way a metaphor is unparaphrasable. This appeals to Wittgenstein's concept of "family resemblance" from the *Philosophical Investigations*, which rests on the observation that without Platonic meanings as outside constraints, there need be no standards for the application of a predicate in other terms.[15]

Unamended Davidsonism, by making the typical metaphor false, solves one problem I should address: an utterance that is true if taken metaphorically but literally false would seem to make some term both apply and not apply, on amended Davidsonism. That is, when I am (a) crushed by the Princess's refusal, but (luckily) (b) not crushed by the boulder her servants drop from the castle wall as a parting gesture, Davidson says that (a) is false and (b) is true, whereas my amended account makes both (a) and (b) true applications of the same predicate. The amended account must characterize such cases as *kinds* of crushing, aspects with respect to which one is crushed, or *ways* in which one is crushed.

When both literal and metaphorical understandings of an utterance are possible, a relativization can explain how both understandings can coexist. There are familiar arguments[16] that relativizations can save us from multiple homonymy.

We still have to acknowledge the cases to which Davidson assimilates all metaphor interpretation. A metaphor is often *not* a serious claim about reality, and the consideration that the sentence might be true is meant to be amusing, or has some other purpose than pointing out an unnoticed kind of case. At other times, the metaphor is serious, but its point is not to convey anything that could be called "information" in any separable sense.[17]

Some really interesting metaphors are cases of other serious intentions than information transmission. These are the kinds of metaphors that change the way we think and feel. They cannot be understood in terms of isolable "cognitive content," but rather in the way Davidson describes. However, on Davidsonian as well as Derridean grounds, the whole notion of "cognitive content," as a separable aspect of what we see and feel, is suspect. Worthwhile "learning" is not just a matter of ingesting propositions, but rather labels a whole complex of states that cannot be divided into the cognitive and "other." A metaphor requiring very radical interpretation, which one takes to be true, eventually, is one of these life-changing metaphors whose effect can better be described in terms of insight than in terms of packets of data.

The process of understanding a "deep" metaphor is not really separable from coming to see that a term applies in an unsuspected case. Suppose someone I respect says that Wittgenstein is a very ironic thinker. I may come to agree by thinking about Wittgenstein and irony, perhaps changing my mind about both. My coming to understand "what she meant" will not easily be put into propositional form, but is a mix of attitudes on these and related topics. This inseparable mix of the "cognitive" with the "other" is characteristic of learning generally, not just of the kind of learning we derive from poetry. (I think I learned this from Davidson.)

Let us see how two kinds of problems are dealt with, the movement from live to dead metaphors and the distinction between a metaphorical use and a new application of a term.

First, de Manian supplementation is made to deal with the transition from live to dead metaphor, given that all predications are really founded in metaphor. On Davidson's view, "Celeste is an eggplant" is false until enough people call guinea pigs eggplants, so that that becomes part of the real extension of the term, a dead metaphor that can be part of a truth-definition clause. But the death of a metaphor is an insensible drift from the novel to the old hat. There is no sharp line between such dead metaphors as "My heart is broken" and the still-live ones. Truth, though, could not have degrees. Thus dead and live metaphors should not differ by the live being always false and the dead sometimes true. Amended Davidsonism, by viewing routine predication and exotic metaphor as end points on a continuum, fits well with the lingering illnesses of metaphor.

Second, the failure to reflect some intuitive line between the metaphorical and the literal is justified. One of Davidson's objections on page 249 of "What Metaphors Mean" was that "all sense of metaphor evaporates" if metaphors are extended applications of terms. This seems altogether fitting and proper, since the "sense of metaphor" does not give clear results. On a revised Davidsonism, there is no rigorous theoretical definition of what it takes to be a genuine metaphor. We apply "metaphor" in ways that resist systematization and seem to admit of degrees.[18]

When a metaphorical utterance is produced that one is inclined to accept as true, how does one know what to keep and what to abandon among the general beliefs associated with a term? Performing the kind of interpretation intended by the utterer of a metaphor is like creating a scientific theory in response to data that make the old theory impossible to retain. Just as there are no rules and no algorithm for scientific theory-creation, so there is no algorithm for the interpretation of metaphor. In both situations, we have "recalcitrant data" that exert pressure to become part of our thinking. In this case, the "recalcitrant data" are the proposed new cases where the predicate is to apply. The "adjustments in theory" are changes in connection and inferences that must be made to accept the new cases as cases of the same predicate.

So how is metaphor to be interpreted? There can be no prior absolutely controlling guides, nothing like an algorithm, because such an algorithm would be in language that was itself subject to interpretation. There can be no determining guides to a project of, essentially, changing language, because there is no system of meaning bearers prior to language to be the basis of such controls. We cannot take an "outside" point of view from which to oversee or evaluate our adjustments in beliefs and language. There is no point of view outside our beliefs, desires, and other propositional attitudes and so no point of view outside our language. Adjustments in propositional attitudes are inseparable from adjustments in language if there are no meaning bearers prior to language, since the contents of propositional attitudes must then be in language-like form.

In interpreting a metaphor, then, there may well be no single answer, especially when the figure is really interesting. There can be wrong answers, however, and criticism can point them out. Getting a metaphor right does not mean following the intentions of the utterer. The utterer of the metaphor does not control how the metaphor is rightly taken. The first person who extended the steam-boiler expression "all fired up," for instance, may not have thought that a team that is all fired up is angry, even though that connection is there in the words. A metaphor is a text.

Coming to accept original metaphors as true, then, is changing language and theory. If there are no semantic bearers below the language-like, changing and adapting language cannot proceed by an algorithm or a routine. Without Platonic Forms or the like, there is no prior code in which the meanings of words exist, and thus no foundation that can provide the basis for changing language to adjust to the Truth. Platonic Forms or the like are required for there to be a general background language from which changes of language can be plotted. Given that there are no prior meaning bearers, the extension of predicates demands creativity, since absolute outside constraints are lacking. This does not mean that such interpretation is groundless, just that the grounding relation is not external absolutes but rather practices. In a phrase, the theory is Wittgensteinian.[19] Only on the basis that nothing but impossibly rigorous rules could control practice would the lack of standard-providing Platonic Forms mean chaos.

There are no algorithms or genuine rules more helpful than "Call all and only roses 'roses' " for extending predicates. The kind of interpretation that applies to live metaphors applies in attenuated form to predication generally. The *routine* for extending predicates in any new case is not fixed by an outside standard, because there are no meaning bearers more intrinsically connected to what they fit than language. Thus every application of a predicate is an extension to a new case that is not fixed either in the nature of things or in the language.

"Nonmetaphoric" interpretation is just routine, in more generally following old patterns. It is not essentially different from the "creative" interpretation required of original metaphors. There are, after all, some old generalizations falsified and some new generalizations coming true whenever a new case of a predicate is discovered. The discovery of a frog in my bed falsifies the previously believed generalization that there are no green frogs in my bed. In every case where some new instance in which it is fitting that a term be applied to a new case, there is some adjustment of old belief required. The more radical the adjustment, the more the utterance seems metaphorical, other things being equal.

So, extensions to new kinds of cases, if such extensions are not controlled by the very nature of things, but rather by a combination of conceptual equipment and the world, are not essentially different from extensions to new cases of the same kind. That is, the very notion of a kind of case is something in part shaped by the linguistic practices. Routine categorization is thus not a matter of just fitting the raw facts either.[20]

B. Why Davidson Really Already Believes This

The main amendment borrowed from de Man is a change in how the use of general terms is conceived. In this last section I argue that this conception of predication is really implicit in Davidson's thinking. (Of course this also amounts to a kind of defense of de Man's ideas, as reconstrued here, on these topics.)

For de Man, metaphor, which in analytic philosophy has been treated as a marginal phenomenon, is made the paradigm of the most central operation of saying things, predication. Normal predication, which has always been treated as property ascription determined by the presence or absence of an external control, namely, the real language-independent property, is on this account a degenerate kind of metaphor. Metaphor, which has always been treated as a deviant exception to the correct use of language, a fallen misuse justifiable only for aesthetic effects, is made the central model of how language functions. On Davidsonian grounds, metaphor and ordinary predication ought to be cases of the same phenomenon.

What, after all, are the bases for extensions to new kinds of cases? Aristotle's account is that such extensions take place on the basis of real analogies in the natures of things. The basis for taking "broken" to apply to hearts when a person is emotionally crushed is obviously that crushed things are broken, this heart is crushed, so this heart is broken. Here, this "natural" connection itself depends on another metaphor, since "crushed" does not just naturally apply to the heart of a person who still survives. That is, the basis of this analogy is partially linguistic, or more dramatically, "contaminated by the linguistic." The fact that crushing things lowers or depresses them does not help either, unless there is something in the nature of things that connects depressions and depressions. These are not raw facts of analogy isolable from the background of language in which they are thought.

Our world, although perhaps not unconnected with the natures of things, is contaminated by the merely linguistic. There is no pure exposition by terms that have exactly the one property of referring to their referents. In explicating the analogy by which a metaphor is justified, we either have an endless trail or metaphors, or catachresis. In either case, the analogies are mediated by the language in which they are framed.

If the analogy could be stated in terms that required no metaphorical extensions, then we would be extending terms to new cases on the basis of the raw facts, the facts that are there prior to any conceptualization. But Davidson has argued that there can be no such level of fact (see "On the Very Idea of a Conceptual Scheme"). There is no removing the linguistic varnish from the raw facts.

The de Manian account of metaphor is thus implicit in the antifoundationalism required by the complex of views about necessity and language that Davidson shares with Quine and Derrida. Part of this complex is the denial that there are any purely natural analogies that are there independently of any way of looking or thinking. Such analogies would require a nature of things that would be capable of being a pure external determiner of meaning. In effect, such prelinguistic analogies would be features of the "manifold" that exist prior to any conceptual scheme and that are organized by that conceptual scheme. Davidson's rejection of "very idea of a conceptual scheme" is thus a rejection of the purely natural analogies that could found metaphorical extensions of a basis independent of the language. If all analogies are mediated by language, then all metaphor based on analogies is mediated by language.

The picture of the relation of language and the world can no longer be that of a code or algorithm. If all external anchors for the analogies that support metaphors are contaminated by the linguistic, then there is little reason to expect the analogies to form a system. There may be no single system of connections, so a given term may connect with other terms in contradictory ways. As de Man's investigations of figuration show (for instance, in the essay on Proust in *Allegories of Reading*), typical systems of metaphor are nonsystems, patterns of connection that assign central terms contradictory roles. The impossibility of purifying our access to the extensions of our terms from the linguistic shaping of what we say is what means that our words are cut loose from the possibility of raw reflection of the real. Without a foundation in something guaranteed to be coherent, such as a single world or the magic language, there is nothing to force the patterns of connection and association among words and texts to simplify into a single set of connections that is free from contradiction. The model of metaphor as the primary linguistic operation removes the misleading metaphor of the algorithm or world code as the basis for what we say.

So, on Davidson's principles, predication is essentially figuration. Without pure natural kinds uncontaminated by language, any extension to an *old* kind of case is a leap not determined by the nature of things. Predications of the most elementary sort are very dead metaphors, metaphors, perhaps, by etymology alone. The most exotic metaphor is continuous with the most fundamental operation of language.

Notes

1. This essay originated as a reaction to an early version of Richard Rorty's "Hesse and Davidson on Metaphor."

2. Where there is disagreement within a speech community, it may be indeterminate exactly where the disagreement is. When my friend says "Kissinger has physical charm," I can decide that she means something different by "physical charm," that one of us is wrong about Kissinger, or that she is trying to annoy me, for instance. The odd remark can be taken as the utterance of a rational being by adjusting ascriptions of meaning, belief, or rhetorical force. Given further disagreements, more discussion may not resolve the question. Since there is nothing more semantically elementary than the words, there is no answer to what is really meant when two systems of what is said, and when, fail to match up in an isomorphism of roles. There are no "behind the scenes" facts to determine where the deviation should be located. When there is indeterminacy of translation or interpretation, there is no fact of the matter.

3. Davidson's semantics is set out in the papers in the first section of his collection *Inquiries into Truth and Interpretation*, including "Truth and Meaning," "Theories of Meaning and Learnable Languages," "True to the Facts," "Semantics for Natural Languages," and "In Defense of Convention T."

4. This example is borrowed from Rorty's "Hesse and Davidson on Metaphor."

5. I have discussed some difficulties about the determinateness of truth-values of sentences in "Reference and Vagueness" and "On That Which Is Not."

6. Since such representation of what is strictly not is a necessary part of language, it turns out that the "purely referential," de Man's term for the literal object-language assertion, is a heuristic fiction. Note here that "true" for de Man, following Austin in many ways, is a predicate of speech acts, rather than their contents.

7. The "decentering of the self" questions exactly the kind of access a person is supposed to have to her real intentions. The self that knows its thoughts by thinking them in the magic language could be a unitary self whose intentions would be clear to itself. Such a self requires and supports the idea of a magic language. But if the self has textlike, language-like thoughts, then levels of self-consciousness are like sequences of texts and commentaries. In that situation, "privileged access" does not supply final answers. I find the decentering arguments persuasive on Quinean-Davidsonian as well as Freudian grounds. Someone who accepts Chisholm's ideas about the self, as expressed in *Person and Object* and *The First Person*, requires very different ideas about meaning and thought, and will be committed to denying de Manian premises needed for rhetorical indeterminacy. A self-presenting self, that is, must present itself to itself in the magic language.

8. One place where this point is made most thoroughly is Derrida's "Signature Event Context" and the subsequent "Limited Inc abc."

9. Given that he wants to say that there is slippage at every level, the temporary supposition that there is a starting point, namely, an inner thought at which logocentric principles hold, allows that slippage to be described as the thought moves from the intention to the language. But this is an "as if" to be abandoned as soon as the point is made.

10. For de Man, the main precursors for meditation on this kind of groundlessness are the thinkers concerned with self-reflection, including the German romantics Fichte and Hegel, who conceived irony in terms of consciousness of consciousness. Given the possiblity of a sequence of levels of irony, it is a short step to the generalization to the questioning of rhetorical force at each level of self-reflection on the previous self-reflection. Given de Man's rhetorical analysis of figuration and meaning, it is again a short step to a deep indeterminacy of meaning.

Davidson's precursors for the formulation of the impossibility of rhetorical force markers are clearly Frege's attempt to have a judgment stroke as a part of an object-language notation, Wittgenstein's commentary on that in *Tractatus* 4.442, and subsequent analytic discussion. A modern version of romantic irony is Quine's "Ontological Relativity," where he shows that indeterminacy of translation relative to a background language continues as far back as one wishes to push the regress to background languages. That is, as soon as one asks what one means, alternative interpretations arise. De Man's discussion can be thought of as a Quinean indeterminacy thesis applied to rhetorical force, rather than, as in Quine's case, applied under the assumption that assertions can be detected unproblematically.

11. De Man here follows Goodman, who has argued in *Ways of Worldmaking* and elsewhere that "resemblance" of some kind holds between any pair of objects, so that no coherent system of groupings need follow from grouping things by resemblance. For de Man, the incoherence in a metaphorical "system" like Proust's (see the discussion in "Reading (Proust)," in *Allegories of Reading*, especially the note on 60–61) is a case of the incoherence of predicate systems generally.

12. Such a supposition would require that somehow the whole extension of "is a frog" is hidden in the use of the term. Only the magic language could manage this predetermination of the future frogs.

13. This needs to be qualified in numerous ways. For instance, given our opinions about the epistemological capacities of organisms and the environment of the other, we may not seek agreement on contents of beliefs.

14. Interpretation accurately construed maximizes agreement, as qualified in the previous note, in all propositional attitudes. The constraints on assigning intentions to speech acts, for instance, maximize agreement in desires, among other things.

15. Davidson's and Quine's denial that there is a magic language behind words supplies a theoretical background for, say, Cleanth Brooks's "The Heresy of Paraphrase." Given that every term has its own pattern of occurrence, that what is said, and when, determines meaning, and that such accidents as literary citation, rhyme, and personal history determine how we make adjustments to understand metaphor, the unparaphrasability of metaphor is to be expected. Benson Mates's demonstration in "Synonymy" that, on the most plausible criterion of synonymy, there are no synonyms, is relevant here.

16. See, for instance, my "How Paintings Can Be Joyful" and "Attributives and Their Modifiers" for discussions of how this might work.

17. For amusing illumination, suppose someone says of my guinea pig Celeste, "She's an eggplant with fur and feet." This is very perceptive, even illuminating, as anyone with guinea pigs knows, but not true. While it might be possible to take "eggplant" in this utterance to be really true of vegetables and other things having a certain ovoid and dumpy configuration, few would interpret the utterance this way and no one should revise their ideas about eggplants so as to make this a true assertion.

18. So, for instance, the metaphorical use of "all fired up," as in "The Raiders are all fired up," is a far more usual usage than the applications to the steam-driven etymological source. The judgment that some utterance is a metaphor seems to be a matter both of what connections are really routine in interpretation and of etymological opinions.

19. A relevant text here is Wittgenstein's *Remarks on the Foundations of Mathematics*, where exactly this point is made about rules in the setting most favorable to the existence of constraints beyond practice, namely, mathematics.

20. Once, again, this is not to deny that there is a world, and that that world constrains what we say, and when, but to deny that our descriptions of that world are determined by that world exclusively.

Works Cited

Brooks, Cleanth. "The Heresy of Paraphrase." In *The Well-Wrought Urn.* 1947. New York: Harcourt Brace Jovanovich, 1975. 192–214.
Chisholm, Roderick. *The First Person.* Minneapolis: U of Minnesota P, 1981.

_____. *Person and Object*. London: Allen & Unwin, 1976.

Davidson, Donald. "Communication and Convention." In *Inquiries into Truth and Interpretation.* 265–80.

_____. *Inquiries into Truth and Interpretation*. Oxford: Clarendon Press, 1984.

_____. "On the Very Idea of a Conceptual Scheme." 1974. In *Inquiries into Truth and Interpretation*. 183–98.

_____"What Metaphors Mean." 1978. In *Inquiries into Truth and Interpretation*. 245–64.

de Man, Paul. *Allegories of Reading*. New Haven, Conn.: Yale UP, 1979.

_____. "The Epistemology of Metaphor." *Critical Inquiry 5, No. 1* (Autumn 1978): 13–30.

Derrida, Jacques. "Limited Inc abc." *Glyph* 2 (1977): 162–254.

_____. "Signature Event Context." In *Margins of Philosophy*. Chicago: U of Chicago P, 1982. 307–30.

Goodman, Nelson. *Ways of Worldmaking*. Indianapolis: Hackett, 1978.

Mates, Benson. *"Synonymy."* 1950. Reprinted in Leonard Linsky, ed., *Semantics and the Philosophy of Language*. Urbana: U of Illinois P, 1952. 111–36.

Nietzsche, Friedrich. "On Truth and Lies in the Extra-Moral Sense I." In Walter Kaufman, ed., *The Portable Nietzsche*. New York: Viking Press, 1954. 42–47.

Quine, W. V. "Ontological Relativity." In *Ontological Relativity and Other Essays*. New York: Columbia UP, 1969. 26–68.

Rorty, Richard. "Hesse and Davidson on Metaphor." *Proceedings of the Aristotelian Society*, supplementary volume 61, 1987.

Rousseau, Jean-Jacques. *Discourses and Essay on the Origin of Languages*. Trans. Victor Gourevitch. New York: Harper & Row, 1986.

Wheeler, Samuel C. III. "Attributives and Their Modifiers." *Noûs* 6, No. 4 (November 1972): 310–34.

_____. "The Extension of Deconstruction." *Monist*, 69, No. 1 (January 1986): 3–21.

_____. "How Paintings Can Be Joyful." In *Philosophic Essays in Honor of Martin Eshleman*. Carleton College, Northfield, Minn., 1971. 83–95.

_____. "On That Which Is Not." *Synthèse* 41 (1979): 155–73.

_____. "Reference and Vagueness." *Synthèse* 30 (1975): 367–379.

Wittgenstein, Ludwig. *Philosophical Investigations*. New York: Macmillan, 1953.

_____. *Remarks on the Foundations of Mathematics*. Oxford: Basil Blackwell, 1956.

7

Reading with Wittgenstein and Derrida

Jules David Law

I. Openings and Closures: Pictures in and of Discourse

> PHILONOUS: *Look you, Hylas, when I speak of objects as existing in the mind, or imprinted on the senses, I would not be understood in the gross literal sense; as when bodies are said to exist in a place, or a seal to make an impression upon wax. My meaning is only that the mind comprehends or perceives them; and that it is affected from without, or by some being distinct from itself.*
>
> *. . . Nor is there anything in this but what is conformable to the general analogy of language; most part of the mental operations being signified by words borrowed from sensible things; as is plain in the terms* comprehend, reflect, discourse, *&c., which, being applied to the mind, must not be taken in their gross, original sense.*
>
> —Berkeley, *Three Dialogues between Hylas and Philonous* 346-47

Philonous's defense of "the general analogy of language" in Berkeley's *Three Dialogues* outlines a critical dilemma whose apparent potential for either infinite extension or pragmatic closure should be familiar to students of literary theory. A critical extension of Philonous's discourse would point to the rhetorical nature of his attempt to articulate and enforce the distinction between "gross literal" and "borrowed" senses. Thus the passage might be seen as complicating its original premises as Philonous explicitly "borrows" a term that in its "gross, original sense" describes sensible actions ("*comprehend*") in order to describe the action by which the sensible world is interiorized ("My meaning is only that the mind comprehends . . . ''). Not only does the passage fail to explain the nature of the "borrowing" involved in Philonous's discourse; it opens up the much larger question of whether the distinction between literal and figurative terms helps explain the distinction between "the mind" and "sensible things," or vice versa.

A quite different critical reading could be given of Berkeley's text, however, in an attempt to close off the apparent textual aporia opened by rhetoric. In this case, Philonous's comments could be read as a plea to distinguish apparently identical signs (i.e., the literal and figurative instances of "comprehend") by their different *uses*. Such a practice of differentiation—in Wittgenstein's terms, establishing the "grammar" of the sign in question—would reveal overlapping or contiguous practices rather than contradictions. In this case Philonous would in effect be entering much the same plea as the Wittgenstein who writes: "But the figurative [*bildliche*] employment of the word can't get into conflict with the original one" (*Investigations* p. 215).[1] The literal and the figurative would not be conflicting realms of sense, but simply different uses.

To dwell on, or to pass over, the paradoxes intrinsic in discourse about discourse—that seems to be the question. If it seems risky to ignore a text's instructions about its own mode of *representing*, is there not also a risk of never passing beyond questions about the nature of representation? And which, then, is the greater trap for a reader? To treat the constantly shifting line between literal and figurative expressions as a matter of course, or to insist on a full elaboration of all possible understandings and misunderstandings of rhetoric before proceeding in one's reading? In various forms these questions present themselves insistently in the contemporary criticism and theory of literature, and it is not entirely inappropriate that Derrida's and Wittgenstein's names be associated with the schematic alternatives such questions imply. For no partisan of either thinker's work would disavow entirely the slogans of deconstruction or ordinary-language philosophy—Derrida's "Il n'y a pas de hors-texte" (*Of Grammatology* 158) and Wittgenstein's "The meaning of a word is its use" (remark 43)—and these assertions do indeed seem to point, respectively, to "close-reading" and to the semantic demystification of rhetoric. Nevertheless, neither of these (in)famous axioms describes a critical program, and that is not simply because both statements in context are hedged about with qualifications,[2] but also because both Wittgenstein's and Derrida's critical operations take aim at the very figurative conventions by which we might presume to put these axioms to use: the picture of language as divided into regions of greater and lesser semantic content, and the picture of language as possessing an interior and an exterior.

It is my intention in this essay to show that Derrida and Wittgenstein offer similar kinds of resistance to our conventional ways of *describing* and *practicing* textual interpretation. This is not to suggest that Wittgenstein and Derrida have similar theories of language or of meaning. I believe that it is in a certain fundamental way mistaken to describe either of them as having *theories* of language or meaning at all, though both have theories about the *accounts we give of language*. Both thinkers are concerned with the following questions: First, what should we make of the ways in which language is *described*, and is there any possibility of identifying and disengaging a second—or "meta"—order of discourse in such cases? And second, how can it be that we are tempted or misled *by language* into giving a distorted account of how we use language? (It is important here to keep in mind that the conception of language as an autonomous, coercive force, though popularly associated with philosophers in the Continental tradition such as Heidegger and Derrida, is in fact no less characteristically Wittgensteinian.)[3]

In response to the first question(s), both Wittgenstein and Derrida suggest that our language about language can in no fundamental way differ from our language in general. For Derrida this means on the one hand that there is no language, properly speaking, disengaged from traditional philosophical discourse and implications, and on the other hand that philosophical discourse cannot distinguish itself categorically from ordinary language:

> There is no sense in doing without the concepts of metaphysics in order to shake metaphysics. *We have no language—no syntax and no lexicon—which is foreign to this history.* ("Structure, Sign, and Play" 280; my emphasis)

> And here one would have to meditate even more patiently the *irreducible complicity*, despite all of the philosopher's rhetorical efforts, *between everyday language and philosophical language.* ("Violence and Metaphysics" 113; my emphasis)

For Wittgenstein, this "irreducible complicity" between philosophical and ordinary language means that the words we use in doing philosophy (especially philosophy of language) must be used roughly in the same way we use familiar, everyday words:

> . . . of course, if the words "language", "experience", "world", have a use, it must be as humble a one as that of the words "table", "lamp", "door".

> One might think: if philosophy speaks of the use of the word "philosophy" there must be a second-order philosophy. But it is not so: it is, rather, like the case of orthography, which deals with the word "orthography" among others without then being second-order. (remarks 97, 121).

What underlies all of these passages is a recognition that the philosophical impulse par excellence is the impulse to isolate a region of language that can be used to handle, control, or explain language in its totality. The consequences of this impulse, and of the pictures or figurations given to such a separation, are of immense interest to Wittgenstein and Derrida. Both attempt to ironize the internal segregations of language by insisting on the essential analogy between the most neglected, derivative, or superficial aspects of language (e.g., writing, orthography) and the privileged discourse of philosophy.

It is Wittgenstein's and Derrida's attempts to *extend* the field of language by breaking down its *internal* barriers that I will focus on in this essay, but before elaborating on that subject I want to consider briefly the second question outlined above (how is it that language deceives us about its own nature?). Derrida's and Wittgenstein's answers to this question are tentative and, I think, ultimately inconclusive. For Wittgenstein, illusions in and about language seem to derive from the narrowness of language as a limited set of formal gestures compared to the endless variety of uses to which language is put. This relative poverty of linguistic *form* results in false resemblances. Inverting Plato, but retaining the traditional Neoplatonic metaphor, Wittgenstein argues that "we remain unconscious of the prodigious diversity of all the everyday language-games because the clothing of our language makes everything alike" (p. 224). Where Plato saw ideal forms betrayed and obscured by the flux of the phenomenal world, Wittgenstein sees the prodigious variety of our linguistic games obscured by the comparatively "uniform appearance" of the words we play with:

> Of course, what confuses us is the uniform appearance of words when we hear them spoken or meet them in script and print.
> Misunderstandings concerning the use of words, [are] caused, among other things, by certain analogies between the forms of expression in different regions of language.
> Impressed by the *possibility of a comparison*, we think we are perceiving a state of affairs of the highest generality. (remarks 11, 90, 104; my emphasis)

Wittgenstein does not seem concerned to decide whether the problem is lodged metaphysically in the very existence of a "possibility of a comparison," or historically in the instituting and development of language, or perhaps psychologically in the teaching of language. It is enough for him to call to our attention how insistently our discussions of language assimilate and idealize our forms of expression, and to tease us out of such habits by "finding and inventing *intermediate cases*" (remark 122).

Derrida's explanation of our tendency to be misled by language involves more historicist gestures than Wittgenstein's, but ultimately it is just as speculative.[4] In *Of Grammatology*, Derrida criticizes Saussure's claim that the graphic nature of script makes writing physiologically more striking than the "true," phonic, substance of language from which it distracts and derives (see particularly 35–44). The myth that writing is responsible for our failure to understand clearly the workings of language is of course not to be attributed to Saussure alone. Throughout much of *Grammatology* Derrida is concerned with demonstrating the persistence of such a myth *throughout the history of Western philosophy*. However, the *origin* of this myth (and of the various systematically interrelated myths about language that are the subject of *Grammatology*) remains obscure. In "White Mythology," Derrida fastens on an analogy that appears in Aristotle's *Poetics* (the ostensibly self-evident similarity between the sowing of seeds and the sun's casting forth of flames [*Poetics* 1457b25–30]), and argues that despite the analogy's actual arbitrariness, it "imposes itself" on Aristotle. Nonetheless, writes Derrida, the source of this imposition cannot be exhibited:

> Where has it ever been *seen* that there is the same relation between the sun and its rays as between sowing and seeds? If this analogy imposes itself — and it does — then it is that within language the analogy itself is due to a long and hardly visible chain whose first link is quite difficult to exhibit, and not only for Aristotle. (243)

The source of language's apparent ability to impose on us is indeed difficult to exhibit, and neither Wittgenstein nor Derrida is able successfully to display it. Derrida is certainly more interested than Wittgenstein in emphasizing the historical narrative and ideological stakes attached to those pictures in (and of) our language that seem inescapable to us. Yet it is important to recognize that both Wittgenstein and Derrida at a certain point rest content with references to mysterious, ineluctable tendencies in our language. In this sense, neither is more metaphysical than the other.

Much contemporary commentary on the relationship between Wittgenstein and Derrida suffers from a tendency to see them as philosophers whose work examines the very possibility of meaning in language. This view, whether used to distinguish or to assimilate Derrida and Wittgenstein, results in the description of their work as versions of, or responses to, skepticism, relativism, metaphysics, and ontology. Thus Charles Altieri, Christopher Norris, and James Guetti have all described deconstruction as a form of skepticism, in relation to which the work of Wittgenstein appears as either corrective or uneasy cohort.[5] On the other hand, Stanley Fish, Richard Rorty, and Henry Staten have all emphasized the ways in which deconstruction and ordinary-language philosophy constitute themselves as theories of *perspectival meaning* — opposed to, and offering critiques of, correspondence theories of meaning.[6] Although all of these writers are attentive to Wittgenstein's and Derrida's concentration on *descriptions of language*, all of them are eager to assimilate such observations about language to more general theories of "meaning" and "context," an assimilation of which Wittgenstein and Derrida themselves are suspicious. The result of this concentration on "meaning" in the analysis of Derrida's and Wittgenstein's work is to separate the very two categories — language and meaning — whose inseparability both thinkers work so hard to demonstrate. The result is often to portray Wittgenstein or Derrida as making a point about "meaning" alone, when the entire point was to frustrate such a move. Such is the case in the following remark by Jonathan Culler: "Wittgenstein's suggestion that one cannot say 'bububu' and mean 'if it does not rain I shall go out for a walk' has, paradoxically, made it possible to do just that. Its denial establishes a connection that can be exploited" ("Convention and Meaning" 25). Quite aside from the fact that the original remark in the *Philosophical Investigations* (p. 18) does not deny the possibility of "meaning" (the remark is in the form of a question, and one might expect a critic of Culler's persuasion to be more attentive to the complexities of an apparently "rhetorical" question), Wittgenstein's point in the passage is expressly about "*the grammar* of 'to mean' " (my emphasis), and is simply not an axiomatic or regulatory statement about the relationship of language to meaning in general.[7] Culler's account of Wittgenstein is, I believe, symptomatic of the way in which both Wittgenstein and Derrida get paraphrased by theorists interested in applying deconstruction and ordinary-language philosophy to questions of literary meaning. (It is astonishing, for instance, how little Derrida in particular is actually *quoted* in the literature dealing with the relationship of deconstruction to ordinary-language philosophy. Nowhere is the tendency to assimilate Wittgenstein and Derrida to general theories of meaning more evident than in this tradition of critical paraphrase.)

To characterize Derrida and Wittgenstein as philosophers who have something to say about "meaning" and "context" is to make a leap beyond their fundamental practices of reading—whether the reading of conventional philosophical texts or of idiomatic expressions "cited" from ordinary discourse.[8] Although this leap is one Derrida and Wittgenstein themselves undoubtedly often make, the first step in coming to terms with the complicated relationship between these two thinkers consists in tracing with them the ways our language *pictures* such a leap or escape to meaning. Consequently, the rest of this essay will attempt to remain, with Wittgenstein and Derrida, "within" various instances of language in order to examine how the temptation to escape is figured by our linguistic practices, and how it is connected to the cutting short of reading.

II. Reading and Writing

It may seem absurd, on the face of it, to compare two philosophers who profess such antithetical attitudes toward their common activity of "doing philosophy." For Wittgenstein, "the real discovery is the one that makes me capable of stopping doing philosophy when I want to" (remark 133), whereas for Derrida, "the passage beyond philosophy does not consist in turning the page of philosophy (which usually comes down to philosophizing badly), but in continuing to read philosophers *in a certain way*" ("Structure, Sign, and Play" 288). Presented in these terms, the difference between the two seems to come down to the question of "reading." Deconstruction, it appears, is at least an exhortation to read closely, and perhaps a method or style of reading, whereas ordinary-language philosophy is suspicious of any interpretive activity that pictures itself as *compelled* by mysterious semantic problems (see, for instance, *Philosophical Investigations*, remarks 435 and 436).[9] This will seem the most fundamental difference between Derrida and Wittgenstein, then: one wishes to *read*, the other to be *able* to stop reading. It is this distinction that, as James Guetti has noted, makes Wittgenstein's work appear at certain moments to be antagonistic to literary "close reading."[10] By contrast, Derrida's essays are close "readings" in the sense that should be roughly familiar to literary critics: interpretations of individual texts (in this case the texts of Western philosophy) by means of detailed quotation, painstaking rhetorical analysis, and the polemical juxtaposition of passages. Some of the most basic assumptions of Derrida's reading process repeat in fact the very underpinnings of literary modernism—the idea of a text at once self-reflexive and decentered in relation to authorial intention:

> Rousseau's text must constantly be considered as a complex and many-leveled structure; in it, certain propositions may be read as interpretations of other propositions that we are, up to a certain point and with certain precautions, free to read otherwise. Rousseau says A, then for reasons that we must determine, he interprets A into B. A, which was already an interpretation, is reinterpreted into B. After taking cognizance of it, we may, without leaving Rousseau's text, isolate A from its interpretation into B, and discover possibilities and resources there that indeed belong to Rousseau's text, but were not produced or exploited by him, which, for equally legible motives, he *preferred to cut short* by a gesture neither witting nor unwitting. (*Of Grammatology* 307)

The "free[dom] to read otherwise" that Derrida insists upon here seems to open up the possibility of endless interpretation, and this would appear to be precisely the possibility Wittgenstein wishes to preempt when he asserts, at the beginning of the *Investigations*, "Explanations come to an end somewhere" (remark 1). The characterization of deconstruction as prolonging indefinitely the activity of interpretation, and of ordinary-language philosophy as wanting to demystify that activity in order to free us from its compulsions, is in many ways harder to refute than the picture of deconstruction as aimed inwardly at the text and ordinary-language philosophy as aimed outward—a picture I will challenge in the next section of this essay. But Derrida's apparent desire to prolong indefinitely the activity of reading ("continuing to read" as opposed to "turning the page") and Wittgenstein's reservations about the interpretive itch are two positions that in crucial ways *meet at the extreme*.

Wittgenstein would at first glance seem prepared to acknowledge as "reading" a great range of casual, spontaneous, semiattentive activities—as far removed as possible from "close," "literary," or critical reading. Reading, for Wittgenstein, would surely include paraphrase, reading for the plot, skimming, and a disposition not to be distracted by rhetorical language. Wittgenstein wishes to dislodge from its privileged place the kind of language use (here, specifically, the kind of reading) that appears to us more immediate, more intense, more self-conscious, than our ordinary use of language. Seen from this perspective, the exhortation to read *closely*, and to dwell systematically over the rhetorical dimension of the text, seems only to be the privileging of a quite particular case of reading at the expense of a whole range of activities we might just as legitimately call "reading." At the beginning of his discussion on the subject, (remarks

156–71), Wittgenstein seems almost to invert the traditional hierarchical configuration of types of reading:

> This will become clearer if we interpolate the consideration of another
> word, namely "reading". First I need to remark that I am not counting the
> understanding of what is read as part of 'reading' for purposes of this in-
> vestigation: reading is here the activity of rendering out loud what is writ-
> ten or printed; and also of writing from dictation, writing out something
> printed, playing from a score, and so on. (remark 156)

The relegation of "understanding" to a purely contingent aspect of reading
might seem at first to exclude precisely the kind of meditative attention to texts
required by deconstruction. Yet there is ultimately no exclusion here ("we also
use the word 'to read' for a family of cases" [remark 164]), and as we shall see,
what Wittgenstein argues for in the case of reading, Derrida argues similarly for
in the case of writing.

In the section from *Of Grammatology* devoted to Lévi-Strauss's "dissertation
on the Nambikwara" and *Tristes Tropiques*, Derrida criticizes Lévi-Strauss for
refusing to count as "writing" the Nambikwara tribe's various kinds of drawing.
"That the Nambikwara could not write goes without saying," writes Lévi-
Strauss in *Tristes Tropiques* (cited in *Of Grammatology* 122). Yet elsewhere, Derrida points out, it appears that the Nambikwara can *imitate* writing, and furthermore that they have a *word* for this activity:

> 1. This small group of Nambikwara nevertheless uses a word to desig-
> nate the act of writing, at least a word that may serve that end. . . . This
> detail, omitted from *Tristes Tropiques*, was indicated in the thesis:
>
>> The Nambikwara of group (a) do not know anything about design, if
>> one excepts some geometric sketches on their calabashes. For many
>> days, they did not know what to do with the paper and the pencils
>> that we distributed to them. Some time later, we saw them very
>> busily drawing wavy lines. In that they imitated the only use that they
>> had seen us make of our notebooks, namely writing, but without un-
>> derstanding its meaning or its end. They called the act of writing ie-
>> kariukedjutu, namely: "drawing lines."
>
> It is quite evident that a literal translation of the words that mean "to
> write" in the languages of peoples with writing would also reduce that
> word to a rather poor gestural signification. It is as if one said that such a
> language has no word designating writing — and that therefore those who
> practice it do not know how to write — just because they use a word mean-
> ing "to scratch," "to engrave," "to scribble," "to scrape," "to incise,"
> "to trace," "to imprint," etc. As if "to write" in its metaphoric kernel,
> meant something else. (*Of Grammatology* 123)

Why would Derrida want to extend the definition of "writing" to include a mode
of inscription apparently as far removed as possible from the highly self-con-

scious, rhetorical, and philosophical texts that constitute the main focus of his philosophical enterprise? Because Derrida, like Wittgenstein, recognizes that the first impoverishment of any theory of reading or writing would come from its programmatic exclusion of certain forms of reading and writing, or from the characterization of those forms as illegitimate, parodic, or parasitic. While from one perspective Derrida's scrupulous attention to written texts appears to be the privileging of a certain mode or style of textual self-reflexivity, from another perspective it is rather a refusal to count as nonsignificant the entire range of readinglike and writinglike activities that literature and philosophy traditionally constitute themselves in contrast with (a contrast represented by the texts of philosophy and literature as a view of the outside from the inside).

Derrida and Wittgenstein are both profoundly suspicious of philosophical attitudes that systematically depreciate a particular category of linguistic elements. Thus both, for instance, note classical philosophy's tendency to neglect those elements in a language that does not name objects:

> Augustine does not speak of there being any difference between kinds of word. If you describe the learning of language in this way you are, I believe, thinking primarily of nouns like "table", "chair", "bread", and of people's names, and only secondarily of the names of certain actions and properties; and of the remaining kinds of word as something that will take care of itself. (remark 1)

> Above all, there are whole "words" which play an indispensable role in the organization of discourse, but still remain from Aristotle's point of view, totally without meaning. The conjunction (*sundesmos*) is a *phōnē asēmos*. This holds equally for the article, for articulation in general (*arthron*), and for everything that functions *between* signifying members, between nouns, substantives, or verbs (*Poetics* 1456b38–1457a10). ("White Mythology" 240)

The point here for Derrida and Wittgenstein is that any philosophical gesture that axiomatically excludes a certain region of language from significance or seriousness is already determining in advance not only the range of possibly significant expressions in a language, but the very *picture* we will have of that language's functioning. Thus, as we shall see, the picture of a language *divided* into regions of greater and lesser (perhaps even full and null) semantic content calls up the picture of a language possessing an interior and an exterior (and vice versa), a picture that—to borrow Wittgenstein's phrase—"already points to a particular use" (p. 184).

We can see a similar attempt by both thinkers to expand the category of significant linguistic gestures when we turn to their remarks on the relation of language to "communication." According to Derrida there is a tendency in the Western philosophical tradition to view language in general, and writing specifically, exclusively as a mode of communication. In "Signature Event Context,"

Derrida cites Condillac's *Essay on the Origin of Human Knowledge* as an exemplary text within this tradition, and he summarizes Condillac's view of writing as follows:

> If men write, it is (1) because they have something to communicate; (2) because what they have to communicate is their "thought," their "ideas," their representations.
>
> Representative thought precedes and governs communication which transports the "idea," the signified content. (312)

Derrida points out that this conception of language as communication already depends on a narrowly instrumentalist definition of "communication":

> Now, the word *communication*, which nothing initially authorizes us to overlook as a word, and to impoverish as a polysemic word, opens a semantic field which precisely is not limited to semantics, semiotics, and even less to linguistics. To the semantic field of the word *communication* belongs the fact that it also designates nonsemantic movements. Here at least provisional recourse to ordinary language and to the equivocalities of natural language teaches us that one may, for example, *communicate a movement*, or that a tremor, a shock, a displacement of *force* can be communicated — that is, propagated, transmitted. It is also said that different or distant places can communicate between each other by means of a given passageway or opening. What happens in this case, what is transmitted or communicated, are not phenomena of meaning or signification. (309)

Although a Wittgensteinian might suspect that a false sense of scandal is created by the initial reference to an absent authority ("nothing immediately authorizes us to overlook"), Derrida's delineation of the various nonsemantic uses for the word "communication" is precisely what Wittgenstein would call the "grammar" of the word "communicate." If language *communicates*, according to Wittgenstein, then communication must indeed be understood in the widest possible sense — at the very least, in a sense commensurable with all the various uses of that word that Derrida himself outlines. For the traditional philosophical conception of language as the conveyance of a semantic content is indeed one of those captivating "pictures" against which Wittgenstein inveighs:

> The paradox disappears only if we make a radical break with the idea that language always functions in one way, always serves the same purpose: to convey thoughts — which may be about houses, pains, good and evil, or anything else you please.
>
> . . . we are so much accustomed to communication through language, in conversation, that it looks to us as if the whole point of communication lay in this: someone else grasps the sense of my words — which is something mental: *he as it were takes it into his own mind*. If he then does something further with it as well, that is no part of the immediate purpose of language.

Not: "without language we could not communicate with one another"—but for sure: without language we cannot influence other people
in such-and-such ways; cannot build roads and machines, etc. And also:
without the use of speech and writing people could not communicate. (remarks 304, 363 [my emphasis], 491)

For Wittgenstein, the picture of language as *communication* is tied to the picture
of an *internal content* made manifest ("As if the purpose of [a] proposition were
to convey to one person how it is with another: only, so to speak, in his thinking
part and not in his stomach" [remark 317]). If language is to be conceived as a
more complicated and nuanced phenomenon than is allowed by our theories of
semantic transport, then we must develop more inclusive and differentiated pictures of what counts as language in the first place. This involves extending the
definition of language to include all sorts of gestural or game-playing activities
(as both Wittgenstein and Derrida do). But it also involves a suspension of categorical distinctions within language (here more narrowly defined), distinctions
that treat certain parts of a text or discourse as less essential to the establishing of
meaning or affect than others—as if certain words or kinds of discourse were
mystically *imbued* with significance. The picture of language that colludes the
most in sustaining such distinctions is the picture of language as possessing an
interior and an exterior, and it is to Wittgenstein's and Derrida's examination of
that distinction that we must next turn our attention.

III. The Inside/Outside Picture

There is nothing outside of the text *[there is no outside-text;* il
n'y a pas de hors-texte*]*. . . . *In what one calls the real life of
these existences "of flesh and bone," beyond and behind what
one believes can be circumscribed as Rousseau's text, there has
never been anything but writing.*

—Of Grammatology *158–59*

We are not concerned with the difference: internal, external.

—The Blue Book *13*

*One ought to ask, not what images are or what happens when
one imagines anything, but how the word "imagination" is
used.* But that does not mean that I want to talk only about
words. *For the question as to the nature of the imagination is
as much about the word "imagination" as my question is.*

—Philosophical Investigations, *remark 370 (my emphasis)*

"The mind seems able to give a word meaning"—isn't this as
if I were to say "The carbon atoms in benzene seem to lie at
the corners of a hexagon"? But this is not something that
seems to be so; it is a picture.

—Philosophical Investigations, *p. 184*

Throughout their work, Derrida and Wittgenstein both question the distinction between an inside and an outside of language, a distinction that has allowed literary theorists to describe certain critical practices as either remaining trapped within, or appealing beyond, the text. Wittgenstein's critical method has traditionally been seen by literary theorists as one that allows us to move outside the text. This critical move has been conceived of variously as an escape from the confines of close reading, as a connection of the text to "forms of life," or as the contextual situating of literary usage within the larger "grammar" of ordinary usage. But in Wittgensteinian terms, the appeal to a form of life, to an ordinary-language game, or to a "use," is quite simply not an appeal to something surrounding or supporting an individual text. (Note that what is being questioned here is not the concept of "appeal" or the concept of explanation by reference— or comparison—to a practice. What is at issue is the specific *picture* or figuration given to such appeals.)

There are two senses in which Wittgenstein might be thought to endorse the interior/exterior model in his descriptions of language use, and in which he might be thought to privilege the exterior over the interior. The first, and simpler sense arises from his frequent references to philosophical problems as entanglements or enclosures:

A *picture* held us captive. And we could not get outside it, for it lay in our language and language seemed to repeat it to us inexorably.

What is your aim in philosophy?—To shew the fly the way out of the fly-bottle. (remarks 115, 309)

The appeal of these conventional tropes is powerful, and one is quickly tempted to point to the tension between such sentiments and the theme, expressed elsewhere in the *Investigations*, of ordinary language as a home from which philosophical discourse has strayed (e.g., remarks 38, 116). Simply pointing to such a contrast, however, would only be, in Derrida's words, the "multiplication of antagonistic metaphors in order better to control or neutralize their effect" ("White Mythology" 214). Wittgenstein's critique of the interior/exterior distinction has to be understood as something more complex than the strategic employment of self-contradiction.

The second and more important sense in which Wittgenstein seems to privilege "outer" processes or criteria has to do with his notion of context. It would seem that if any phenomenon deserves to be figured as something external, it would be *context*:

An 'inner process' stands in need of outward criteria.

An expectation is imbedded in a situation, from which it arises. . . .

. . . What is happening now has significance—in these surroundings. The surroundings give it its importance. . . .

Now suppose I sit in my room and hope that N.N. will come and bring me some money, and suppose one minute of this state could be isolated, cut out of its context; would what happened in it then not be hope? (remarks 580, 581, 583, 584)

In all of these remarks, certain circumstances are figured as external to others, with the former giving significance to the latter. But of course this exteriority is of several different kinds: at the very least, the exteriority of the phenomenal world to consciousness, the exteriority of environment in the most general sense to individual subjects, and the temporal "surrounding" of a moment by other moments. And which of these would describe the context a sentence provides for a word within it (pp. 181–82)? In the case of temporal context particularly, the sense in which circumstances can be represented as exterior starts to get complicated. The way in which a given context might be incomplete or inadequate is not a structurally identifiable gap or lack in present circumstances, but is rather the possibility of other circumstances arising. For instance, in the case of a visual representation of the experience Wittgenstein calls a "change in aspect," the adequacy of the exterior representation to the interior experience is doubly contingent:

Then is the copy of the figure an *incomplete* description of my visual experience [i.e., the experience of seeing the figure "in a new way"]? No. — But the circumstances decide whether, and what, more detailed specifications are necessary. — It *may* be an incomplete description; if there is still something to ask. (p. 199)

If context is *outside* what it contextualizes, then the perceived "incompleteness" of a given piece of language (here, a "description") should be referable to something in the immediately surrounding "circumstances." But the incompleteness may be referable either to present or to future circumstances, and thus to external criteria of very different sorts.

It is important to see that for Wittgenstein, arguments against the picture of an "inner" state of mind (or "inner" process) are equally telling against the picture of an "outer" context. Consider remark 305, in which Wittgenstein criticizes the representation of "remembering" as an "inner process":

"But you surely cannot deny that, for example, in remembering, an inner process takes place." — What gives the impression that we want to deny anything? When one says "Still, an inner process does take place here" — one wants to go on: "After all, you *see* it." And it is this inner process that one means by the word "remembering". — The impression that we wanted to deny something arises from our setting our faces against the picture of the 'inner process'. What we deny is that the picture of the inner process gives us the correct idea of the use of the word "to remember". We say that this picture with its ramifications stands in the way of our seeing the use of the word as it is.

If Wittgenstein does not exactly want to "deny" the idea that remembering is an inner process, then how is it that the "picture of the inner process . . . stands in the way"? It stands in the way because it is modeled on the picture of an "outer process." But why should *that* analogy stand in the way? Not because it models purely hypothetical processes on processes we can actually *see*, but because it substitutes a scheme (inner/outer) for an investigation of the words at issue (e.g., "remembering"). An investigation would point to the discrepancies as well as the similarities among the various activities of, say, remembering a face, remembering an appointment, remembering how to proceed (in a game, on a journey, with a puzzle or solution, etc.). In each of these cases there is a different relationship between what we imagine the "inner process" to be and the "outer process" we imagine it to be modeled on.

The appealing binary distinction between "inner" and "outer" is misleading because it is taken to account for the difference between "inner processes" and "outer processes," when in fact we are already using the word "process" quite differently in the two cases, *regardless of whether we assimilate the interior/exterior distinction to that difference or not*. This becomes clearer if we look at Wittgenstein's treatment of the terms "inner" and "outer" in yet another case:

> And above all do *not* say "After all my visual impression isn't the *drawing*; it is *this*—which I can't shew to anyone." —Of course it is not the drawing, but neither is it anything of the same category, which I carry within myself.
>
> The concept of the 'inner picture' is misleading, for this concept uses the '*outer* picture' as a model; and yet the uses of the words for these concepts are no more like one another than the uses of 'numeral' and 'number'. (p. 196)

The adjectives "inner" and "outer" simply cannot account for the difference between the inner and outer picture, for the difference between the two uses of "picture" is grammatical rather than schematic. The phrases "inner picture" and "outer picture" are related grammatically; that is to say, the two phrases must be related to one another in a way that would be made "perspicuous" by the elaboration of "*intermediate cases*" (remark 122).

Does conceiving of the grammatical relationship between "inner" and "outer" in this way mean that the two cannot be categorically distinguished? Not exactly, since it is at the same time a feature of our language that certain grammatically related phrases may logically exclude one another. This is the case, for instance, in our discourse about "belief":

> I say of someone else "He seems to believe . . . " and other people say

it of me. Now, why do I never say it of myself, not even when others *rightly*
say it of me? . . .

My own relation to my words is wholly different from other people's.

That different development of the verb would have been possible, if
only I could say "I seem to believe". (pp. 191–92)

If operating with language was not at all a personal experience (as Wittgenstein is
often thought to say), then there would be nothing to prevent people from saying
of themselves what other people might say of them. That is, it would make no
less sense to say "I believe x is the case, and I am right" (or "I seem to believe
x is the case") than to say "He believes x is the case, and he is right" (or, "He
seems to believe x is the case"). But there is a difference in our language; the
former expression is considered to be tautological, the latter to be quite proper.
Wittgenstein thinks of the difference that divides talk about one's own beliefs
from talk about other people's beliefs as a "grammatical" difference, and here
perhaps we can see how "grammar" may allow for differences that are absolute
even among terms that are connected by intermediate cases or uses. We have an
undeniably different relation to our own words (often figured as an internal relationship) than we do to other people's words (often figured as an external relationship), but what this difference illuminates is as much a fact about grammar
(in this particular case, the grammar of "belief") as it is a fact about the relationship between "internal" and "external" experiences. The quite literal difference between what we may say about ourselves and what we may say about
others is in fact a central feature of our grammar. And what is "grammatical,"
then, is neither exclusively personal nor exclusively social, but a fact about the
way the two are brought together and regulated in language. This makes of *context* something other than a simple appeal outward from a text to an external community or situation. It is not that there are no such things as successful appeals or
justifications or substantiating contexts, but rather that the pictures we give of
them are misleading.

To find a meaningful context for a given phrase or figure in a literary text
might involve *any* of the following: imagining how the phrase is used in other
texts or situations (even here the picture of the "outside" of the text is not entirely clear since we might be searching either for "the language-game which is
its original home" [remark 116] or a "fiction" to "surround" the text with [p.
210]); substituting an equivalent expression ("We speak of understanding a sentence in the sense in which it can be replaced by another which says the same"
[remark 531]);[11] finding a phrase that *supplements* rather than replacing the original one (p. 188); or searching elsewhere in the text itself for other uses of the
same figure, phrase, or expression. This last possibility is not articulated by Wittgenstein, since his work does not deal with individual, extended documents —
with *texts* in the traditional sense. But it is important to see that his conception of
context could not *exclude* investigations of a text's internal grammar.

It is important to keep in mind, of course, that Wittgenstein does not simply *reject* the model in which language is conceived of as the exterior to thought, or the correlative model in which context is exterior to language, that is, is the medium in which language is "applied." Rather, he insists on our retaining this picture and comparing the various ways in which it is invoked. In challenging the assumption that language is an approximate representation of private mental contents he writes:

> The great difficulty here is not to represent the matter as if there were something one *couldn't* do. As if there really were an object, from which I derive its description, but I were unable to shew it to anyone. — And the best that I can propose is that we should yield to the temptation to use this picture, but then investigate how the *application* of the picture goes.

This remark is paradigmatic of Wittgenstein's way of approaching questions about language. For the remark makes no claims about what language can or cannot do; rather Wittgenstein concerns himself here with the question of how we *describe* the operations of language. At one level the passage seems to recommend that we substitute talk about "application" for talk about "derivation." Language is now to be described as applying or failing to apply in certain circumstances, and not as a more or less satisfactory representation of inner experience. But at another level, "application" does not supplant "derivation"; rather it is the *application of the picture of derivation* that is to be investigated. Recourse to the concept of "application" does not *resolve* problems generated by the picture of language as exteriority. The investigation of "applications" can help us construct only a "grammar," not an "outside."

For Derrida as for Wittgenstein, there is no appeal to an "outside" of language. But Derrida is much fonder than Wittgenstein of interpreting this fact as the necessity or importance of remaining *within a text* — of continuing to read. Since Derrida at many points denies the existence of either an exteriority *or* an interiority to texts, however, we need to investigate how he conceives the possibility of remaining within a text of which there can be, properly speaking, no inside.[12]

When he reads, Derrida seeks to trace the line of thought in a text that runs endlessly between — while constantly dividing — the opposing terms in each of the following pairs: speech and writing, the literal and the metaphoric, the inside and the outside. Derrida discusses these oppositions as they arise in the texts themselves, either as explicit topics or as rhetorical tropes. But for Derrida it is not enough to recognize the mutual constitution of the opposing terms within each of these pairs. It is necessary as well to see how *each pair entails the others*. Further, it is important to see how the philosophical categories named by these terms arise *inevitably* in our readings of texts.

In order to understand what Derrida means by "Il n'y a pas de hors-texte" we must first consider his claim that in the tradition of Western philosophy, the interior/exterior distinction has never become disengaged from the thought

/language, speech/writing, and literal/metaphoric distinctions. ("It is a question at first of demonstrating the systematic and historical solidarity of the concepts and gestures of thought that one often believes can be innocently separated" [*Of Grammatology* 14]). Of course, to call the mutual dependence of these distinctions a *principle* is already to give an axiomatic if not metaphysical appearance to the argument, and here I believe it is important to note three somewhat distinct explanations offered by Derrida for this "systematic and historical solidarity." Those three explanations may be described, roughly, as the ontological, the Freudian, and the literary, and though perhaps these categories too should be investigated jointly, I will for the purposes of this argument separate them here.[13]

The "ontological" or "ontotheological" impulse in Derrida's work derives from his insistence on the foundational (or perhaps better *pre*foundational) status of such categories as "différance," "play," "writing," the "trace," and "supplementarity."[14] This impulse in Derrida's work emerges in those passages where the precedence of certain conceptual categories is presented in the form of an abstract, retrospectively deduced, logically necessary precedence. Thus, "différance" is described as "no longer simply a concept, but rather the possibility of conceptuality" ("Différance" 11); the "*trace*" is touted as "*the absolute origin of sense in general*" (*Of Grammatology* 65); and "supplementarity" is defined as a "law," itself governed by a "formal necessity" ("White Mythology" 229). "Writing," too, is one of these prefoundational categories: "The problem of the soul and body is no doubt derived from the problem of writing from which it seems—conversely—to borrow its metaphors" (*Of Grammatology* 35).[15] Writing, for Derrida, is both the *precondition* and the model for all distinctions between an interior and an exterior. To speak of writing, in our culture, is to speak simultaneously of the ground for the interior/exterior distinction, and of the motive for articulating that distinction:

> If "writing" signifies inscription and especially the durable institution of a sign (and that is the only irreducible kernel of the concept of writing), writing in general covers the entire field of linguistic signs. In that field a certain sort of instituted signifiers may then appear, "graphic" in the narrow and derivative sense of the word, ordered by a certain relationship with other instituted—hence "written," even if they are "phonic"—signifiers. The very idea of institution—hence of the arbitrariness of the sign—is unthinkable before the possibility of writing and outside of its horizon.
>
> Now we must think that writing is at the same time more exterior to speech, not being its "image" or its "symbol," and more interior to speech, which is already in itself a writing. Even before it is linked to incision, engraving, drawing, or the letter, to a signifier referring in general to a signifier signified by it, the concept of the *graphie* [unit of a possible graphic system] implies the framework of the *instituted trace*, as the possibility common to all systems of signification. (*Of Grammatology* 44, 46)

According to Derrida, the interior/exterior distinction derives from attempts to define one part of language (''writing'' in the narrow, graphic sense) in relation to, and *against*, the complete field of that concept. Thus, at a certain level, or at a certain moment, of Derrida's argument, it appears that to speak of texts in terms of an inside and an outside is already to accept the whole ontology of derived, debased, and inadequate signs that follows from the categorical partitioning of language against itself.

Derrida's second argument for the mutual dependency of certain philosophical categories and distinctions is also retrospectively deduced and a priori, and might best be characterized as a Freudian logic, by way of Lacan. This logic can be seen operating in those passages where Derrida describes the constitution of the individual subject:

> For what is reflected is split *in itself* and not only as an addition to itself of its image. The reflection, the image, the double, splits what it doubles. The origin of the speculation becomes a difference. What can look at itself is not one; and the law of the addition of the origin to its representation, of the thing to its image, is that one plus one makes at least three.
>
> . . . The speculary dispossession which at the same time institutes and deconstitutes me is also a law of language.
>
> Society, language, history, articulation, in a word supplementarity, are born at the same time as the prohibition of incest. That last is the hinge [*brisure*] between nature and culture. (*Of Grammatology* 36, 141, 265)

Here, Derrida's emphasis is less on logical *derivation* or *priority* than on the *simultaneous* institution of certain conceptual categories. And that simultaneous institution—which gathers together language, the subject, and social space—once again links writing indissolubly with the distinction between interiority and exteriority. Paraphrasing (and then questioning) the argument he finds in a particular passage from Condillac's *Essay on the Origin of Human Knowledge*, Derrida writes:

> . . . it is at the moment that the social *distance*, which had led gesture to speech, increases to the point of becoming *absence*, that writing becomes necessary. . . . From then on, writing has the function of reaching *subjects* who are not only distant but outside of the entire field of vision and beyond earshot.
>
> Why *subjects?* Why should writing be another name for the constitution of *subjects* and, so to speak, of *constitution* itself? of a subject, that is to say of an individual held responsible (for) himself in front of a law and by the same token subject to that law? (281)

In Derrida's reading of Condillac, *writing* is instituted only at the moment that an *absence* is recognized, which is also the moment at which the latter is conceptualized as an absolute *exteriority*. Writing, according to this psychoanthropological scheme, is a trace that expresses alienation in its very form. ''Writing'' and exteriority are one in our culture, and any invocation of an interior/exterior distinction to describe the effect or the signified of writing will thus suffer from what Derrida elsewhere calls the "implication of the defined in the definition" ("White Mythology" 253). Like the ontological argument—in which writing is connected to the interior/exterior distinction by a relation of logical precedence—Derrida's Freudian argument is an abstract and deductive one. But the passage from *Of Grammatology* just cited already points toward a third—and in Derrida's work, the most comprehensive—argument against letting any investigation of writing be governed by an interior/exterior distinction. For the argument linking writing to absence and exteriority in the preceding passage was ostensibly *Condillac's* rather than Derrida's. What Derrida sees as the necessary link between writing and exteriority in our culture is not only deducible through an abstract ontological or psychoanthropological analysis, but can be discovered—through careful reading—as the more or less explicit postulate of innumerable texts in the Western philosophical tradition.

Throughout *Of Grammatology*, the linking of writing to exteriority and to metaphor (all three opposed, always, to speech, interiority, and the literal) is discovered over and over again as Derrida reads the texts of Plato, Saussure, Lévi-Strauss, and Rousseau. Any paraphrase, critique, or account of Derrida's work that does not grapple with these readings, and with the critical practices staked out in them, simply reduces Derrida's work to a set of epigrammatic philosophical axioms—as striking, as representative, and of about as much consequence as "meaning is use" or "a picture held us captive." Furthermore, to ignore Derrida's readings of individual texts is effectively to isolate the ontological and Freudian tropes in his argument, tropes whose historical production and complex applications in individual texts it is Derrida's whole project to display. In the final analysis, Derrida's work is not intended to function or to persuade through the demonstration of logical derivation, a priori necessity, or retrospective deduction. Although the elaboration of his argument by these means occupies an important place in his work, his practice of reading shows how these traditional "philosophemes" themselves emerge, and are used, in specific texts.

To see how the linkage of the interior/exterior distinction with writing arises through Derrida's *reading*, we must turn briefly to his reading of Plato's *Phaedrus*, a text Derrida considers to be practically inaugural within the logocentric tradition. Derrida's fullest reading of the *Phaedrus* is to be found in "Plato's Pharmacy" (1972), but for our purposes it will be sufficient to consider some of the passages he discusses in *Of Grammatology*. Those passages are drawn from the famous condemnation of writing at the end of the *Phaedrus* where Socrates contrasts "writing," characterized as "external marks" (275a), with "those lessons on justice and honour and goodness that are expounded and set forth for the sake of instruction, and are veritably written in the soul of the listener" (278a). How does one respond to this curious rhetorical echo, this implication of the defined in its *other?* Our Berkeleyan straight man Philonous has already provided us with one response: "Look you, Hylas, when I speak of objects as existing in the mind, or *imprinted* on the senses, I would not be understood in the *gross literal sense*" (my emphasis). But this depreciation of gross literality only repeats at another level the depreciation of "writing" or "imprinting" *without explaining the latter concepts*. It still leaves undecided just how we are to understand the figurative or nonliteral sense in which writing/imprinting is being used. And it leaves undecided as well whether the interior/exterior distinction ("in the soul" vs. "external marks") is meant to be explained by the figurative/literal distinction or instead to give meaning *to it*. In reading Plato's text we confront the fact that the writing/speech distinction cannot be elaborated or investigated independently of the literal/figurative or exterior/interior distinctions. That is why, according to Derrida, we cannot "solve" the apparent contradiction in Plato's text by deciding to read figuratively where we once read literally, that is, by privileging external marks, but now only as metaphors:

> . . . the writing of truth in the soul, opposed by *Phaedrus* (278a) to bad writing (writing in the "literal" [*propre*] and ordinary sense, "sensible" writing, "in space") . . . all that functions as *metaphor* in these discourses confirms the privilege of the logos and founds the "literal" meaning then given to writing: a sign signifying a signifier itself signifying an eternal verity, eternally thought and spoken in the proximity of a present logos. The paradox to which attention must be paid is this: natural and universal writing, intelligible and nontemporal writing, is thus named by metaphor. A writing that is sensible, finite, and so on, is designated as writing in the literal sense; . . . Of course, this metaphor remains enigmatic and refers to a "literal" meaning of writing as the first metaphor. This "literal" meaning is yet unthought by the adherents of this discourse. It is not, therefore, a matter of inverting the literal meaning and the figurative meaning but of determining the "literal" meaning of writing as metaphoricity itself. (*Of Grammatology* 15)

To what extent is this a *reading* of the *Phaedrus*, and to what extent is it a speculative ontology? On the ontological side we have the assumption—apparently not drawn from anything in the *Phaedrus* itself—that writing is not only a metaphor, but "the first metaphor." That "writing" is used as a metaphor in *Phaedrus* 278a seems clear; but why should it necessarily be the *first* metaphor? The argument presumably goes something likes this: before the emergence of "writing" (in the narrow sense of graphic inscription) there could have been no other activity derivative from (and yet analogous to) speech and thought, with which we might describe speech and thought. The first falling away from the *logos*, then, would have been the first means of figuring it—writing would be *essentially* figurative.

However, Derrida's phrase "first metaphor" (*première métaphore*) might also be understood in the sense of an exemplary, not a historically anterior, metaphor. (It is worth noting that the phrase "first metaphor" is replaced by the phrase "metaphoricity itself" [*métaphoricité elle-même*] in the course of the paragraph.) In fact, if we insist on reading the passage *as a reading* of the *Phaedrus*, the attribution of anteriority to writing and to metaphor does not seem to work. For if Plato paradoxically opposes "writing" in its figurative sense to literal "writing," the effect is neither an ironic, infinite regress ("Without this recognition and this respect, critical production would risk developing in any direction at all" [*Of Grammatology* 158]), nor an "inversion" in which metaphorical sense would now be recognized as primary, nonderivative, and so on. ("Deconstructing this tradition will therefore not consist of reversing it, of making writing innocent" [*Of Grammatology* 37].) The only way to respect both the literal and the figurative in Plato's text would be to see them both as nonderived. Attributing priority or anteriority to metaphor would only reinstitute the value of natural signification, which is precisely what Plato's figure of *writing in the soul* problematizes. The latter point is particularly important because it qualifies Derrida's ontological-sounding assertion that "the problem of body and soul is no doubt derived from the problem of writing." If mutually defining terms (e.g., speech and writing) exclude the possibility of derivation from one another, then mutually defining relationships *among pairs of terms* must also exclude derivation. We cannot arrive at a categorical distinction between speech and writing through an appeal to the literal/figurative model, or to the distinction between interior and exterior, because these sets of distinctions are mutually constituting in Plato's text. This does not mean that significances cannot be attached to, or critical readings produced from, the text. But it means that literary criticism's privileged model of the text as a structure possessing an inside and an outside (whether conceived as content and form, affect and reference, authorial intention and historical context, etc.) is inseparable from a division of the text into literal and figurative significations. Furthermore, each of the various interior/exterior models we employ draws the line between figurative and literal expressions differently, with corresponding assumptions about the relative values of literal and figurative meaning. To Derrida's way of thinking, this critical predetermination of the line separating figurative from literal expressions in a given text constitutes an evasion of the critic's responsibility to *arrive at* a complex picture of the text's dynamic relationships *through reading*. Since the text may often employ the same expression literally in one place and figuratively in another, any predetermination of the text's structure will tend toward the glossing over of its most productive and important complexities.[16]

The idea of a comprehensive, complex reading that attempts to account for as many as possible of the text's details and for their potentially conflicting values, is familiar to literary critics both in its romantic-organic and its New Critical versions. Derrida endorses this mode of reading, and provisionally terms it "intrinsic," while continuing to oppose the conventional choices of intrinsic and extrinsic criticism.[17] In describing the "signifying structure" that he believes a "critical reading should *produce*," Derrida argues that those critical operations that either aim outwardly at the text's "reference" or inwardly at the author's "intention" (inward, because the text in this case is seen as a successful expression of meaning that needs only to be mirrored by or reproduced in the act of reading) are equally evasive of the text's complex and self-conflicting dynamic:

> To produce this signifying structure obviously cannot consist of reproducing, by the effaced and respectful doubling of commentary, the conscious, voluntary, intentional relationship that the writer institutes in his exchanges with the history to which he belongs thanks to the element of language. This moment of doubling commentary should no doubt have its place in a critical reading. To recognize and respect all its classical exigencies is not easy and requires all the instruments of traditional criticism. Without this recognition and this respect, critical production would risk developing in any direction at all and authorize itself to say almost anything. But this indispensable guardrail has always only *protected*, it has never *opened*, a reading.
>
> Yet if reading must not be content with doubling the text, it cannot legitimately transgress the text toward something other than it, toward a referent (a reality that is metaphysical, historical, psychobiographical, etc.) or toward a signified outside the text whose content could take place, could have taken place outside of language, that is to say, in the sense that we give here to that word, outside of writing in general. . . .
>
> Although it is not commentary, our reading must be intrinsic and remain within the text. . . . *The security with which the commentary considers the self-identity of the text, the confidence with which it carves out its contour, goes hand in hand with the tranquil assurance that leaps over the text toward its presumed content, in the direction of the pure signified.* (*Of Grammatology* 158–59)

Critical reading, in Derrida's view, must attempt to articulate a text's complex details without assuming either clarity and consistency of authorial intention (which would obviate the need for external supplements or keys—for *interpretation*) or the existence of authoritative *contexts* (which would dissolve concrete textual tensions and ambiguities). For Derrida no act of reading or interpretation should structurally *negate* or *exclude* certain parts of a text, allowing us in effect to treat one part of the text as uniquely, structurally representative of the whole— yet this is precisely what extrinsic criticism and criticism-as-doubling-commentary (i.e., respectful paraphrase) end up doing. Both these models of criticism imply the interior/exterior distinction, and attempt to represent the entire text synecdochically, by way of textual details that are pictured as either connecting the text to its authoritative context or synthesizing and ordering the text from within. The rush to represent the text in its own terms and the rush to connect it to something else are in many ways mirror images of one another, both being critical evasions.

There are, of course, ironies and paradoxes involved in Derrida's critique. For textual criticism *always* proceeds according to some formula for reduction and *re*presentation; interpretations are rhetorical representations, in both the general and technical sense of "rhetorical." Furthermore, Derrida ultimately chooses to designate his own critical program of reading as "intrinsic," acknowledging the inevitability of the very hermeneutic model against which he inveighs. Derrida's response to these two ironies is one and the same: we simply cannot dispense with the deepest figurative and critical concepts in our culture, but by tracing the obsessiveness with which they appear in our writings, and the obsessiveness with which they attach to one another, we can hope to deny their claims to *naturalness*, and thus to *rightness*:

> As Saussure will do, so does Rousseau wish at once to maintain the exteriority of the system of writing and the maleficent efficiency with which one singles out its symptoms on the body of the language. But am I saying anything else? Yes, in as much as *I show the interiority of exteriority, which amounts to annulling the ethical qualification* and to thinking of writing beyond good and evil. (*Of Grammatology* 314; my emphasis)

In Derrida's reading of Western philosophy, the interior/exterior distinction is above all an ethical, hierarchizing, exclusionary distinction. Although it is only one picture of textual meaning among many, it is that picture that in most texts discourages us from looking for other pictures. Whether this observation of Derrida's is ultimately a historicist or an abstractly philosophical one, it stands as a caution to certain textual practices, and to certain ways of picturing the texts we read. As a picture of *where meaning is to be got from texts*, Derrida's "intrinsic" criticism seems no different in principle from any other textual model. But if the interior/exterior model is indeed a picture in (and of) our language that we cannot get around, then Derrida's insistence that we trace its inevitable repressions and returns may end up sounding very much like Wittgenstein's advice that we *yield to the temptation to use the picture, but investigate how the application of the picture goes* (remark 374).

IV. Conclusion

Both Wittgenstein and Derrida examine the classical subordination of reading and writing to "understanding," as well as the traditional figuring of the latter as a controlling interior activity corresponding—and giving meaning—to exterior gestures. But it is in their respective alternatives to the classical account that they appear to part ways. To the ordinary-language camp, Derrida seems stuck within—fascinated by—the very oppositions between interior and exterior, between writing and its *other* (speech, thought, gesture), that he deconstructs. In tracing the textual phenomenon he describes as "re-inscription," Derrida recognizes that he cannot relinquish the formal oppositions whose inadequacy he has intimated, and chooses instead to invest the opposing members of a given conceptual pair with all the implications of what had previously been considered their marginal, exceptional, or even antithetical cases.[18] Thus Derrida does not *move beyond* those passages in a given text that explicitly oppose, e.g., writing and *logos*, as one might move beyond a problem that has been solved or a false distinction that has been exposed. By contrast, Wittgenstein performs his deconstructions of binary oppositions by articulating the *"intermediate cases"* (remark 122) and "continuous series of transitional cases" (remark 161) that join them according to the "grammar" of our language.

To what extent, then, can Derrida and Wittgenstein be said to offer us similar strategies for reading texts? From the ordinary-language philosopher's point of view, deconstruction seems bent on making of certain rhetorical features of language a metaphysical dilemma, extending to issues of identity, knowledge, and communication. Ordinary-language philosophy would dissolve those dilemmas, but what it would leave in their place is less clear—especially once we recognize that the picture of recourse to a context is a picture fraught with ambiguities and difficulties—*by Wittgenstein's own account*. (Even the picture of application has to be *applied* [remark 141].) Certainly, once we step outside their practices of reading, we might say that Derrida's great theme is the inescapable (and constituting) presence of philosophical categories in our language, whereas Wittgenstein's theme is the possibility of thinking clearly about our use of language *without acceding* to the philosophical categories built into it.[19] This characterization returns us to the familiar notion of deconstruction and ordinary-language philosophy as divided or related along the lines of such epistemological and metaphysical themes as the necessity of perspective, the possibility of meaning, and the escape from language. As I have tried to show, however, this view of Wittgenstein and Derrida passes too quickly over their patient investigations of the *linguistic* constraints on language—not the historical, metaphysical, or psychological constraints (for neither philosopher's work in itself points to, or points away from, an explanation of such constraints), but the *pictures* of our language that emerge repeatedly in our discourse, representing language as divided against itself and throwing up obstacles to its own comprehension. The investigation of these pictures, and of their various relationships to one another, cannot constitute a *reading* of a text. But if it is true that we must *read* before we construct *readings*, then both Wittgenstein and Derrida point to the many and complexly related *forms* of reading that we can neither assimilate nor neglect. Whether our pictures of reading are related *rhetorically* or *grammatically* to one another (and to the pictures we have of other activities), and whether there is a distinction between these two kinds of relationships, are questions that need to be investigated in their own right. But what both Wittgenstein and Derrida may be said to recognize is that we operate with various pictures of what reading is like, and that these pictures themselves are built into our language. Getting around them is not the issue; connecting them to other pictures of our lives may well be.

Notes

1. All citations of Wittgenstein's work in this essay are from the *Philosophical Investigations*. Citations from this point on will thus omit title, and will be identified in simply by "remark" number (for Part I of the *Investigations*) or page number (for Part II).

2. Derrida's statement comes in the middle of a lengthy discussion concerning the alternatives of intrinsic and extrinsic criticism, in which the model of textual interiority/exteriority is both invoked and criticized. See my discussion below, pp. 160–62. Wittgenstein's "meaning is use," as has often been pointed out, is qualified *explicitly* from the start: "For a *large* class of cases—though not for all—in which we employ the word 'meaning' it can be defined thus: the meaning of a word is its use in the language" (remark 43).

3. In "Building Dwelling Thinking" Heidegger writes: "Man acts as though *he* were the shaper and master of language, while in fact *language* remains the master of man" (146). In *Of Grammatology*, Derrida implicitly concurs: "The writer writes *in* a language and *in* a logic whose proper system, laws, and life his discourse by definition cannot dominate absolutely. He uses them only by letting himself, after a fashion and up to a certain point, be governed by the system" (158). Compare with these statements Wittgenstein's various remarks concerning the coercive effects of the linguistic system: "Our forms of expression prevent us in all sorts of ways from seeing that nothing out of the ordinary is involved" (remark 94); "A *picture* held us captive. And we could not get outside of it, for it lay in our language and language seemed to repeat it to us inexorably" (remark 115); "We have only rejected the grammar which tries to force itself on us here" (remark 304).

4. Edward Said ("The Problem of Textuality") points to the absence in Derrida's work of any extended historical explanation for the endurance of certain philosophical categories and rhetorical tropes: "All of Derrida's work has magnificently demonstrated that such a contract exists, that texts demonstrating logocentric biases are indications that the contract exists and keeps existing from period to period in Western history and culture. But it is a legitimate question, I think, to ask what keeps that contract together, what makes it possible for a certain system of metaphysical ideas, as well as a whole structure of concepts, praxes, ideologies derived from it, to maintain itself from Greek antiquity up through the present. What forces keep all these ideas glued together? What forces get them into texts? "(701). These are crucial questions, and form the basis for an indispensable critique of deconstruction. But, it is important to point out, these questions are equally relevant to ordinary-language philosophy, whose discussion of context (from Wittgenstein to Austin and Searle) is certainly no more historical or political than Derrida's discussion of texts.

5. Altieri describes Derrida as a popularizer of "skeptical perspectives on language, consciousness, and meaning," and claims that the "ontology implicit in Wittgenstein's work helps us recover the force of humanistic claims about literature that have come to seem mere truisms" ("Wittgenstein on Consciousness and Language" 1397–98). According to Norris, "Deconstruction is at present the most rigorous and (to its opponents) the most perverse of all attempts to reckon the consequences of skeptical doubt." Although Wittgenstein is often invoked to counter the claims of skeptics, argues Norris, Wittgenstein's writings in fact "stand in a distinctly ambivalent relation to those very forms of self-induced skeptical doubt which Wittgenstein professedly chased off limits" (*The Deconstructive Turn* 34–35). For Guetti, deconstruction is a "peculiarly extravagant" form of "philosophical skepticism" which "becomes, from a Wittgensteinian perspective, much ado about nothing" ("Wittgenstein and Literary Theory—I" 74).

6. According to Rorty's earliest and most sympathetic assessment of deconstruction, Derrida advocates that we abandon certain cognitive frameworks or world views, e.g., the Kantian: "He [Derrida] is suggesting how things might look if we did not have Kantian philosophy built into the fabric of our intellectual life" ("Philosophy as a Kind of Writing" 98). This assessment is shared by Samuel Wheeler in his essay on Derrida and Donald Davidson, though Wheeler is more interested than is Rorty in Derrida's practice of reading (see note 16): "The core problem which drives the analyses of both Derrida and Davidson, it seems to me, is that allegedly non-Aristotelean and non-essentialist accounts of the world (e.g. Kantian and 'linguistic' ones) still seem to rest on essentialism about conceptual or linguistic items" ("Indeterminacy of French Interpretation" 484). See also Stanley Cavell's remarks in "Politics as Opposed to What?" Cavell refers to the "intimacy and . . . abyss" between Anglo-American and new French philosophies: "The intimacy is that both define themselves as critiques of metaphysics, which just says that we are all children of Kant" (173). Fish, in an essay on Derrida and J. L. Austin, suggests that ordinary-language philosophy and deconstruc-

tion are both philosophies that emphasize "the necessity of interpretive work, the unavoidability of perspective, and the construction by acts of interpretation of that which supposedly grounds interpretation, intentions, characters, and pieces of the world" ("Compliments of the Author" 700). Derrida, writes Fish, "is very much a philosopher of common sense, that is, of the underlying assumptions and conventions within which the shape of common sense is specified and acquires its powerful force" (712). Even Staten, far more subtle in his attentiveness to the centrality of the "spatiotemporal phenomenon of language" in Wittgenstein and Derrida, tends to describe their projects in terms of the critique of "meaning" and "context": "We can see the convergence between Derrida and Wittgenstein in this notion of continually different contextualized meaning as the focus of investigation" (*Wittgenstein and Derrida* 25).

7. See also Wittgenstein's elaboration of this point in remark 665: "But—can't I say 'By "abracadabra" I mean toothache'? Of course I can; but this is a definition; not a description of what goes on in me when I utter the word."

8. Both John Ellis and Henry Staten have taken up the question of what *texts* Wittgenstein might be said to *read*. According to Ellis, "The implied text which Wittgenstein annotated was the very well-known kind of philosophical argument which begins from assertions about the nature of language and the meaning and structure of propositions, and then deduces from these premises a comprehensive set of conclusions about the whole range of philosophical problems; in other words, the implied text was the dominant strain of philosophical thought in England in the preceding quarter century" ("Wittgensteinian Thinking" 438–39). Staten agrees that Wittgenstein's "critical" method is "a way of attacking another style of language, the traditional style of philosophy" (*Wittgenstein and Derrida* 75). However Staten points out, importantly, that this critique is achieved not through implicit citations of texts, but through a critique of the very mechanism of "citation," a critique that can be performed with the help of any "sample" piece of language, referred to by the demonstrative pronoun "this," and with the help of quotation marks. See Staten's chapter "Wittgenstein Deconstructs," particularly 68, 86–88. It is in the latter, restricted sense of reading actual cited samples of language, and not in the more general sense of reading a tradition, that I will be referring to Wittgenstein's "practice of reading" throughout this essay.

9. Christopher Norris is one of the few critics to emphasize the centrality of "reading" and "writing" to Wittgenstein's investigations of language: "Problems about language—however illusory Wittgenstein considers them—are focused most sharply on the instances of *writing* and *reading*" (*The Deconstructive Turn* 50).

10. See Guetti, "Wittgenstein and Literary Theory—II," 68–70.

11. See also remarks 90–91, where Wittgenstein suggests that obscure expressions in our language may on occasion be resolved by substituting equivalent or analogous expressions, even though this process cannot be considered as a preliminary step toward some *final* or *comprehensive* analysis: "Our investigation is therefore a grammatical one. Such an investigation sheds light on our problem by clearing misunderstandings away. Misunderstandings concerning the use of words, caused, among other things, by certain analogies between the forms of expression in different regions of language.— Some of them can be removed by substituting one form of expression for another; this may be called an 'analysis' of our forms of expression, for the process is sometimes like one of taking a thing apart.

But now it may come to look as if there were something like a final analysis of our forms of language, and so a *single* completely resolved form of every expression."

12. Cf. Rodolphe Gasché, in "Deconstruction as Criticism": "It is true, that far from being an operation *in the limits* of the text, deconstruction proceeds *from and at the limit of* the text. But the outside of the text, that which limits its reflexive stratas and cognitive functions, is not its empirical and sensible outside. The outside of the text is precisely that which *in* the text makes self-reflexion possible and at the same time limits it" (182–83).

13. I believe that this tripartite division is roughly consistent with Samuel Wheeler's recent formulation of three "ways . . . deconstructive arguments proceed" ("Wittgenstein as Conservative Deconstructor" 243–44). The first way deconstruction operates, Wheeler argues, is "to show sys-

tematically that no dichotomy drawn in the way that a given dichotomy is will work,'' essentially because the two sides of the dichotomy ''presuppose'' one another conceptually. The second way is to ''undercut the dichotomy by showing that what the theory takes to be a natural division is in fact a product of other factors entirely. This shows that a position is ideological, not scientific — that, for instance, economic factors, gender practices, diseased spirits, Freudian phallism, or other extralogical factors actually motivate a dichotomy.'' Thirdly, ''the most characteristic strategy of deconstruction as practiced by Derrida is to discuss a particular text and show how that text undermines itself, in that the division that it is arguing for is implicitly denied in the text itself.'' Wheeler goes on to outline a ''fourth'' possible deconstructive strategy which he argues is Wittgensteinian in spirit, and which avoids what Wheeler takes to be the alternately totalizing and anarchic tendencies of Derridean deconstruction. As can be seen from my discussion above, I believe that the putative totalizing tendency of deconstruction (which would appear to undercut its anti-foundational claims) is more complicated than analytic philosophers have generally allowed. If deconstruction seems to depend on implicitly totalizing philosophical principles, then those principles are heterogeneous enough (historical, psychological, textual) to make the whole of Derrida's argument *less* totalizing than the sum of its parts.

14. Richard Rorty has been the most recent to label Derrida an ''ontotheologist.'' Rorty argues that Derrida's conception of language as essentially a ''trace'' betrays his ontological presuppositions. See ''Philosophy as a Kind of Writing'' (100) and ''Deconstruction and Circumvention'' (3, 9, 17). The same point was made earlier by Fredric Jameson in *The Prison-House of Language* (173–86). Jameson writes that ''Derrida's notion of the trace [looks] suspiciously like yet another ontological theory of the type it was initially designed to denounce'' (183). On the question of Derrida's supposed ''theology'' or ''negative theology,'' see Edward Said (''The Problem of Textuality'' 675), Rodolphe Gasché (''Deconstruction as Criticism'' 180), and Frank Lentricchia (*After the New Criticism* 171).

15. Why there should be ''no doubt'' about this sequence (whether logical or historical) is not clear, especially given Derrida's critique of the whole concept of ''deriving.'' I believe many of Derrida's claims about logical priority are finally best understood with the following passage, from ''Structure, Sign and Play,'' in mind: ''Play is always play of absence and presence, but *if it is to be thought radically*, play must be conceived of before the alternative of presence and absence. Being must be conceived as presence or absence on the basis of the possibility of play and not the other way around.'' (292; my emphasis). The crucial clause in this passage is clearly ''if it is to be thought radically.'' The passage thus is not the revelation of Derrida's own ontotheology (i.e., ''play'' as origin), but rather a statement about the necessity of reversing certain traditional conceptual sequences *if* one is to be able to think critically about the individual concepts that form the sequence. In order to reexamine certain philosophical themes, their *histories* must be reversed — especially when the traditional accounts of those histories have no logical necessity to them in the first place (see Derrida's critique of Jakobson and Halle, *Of Grammatology* 54). In this light, Derrida's more metaphysical sounding statements may appear as phases of his argument lodged between the moment of deconstruction-as-reversal and the moment of deconstruction-as-reinscription, or perhaps as reinscriptions that fail to get recognized as such (e.g., the ''writing'' to which logical priority is now attached is not only no longer the narrow, graphic ''writing'' of traditional philosophy, but no longer even a strictly delimitable phenomenon at all — in which case ''derivation'' would cease to have quite the threatening implication of *determination* that it previously had). All that having been said, I nonetheless wish to preserve the sense that something *along the lines of* a metaphysical or ontological claim is being made when Derrida says ''the problem of body and soul is no doubt derived from the problem of writing,'' since this *kind* of claim differs from other accounts he gives of the linkage of philosophical categories.

16. Cf. Samuel Wheeler (''Indeterminacy of French Interpretation'' 490): ''Derrida illustrates this kind of plague-like displacement [endless indeterminacy] in interpreting particular texts. A given assertion doesn't fit with other parts of a text, somehow. The interpretation of that part of a discourse then proceeds to unhinge the prior interpretation of the rest of the discourse.''

17. What distinguishes Derrida's own conception of patient, intrinsic, nonexclusive *reading* from the romantic ideal of structural totality and unity (of which structuralism is only the latest instance) is that Derrida's desire to *account* for all a text's details is not a desire to label them as either "consistent" or "aberrant." In Derrida's view, romantic organicism censures any textual details that cannot be incorporated functionally into the whole, while structuralism *finds ways* of incorporating all details into the whole. In either case, the consistent/aberrant distinction (a manifestation of the interior/exterior distinction) cannot account for the shifts among, tensions between, or anticipations of *different structures* in the same text. See "Force and Signification" (especially 24–27) and *Of Grammatology* (294–95).

18. On reinscription, see Derrida's comments in *Positions* (40–44), and Rodolphe Gasché's in "Deconstruction as Criticism" (192–93).

19. Samuel Wheeler ("Wittgenstein as Conservative Deconstructor" 258) writes: "Much depends here on just how central philosophy is to our forms of life, how much the tradition from Plato on has transformed things. This *may* be the central difference between Wittgenstein and Rorty, on the one hand, and Derrida and Heidegger on the other." As for the characterization of Wittgenstein as exemplary "clear thinker," cutting through philosophical tangles and sorting out muddled thinking about language, see John Ellis's "Wittgensteinian Thinking in Theory of Criticism." Ellis sees Wittgenstein's importance for literary theory lying in his "matchless analytic technique," and in his "alert[ness] to the logical traps in the language we use and in the hidden assumptions of our everyday attitudes" (451, 441). Ellis recommends that we apply Wittgenstein's "remarkably direct, clear as well as subtle" thinking to "the conceptual problems central to literary theory" (439). Although I share this view of Wittgenstein's clarity and subtlety, the invocation of Wittgenstein as clear thinker does not capture what is most distinctive about his work: the insistence on remaining *within* the varied and inconsistent pictures and expressions that our language gives to us, and a suspicion of the specular tradition in philosophy that pictures analysis as a technique of *penetration, clarification,* or *illumination*.

Works Cited

Altieri, Charles. "Wittgenstein on Consciousness and Language: A Challenge to Derridean Theory." *MLN* 91 (1976): 1397–1423.

Berkeley, Bishop George. *Three Dialogues between Hylas and Philonous. The Works of George Berkeley*. Vol. 1. Ed. Alexander Campbell Fraser. Oxford: Clarendon, 1871.

Cavell, Stanley. "Politics as Opposed to What?" *Critical Inquiry* 9 (1982): 157–78.

Culler, Johnathan. "Convention and Meaning: Derrida and Austin." *New Literary History* 13 (1981): 15–30.

Derrida, Jacques. *Dissemination*. Trans. Barbara Johnson. Chicago: U of Chicago P, 1981.

———. "Force and Signification." 1965. In *Writing and Difference*. 3–30.

———. *Margins of Philosophy*. Trans. Alan Bass. Chicago: U of Chicago P, 1982.

———. *Of Grammatology*. 1967. Trans. Gayatri Chakravorty Spivak. Baltimore: Johns Hopkins UP, 1976.

———. "Plato's Pharmacy." 1972. In *Dissemination*. 61– 171.

———. "Signature Event Context." 1977. In *Margins of Philosophy*. 307–30.

———. "Structure, Sign, and Play in the Discourse of the Human Sciences." 1967. In *Writing and Difference*. 278–94.

———. "Violence and Metaphysics: An Essay on the Thought of Emmanuel Levinas." 1964. In *Writing and Difference*. 79–153.

———. "White Mythology: Metaphor in the Text of Philosophy." 1974. In *Margins of Philosophy*. 207–72.

———. *Writing and Difference*. 1967. Trans. Alan Bass. Chicago: U of Chicago P, 1978.

Ellis, John M.. "Wittgensteinian Thinking in Theory of Criticism." *New Literary History* 12 (1981): 437–52.

Fish, Stanley. "With the Compliments of the Author: Reflections on Austin and Derrida." *Critical Inquiry* 8 (1982): 693–721.

Gasché, Rodolphe. "Deconstruction as Criticism." *Glyph* 6 (1979): 177–215.

Guetti, James. "Wittgenstein and Literary Theory—I." *Raritan* 4, No. 2 (1984): 67–84.

———. "Wittgenstein and Literary Theory—II." *Raritan* 4, No. 3 (1985): 66–84.

Heidegger, Martin. "Building Dwelling Thinking." In *Poetry, Language, Thought.* Trans. Albert Hofstadter. New York: Harper & Row (Harper Colophon), 1971. 143–61.

Jameson, Fredric. *The Prison-House of Language: A Critical Account of Structuralism and Russian Formalism.* Princeton, N.J.: Princeton UP, 1972.

Lentricchia, Frank. *After the New Criticism.* Chicago: U of Chicago P, 1980.

Norris, Christopher. *Deconstruction: Theory and Practice.* New York: Methuen, 1982.

———. *The Deconstructive Turn: Essays in the Rhetoric of Philosophy.* New York: Methuen, 1983.

Plato. *Phaedrus.* Trans. and intro. R. Hackforth. New York: Cambridge UP, 1952.

Rorty, Richard. "Philosophy as a Kind of Writing." In *Consequences of Pragmatism: Essays 1972–1980.* Minneapolis: U of Minnesota P, 1982. 90–109.

———. "Deconstruction and Circumvention." *Critical Inquiry* 11 (1984): 1–21.

Said, Edward. "The Problem of Textuality: Two Exemplary Positions." *Critical Inquiry* 4 (1978): 673–714.

Staten, Henry. *Wittgenstein and Derrida.* Lincoln: U of Nebraska P, 1984.

Wheeler, Samuel C. III. "Indeterminacy of French Interpretation: Derrida and Davidson." In *Truth and Interpretation: Perspectives on the Philosophy of Donald Davidson.* Ed. Ernest LePore. Oxford: Basil Blackwell, 1986. 477–94.

———. "Wittgenstein as Conservative Deconstructor." *New Literary History* 19 (1988): 239–58.

Wittgenstein, Ludwig. 1958. *The Blue and Brown Books.* Oxford: Basil Blackwell, 1969.

———. *Philosophical Investigations.* 1953. Trans. G. E. M. Anscombe. Oxford: Basil Blackwell, 1967.

8

Text Acts: Recasting Performatives with Wittgenstein and Derrida

Steven Winspur

Although the Derrida-Searle debate underscored a key distinction between Continental perspectives on the linguistic sign and those of contemporary Anglo-American philosophy (a distinction hinging on the importance one grants to speakers' intentions),[1] one can nevertheless discern traces of the common horizon where these perspectives would converge. Within the Anglo-American tradition this horizon was already visible in J. L. Austin's break with British empiricist thought by claiming that utterances should not be viewed primarily as descriptions. "It was for too long the assumption of philosophers that the business of a 'statement' can only be to 'describe' some state of affairs," wrote Austin on the first page of his epoch-making *How to Do Things with Words*. By shifting the focus away from Russellian descriptions of sense-data and toward the various social uses to which speech is put, Austin's first revolution was to discard most mental descriptions as irrelevant.[2] Speech acts such as promising, stipulating, or apologizing are not descriptions of mysteriously " 'inward and spiritual act[s]' " (Austin 9), but rather the performance of scenarios of social responsibility that are regulated by a complex system of public rules.

Working within a different, nonempiricist, framework, Jacques Derrida approaches the problem of how statements get their meaning in a way similar to Austin's. The shift of focus that Derrida inaugurates also pulls us away from a theory of descriptions—namely, Husserl's phenomenology[3]—and in so doing it too accentuates the conventionalized rules of public language that dissolve the false immediacy and apparent priority of the "inward and spiritual act" of thought (to use Austin's terms).

Despite the fact that Derrida criticizes Austin's project in his article "Signature Event Context," the criticism is not an out-and-out rejection. Instead, Derrida focuses on the presupposition of consciousness-to-oneself in the act of speaking that still seems to haunt the English philosopher. The presupposition crops up, for instance, in Austin's stipulation that performative utterances must always be reducible to statements in the first person and the indicative mood, so that they reveal the "utterance-*origin*" apparently lying behind performatives, an origin hinted at by the pronoun I (60–61). This stipulation effectively conflates the *force* of the performative with *apparently self-conscious acts of utterance*, so that performative force seems to be "tethered," as Austin puts it (61), to the speaker's awareness of her own "serious" intentions at the moment of speaking. For instance, if I tell someone "I bet you I'm right!" the strength of my bet (or what makes it a bet rather than a mere statement of belief) apparently depends on the self-conscious seriousness of my statement (I don't make bets lightly but instead weigh up the consequences of possibly being mistaken before I venture to put my word on the line). In short, all this serious deliberation seems to be wrapped up in my apparently self-reflexive use of the present tense of the indicative accompanied by the pronoun I: "I bet you now, in this very moment of uttering the phrase on which I'm staking my life (or at least some of my money), that I'm right." There are, however, major flaws in this Austinian view of how performatives are tethered to their utterance origin. First, the reflexivity entailed by using the first-person pronoun and the present tense of the indicative is an illusory one since there is a logical distinction between the grammatical subject of a statement (the word "I" in "I bet") and the speaking subject who utters the statement. To utter "I bet you I'm right" does not in fact accomplish a self-reflexive act in which the grammatical "I" mirrors the force of the speaking "I." The two I's are structurally distinct and hence the two ends in the circle of self-reference can never meet. As Derrida goes on to point out, the very status of the speaking subject becomes impossible to determine in many performatives where the force of the utterance simply cannot be pinned down to an authority that the speaker is alone supposed to possess ("Limited Inc abc" 216). What give bets their authority, then, is not so much their utterers as what Derrida calls "societies which are (more or less) anonymous, with limited responsibility or liability" (216)—that is, forms of language use that transcend their users (whether these be horse-betting addicts or merely speakers saying "I bet you . . . "), and yet whose power depends on these users' participating unwittingly in a "Limited Inc." betting company that is constituted by the specific rules and power relations of this performative. It is a company (or *société*—the French word conveying the important parallel between social groups and financial ones) since no one person lies at the root of its power, and those who invest in the company (those who bet, that is) each have limited liability in case their bets misfire. Put simply, our membership in this betting company does not entail our accepting full responsibility for betting according to the rules, since the rules, and hence their authority, are not totally ours, with the result that we can in some instances cheat when we bet. It is the very institution of the betting company (with its limited liability and diffuse network of authority) that enables us to do this, and not some "flaw" in human nature or in our subjective intentions. Consequently, we begin to see why a rigorous speech-act theory will search for performative force not in the depths of intentionality (as Searle tries to do) nor in a putative "utterance-*origin*" (as proposed by Austin), but rather in the very structures of convention that make up the performative contracts in which we engage.

The second flaw in Austin's account, and to which Derrida devotes most of his attention in "Signature Event Context," is the notion of seriousness. How can our seriousness be guaranteed (so that performatives can be protected from "misuse") and indeed are performatives always serious, for haven't we just seen how the speech act of betting *lends itself* to cheating? (Moreover, don't we bet in haste, for example, without seriously pondering our act, or even in jest, and yet still live up to the rules of betting?) When Austin anchors his entire notion of performatives on their serious use, or on what he calls "ordinary circumstances" (22), but then fails to seal this off completely from nonserious uses, it is clear that the purely *moral* opposition between the serious and the nonserious covers up major difficulties.[4] For does he not admit that "as *utterances* our performatives are . . . heir to certain . . . kinds of ill which infect *all* utterances" (21), namely, the possibility of being used ironically or nonseriously? Far from making this "ill" seem independent of performatives, Austin's admission is a telling one since it hints at a fundamental problem in his argument: namely, that it is in the very nature of the theory of performatives to bring into question the hierarchy of seriousness versus nonseriousness (Felman 37–40). As if aware of this problem, Austin makes up his own metaphor for nonserious performatives: "the *etiolations* of language" (22)—a figurative term whose moral force is plain (since an etiolated plant, deprived of sunlight, is one whose life can only be seen as "deformed" or morally derivative of "normal, healthy" plant life).

The Derrida-Searle debate that followed the former's article "Signature Event Context" unfortunately obscured the common ground shared by Austin's initial theory and by Derrida's critique. For by bolstering Austin's criterion of seriousness with a full-blown theory of how speakers are aware of their intentions ("Reiterating the Differences"), John Searle subtly shifted the focus of Austin's argument. Instead of continuing Austin's attacks against the mentalist tradition in philosophy and against the language-as-description theory, Searle slotted Austin back into this traditional framework.[5] The unfortunate effect of this shift of emphasis has been a general misunderstanding of the entire debate between Derrideans and Austinians. On the one hand, followers of Searle's critique of Derrida have failed to see the radical strain common to Austin and Derrida's arguments (e.g., Altieri 25–39), while on the other hand, those readers of Derrida who accept Searle's defense of Austin as an adequate representation of the latter's theory run the risk of cutting themselves off, as Searle himself does, from the lessons of the initial debate. Searle's defense of Austin is therefore doubly misleading. First, it plasters over some of the real issues on which speech-act theory rests: ethical and political questions relating to how speakers in fact get their perlocutionary force or how certain statements acquire seriousness. Second, it obscures the central thrust of Austin's initial argument—an attempt to get beyond the two "fetishes" of truth-falsity and value-fact that have lent credence to the misleading view of language as being essentially descriptive (Austin 139–47).

There is, then, an important way in which the radical core of Austin's theory can actually be salvaged by Derrida's critique. Indeed, it could emerge even stronger from the skirmish since, by revealing the dependence of performatives on *"a general theory of action"* and on "predicates [that are] *graphematic in general"* ("Signature Event Context" 186, 187), Derrida hints at an alternative explanation of performative force. Such an alternative would develop Derrida's claim that performatives function essentially as quotations of preestablished formulas ("Signature Event Context" 191–92) by demonstrating the links between such formulas and patterns of human activity.

This, at any rate, is the point I wish to prove in the following pages. My first step toward resituating Austin's theory will be to compare it to the later work of Ludwig Wittgenstein, who also sought to wrest philosophy away from an oversimplified notion of language as description. Indeed, Austin's initial attack against the assumption "that the business of a 'statement' can only be to 'describe' some state of affairs" bears a striking resemblance to the following observation near the beginning of Wittgenstein's *Philosophical Investigations* (first published in 1953, two years prior to Austin's William James Lectures, which were later reprinted as *How to Do Things with Words*):

> But how many kinds of sentence are there? Say assertion, question, and command?—There are *countless* kinds: countless different kinds of use of what we call "symbols," "words," "sentences." And this multiplicity is not something fixed, given once for all; but new types of language, new language-games, as we may say, come into existence. . . .
> Here the term "language-*game*" is meant to bring into prominence the fact that the *speaking* of language is part of an activity, or of a form of life. (remark 23).[6]

In the second section of my essay I shall use insights from Wittgenstein and Derrida to demonstrate the textuality implicit in every speech act. The influence of literary performatives on this underlying textual network will be examined in my concluding section.

I. Positive Deconstruction

Investigations in the philosophy of language (whether conducted by Austin, Wittgenstein, or Searle) generally aim at explaining how sentences function "in real life" (Searle, "Reiterating the Differences" 205). Invoking reality cuts two ways, however. For whereas Wittgenstein proposes the notion of a "form of life" only to insist that there exist an indefinite number of *distinct* forms of life,[7] Austin and Searle invoke real life in order to legislate between primary uses of performatives (e.g., in law courts) and secondary uses (e.g., on a theatrical stage).[8] "Real life" for the last two writers thus becomes a normative concept (the law courts are serious stages whereas theaters are not), and as such it exposes Austin and Searle to the criticism that their theories rest on an ideological view of real life rather than on a thorough analysis of the power structures and contradictions that together make up what is "real."[9]

By contrast, the main effect of Wittgenstein's arguments is to tear philosophy away from oversimplified models of language and life. Wittgenstein's premise is not that the normative term "reality" needs a complex *explanation* but rather that all forms of living are traversed by contradictions, and that when these plague our thinking the only cure is to rediscover our peace with the world. "The real discovery is the one that makes me capable of stopping doing philosophy when I want to," he writes. " — The one that gives philosophy peace, so that it is no longer tormented by questions that bring *itself* into question" (remark 133). The philosophy of language, for Wittgenstein, is consequently an enterprise with a fundamentally *ethical* goal. It does not set out to explain all possible language usage,[10] but instead helps us, language's users, to stop bumping our heads against problems that our own language creates (remark 119). The issue at stake is our own happiness-through-living, or striking the proper balance between ourselves and our speech acts, so that we reach a sort of Aristotelian *eudaimoneia* (or happiness-in-act) with our words (and therefore with ourselves).[11] Hence the "therapeutic" simile that Wittgenstein repeatedly draws in connection with his writings. "There is not *a* philosophical method," he remarks, "though there are indeed methods, like different therapies" (remark 133). And elsewhere: "The philosopher's treatment of a question is like the treatment of an illness" (remark 255, cf. remark 593).

One cause of such ailments is a poor philosophical diet (that is, basing our views of language on too narrow a range of illustrative examples; see remark 593). In these cases the best form of treatment is to vary the diet — to broaden the realm of examples and counterexamples (and view words not only as names but also as commands, wishes, etc.; remarks 11–14, 23–24) so that the overdependence on misleading illustrations dissolves itself. As Kevin Mulligan has shown, there is a striking parallel between this technique of Wittgenstein's and Derrida's overall strategy of pulling us away from our narrow view of language as speech so that we confront hitherto ignored (or at least marginalized) types of sign use (Mulligan 62; cf. Staten). For Derrida's deconstructions are not mere *negations* of philosophical myths (phonocentrism, presence, and so on); instead, traditional examples of speaking (whether in Saussure's linguistics, Husserl's phenomenology, or Plato's epistemology) are shown to depend for their meaning on the concept of an essentially nonspoken trace with its associated space of writing. The philosophical texts Derrida deconstructs are thus shown to suffer from an internal strain or ailment — whereby the primacy of traces, as Derrida shows in *Of Grammatology*, is repressed by the apparently self-evident equation between thinking and talking. The self-evidence of this equation is in fact merely a symptom of its circularity: thinking is defined as speaking (silently) to oneself, while speaking (aloud) to someone is defined as communicating one's thoughts. Deconstructing this vicious circle means showing the damage it causes whenever we try to explain acts of thought and speech. For as long as we hold on to the equation we just keep banging our heads against the limits it imposes on us.[12]

Wittgenstein's own technique of "show[ing] the fly the way out of [this logocentric] fly-bottle" (remark 309) is to let the speech-thought model reveal its inherent ridiculousness. Thus we find him engaged in the following sparring match:

"The purpose of a language is to express thoughts."—So presumably the purpose of every sentence is to express a thought. Then what thought is expressed, for example, by the sentence "It's raining"?—(remark 501)

Here the traditional notion of thought (as indicated by the quotation marks around the first statement) is pushed to its logical conclusion: meaningful words get their meaning from the ideas they express. This conclusion is then deflated by the simplicity of the final example—a statement whose meaning depends solely on its conventionalized use in certain contexts, and which, therefore, needs no further grounding in a hypothetical realm of "thought." Philosophical ailments are not easily cured, however, and even when confronted by our own nonsense we are loath to give it up: "But isn't it our *meaning* it that gives sense to the sentence?" remarks Wittgenstein's imaginary opponent (remark 358). He goes on: "And 'meaning it' is something in the sphere of the mind. But it is also something private!" (remark 358). Wittgenstein's rejoinder is both sympathetic and ironic (his sympathy is provoked by the extent of our philosophical ailment, while his irony cuts to the core of the problem): "How could this seem ludicrous? [I.e., Yes, indeed, isn't it *natural* to say that meaning is private! And yet such a view is ludicrous since most meanings are *publicly* constituted rules; remarks 243, 692, p. 218.] It is, as it were, a dream of our language" (remark 358). In other words, postulating a private realm of meaning is not something we as individuals dream up in order to explain language to ourselves; it is a dream already mapped out for us by the confusions inherent in language itself.[13]

Consequently, the philosophical treatment of these confusions is a long, painstaking endeavor. Every twisted strand in our language must be retraced so that the snarls can be undone. Certain metaphors must be shown to be misleading, for instance, the phrase "the speed of thought": "Suppose we think while we talk or write . . . we shall not in general say that we think quicker than we talk; the thought seems *not to be separate from the expression*. On the other hand, however, one does speak of the speed of thought" (remark 318). In addition, certain "evident" truths about speech and thought have to be challenged:

"Can one think without speaking?" — And what is *thinking?* Well, don't you ever think? Can't you observe yourself and see what is going on? It should be quite simple. (remark 327)

But the simplicity of this experiment covers up a methodological flaw: one cannot establish criteria for defining public concepts such as meaning, speech, or thought on the basis of essentially private introspection: "If I know it only from my own case, then I know only what *I* call that, not what anyone else does." (remark 347, cf. remark 314). Moreover, what instructions must we follow in order to observe our thoughts (for if it is indeed a bona fide experiment, then its steps should be clear enough for everyone to follow and its results publicly verifiable; remark 380)?[14] Gradually, through this long process of conceptual teasing we are pulled away from our initial speech model of thought — "Isn't the thinking subject in the last resort mere superstition?" Wittgenstein had asked earlier (*Notebooks* 80) — and led to acknowledge the validity of other models (for instance, reading, playing music, or following mathematical rules).[15] These models help us to make "a radical break with the idea that language always functions in one way, always serves the same purpose: to convey thoughts" (remark 304), and as a result we overcome the tensions between our linguistic capabilities (or what we can already *do* with our language) and our metalinguistic knowledge (that is, our anguished attempts at *explaining* in a traditional philosophical manner how language works; see Ryle 9–11).

Wittgensteinian therapy consists, then, of letting certain problematic views of language work themselves out of our system, so to speak. The conceptual malady is pinpointed, then allowed to spread until the point where it begins to show its own weakness and thus lose its grip on our thinking, or as Wittgenstein put it: "In philosophizing we may not *terminate* a disease of thought. It must run its natural course, and *slow* cure is all important" (*Zettel* 382). Deconstruction is a most appropriate term here since what both Wittgenstein and Derrida do is let certain statements or texts reveal their own tensions, allow these tensions to increase and hence "run their natural course" until the ailment begins to pass.[16] What is important is that the therapeutic model behind such strategies is not aimed at giving us the so-called correct view of language,[17] but rather at restoring equilibrium to troubled language users.

In an obvious way the *Philosophical Investigations* are Wittgenstein's own self-therapy,[18] but in a less obvious way they are also our own therapy since the "Ludwig Wittgenstein" we read is not so much a troubled individual as a battleground for conflicting notions that trouble us all. Or, as he put himself, "I ought to be no more than a mirror, in which my reader can see his own thinking with all its deformities so that, helped in this way, he can put it right" (*Culture and Value* 18). The question now arises, of course, "How does language appear to us *after* we have undergone deconstructive treatment?"

II. Acts, Traces, and Texts

When Wittgenstein examines reading as an alternative thought model to speaking he discovers two things. First, from the point of view of what the reader *feels*, there is "not any one feature that occurs in all cases of reading" (*Philosophical Investigations*, remark 168). In other words, if we look at reading in order to find criteria for defining "thoughtful activity" we shall not find such criteria in the realm of readers' inner experiences. The second discovery is that such criteria *are* present in the reader's ability to explain what she is doing, and, furthermore, to quote from the text in front of her, to discuss the text, fill it out, build on it, and so on. By doing these things she proves that she can read "thoughtfully." Consequently, thought appears not as a mysteriously inner process that would somehow accompany publicly learned actions (such as reading), but simply as the ability to do such actions according to the rules by which we learn them. Just as our words get their meaning by being used in accordance with the rules of grammar (and not by some shadowy accompaniment of thoughts; see remark 329), so our behavior gets its meaning simply from our following certain cultural rules that we have also come to learn. "Nothing is more wrong-headed than calling meaning a mental activity," we read in the *Investigations*. "(It would also be possible to speak of an activity of butter when it rises in price . . .)" (remark 693).

Wittgenstein's other alternative thought models underline this primacy of rule-governed action over private mental life. Doing sums in arithmetic, or other mathematical problems, means that one has mastered a set of rules—in other words, one is not merely repeating *examples* of addition that one has learned previously (e.g., $2 + 3 = 5$), but one has learned to apply the principles of arithmetic (addition, subtraction, and so on) so as to generate sums that one has not done before. Playing music similarly entails our combining notes in accordance with the rules of harmony and, if we are good musicians, the creation of new note combinations that extend or even modify these rules.

Two important consequences arise from all this. First, what is traditionally called "thought" is in fact constituted by purposeful actions—a thoughtful statement, a profound insight in mathematics, or an inspiring musical phrase all appear as such because they affect the lives of their respective listeners and change the way these listeners *do* things (math, music, or whatever). Even statements that are not radically innovative derive their meaningfulness from the pragmatic goals they accomplish: most of everyday conversation is directed to specific aims, as are most applications of arithmetic, and the mass transmission of music (in cars, stores, and elsewhere) is also done for its effects on the audience-as-consumer. In other words, what appear basic in all these instances of language use are patterns of human activity that ground the appropriateness of each particular exchange of signs. Or, as Wittgenstein put it, "It is not a kind of *seeing* on our part [that is conveyed whenever we communicate]; it is our *acting* which lies at the bottom of the language-game" (*On Certainty* 204; cf. 110). The second consequence of Wittgenstein's shift of focus has a direct bearing on the theory of performatives. Given that language use is now situated squarely within the context of a general theory of action, whereby human life is defined in an Aristotelian fashion as the fabric of a person's acts and purposes,[19] then so-called speech acts are no different in kind from other language uses,[20] nor are they distinct in essence from the other acts that make up a person's life.

The shift that takes place, then, when we move from Searle's speech-act theory to a Wittgensteinian one is the replacement of the paradigmatic concepts of speaking and thinking by those of action and rule. What sort of rules emerge from Wittgenstein's discussion? The most common sort he examines is the rule that allows me to continue a series (whether of numbers, musical notes, or else a series of propositions in a text that I'm reading; see *Philosophical Investigations*, remarks 156–71, 692–93; *Zettel* 90–98). Here the rule boils down to the power of inferring from a set of examples (e.g., $2 + 3 = 5$ and $7 + 1 = 8$) certain principles that allow us to generate other propositions adhering to the same principles. In other words, learning a rule allows us to construct statements that all carry within them a trace of the rule in question, and whose authority is guaranteed by this trace. It is therefore clear why performative utterances, as Derrida points out in "Signature Event Context" (179–80), rest on the repetition of some coded formula (for instance, "I pronounce you man and wife") since it is this repetition that unveils the basic rule structure underlying all utterances. The force of the performative resides not in its being stated with the proper intentions but rather in its being used according to the rules attached to it. When a dignitary christens a ship or a student promises to hand in a paper the next day or a county clerk pronounces a couple "man and wife," they all do so by certain "powers," not "invested in them" as individuals but invested in their respective *social* roles (dignitaries play the role of baptizing ships, students of living up to their promises, county clerks of marrying couples). As Barbara Johnson has shown, the role-playing nature of performatives undermines Austin and Searle's exclusion of theatrical performatives as "parasitic" upon "real" ones since *all* performatives turn out to be essentially theatrical — as one might have already guessed from the terms "speech *act*" and "performance" (60–66).

A further consequence of this inbuilt theatricality is that the formulas used in performatives ("I pronounce you man and wife," etc.) are essentially scripts, or short texts, quoted by their speakers, and as such their existence is logically independent of each actual utterance that invokes them. Derrida underlines this point by arguing that the performative's utterability depends on its iterability ("Signature Event Context" 180), and in his commentary on this argument John Llewelyn coins the term "paracitation" to show the necessary link between the performative's status as a quotation and its consequent tendency to be mimicked, cited, and generally removed from an apparently original or "proper" use (60). There can be no such thing as a one-off speech act since for such acts to occur at all they must play out a previously coded script. It is *because* performatives are already textual that they give rise to this apparently parasitic (but in fact inevitable) paracitation. It is also because of their textual nature that performatives can only function in front of an audience—there can be no such thing as a private speech act (as Wittgenstein conclusively demonstrated: *Philosophical Investigations*, remarks 267–75) because the effect of the act (which determines whether the act has indeed come off) is always on the side of its receiver (or reader) and not on the side of the utterer. The text act relies therefore on potential readers for its completion and interpretation.

When we place these considerations in the context of the general theory of life-as-action outlined earlier the reader's role in activating performative force becomes central. For our everyday actions acquire their meaning not from our private decisions to do them but rather from their impact on, and interconnections with, other people's acts, as well as other acts we ourselves did previously. That is why we are often better placed to understand what we do when we stand outside ourselves, so to speak, and judge the effects our actions have had on others. Family interactions illustrate this point well since very often how we *intend* to help our children or spouses is thwarted by what our initially helpful act actually achieves. It is only by putting ourselves in the audience's position, and interpreting our act from the outside, that we can acknowledge this dissonance and hence resolve the family tension. When read in this way our acts often show up patterns of contradiction (between our goals—say, helping one's child—and our attempts at reaching them), and sometimes these contradictions rock the very foundations of the socially created roles that we take over in our speech acts: for instance when we promise our children that we will be home early (to help take care of them) but extra work, which we have to do in order to pay for their care, prevents us from living up to our word. Pierre Bourdieu has shown to what extent the power structures in society underlie the effectiveness of almost every type of speech act—it becomes more difficult to "promise," for instance, if one is unemployed. Reading performatives consequently entails reading the tensions and contradictions that underlie their usage, to the point where such a study becomes fundamentally *ethical*, in an updated Aristotelian sense. For whereas classical ethics elaborated its system of actions, means, and goals in order to teach people "the good life," or happiness-through-acts, it is one of the more obvious features of the modern world that no theory of *eudaimonia* is around to tell us how to bring together an overarching notion of the Good with our multifarious speech-act roles (whereby we are often simultaneously children-to-our-parents, parents-to-our-children, spouses, employers and employees).[21]

There are, nevertheless, some solutions to this problem. Wittgenstein's therapeutic treatment of certain discourse ailments is one; another is the reading of poetry. It is to this last and especially powerful form of text act that I now turn.

III. Textual Power

Since romanticism, if not before, the reading of poetry has been modeled on a form of seeing (as underscored by the ubiquitous expression "poetic image").[22] By applying to poetry Wittgenstein's important claim that understanding a language game is "not a kind of *seeing* on our part [but discovering a form of] *acting*, which lies at the bottom of the language-game" (*On Certainty* 204), we are better able to explain poems that are quite obviously not descriptive in nature.[23] Moreover, by jettisoning image-based theories of poetry, which must always reduce a poem's verbal innovations to *previously* coded ways of seeing (and thus suppress the force of the text's innovations), we can understand how certain poems *question* traditional codes of seeing and of authority. In short, by viewing certain poems as text acts we will be able to better appreciate both their aesthetic and their ethical power.

My first example is the opening poem to Stéphane Mallarmé's major collection *Poésies*, itself entitled "Salut" (Greeting or Good health):

> Rien, cette écume, vierge vers
> A ne désigner que la coupe;
> Telle loin se noie une troupe
> De sirènes mainte à l'envers.
>
> Nous naviguons, ô mes divers
> Amis, moi déjà sur la poupe
> Vous l'avant fastueux qui coupe
> Le flot de foudres et d'hivers;
>
> Une ivresse belle m'engage
> Sans craindre même son tangage
> De porter debout ce salut
>
> Solitude, récif, étoile
> A n'importe ce qui valut
> Le blanc souci de notre toile. (27)

> (Nothing, this foam, virgin verse
> To designate naught but the cup;
> Thus far-off drowns a troop
> Of sirens many upside down.
>
> We navigate, O my diverse
> Friends, I already on the stern
> You the festive prow that cuts
> The wave of lightnings and winters;
>
> A beautiful drunkenness incites me
> Without fearing even its rocking
> To carry erect this greeting [or toast, or health]
>
> Solitude, reef, star
> To whatever was worth [the effort of]
> The white care of our [sail-]cloth.)[24]

The sonnet's performative status is hinted at by the fact that both its title and the event mentioned in the first tercet — proposing a toast — are themselves speech acts. They are not necessarily the same speech act, however, since the exclamation "*Salut!*" will in some contexts wish us good health but in others it will simply welcome us. This performative ambiguity is important since the poem is not the mere recording of one particular speech act (namely, the actual toast that was this poem read out by Mallarmé on February 15, 1893, during the banquet honoring the Symbolist literary review *La Plume*).[25] Instead, the poem celebrates the performative force inherent in every speech act, as the poem's last two stanzas point out. The salutation is addressed to "whatever" has given rise to the "care," time, and effort that go into any poem's fabrication (whose metonymic "white" page is conjoined in the final line with the metaphoric "sail" of poetic voyages). It is the translation of circumstance into text act that is commemorated here — a translation lying at the heart of so many of Mallarmé's apparently "circumstantial" poems (the "Hommages et Tombeaux," for instance, or the "Vers de circonstance"). The circumstance is not a referential hindrance to the creation of "pure poetry," a hindrance from which the latter has to escape;[26] on the contrary, because of their essentially pragmatic nature, making them the meeting point of specific actions and goals in the public world, circumstances carry within themselves the very trace of public action on which poetic performativity depends. In short, with Mallarmé we move from an expression theory of literature to an action theory, or, as he put, "Your act is always put to paper; for meditating without tracing merely vanishes." (369, cf. Johnson 58).

"Salut" clearly points to this shift from expression to action. Both the narrator and we, the readers, are bound up by the power of the text act ("A beautiful drunkenness incites me . . . "), so that we are carried along by the very act of salutation, which merely serves to underscore the nature of illocutionary commitment. For the poem does not *express* a Mallarméan wish; rather the narrator is buoyed up by the act of well-wishing, as we are also: "We navigate, O my diverse / Friends [i.e., not merely Mallarmé's actual audience one February evening in 1893 but all future readers of the poem, from *diverse* ages and backgrounds], I already on the stern / You the festive prow that cuts / The wave . . ." In other words, poetry's standard romantic voyage to imaginary, private worlds has here been rerouted for the reader and is now afloat on the giddy seas of public discourse. Consequently, the title of Mallarmé's poem, beckoning us into his collected works, is not really a prefatory "Welcome" from the author, but rather poetry's own salutation for every reader *and writer* who happens to stumble upon its performative force. It is the "good health" (or *salut*, as a noun, that the title proposes) performatively bestowed on us by poetry's own salutation — *salus*. The Latin word *salus* pinpoints what is at stake here, for it is not some vague ideal of salvation that is being offered by the text, but rather the *continuation of life* (*salus*'s definition) that comes through our *actions* with words.

Hence the characterization of poetry's power as nonconstative: it is a form of discourse that has "nothing" to report ("Nothing, this foam, virgin verse") but much to accomplish. To begin with, it must dispense with the purely descriptive thematics of earlier romanticism: "Thus far-off drowns a troop / Of sirens many upside down." Sinking the sirens and their legendary song is not just minor poetic vengeance; it short-circuits an entire expressive theory of poetry. Moreover, by refusing to state anything except its own performative function and effect ("A beautiful drunkenness incites me . . . To carry erect this greeting"), the poem sets itself up as a model (or "star" — line 12) that guides us, its readers, toward solving specific problems in our own lives. "Salut" 's own reshuffling of the themes and goals of romanticism in turn prompts us to reorganize the model text acts to which we previously clung, with the result that our lives (our pattern of actions and goals) are radically changed.

My final example of such ethical change through the power of textuality is an extract from Lautréamont's *Les Chants de Maldoror* (The songs of Maldoror).[27] This work openly presents itself as an antidote for curing the cultural damage of romanticism, as one can tell from the following aside to the reader that occurs in the middle of the fifth canto:

> Puisque la répulsion instinctive, qui s'était déclarée dès les premières pages [of the *Chants*] a notablement diminué de profondeur, en raison inverse de l'application à la lecture, comme un furoncle qu'on incise, il faut espérer, quoique ta tête soit encore malade, que ta guérison ne tardera certainement pas à rentrer dans sa dernière période. Pour moi, il est indubitable que tu vogues déjà en pleine convalescence. (189)

> (Since the instinctive repulsion that had announced itself from the outset [of the *Chants*] has notably diminished in intensity, in inverse proportion to your applying yourself to your reading, like a boil that has been cut out, we must hope, despite the fact that your head is still sick, that your healing will not slow down before entering its final phase. As for me, it is beyond question that you are already forging ahead in complete convalescence.)

Lautréamont sets out to heal his readers from ailments they have received at the hands of such writers as Hugo, Lamartine, and Vigny. He succeeds in correcting his readers by correcting these intertexts with which they were raised. An example of such reform occurs in the twelfth stanza of the first canto of the *Chants* where we find a nocturnal graveyard scene. The book's hero, Maldoror, is about to address a gravedigger who is suffering, like *Maldoror*'s readers, from romantic malady. "Isn't it true, gravedigger, that you will want to talk to me?" asks Maldoror, to which the other replies: "Friend, it is impossible for me to exchange ideas with you. . . . I have to finish digging this grave, with my tireless spade, so that it will be ready tomorrow morning. In order to do serious work one mustn't do two things at once."[28] But then the gravedigger does begin to talk, and talk interminably as if to an analyst, so that little by little his own contradictions become apparent. "Digging a ditch often surpasses our natural strength," he bemoans, and then continues:

Comment veux-tu, étranger, que la pioche remue cette terre . . . lorsque celui qui tient la pioche, de ses tremblantes mains, après avoir toute la journée palpé convulsivement les joues des anciens vivants qui rentrent dans son royaume, voit, le soir, devant lui, écrit en lettres de flammes, sur chaque croix de bois, l'énoncé du problème effrayant que l'humanité n'a pas encore résolu: la mortalité ou l'immortalité de l'âme. Le créateur de l'univers, je lui ai toujours conservé mon amour; mais si, après la mort, nous ne devons plus exister, pourquoi vois-je, la plupart des nuits, chaque tombe s'ouvrir, et leurs habitants soulever doucement les couvercles de plomb, pour aller respirer l'air frais. (69–71)

(Stranger, how can my pickax possibly turn over this earth . . . when the one holding the pickax in his quivering hands, after convulsively touching the cheeks of the once living bodies that are returning to his kingdom, sees before him in the evening, written in flaming letters upon each wooden cross, the statement of the terrifying problem that humanity has not yet resolved: the mortality or immortality of the soul. For the Creator of the universe I've always kept a special affection; but if, after death, we are no longer supposed to live, why can I see almost every night each grave opening up and its inhabitants gently lifting up the leadened coffin lids so as to go and breathe in the fresh air.)

As a solution to this ethical dilemma (for how indeed could a gravedigger justify his own occupation if he suspected that you can't keep bodies in the ground?) we have Maldoror's response:

Arrête-toi dans ton travail. L'émotion t'enlève tes forces; tu me parais faible comme le roseau; ce serait une grande folie de continuer. Je suis fort; je vais prendre ta place. Toi, mets-toi à l'écart. (71)

(Stop your work. Your emotion is sapping you of your strength; you seem to me to be weak like the reed; it would be madness to go on like this. I'm strong; I'm going to take your place. You, stand over there to one side.)

Maldoror tells the poor man to literally step aside from the contradiction that is ruining his life: "Stop digging for a moment and listen!" he says in effect. "Follow your own maxim that 'in order to do serious work one mustn't do two things at once'—namely, your digging and your metaphysical speculations." *Too* much nocturnal thinking has turned the poor gravedigger into a perfect illustration (and hence parody) of one of his romantic intertexts—Pascal's "thinking reed" whose so-called strength is to be blown in any direction without resistance ("you seem to me to be weak like the reed").

Maldoror continues his treatment:

Il ne faut pas qu'un doute inutile tourmente ta pensée . . . Les hallucinations dangereuses peuvent venir le jour; mais elles viennent surtout la nuit. Par conséquent, ne t'étonne pas des visions fantastiques que tes yeux semblent apercevoir. Pendant le jour, lorsque l'esprit est en repos, interroge ta conscience; elle te dira, avec sûreté, que le Dieu qui a créé l'homme avec une parcelle de sa propre intelligence possède une bonté sans limites. (71–72)

(You mustn't let a useless doubt torment your thinking . . . Dangerous hallucinations can occur in the daytime; but they come especially at nighttime. Consequently, don't be surprised by fantastic visions that your eyes seem to encounter. During the daytime, when your mind is at rest, examine your conscience, for it will tell you with certainty that the God who endowed man with a grain of his own intelligence also has unlimited kindness.)

In other words, thinking should be done only in the daytime when it can be applied to public action and reason; do not let yourself be troubled by the *useless* nocturnal specters of romanticism. For, once you view life as a series of actions leading to goals, then aimless *inaction* or metaphysical speculation just evaporates as irrelevant. Or, as Wittgenstein put it, "Philosophical problems [such as the speculative issue of life after death] arise when language *goes on holiday*," that is, when our speech becomes unhitched from the specific public uses for which it functions, so that its wheels spin aimlessly (*Philosophical Investigations*, remark 38). "We dream only when we're asleep," wrote Lautréamont later in his *Poésies* (a work published under his real name, Isidore Ducasse, rather than the earlier pen name Lautréamont: 259). Consequently, dreaming of ghosts or other visions simply has no place in our activity. This is because sleep, by definition, is a nonactivity, the very opposite of life since "everything lives by action" ("*Tout vit par l'action,*" *291*).

How does the gravedigger respond to such ethical counseling? His first reaction is to blurt out the question "Where am I?"

—Où suis-je? N'ai-je pas changé de caractère? Je sens un souffle puissant de consolation effleurer mon front rasséréné, comme la brise du printemps ranime l'espérance des vieillards. Quel est cet homme dont le langage sublime a dit des choses que le premier venu n'aurait pas prononcées? (72)

(—Where am I? Hasn't my character changed? I feel a strong breath of consolation blowing across my quietened brow, like the spring breeze that reawakens the hopes of old men. Who is this man whose sublime tongue has uttered things that the first passerby would never have been able to pronounce?)

Of course, the man to whom the gravedigger is referring is nobody: a fictional hero (Maldoror) of a fictional writer (Lautréamont). And it is this very multiplication of masks that points to the source of the character's discursive power: it is not *who* is talking here that amazes us, but *what* is talking—a language of performatives ("Stop your work!" "Stand aside!" "Examine your conscience!") reverberating far beyond the fictional confines of Lautréamont's text and reaching the reader's own lived contradictions. Lautréamont has pushed the graveyard intertexts of romanticism through to their extreme and in so doing has revealed their ethical bankruptcy: they reject the utility of public action (in favor of private reverie) while accepting at the same time literature's role as a (moral) guide for its reader. Romantic torment thus loses its hold upon us, as it does for *Maldoror*'s gravedigger, and we are free to find other intertexts on which to model our lives.

Therein lies the pragmatic power of literature. Our actions are always grounded in preexistent textual models (whether these be poetic, journalistic, filmic, or whatever), and the power of certain literary texts (such as Lautréamont's or Mallarmé's) resides precisely in their *recasting* the performative force inherent in such models. Hence Mallarmé's partiality for "circumstantial verse," or Lautréamont's fascination with the genre of the maxim, which openly parades its social, yet at the same time literary-formal, power. Such texts can in no way be seen as "parasitic," second-order copies of "normal" spoken performatives (Austin 22), since their function does not consist of *copying* anything. Their function is rather, as Derrida argues in *Of Grammatology*, to bring into question, and hence change, the norms of speaking power that traditional philosophers assume to be normal, "everyday" language (139–42). Text acts ground their speech-act cousins, and not the other way around. Is it not significant, in this regard, that one of Austin's own examples of the exemplary speech act of promising (Felman 9) should be a line from the classical play *Hippolytus* (Austin 9–10) — a line, moreover, whose *literary* statement "My tongue swore to, but my heart did not" later served as a model for postromantic nonliterary speculation on the role of "sincerity" and "intentions" in language use? Since literary texts are in this way always *in advance of* nonliterary clichés, or of so-called ordinary language, it is hardly surprising that "ordinary-language philosophers" who seek to define complex acts on the basis of seemingly simple ones (like flipping a light switch [Davidson 4] or stepping on a car brake [Davis 12]) come up empty-handed when pressed for a general theory of action that would explain complex ideological acts such as literature. Only by turning the inquiry around and examining the textual (and hence ideological) ingredient in all patterns of action can the dialogue between literature and philosophy continue to bear fruit. For it is precisely literary texts that teach us, in Wittgenstein's words, to "make a radical break with the idea that language always functions in one way, always serves the same purpose: to convey thoughts" (*Philosophical Investigations*, remark 304).

Notes

1. The critique of J. L. Austin put forward by Jacques Derrida in "Signature Event Context" amounts to an undermining of the notion that a statement's meaning could be exhaustively understood by reconstructing the ideal moment when the speaker's intentions coincided with the moment of uttering her statement. This, in turn, questions the very authority of a person's thoughts and intentions for an understanding of what that person says. John Searle's adaptation of Austin's concept of performatives places intentions (and hence the speaker's authority) at the heart of the concept of a speech act. See, for instance, p. 16 of his book *Speech Acts*: "When I take a noise or a mark on a piece of paper to be an instance of linguistic communication, as a message, one of the things I must assume is that the noise or mark was produced by a being or beings more or less like myself and *produced*

with certain kinds of intentions" (my emphasis). Although Derrida does *not* deny the existence of intentions in the acts of speaking or writing—see "Limited Inc abc" 193—he brings into question the usefulness of intention as a measuring stick for determining any statement's meaning. ("Limited Inc abc" 193–95)

2. A clear presentation of Bertrand Russell's theory, whereby language is a set of propositions based on elementary descriptions of sensory experience, can be found in Pears (ed.), *Russell's Logical Atomism* 31–43.

3. Derrida's first two books have Husserl as their object: his translation of, and introduction to, Husserl's *Origin of Geometry*, and then his critique of Husserl's theory of the sign, *La Voix et le phenomene*, especially 67–77 and 98–117.

4. See Derrida, "Limited Inc abc"': "The necessity, assumed by classical theory, of submitting itself to the very normativity and hierarchy that it purports to analyze, deprives such theory of precisely what it claims for itself: seriousness, scientificity, truth, philosophical value, etc." (211). Cf. p. 232: "If what [Austin and Searle] call the 'standard,' 'fulfilled,' 'normal,' 'serious,' 'literal,' etc. is *always capable* of being affected by the non-standard, the 'void,' the 'abnormal,' the 'nonserious,' the 'parasitical' etc., what does that tell us about the former?"

5. See "Reiterating the Differences"': "Derrida . . . has misunderstood and misstated Austin's position at several crucial points, as I shall attempt to show. . . . Understanding [an] utterance consists in recognizing the illocutionary intentions of [its] author" (198, 202). But if the serious intentions embedded in speakers' performatives are indeed the foundations of a viable speech-act theory then performative force as such loses most of its conceptual power and instead becomes dependent on a traditional epistemology of thought processes, beliefs, and "all the offstage performers" that Austin tried to cast aside (10 n.1). As if aware of this problem, Searle argues in "Reiterating the Differences" that intentions do not have to exist independently of the speech acts in which they are manifested (202). But if the act of speaking is the only trace we have of such intentions, then why encumber our understanding of such public acts with a purely hypothetical private, and hidden, dimension? As we shall see later in this essay, Searle is drawn into such difficulties because of his use of the term "expression," which logically entails the existence of something-to-be-expressed ("there need be no *gulf* at all between the illocutionary intention and its expression," he writes [202]). As I shall argue later, a rigorous theory of performatives dissolves the (still descriptive) notion of language as the expression of something-or-other (thoughts, intentions, or whatever).

6. Cf. Wittgenstein's remark from circa 1945 that "words are deeds" (*Culture and Value* 46). This comment on the pragmatic dimension of speaking (which is strikingly Austinian yet ahead of its time) also appears in parentheses in the *Philosophical Investigations* at remark 546.

7. See *Philosophical Investigations*: "What has to be accepted, the given, is—so one could say—*forms of life*" (p. 226).

8. See Austin: "A performative utterance will . . . be *in a particular way* hollow or void if said by an actor on the stage, or if introduced in a poem or spoken in a soliloquy. Language in such circumstances is in special ways—intelligibly—used not seriously, but in ways *parasitic* upon its normal use" (22). Cf. Searle, "Reiterating the Differences" 204–5.

9. See Barbara Johnson: "The speaking subject is only a persona, an actor, not a person. But if one considers the conventionality of all performative utterances . . . , can it really be said that the chairman who opens a discussion or the priest who baptizes a baby or the judge who pronounces a verdict are persons rather than personae? . . . The performative utterance thus automatically fictionalizes its utterer when it makes him the mouth-piece of a conventionalized authority. . . . If people are put to death by a verdict and not by a poem, it is not because the law is not a fiction" (60). In chapter 9 of *Is There a Text in This Class? The Authority of Interpretive Communities*, 197–245, Stanley Fish similarly refutes Austin and Searle's distinction between "serious" discourse and secondary "literary" discourse—although his refutation follows a different line from Johnson's. Cf. Derrida's remark in "Limited Inc abc": "As though the meaning of these words ('real life') could immediately be a subject of unanimity, without the slightest risk of parasitism: as though literature, theater, deceit, infidelity, hypocrisy, parasitism, and the simulation of real life were not part of real life!" (232).

10. "It is not our aim to refine or complete the system of rules for the use of our words in un-heard-of ways" (*Philosophical Investigations*, remark 133).

11. Cf. Wittgenstein's remark in *Culture and Value* that "the way to solve the problem you see in life is to live in a way that will make what is problematic disappear" (27). Aristotle's concept of *eudaimonia* is clarified in his *Nicomachean Ethics*, and I shall return below to its usefulness as a bridge between theories of language and a general account of human action.

12. Cf. Derrida's comment that grammatology is the following through of a tension between metaphysical presuppositions and critical concepts—in his closing remarks in the interview on "Semiology and Grammatology" reprinted in *Positions* 36.

13. Cf. *Culture and Value*: "Language sets everyone the same traps; it is an immense network of easily accessible wrong turnings. And so we watch one man after another walking down the same paths and we know in advance where he will branch off, where walk [sic] straight on without noticing the side turning, etc. etc." (18). Cf. Derrida's comment in *Positions* that " 'ordinary language' is not innocent or neutral. It is the language of Western metaphysics and it carries with it not only a considerable number of presuppositions of all sorts but also presuppositions inseparable from one another, . . . and tied together in a system" (29).

14. Cf. Wittgenstein's comment in *On Certainty* 589: "For how does a man learn to recognize his own state of knowing something?" I.e., how can he *be taught* this, how can we give him criteria for distinguishing between mistaken "states of knowing" and correctly identified "states of knowing"?

15. See *Philosophical Investigations*: "Is thinking a kind of speaking? One would like to say it is what distinguishes speech with thought from talking without thinking. . . . Say: 'Yes, this pen is blunt. Oh well, it'll do.' First, thinking it; then without thought; then just think the thought without the words. . . . But what constitutes thought here is not some process which has to accompany the words if they are not to be spoken without thought.

Imagine people who could only think aloud. (As there are people who can only read aloud.)" (remarks 330–31).

The analogy between thinking and reading is further explored in remarks 156–71, while the one between thinking and playing music is developed in remark 341, and the resemblance between thinking and following mathematical rules is developed in remark 692.

16. Cf. John Llewelyn: "Deconstruction is an anonymous middle-voiced going on: *il s'agit, il se passe*, it travels, to take a simile from Gilles Deleuze and Félix Guattari, like a rhizome" (63).

17. See *Philosophical Investigations*: "The work of a philosopher consists in assembling reminders, *for a particular purpose*" (remark 127, my emphasis). It is the specific *purpose* of the philosophical treatment that dictates what views of language the treatment will lead to.

18. Hence the profusion of remarks that begin with such phrases as "I should like to say . . . " or "Here there is an inclination to say . . . ". For a detailed examination (and revision) of the notion that the *Investigations* is a form of self-confessional text, see Winspur, "Wittgenstein's Semiotic *Investigations*" 35–49.

19. See Aristotle's definitions of the three types of life possessed by plants (nutrition and growth), animals (nutrition, growth, perception, and movement), and humans (nutrition, growth, perception, movement, and the rational organization of these functions in view of planned goals) in his *Nicomachean Ethics* 13. In other words, what distinguishes the "souls" of these three life forms is not forms of consciousness but forms of *action*, and what makes humans human is that they construct their actions amid frameworks of goals and justifications that they can explain, alter, or adapt.

20. The action model underlying all speech is acknowledged by Austin when he abandons his initial distinction between constative and performative utterances, and instead views all utterances as acts: "Once we realize that what we have to study is *not* the sentence but the issuing of an utterance in a speech situation, there can hardly be any longer a possibility of not seeing that stating is performing an act. . . . The truth or falsity of a[n apparently constative] statement depends not merely on the meanings of words but on what act you were performing in what circumstances" (139, 145).

21. Cf. Theodor Adorno: "Our perspective of life has passed into an ideology which conceals the fact that there is life no longer" (15).

22. For justifications of this claim, as well as an approach toward rethinking modern poetry without resorting to images, see my "Reading a Poem's Typographical Form: the Case of Paul Eluard" and *Saint John Perse and the Imaginary Reader* 145-52.

23. My transferring of Wittgenstein's arguments into the realm of literary analysis differs from two earlier transfers, done by Charles Altieri and Reed Way Dasenbrock. For whereas these critics use Wittgenstein to refine the (romantic) concept of artistic expression, I instead view certain Wittgensteinian arguments as an undermining of this notion. Consider, for example, the confusions concerning the term "image" that Wittgenstein pinpoints in his *Lectures and Conversations*: "Aesthetic puzzles—puzzles about the effects the arts have on us. . . . There is a tendency to talk about the 'effect of a work of art'—feelings, images, etc. Then it is natural to ask: 'Why do you hear this minuet?', and there is a tendency to answer: 'To get this and that effect.' And doesn't the minuet itself matter?—hearing *this* [particular musical text]; would another have done as well?" (28–29).

24. Translation by Robert Greer Cohn 33, 35. Other translations from French in this essay are my own unless stated otherwise.

25. R. A. York offers a different interpretation of Mallarmé's sonnet from the one I outline here (see York 47–48). By focusing on a specific moment of utterance apparently "expressed" in the poem, York situates the text's pragmatic force not in its reader's decoding (as I do) but rather in the poet's putative act of imaginative creation.

26. Such is the traditional view of Mallarmé's poetics as presented, for instance, by Scherer 9–17. Two important reevaluations of the circumstantial nature of Mallarmé's poems can be found in Johnson 52–66, and in Chambers.

27. The analysis that follows is a shortened version of pages 87–89 of my article "Ethics, Change, and Lautréamont," where I explore in detail the interconnected concepts of intertextuality and models for human action. For an important discussion of the ethical dimension to Lautréamont's writings, see Pierssens 10–13, 19–34, and passim.

28. Lautréamont: "N'est-ce pas, fossoyeur, que tu voudras causer avec moi? . . . —Ami, il m'est impossible d'échanger des idées avec toi. . . . Je dois finir de creuser cette fosse, avec ma bêche infatigable, afin qu'elle soit prête demain matin. Pour faire un travail sérieux, il ne faut pas faire deux choses à la fois" (70). Cf. Pierssens 47–49.

Works Cited

Adorno, Theodor. *Minima Moralia: Reflections from Damaged Life*. 1951. Trans. E. F. N. Jephcott. London: Verso, 1978.

Altieri, Charles. *Act and Quality: A Theory of Literary Meaning and Humanistic Understanding*. Amherst: U of Massachusetts P, 1981.

Aristotle. *The Nicomachean Ethics*. Trans. David Ross. Oxford: Oxford UP, 1980.

Austin, J. L. *How to Do Things with Words*. Ed. J. O. Urmson and Marina Sbisa. 2nd ed. Cambridge, Mass.: Harvard UP, 1975.

Bourdieu, Pierre. *Ce que parler veut dire: l'économie des échanges linguistiques*. Paris: Fayard, 1981.

Chambers, Ross. "An Address in the Country: Mallarmé and the Kinds of Literary Context." *French Forum* 11, No. 2 (1986): 199–215.

Cohn, Robert Greer. *Towards the Poems of Mallarmé*. Berkeley: U of California P, 1965.

Dasenbrock, Reed Way. "Accounting for the Changing Certainties of Interpretive Communities." *MLN* 101, No. 5 (1986): 1022–41.

Davidson, Donald. *Essays on Actions and Events*. Oxford: Clarendon Press, 1980.

Davis, Lawrence H. *Theory of Action*. Englewood Cliffs, N.J.: Prentice-Hall, 1979.

Derrida, Jacques. *De la grammatologie*. Paris: Editions de Minuit, 1967. [*Of Grammatology*. Trans. Gayatri Chakravorty Spivak. Baltimore: Johns Hopkins UP, 1976.]

———. Introduction. *L'Origine de la géométrie*. By Edmund Husserl. Paris: Presses Universitaires de France, 1962. 3–171. [*Edmund Husserl's Origin of Geometry: an Introduction*. Trans. John P. Leavey, Jr. Stony Brook, N.Y.: Nicholas Hays, 1978.]

_____. "Limited Inc abc." *Glyph* 2 (1977): 162–254.

_____. *Positions*. Paris: Editions de Minuit, 1972. [*Positions*. Trans. Alan Bass. Chicago: U of Chicago P, 1981.]

_____. "Signature événement contexte." *Marges de la philosophie*. Paris: Editions de Minuit, 1972. ["Signature Event Context." Trans. Samuel Weber and Jeffrey Mehlman. *Glyph* 1 (1977): 172–97; rpt. in *Margins of Philosophy*. Trans. Alan Bass. Chicago: U of Chicago P, 1982.]

_____. *La Voix et le phénomène*. Paris: Presses Universitaires de France, 1967. [*Speech and Phenomena*. Trans. David B. Allison. Evanston: Northwestern UP, 1973.]

Felman, Shoshana. *Le Scandale du corps parlant: Don Juan avec Austin ou La séduction en deux langues*. Paris: Seuil, 1980. [*The Literary Speech Act: Don Juan with J. L. Austin, or Seduction in Two Languages*. Trans. Catherine Porter. Ithaca, N.Y.: Cornell UP, 1983.]

Fish, Stanley. *Is There a Text in This Class? The Authority of Interpretive Communities*. Cambridge, Mass.: Harvard UP, 1980.

Johnson, Barbara. *The Critical Difference: Essays in the Contemporary Rhetoric of Reading*. Baltimore: Johns Hopkins UP, 1980.

Lautréamont and Germain Nouveau. *Oeuvres complètes*. Paris: Gallimard, Pléiade, 1970.

Llewelyn, John. *Derrida on the Threshold of Sense*. London: Macmillan, 1986.

Mallarmé, Stéphane. *Oeuvres complètes*. Ed. Henri Mondor and G. Jean-Aubry. Paris: Gallimard, Pléiade, 1945.

Mulligan, Kevin. "Inscriptions and Speaking's Place: Derrida and Wittgenstein." *Oxford Literary Review* 3, No. 2 (1978): 62–67.

Pears, David. *Russell's Logical Atomism*. London: Collins/Fontana, 1972.

Pierssens, Michel. *Lautréamont: Ethique à Maldoror*. Lille: Presses Universitaires de Lille, 1984.

Ryle, Gilbert. *The Concept of Mind*. 1949. Harmondsworth: Penguin, 1973.

Scherer, Jacques. *Le "Livre" de Mallarmé*. Paris: Gallimard, 1977.

Searle, John. "Reiterating the Differences: A Reply to Derrida." *Glyph* 1 (1977): 198–208.

_____. *Speech Acts: An Essay in the Philosophy of Language*. Cambridge: Cambridge UP, 1969.

Staten, Henry. *Wittgenstein and Derrida*. Lincoln: U of Nebraska P, 1984.

Winspur, Steven. "Ethics, Change, and Lautréamont." *L'Esprit Créateur* 27, No. 2 (1987): 82–91.

_____. "Reading a Poem's Typographical Form: The Case of Paul Eluard." *Teaching Language through Literature* 23, No. 1 (1983): 38–46.

_____. *Saint-John Perse and the Imaginary Reader*. Geneva: Droz, 1988.

_____. "Wittgenstein's Semiotic *Investigations*." *American Journal of Semiotics* 3, No. 2 (1984): 33–57.

Wittgenstein, Ludwig. *Culture and Value*. Ed. G. H. von Wright. Trans. Peter Winch. Chicago: U of Chicago P, 1980.

_____. *Lectures and Conversations on Aesthetics, Psychology and Religious Belief*. 1966. Ed. Cyril Barrett. Oxford: Basil Blackwell, 1978.

_____. *Notebooks, 1914–1916*. 1961. Ed. G. H. von Wright and G. E. M. Anscombe. Trans. G. E. M. Anscombe. New York: Harper & Row, 1969.

_____. *On Certainty*. 1969. Ed. G. E. M. Anscombe and G. H. von Wright. Trans. Denis Paul and G. E. M. Anscombe. Oxford: Basil Blackwell, 1974.

_____. *Philosophical Investigations*. 1953. Trans. G. E. M. Anscombe. Oxford: Basil Blackwell, 1968.

_____. *Zettel*. Ed. G. E. M. Anscombe and G. H. von Wright. Trans. G. E. M. Anscombe. Oxford: Basil Blackwell, 1967.

York, R. A. *The Poem as Utterance*. London: Methuen, 1986.

9

Philosophy as *Not* Just a "Kind of Writing": Derrida and the Claim of Reason

Christopher Norris

I

As Derrida recently reminded us in "An Idea of Flaubert," this novelist had very little patience with philosophy and regarded all that strenuous seeking after truth as a stupid waste of time. At least, such is the lesson to be read in *Bouvard et Pécuchet*, where those twin autodidacts set out to master all the great philosophical systems, and in so doing reduce the whole business to an absurd catalogue of *idées recues*. What is in question here is not just Flaubert's personal distaste for philosophy or his preference for the claims of "literary" style over those of conceptual understanding. Rather, as Derrida suggests, it is in the nature of philosophy to invite this kind of treatment, to leave itself open to parody as an endless recycling of empty words and phrases. "In philosophy, the delivery, transmission and reception of ideas, coded arguments and classifiable responses or solutions lends itself more readily to stereotyping than anywhere else" (750). And this because philosophers are fatally willing to treat their ideas with misplaced reverence and imagine that they are actually propounding *solutions* when in fact they are just rehearsing the same old problems. From Plato to Hegel, the whole bad tradition is passed in review and found to be nothing more than a stupid repetition of clichéd arguments, all the more offensive for thinking themselves original at every turn.

What simultaneously disgusts and fascinates Flaubert is this constant capacity of philosophers to forget just how long the game has been playing and how unlikely it is that they will now come up with some remarkable new move. Their stupidity is twofold, he seems to suggest. On the one hand it consists in wanting to reach conclusions, in believing that there are indeed answers to be found and that philosophy is the discipline best placed to find them. On the other it is a question of their not having grasped that philosophy is a *textual* activity, one kind

189

of writing among others, and is therefore not to be treated as a privileged, truth-telling discourse. Flaubert most effectively makes this point by having his Bouvard and Pécuchet assemble all the great opposing creeds of philosophical history (like "spiritualism" and "materialism") into a mere succession of passing fads where their differences collapse into nonsense. Like Mallarmé, he dreams of an ideal "book about nothing" that would finally undo the various illusions (of truth, reference, "concepts" as distinct from mere words) that have so stupefied the discourse of philosophy. The novelist and the poet both (according to Derrida) "manipulate philosophemes" in a way that undermines every received idea, every last system of articulated theory. These "philosophemes" can exist henceforth only "as a sort of metalanguage instrumental to the display of their writing." Hence Flaubert's amused contempt for those slaves of the Idea who think to build an edifice of concepts against all the lures of writing and literary style. His response is to set these thinkers up as mere dupes of a chronically self-deceiving enterprise whose pretensions are reduced to absurdity by Bouvard and Pécuchet's labors. What survives this process is nothing but an endless and stupid repetition of received ideas. "They [Flaubert and Mallarmé] resort . . . to a simulacrum of the dialectic and of the idea in both its Platonic and Hegelian guises, a simulacrum that would allow them to reassemble the philosophical, marking its limits as they discredit its oppositions" (762). And among these oppositions are all the great system-building terms (like Flaubert's favorites, "materialism" and "spiritualism") on which philosophers have hitherto depended for their sense of having something distinctive and important to say.

One could take this reading of Flaubert as a typecast example of what deconstruction does when it approaches the texts of philosophy with an eye to their rhetorical (or "literary") aspects. Certainly it seems to recapitulate some of Derrida's most characteristic arguments with regard to that deep-laid "metaphysics of presence" that marks the whole tradition of philosophical thinking, from Plato to Heidegger and beyond. Thus Flaubert can be seen as calling into question the three main assumptions that underpin the discourse of philosophy as a quest for ultimate, self-validating truth. First there is the idea that writing is a strictly subordinate means for communicating knowledge, such that any problems of philosophical "style" are a matter of secondary concern, so long as one knows that the thinker has something of genuine importance to communicate.[1] On the contrary, says Derrida, philosophy is preeminently a *collection of texts*, a written archive whose authoritative claims are oddly bound up with a strong disposition to deny or efface its own textual character. Second, there is the notion (associated mainly with Hegel) that consciousness evolves through a history of progressive approximations to truth, a narrative whose unfolding provides both the theme and the method of a properly reflective philosophical grasp. It is precisely this delusive totalizing movement—its presumption that history must finally make sense from the standpoint of a consciousness ideally possessed of its own self-evident rationality—that Derrida sets out to deconstruct in his several essays on Hegel (see "From Restricted to General Economy"). By exposing such ideas to parody, by reducing them to a mere "simulacrum of the dialectic," Flaubert anticipates much of what Derrida will write about the moments of *excess*, of disruptive or heterological sense, encountered in the reading of Hegel's texts. And this leads on to the third main respect in which Flaubert manages to disconcert the project of philosophical reason. He reminds us (like Derrida) that there is nothing strictly "proper" to philosophy; that intellectual history is everywhere worked over by a covert metaphorics whose tracks have been effaced by philosophy's need to repress the knowledge of its own textual constitution. Thus "Flaubert shows himself a brother to Nietzsche," specifically that Nietzsche who asked "What is truth?" and found it to be simply a collection of metaphors, metonymies, and other such devices, rhetorical figures that had managed to pass themselves off as conceptual truths (see Spivak xxi—xxxviii).

A cursory reading of the Flaubert essay would take it as further proof that Derrida is some kind of antiphilosopher, abandoning all the forms and protocols of argument that have hitherto characterized the discipline. I shall argue that this is a mistaken reading, one that answers more to current institutional needs and prejudices than to anything demonstrably "there" in Derrida's texts. On the one hand there are those like John Searle, philosophers in the mainstream analytic tradition, who regard Derrida as merely playing games and willfully ignoring all the proper, "serious" methods for carrying on debate (see "Reiterating the Differences"). To them it must appear that Derrida is nothing more than a latter-day sophist, one who substitutes rhetorical tricks for the difficult business of arriving at knowledge and truth. By fastening on Derrida's (to them) more outrageous pronouncements, and ignoring the detailed process of *argument* by which those pronouncements are arrived at, his opponents avoid any real confrontation with the issues Derrida raises. Then again, there are neopragmatists like Richard Rorty who approve of Derrida precisely *because* he seems to reject that idea of "philosophy" as a discourse with its own special truth-seeking rigor. Rorty thinks this whole enterprise was misguided from the start, and especially so when it took (with Descartes and Kant) that decisive turn toward epistemology that has since then produced—as Rorty sees it—such a deal of pointless debate (see *Philosophy and the Mirror of Nature*). Much better that philosophy should now give up its privileged truth-claims, accept that final answers are not to be had, and then—rather than shut up shop altogether—accept its new role as a cultural discourse on a level with others like literary criticism.

So what Rorty finds congenial in Derrida is exactly what offends a mainstream practitioner like Searle. It is the idea that philosophy has so far been deluded by its own (intellectual or professional) self-image; that its concepts most often come down to metaphors at root; and that philosophers can best get hold of this belated insight by renouncing all claim to specialized knowledge or expertise. Thus Rorty counts Derrida a kind of half-way pragmatist, still too much concerned with "deconstructing" the old metaphysics, but a useful ally nevertheless insofar as he insists that philosophy is just another "kind of writing," with no privileged access to truth ("Philosophy as a Kind of Writing"). Searle thinks Derrida merely incompetent because he will not acknowledge that Derrida's texts have a rigor that is alien to his own tidy notions of philosophical method. Rorty's attitude is certainly more benign, but he also, like Searle, passes over those aspects of Derrida's work that do not fit in with his own argumentative purposes. For Rorty, this means politely ignoring all the passages of hard-pressed textual analysis where Derrida shows deconstruction actually *at work* on the grounding assumptions of logocentric reason. Here, he thinks, Derrida is largely wasting his time, or falling back into a kind of negative theology that merely replaces one set of absolutes (truth, meaning, clear and distinct ideas) with another (trace, *différance*, and other such deconstructive key terms). To this extent Derrida is still hung up on the same philosophical problems, still partly captive to the old belief that philosophy has special things to say and a special kind of competence for saying them.

I think this involves a misreading of Derrida, and hope to make the argument good in what follows. I shall also be claiming, for connected reasons, that Derrida's influence on literary criticism has helped to obscure the philosophical import of his work, in the sense that he has been either praised or denounced for having turned philosophy into a species of applied rhetoric. Now there are certainly moments in Derrida's writing when he seems to make a choice between ''philosophy'' and ''literature,'' and to come out expressly on the side of literature. One such moment occurs in his earliest published work, *Edmund Husserl's Origin of Geometry: An Introduction*. Here the choice is posed in what would seem quite uncompromising terms. On the one hand is Husserl's rigorous attempt to rethink the grounding intuitions of a science whose history and genesis must somehow be conceived as implicitly *there* at the moment of its first conception. For Husserl, it is imperative to save such primordial intuitions by explaining (1) how their logic is reactivated in subsequent reflection on that same founding moment; (2) how geometry has a ''history'' only insofar as it involves an unimpeded thinking back to that origin; and (3) how the a priori character of geometric truth is ideally unaffected by errors or distortions attendant on the process of historical transmission. In short, Husserl thinks of geometry as the paradigm or test case for a method—that of transcendental phenomenology—that would secure science against the threat of relativism. And if this can be established, then the way is clearly open for philosophy to regain its authentic (Husserlian) vocation. It would point toward the ultimate grounding of reason in a sense of those constitutive structures of knowledge and perception that *cannot be doubted* since thinking and experience itself are simply inconceivable without them.

Husserl's project in the *Origin of Geometry* therefore presents a very striking example of logocentric reason. It is a philosophy at once turned back toward origins and seeking to enclose all the history of thought in a moment of pure, self-present understanding. I shall not attempt to summarize the detailed arguments Derrida brings to bear in his reading of this text. They turn on the fact that Husserl cannot conceptualize geometry or the source of its ''primordial intuitions'' without, in the process, using a language of *inscription, writing*, or graphic representation. And this affects not only the ideal objectivities of geometric truth but also that concept of a timeless access to such truths through a perfectly repeatable interplay of present intuition and past discovery. According to Husserl, "Traditionality is what circulates from one to the other, illuminating one by the other in a movement wherein consciousness discovers its path" (Derrida, *Husserl's Origin of Geometry* 86). But in fact, as Derrida argues, it is only in terms of writing—of inscriptions cut off from any intuitive or self-present source—that Husserl can represent geometry as an object of transmissible knowledge. "The possibility of *writing* will assure the absolute traditionalization of the object, its absolute ideal Objectivity. . . . Writing will do this by emancipating sense from its *actually present* evidence for a real subject and from its present circulation within a determined community" (88; Derrida's italics). And this because writing alone is capable of conferring that ideal permanence, removed from the flux of mere transient perception, that Husserl is so determined to establish. Without this resort to an inscriptionalist idiom there would be no conceiving of geometry as a locus of primordial truth.

But of course this complicates Husserl's other claim, his argument that knowledge is ultimately grounded in acts of self-present *intuition* that properly should involve no detour through writing or other such fallible forms of transmission. This aporia is crucial to Derrida's reading and is taken up subsequently in *Speech and Phenomena*, where he finds it manifest everywhere in Husserl's meditations on language, meaning, and truth. Beyond that, it is the burden (as Derrida argues) of all those "logocentric" thinkers, from Plato to Saussure, for whom *speech* is the proper, authentic medium of language and writing a debased, parasitical, or "supplementary" form. There is no room here for a detailed rehearsal of Derrida's commentaries on Plato, Rousseau, Hegel, Saussure, and others (see esp. *Of Grammatology, Writing and Difference*, and *Dissemination*). Sufficient to say that he presents textual evidence and a rigorously argued case for the strict impossibility of conceiving language on the basis of an ideal speech situation where words and meanings correspond in a perfect (self-present) reciprocity of sense. Always there is the appeal—however covert, metaphorical, or tucked out of sight—to some analogue of *writing* whose role in the argument turns out to be crucial to its whole working system of assumptions. Thus the negative valuations traditionally attached to writing (as a "dangerous supplement" everywhere threatening the ideal spontaneity of speech) cannot be upheld once these texts are read with a vigilant attention to their strategies of argument. It is on these grounds precisely that Derrida can point to the internal contradictions that emerge from Husserl's project in the *Origin of Geometry*.

These arguments amount to a form of Kantian transcendental deduction. That is to say, they pose the question: what must be the necessary *presuppositions* of our thinking about language if language is to make any kind of coherent or intelligible sense? Such arguments have traditionally been used to refute the more extreme forms of philosophical skepticism. They have indeed been used against Derrida himself by opponents who ask how he can possibly expect his writings to be read and properly understood, given his well-known disbelief in the existence of determinate meanings. Where these objections miss the mark is in not discerning how rigorously Derrida argues his way in following out the various contradictory entailments of the texts he reads. The result may be the kind of "unthinkable" aporia that leads philosophers like Searle to dismiss Derrida as simply not knowing the proper rules of the game. But the route of detailed argument by which those conclusions are arrived at is one that philosophers should recognize, since it takes the form (as with Derrida on Husserl) of a transcendental deduction, albeit to what must seem decidedly counterintuitive ends.

Now I said earlier that his essay on the *Origin of Geometry* contained a passage that appeared to pose a choice between "philosophy" and "literature" as in some sense epitomizing rival attitudes to language. More specifically, it is a question of Husserl "versus" Joyce, since the one attempts to reduce language to a pure, univocal order of sense while the other opens language up to a seemingly infinitized *written* textuality beyond any logocentric reckoning. What we find in Joyce, Derrida suggests, is "the generalized equivocation of a writing that, no longer translating one language into another on the basis of their common cores of sense, circulates throughout all languages at once, accumulates their energies . . . , cultivates their associative syntheses instead of avoiding them" (*Husserl's Origin of Geometry* 102). This passage has often been quoted as evidence of a "turn" in Derrida's work, an almost aboriginal turn indeed, since it occurs in the course of his earliest and, in a certain sense, his most "philosophical" book. On this reading, Derrida is taken to reject philosophy as such, since its protocols demand an effacement or repression of writing that cannot be maintained without manifest self-contradiction. What the passage seems to announce is that thinking must henceforth abandon this deluded quest and position itself over and against philosophy by taking up the Joycean challenge. That is to say, deconstruction will no longer be tied to forms of argument that, no matter how radical their upshot, still use the conceptual resources of philosophy and therefore belong within its field. It is on these terms that Derrida has been understood by neopragmatists like Rorty and by literary critics who celebrate Derridean "free play" as a kind of belated revenge against the superior truth-claims of philosophers from Plato to the logical positivists. What Derrida reads in Flaubert—philosophy's discomfiture at the hands of writing or literary style—can then be read as the chief lesson of Derrida's deconstructive enterprise.

But this is to suppose that one escapes philosophy simply by determining no longer to have any truck with it. Such gestures are ineffectual, as Derrida has often pointed out, because they fail to acknowledge how utterly pervasive is philosophy's influence on our language and habits of thought (see esp. *Margins of Philosophy*). One can only work from within, so to speak, using the language that comes to hand (along with its inescapable logocentric residues), but using it in precisely such a way as to bring out its inherent strains and contradictions. And this means continuing to operate with methods—including certain deconstructive variants of transcendental deduction—that at least have the merit of making sense (*philosophical* sense) to those trained in that tradition. So it is wrong to seize on isolated passages—like the set-piece comparison between Joyce and Husserl—and take them as pronouncing an end to "philosophy" and a new dispensation of metaphor, rhetoric, or literary style. For it remains the case that Derrida is only in a position to issue such statements when he has worked through the texts of philosophers from Plato to Husserl with the utmost argumentative rigor. And the same applies to those recent writings of Derrida—most of them intended for translation and aimed at an American readership—where he seems less concerned with arguments and more inclined to exploit the various possibilities of noncommunication and cross-purpose exchange. Even here (most notoriously, in the "response" to John Searle) Derrida is resuming issues and problems that are worked over with meticulous care in his more "philosophical" texts.

Indeed, it was Searle's failure to reckon with this complex background of argument—his assumption that Derrida must either be fooling or just an incompetent philosopher—that made the exchange such a nice demonstration of Derrida's central point. For after all, if Derrida *has* failed to grasp the plain sense of Austin's speech-act theory, then what must this mean for the theory itself, and for Searle's confidently orthodox restatement of it? Searle even concedes at one point (if only by way of polite convention) that "it is possible that I may have misinterpreted him [Derrida] as profoundly as I believe he has misinterpreted Austin" ("Reiterating the Differences" 205). To which Derrida responds with yet another version of the transcendental riposte. What sense can we make of speech-act philosophy, given its commitment to notions of determinate meaning and context, if such misunderstandings are not merely a frequent occurrence but an *inbuilt possibility* of language? And again—more pointedly—what does this imply for the "self-made, auto-authorized heirs of Austin," those (like Searle) who think to expound his meaning with immunity from errors of any kind? If this all strikes Searle as mere sophistry, his reaction is hardly to be wondered at, considering how deeply his thinking invests in the speech-act metaphysics of presence.

I am suggesting that Derrida has *earned* his position, and earned it moreover by distinctly "philosophical" means. To read his essay on Flaubert as a straightforward endorsement of the novelist's attitude ("philosophy is stupid!") is thoroughly to mistake its import. There is one particular episode from *Bouvard et Pécuchet* that Derrida singles out for close attention. It is their reading of Spinoza's *Ethics*—a work of the utmost systematic rigor, complete with all its axioms and corollaries—that creates first excitement, then despair in the two autodidacts. They go through the text picking out occasional sentences and jotting down remarks like "Oh, that would be splendid!" But in the end, as Flaubert writes, the effort is too much for them; they feel themselves suspended "in a bottomless abyss, with nothing around them but the incomprehensible, the immobile, the eternal" ("An Idea of Flaubert" 756). So when the curé asks Bouvard where he had come across such fine ideas, he replies, "In Spinoza." The name makes the curé jump. "Have you read him?" And Bouvard reassures him, "God forbid!" (755).

Now there are three possible ways of reading this episode. The first would take it as a straightforward attack on philosophy from the standpoint of a "literary" attitude that identifies with Bouvard's (and implicitly Flaubert's) hatred of systematizing creeds. The second would somewhat modify this position by dissociating Derrida's from Flaubert's attitude, and Flaubert's in turn from the absurd predicament of Bouvard. (Such elementary refinements are taken for granted in narrative theory but often ignored in the reading of critical or philosophical texts.) And there is a third possibility: that Derrida has selected this episode to make a more specific point about the *kinds and varieties* of philosophical discourse. That is to say, he takes Spinoza as the paradigm case of a philosophical text that *holds out* against reading, not only the "stupid" kind of reading embarked upon by Bouvard and Pécuchet, but also that other, interrogative reading that deconstruction seeks to advance. It would not then be a case of "literature" unmasking the deluded pretensions of "philosophy" in general, but of a certain false *idea* of what constitutes philosophical truth, namely, that massive "immobility" of system and concept that so overwhelms Bouvard and Pécuchet. For them, as Derrida writes, Spinoza represents "the locus of the greatest temptation, but also of a terror which renders him unattainable, distant, inassimilable. His work is too much: too strong and too beautiful" ("An Idea of Flaubert" 755). And it is precisely this feeling about Spinoza—his attempt to build a self-sufficient edifice of theory immune to mere vagaries of reading—that reduces Pécuchet to scribbling his absurd marginalia. What Derrida is surely getting at here is the requirement that philosophy not only be "readable" but in some sense acknowledge its own textuality, rather than take refuge in the heaven of pure concepts.

II

Why Spinoza should figure as something of a test case is perhaps best answered by a passing reference in Vincent Descombes's *Modern French Philosophy*. Descombes provides some very useful background on the shifts of intellectual allegiance that marked the passage from a period dominated by Hegel, Husserl, and Heidegger to one that witnessed the supremacy of those modern "masters of suspicion," Nietzsche, Marx, and Freud. A major influence here was the reading of Hegel propounded by Alexandre Kojève, a reading that emphasized the violent, disruptive, heterogeneous elements in Hegel's text, and resisted the phenomenological drive toward an ultimate reconciliation of history and meaning. Derrida's essays on Hegel suggest that Kojève (along with Bataille) influenced his thinking at a formative stage (see esp. "From Restricted to General Economy"). But Kojève also singled out Spinoza (especially the *Ethics*) as a case of philosophical argument that adopted an omniscient or God's-eye view that could be sustained only by ignoring the constraints of its own discursive production. The *Ethics* laid claim to an ultimate knowledge inaccessible to any but a timeless intelligence whose source lay beyond all mere considerations of enunciative time and place. It could only have been written by God, or by a God-like author possessed of a truth indifferent to the mere relativities of human discourse. Kojève rejected such absolute truth-claims by insisting that philosophy is *always* bound to the limits of what can be understood as spoken—or written—relative to the subject's enunciative role within language. So Spinoza was effectively not making sense by assuming a stance of perfect detachment from the governing conditions of discursive possibility. His texts could be read and understood (on their own terms) only by suspending one's sense of their anomalous status vis-à-vis the conditions of humanly available knowledge.

This is *not* to argue—or not to make the simple point-scoring claim—that "philosophy" is deluded insofar as it fails to acknowledge its own "literary" status. Thus Derrida insists that Flaubert, far from breaking with philosophy, continues to think within the terms handed down by philosophers from Plato to Hegel. That tradition is inscribed in his reflections on the novel, even where Flaubert imagines his ideal "book about nothing," a text that would come out on the far side of all those hateful antinomies ("form" and "content," etc.) that plague the history of aesthetics. Thus Derrida reminds us how frequently the word "Idea" figures in Flaubert's utopian projections for a novel devoid of mere content and theme. It is a word heavy with idealist motifs, one that "unfolds, fixes its own destiny, and seals itself off," a word whose Hegelian pretensions Flaubert can reduce to near nonsense but which still sets the terms for his thinking about art. Thus he imagines a writing all the more perfect for its total lack of content, a "liberation from materiality" whose sign would be the emptying out of subject matter to the point of an ideally "attenuated" prose. At this stage the novel would finally have achieved a consummate indifference to everything extraneous, everything that encouraged the crude opposition between novelistic "content" and "form." Yet this very desire to transcend antinomies ends up by repeating them in a language of purebred formalism that constantly betrays its Platonic-Hegelian lineage. "The idea of that idea, the word 'idea,' remains the philosophical translation of a non-philosophical text. Philosophy has taken place; there is nothing more to be expected of it; it has already saturated our culture and its own field of action" ("An Idea of Flaubert" 763). At the point of maximum resistance to philosophy, literature finds itself always preempted by a covert metaphysics of form, content, and idea.

So there is no question of Flaubert's having "overcome" this whole bad history simply by declaring his impatience with it or his unwillingness to *read* Spinoza or Hegel on their own philosophical terms. No more can Derrida be taken as claiming that deconstruction now operates outside and beyond the "closure" of Western (logocentric) reason. Such arguments must always founder—as he has shown repeatedly—on the fact that any attempt to go "beyond" philosophy will end up by rehearsing well-worn moves in a game that philosophy has long since invented and for which it has established all the operative rules (see "Of an

Apocalyptic Tone Recently Adopted in Philosophy''). So it is mistaken to suppose (like Rorty) that deconstruction gives some kind of warrant for dispensing with all the vexatious problems of traditional philosophy and embracing a full-blown pragmatist creed. The idea that one can step outside that tradition simply by declaring it bankrupt is no more convincing than Flaubert's desire to have done with it even as he launched a new episode in the adventure of idealist metaphysics. Most readings of Derrida ignore the extent to which he conserves philosophy as a distinctive and still very necessary exercise of thought. They draw the lesson *tout court* that philosophy is just another ''kind of writing,'' and that therefore its texts must henceforth be read with an eye to their purely rhetorical complexities, rather than to anything in the nature of argument or conceptual justification. What these readings pass over is Derrida's equal and opposite insistence: that all our thinking about language, rhetoric, and metaphor is conducted in terms that derive from that same (supposedly discredited) tradition (see esp. ''The Supplement of Copula'' and ''White Mythology''). But of course this complicating message has rather less appeal for literary theorists in search of handy arguments against their overweening colleagues in philosophy.

One can find many examples in Derrida's writing of this scrupulous and explicit refusal to countenance any strategy that would simply turn the tables on philosophical reason. His critique of Foucault in the essay ''Cogito and the History of Madness'' is perhaps the best known and certainly the most emphatic. Foucault had claimed to be speaking in some sense *on behalf* of madness, writing not so much a ''history of psychiatry'' — which would inevitably take up a position on the side of diagnostic reason — as a history ''of madness itself, in its most vibrant state, before being captured by knowledge'' (quoted in ''Cogito and the History of Madness'' 34). And a crucial moment in this history was the point at which Descartes, in his first *Meditation*, entertained the ''hypothesis of insanity'' as a means of provisionally exposing to doubt all our commonplace certitudes about knowledge, experience, and waking reality. But of course the whole purpose of Descartes's experiment in hyperbolic doubt was to reconfirm the sovereignty of reason by showing it to be ultimately proof against the trials of insane imagining. Foucault reads this episode as a virtual allegory of modern (post-Cartesian) reason in its relation to madness as the feared and excluded ''other'' of rational discourse. It is this same Cartesian gesture that takes practical shape in the history of those various institutions for the mad — the prisons, hospitals, psychiatric clinics — whose genealogy Foucault sets out to trace. And in doing so he claims to be *speaking on the side* of madness, and against all the forms of protective isolation that reason has devised in its own will-to-power as the voice of authority and knowledge.

Derrida's counterargument once again comes down to a form of transcendental *tu quoque*. That is, he denies that it is possible for Foucault to advance even a single proposition in support of his case without rejoining the discourse of reason by adopting its language and discursive constraints. And this is not a matter of some specific weakness or occasional blind spot in Foucault's strategy.

Quite simply, it is a condition "inherent in the essence and the very project of all language in general; and even in the language of those who are apparently the maddest; and even and above all in the language of those who, by their praise of madness, by their complicity with it, measure their own strength against the greatest possible proximity to madness" ("Cogito" 54–55). Foucault claims to be taking a stand against Descartes, revealing the Cartesian moment of "insanity" as a covert policing operation, a prelude to internment, always safely under control by the agents of rational thought. On the contrary, says Derrida: Foucault has performed "a Cartesian gesture for the twentieth century," a repetition of Descartes's strategic move that is all the more deceptive for flatly denying (unlike Descartes) its investment in the discourse of reason. It is only by choosing specific and isolated *episodes* in that discourse—episodes whose "hyperbolic" strangeness cannot fail to strike us now—that Foucault is able to ignore his own inescapable complicity with it. "To all appearances, it is reason that he interns, but, like Descartes, he chooses the reason of yesterday as his target and not the possibility of meaning in general" ("Cogito" 55). For there is simply no speaking, no thinking or arguing—and certainly no writing an ambitious "history of insanity in the age of reason"—that can claim, without manifest hyperbole, to represent the authentic discourse of madness.

Foucault took this critique as occasion for a contemptuous dismissal of Derrida's entire project.[2] He attacked deconstruction as a mere rhetorical bag of tricks, a neat little "pedagogy" secure in the knowledge that nothing exists outside the text. And this argument has persuaded others—notably Edward Said[3]— that there is a choice to be made between these two divergent paths of poststructuralist thought, the one (Foucault's) encouraging an active involvement with the politics of power and knowledge, while the other (Derrida's) can lead only to a self-imposed condition of "textualist" quietism. But this is to confuse Derrida's rigorous protocols of reading with the vulgarized account of deconstruction that believes it to have severed all ties with the world and entered a zone of polymorphous textual "free play." It is a confusion that Derrida has more than once sought to correct, lately with increasing emphasis. "To distance oneself thus from the habitual structure of reference, to challenge or complicate our common assumptions about it, does not amount to saying that there is *nothing* beyond language" ("Deconstruction and the Other" 124). And this would certainly apply to the context of his difference with Foucault, where what is at stake *on both sides* is a set of institutionalized relations between power, knowledge, and the discourse of reason. Foucault's extreme epistemological skepticism leads him to equate knowledge with power, and hence to regard all ideas of "enlightened" progress (in psychiatry, sexual attitudes, or penal reform) as signs of an increasing sophistication in the mechanisms of social control (see esp. *Power/Knowledge*). Derrida, by contrast, insists that there is no escaping that post-Kantian enlightenment tradition, and certainly no question of our now having emerged at last into a "postmodern" era where its concepts and categories lack all critical force. On the contrary, it is only by working persistently *within* that tradition, but *against* some of its ruling ideas, that thought can muster the resistance required for an effective critique of existing institutions.

Such is the theme of Derrida's recent essays on the politics of knowledge, the "principle of reason," and the role of university teaching and research. It is a superficial irony at most that Derrida should devote himself to defending philosophy's role in the French school and university curriculum while continuing to "deconstruct" its traditional arguments and truth-claims. "Who is more faithful to reason's call, who hears it with a keener ear, who better sees the difference, the one who offers questions in return and tries to think through the possibility of that summons, or the one who does not want to hear any question about the reason of reason?" (Derrida, "The Principle of Reason" 9). One should read this as a two-fold challenge, on the one hand to philosophy, insofar as it remains constitutionally blind to certain of its governing interests and motives, but on the other — more pointedly — to those forms of neopragmatist or "postmodern" thinking that renounce reason itself. For Derrida, the critique of existing relationships between power and knowledge has to go by way of a close engagement with the texts in which those relations are obliquely inscribed. Hence his latest essays on Kant and Hegel, texts in which the deconstruction of philosophical themes goes along with an analysis of the way these ideas have shaped our understanding of liberal education, of the modern university and philosophy's role vis-à-vis the politics of knowledge (see esp. "The Principle of Reason" and "La Philosophie et ses classes").

Certainly Derrida goes far toward dismantling that Kantian conception of philosophy that treats it as a locus of pure, disinterested inquiry, free from the pressures of state interference by virtue of its guaranteed nonparticipation in practical affairs. He shows very clearly how this rhetoric of disinterest serves both to prop up philosophy's truth-claims and, more crucially, to disguise its manifold stakes and investments in the word "outside" the university. Such distinctions are scarcely tenable, as Derrida remarks, at a time when "military programs, especially those of the Navy, can very rationally subsidize linguistic, semiotic or anthropological investigations," and when these disciplines are tied up in turn with "history, literature, hermeneutics, law, political science, psychoanalysis, and so forth" ("Principle of Reason" 14). But to bring these counterarguments against the traditional Kantian ideal — and to link that ideal with the classic epistemology of knowledge, reason, and truth — is *not* to suggest that we henceforth abandon the entire conceptual ground of enlightened understanding. Rather, it is a question of thinking these issues through with a sense of their urgent practical import *and* their distinctive philosophical character. For otherwise — as Gillian Rose has lately argued in a powerful critique of poststructuralist theory, *Dialectic of Nihilism* — there is a tendency simply to forget or repress those real, insistent problems in the history of thought that then return to haunt the discourse of latter-day unreason.

Rose makes a very strong case against Foucault's undifferentiating rhetoric of power and knowledge, his lack of epistemological rigor, and his failure to engage with the crucial "antinomies" (of reason in its practical or legislative aspect) bequeathed by Kant to modern philosophy and the human sciences at large. But she is, I think, less persuasive when she reproaches Derrida for likewise giving way to an irrational "dialectic of nihilism" devoid of any genuine critical grasp. And this misreading comes about precisely through Rose's endorsement of the widespread idea—widespread at least among literary theorists—that deconstruction seeks to put an end to philosophy since it demonstrates how all concepts reduce to metaphors (or effects of writing) in the end. Certainly she is able to quote several passages—including the celebrated Nietzschean epilogue to "Structure, Sign and Play" (293)—that would seem to lend credence to this version of Derrida. But she also has to ignore all the contrary indications (some of which I have assembled here) that Derrida is far from embracing such a simplified view of the issues at stake. This is not just to say that he is still a "philosopher" insofar as he writes about Kant, Hegel, and others who lay special claim to that title. Rather, it is a question of Derrida's engaging their texts at a level of argument that philosophers—some of them at any rate—will recognize as belonging to that same history of enlightened conceptual critique. "Those who venture forth along this path, it seems to me, need not set themselves up in opposition to the principle of reason, nor need they give way to 'irrationalism.' They may continue to assume *within* the university, along with its memory and tradition, the imperatives of professional rigor and competence" ("Principle of Reason" 17). And when Derrida invokes "professional" standards, he is not making terms with that line of ultrapragmatist thought that leads philosophers like Rorty (and literary theorists like Stanley Fish) to collapse the distinction between valid argument and what *counts* as valid argument within any given community of interests.[4] In fact, it is precisely Derrida's habit of raising difficulties with this consensus view of knowledge that strikes both Rorty and Fish as a needless distraction from the communal enterprise. To Rorty it represents a kind of backsliding into the bad old ways of philosophy, a sign that Derrida is still having trouble with problems that the pragmatist can cheerfully ignore (see "Philosophy as a Kind of Writing"). To Fish, it simply figures as one more example of how theory goes wrong when it fails to understand that arguments can *make sense* only within the context of existing "professional" codes and conventions (see "With the Compliments of the Author"). Their combined counterarguments help to make the point: that deconstruction preserves its critical thrust insofar as it engages with properly "philosophical" problems and refuses the accommodating line of least resistance offered by current neopragmatist fashion.

So there is no contradiction or sign of bad faith in Derrida's simultaneously defending the interests of philosophy and subjecting them to the rigors of deconstructive critique. Such work must always involve, as he writes, "a double gesture, a double postulation: to ensure professional competence and the most serious tradition of the university even while going as far as possible, theoretically and practically, in the most directly underground thinking about the abyss beneath the university" ("Principle of Reason" 16). In this passage from "The

Principle of Reason,'' Derrida is alluding on the one hand to certain distinctive topographical features of the Cornell University campus, and on the other to that long tradition in philosophy, from Plato to Heidegger, that has sought to establish grounds or foundations for reason itself. That such grounds may turn out to be simply unavailable—products of the will-to-truth within language, metaphors masquerading as concepts—is the Nietzschean message most often extracted from Derrida's texts. But to take this message at face value, as a break with all forms of enlightened thought, is to ignore Derrida's reiterated point: that deconstruction can operate only through a vigilant critique of inherited concepts and categories. Such ultimate questions about the reason of reason must find themselves suspended, as Derrida writes, ''above a most peculiar void.'' Like that Kantian idea of the modern university, and—more specifically—of philosophy's role within it, they must always verge on the limits of what is thinkable in ''competent'' or ''professional'' terms. So Derrida asks, ''Is it rational to worry about reason and its principle?''; and responds, ''Not *simply*; but it would be over-hasty to seek to disqualify this concern and refer those who experience it back to their own irrationalism, their obscurantism, their nihilism'' (''Principle of Reason'' 14). For it may be in the questioning of reason itself—a questioning nonetheless rigorous or consequent—that philosophy retains a sense of its present-day *critical* pertinence and purpose.

Notes

1. This attitude is present even among some of Derrida's more sympathetic Anglo-American commentators. Thus Newton Garver, in his preface to the English translation of *Speech and Phenomena*: ''Faced with Derrida's unrestrained literary extravagance, one cannot help wondering if the heavy reliance upon metaphor and paradox is not misplaced'' (xxvi).

2. Foucault's response appeared as an appendix to the revised edition of *Folie et déraison* 583–603. It has been translated by Geoff Bennington under the title ''My Body, This Paper, This Fire.''

3. See particularly Edward Said, ''The Problem of Textuality: Two Exemplary Positions.''

4. For a full-dress defense of this ''professionalized'' ethos, see Stanley Fish, *Is There a Text in This Class?*

Works Cited

Derrida, Jacques. ''Cogito and the History of Madness.'' In *Writing and Difference*. 31–63.

_____. ''Deconstruction and the Other.'' Interview with Richard Kearney. In *Dialogues with Contemporary Continental Thinkers*. Ed. Richard Kearney. Manchester: Manchester UP, 1984. 105–26.

_____. *Dissemination*. Trans. Barbara Johnson. Chicago: U of Chicago P, 1981.

_____. *Edmund Husserl's Origin of Geometry: An Introduction*. Trans. John P. Leavey, Jr. Stony Brook, N.Y.: Nicholas Hays, 1978.

_____. ''From Restricted to General Economy: A Hegelianism without Reserve.'' In *Writing and Difference*. 251–77.

_____. ''An Idea of Flaubert: 'Plato's Letter.' '' Trans. Peter Starr. *MLN* 99, No. 4 (September 1984): 748–68.

_____. *Margins of Philosophy*. Trans. Alan Bass. Chicago: U of Chicago P, 1982.

_____. "Of an Apocalyptic Tone Recently Adopted in Philosophy." Trans. John P. Leavey. *Oxford Literary Review* 6, No. 2 (1984): 3–37.

_____. *Of Grammatology*. Trans. Gayatri Chakravorty Spivak. Baltimore: Johns Hopkins UP, 1976.

_____. "La Philosophie et ses classes." In *Qui a peur de la philosophie?* Paris: Flammarion, 1977. 445–50.

_____. "The Principle of Reason: The University in the Eyes of Its Pupils." Trans. Catherine Porter and Edward P. Morris. *Diacritics* 13 (Autumn 1983): 3–20.

_____. *Speech and Phenomena and Other Essays on Husserl's Theory of Signs*. Trans. David B. Allison. Evanston, Ill.: Northwestern UP, 1973.

_____. "Structure, Sign and Play." In *Writing and Difference*. 278–93.

_____. "The Supplement of Copula." In *Margins of Philosophy*. 175–205.

_____. "White Mythology." In *Margins of Philosophy*. 207–71.

_____. *Writing and Difference*. Trans. Alan Bass. London: Routledge & Kegan Paul, 1978.

Descombes, Vincent. *Modern French Philosophy*. Cambridge: Cambridge UP, 1980.

Fish, Stanley. *Is There a Text in This Class?* Cambridge, Mass.: Harvard UP, 1980.

_____. "With the Compliments of the Author: Reflections on Austin and Derrida." *Critical Inquiry* 8, No. 4 (Summer 1982): 693–702.

Foucault, Michel. Appendix. *Folie et deraison*. Rev. ed. Paris: Gallimard, 1972. 583-603. Trans. Geoff Bennington. "My Body, This Paper, This Fire." *Oxford Literary Review* 4 (1979): 9–28.

_____. *Power/Knowledge*. Ed. & trans. Colin Gordon. New York: Pantheon, 1980.

Garver, Newton. Preface to Jacques Derrida, *Speech and Phenomena and Other Essays on Husserl's Theory of Signs*. Evanston, Ill.: Northwestern UP, 1973. ix–xxix.

Rorty, Richard. *Philosophy and the Mirror of Nature*. Princeton, N.J.: Princeton UP, 1979.

_____. "Philosophy as a Kind of Writing." In *Consequences of Pragmatism: Essays 1972–1980*. Minneapolis: U of Minnesota P, 1982. 90–109.

Rose, Gillian. *Dialectic of Nihilism: Post-Structuralism and Law*. Oxford: Basil Blackwell, 1984.

Said, Edward. "The Problem of Textuality: Two Exemplary Positions." *Critical Inquiry* 4, No. 4 (Summer 1978): 673–714.

Searle, John. "Reiterating the Differences: A Reply to Derrida." *Glyph* 1 (1977): 198–208.

Spivak, Gayatri C. Translator's preface to Jacques Derrida, *Of Grammatology*. Baltimore: Johns Hopkins UP, 1976. ix–lxxxvii.

10

Two Meanings of "Logocentrism": A Reply to Norris

Richard Rorty

"The discourse of philosophy" is to early Derrida as "Being" is to late Heidegger. Both terms refer to something we can never simply walk away from, but instead must constantly struggle with. As Christians think God inescapable and Heidegger thinks Being inescapable, so Derrida thinks "the discourse of philosophy" inescapable. All our attempts to do without it are relations to it. It follows us down the nights and down the days. It waits at the end of every road that seems to lead away from it. Just as Freud thought that we never cease from erotic struggle with images of our parents, no matter how long we live or how little we consciously think about them, so the early Derrida thinks that we cannot escape from logocentric discourse. For him, as Norris says, "philosophy's influence on our language and habits of thought is utterly pervasive." Just as Freud thought that we might be able to replace neurotic misery with ordinary human unhappiness by *realizing* that our struggle with those figures of infantile fantasy is interminable, so may we replace self-deception with the endless labor of deconstruction by *realizing* that there will never be a *last* philosophical discourse.

If (but only if) philosophy's influence *is* that pervasive, we have no choice but to use, as Norris says, "the language that comes to hand (along with its inescapable logocentric residues) . . . in precisely such a way as to bring out its inherent strains and contradictions." Just as the abstract knowledge gained from psychoanalysis is useful only insofar as it is artfully applied to particular events in our lives, so the abstract knowledge that the discourse of philosophy is self-contradictory is no help unless we artfully bring it to bear on particular texts. If the premise about philosophy's pervasiveness is true, then American deconstructive criticism—with its dreary and repetitious discovery of tiresomely familiar "inherent strains and contradictions"—may be the best we can hope for.

My own view, as I said in "Deconstruction and Circumvention," is that that crucial premise is false. The "discourse of philosophy" does function as an inescapable parent figure for some people. But for other people it is only an aging great-uncle, briefly glimpsed in childhood at the occasional family celebration. The idea of God is, in part, the idea of the Father of Us All—the parent we all have in common. The idea of Being, or of "the discourse of philosophy," as something we purport to forget only to find ourselves bonded to it anew, is pretty much the same idea. Prophets who claim a personal, quasi-filial, relationship with God tell us that he is as inescapable for us as for them. But, Freud suggested, such prophets may simply be trying to excuse their own idiosyncratic difficulties by taking them to be universal: imagining that their own tiresome and embarrassing parents are also the parents of everyone else. Late Heidegger and early Derrida are, to my mind, this sort of prophet.

My view has, at least, the virtue of explaining why the writings of both men are so important for some of us—those of us for whom the discourse of philosophy actually *has* been important—while looking so absurd, so little worth reading, to many other people. Having myself cathected the discourse of philosophy when young, I find Heidegger and Derrida among the most powerful and fascinating writers of my time. They speak to my condition. But I doubt very much that they speak to a universal human, or even a universal Western, condition. My own imagination is filled with the same images as fill theirs: Socrates and Phaedo, shifty Matter and stalwart Form, dubious mind-dependent redness and reliable mind-independent squareness, the starry a priori above and the grimy a posteriori below, Hegel's rose, Nietzsche's tarantulas, and Quine's rabbit stages. These are powerful, but not universally compelling, images. Their power over me, I take it, comes from the way I happened to acquire them, the way they happened to interlock with, and eventually to symbolize, my own idiosyncratic hopes and fears. Their power over Heidegger and Derrida, I assume, is a result of similarly idiosyncratic interlockings.

Consider, from this point of view, Norris's claim that one cannot "escape philosophy simply by determining no longer to have any truck with it." This is certainly true for those of us who have had a lot of truck with it in the past; nobody escapes his past, his parents, or his Bloomian precursors just by turning his back on them. But, as I suggested in "Deconstruction and Circumvention," a lot of people never have had much truck with philosophy. Even the intellectuals, in recent centuries, have been having less and less truck with it. As science, scholarship, and (especially) literature have ramified, the number of people who cathected philosophy in their youth has steadily decreased. So, to evaluate Norris's argument, we have to look at the premise I have already isolated: the premise about philosophy being "utterly pervasive."

I think this premise seems plausible only if one identifies the "discourse of philosophy" with any and all binary oppositions. Few pieces of writing will not invoke, implicitly or explicitly, some such oppositions as good-evil, noble-base, cause-effect, free-necessary, original-derivative, eternity-time, positive-negative, male-female, and white-black. But it is not plausible to think of *all* these oppositions as equally "philosophical." Their casual ubiquity suggests that they swing free of whatever logocentric assumptions might have been associated with their use, just as the word "atom" has come to swing free of Democritean assumptions. As Barbara Herrnstein Smith has said, if one identifies the whole list of familiar oppositions with "logocentrism" then

> . . . there is no reason to believe that the metaphysics of Western thought is distinct from that of Eastern thought, or tribal thought, or the thought of illiterates or of preverbal or as yet unacculturated children. On the contrary, I am persuaded that "the metaphysics of Western thought" *is* thought, all of it, root and branch, everywhere and always.[1]

Smith's point suggests that we distinguish a narrow from a wide sense of the term "logocentric metaphysics of presence." In the *narrow* sense, this metaphysics consists of something like the doctrines that, toward the beginning of his essay, Norris identifies as "the three main assumptions that underpin the discourse of philosophy as a quest for ultimate, self-validating truth." The notions invoked in aid of this project of self-validation—notions like "self-evident," "intuitive," "directly present to consciousness," "conditions of the possibility of experience," and so on—are are not commonsensical, but obviously philosophical.

But in the *wide* sense, the metaphysics of presence and "the discourse of philosophy" include *all* the invidious binary oppositions listed earlier, and thousands more. These are distinctions some philosophers have been tempted to explicate with reference to the idea of self-validation, but that explication is no more essential to their use than astrophysics is to our casual references to heavenly bodies. It is one thing to say that the quest for ultimate, self-validating truth has "inherent strains and contradictions." It is another to say that "the language of the West" or "the discourse of philosophy" has such strains. The former strains are quite specific, and are the kind Derrida finds in Husserl and other authors who are driven by the quest for certainty, the need for direct, immediate confrontation, and the like. The latter strains are merely the ordinary strains that appear in any and every vocabulary (scientific, political, technical, or whatever) when it meets an anomaly—something with which it was not designed to cope. To develop a new vocabulary that will handle the new, perplexing, cases is not a matter of escaping from philosophy, or from "the structure of previous thought," but simply of reweaving our web of linguistic usage—our habits of responding to marks and noises with other marks and noises. Some such reweavings are relatively easy and painless (e.g., those involved in Kuhnian "normal science" and in reformist politics); others are dramatic and disturbing (e.g., those involved in intellectual and political revolutions).

Although they may appear dramatic to hindsight, revolutions in philosophy, like the Copernican Revolution in science and unlike violent political revolutions, take quite a long time: sometimes a century or two. During the last hundred and fifty years, there has been continually increasing dissatisfaction among philosophers with ideas like "self-validating truth," "intuition," "transcendental argument," and "principles of the ultimate foundation of all possible knowledge."[2] So, as John Searle remarked in his review of Culler's *On Deconstruction*, if deconstruction is no more than another version of antifoundationalism, it is not very exciting. Most philosophers nowadays *are* antifoundationalists. If Derrida were simply telling us that ideas like "self-validation" and "intuition" contain "inherent strains and contradictions," he would be telling us little that we might not have learned from Peirce's criticism of Descartes, T. H. Green's of Locke, Wilfrid Sellars's and W. v. O. Quine's of the various dogmas of empiricism, and Wittgenstein's and Davidson's of "building-block" theories of language learning. Norris is quite right that Derrida does a first-class, highly professional, job on Husserl. But, *mutatis mutandis*, it is pretty much the same job the philosophers I just mentioned did on their respective targets.[3] The basic antiintuitionist and antifoundationalist point common to Derrida and these others is that knowledge is a matter of asserting sentences, and that you cannot validate such an assertion by confronting an object (e.g., a table, the concept "tablehood," or the Platonic Idea of Table), but only by asserting other sentences. This point is linked to lots of other holist and antiessentialist doctrines, doctrines that make it possible to set aside the subject-object, representationalist notions of knowledge we inherited from the Greeks.[4]

I think Norris is wrong when he says that my view requires me to "politely ignore all the passages of hard-pressed textual analysis where Derrida shows deconstruction actually at work on the grounding assumptions of logocentric discourse." The passages I assume Norris would pick out as fulfilling this description seem to me to divide into two sets. The first set offers the standard antiintuitionist, antiessentialist arguments Derrida shares with many of his contemporaries. The second set is made up of all those passages in which Derrida refuses to allow his opponents to invoke some innocuous, commonsensical distinction by pointing out that this distinction can be "brought into question." Bringing it into question often involves no more, as Searle rightly remarks, than pointing out that there are difficult borderline cases, or that some philosopher might attempt to construe the distinction at hand as one more instance of the distinction between self-validating plenitude and non-self-validating deficiency.

The latter set includes, for example, the much-discussed passages in which Derrida questioned Austin's use of the distinction between serious and nonserious uses of a given sentence. Here Derrida seemed either to invoke what Searle calls the "positivistic" assumption that a distinction cannot be used if it cannot adjudicate all borderline cases, or else simply to assume that *all* distinctions (except, for some reason, his own) are somehow "complicit" with "the discourse of philosophy." The positivistic assumption is as bad as Searle says it is, and the notion of "complicity" is too vague to have any argumentative force; its use would be defensible only if any binary opposition were dubious just because it is binary, or just because one side of the opposition has traditionally been taken as superior to the other. But such an opposition becomes dubious only when the purpose it is serving is dubious.[5] In itself, it is just a tool that can be used for good or for ill.

I confess that I find the knee-jerk suspicion of binary oppositions among deconstructionists baffling. To say, as they often do, that the "preferred" term of such an opposition "presupposes" the other term is true enough, if all it means is that you will not understand the meaning of, for example, "white" unless you understand that of "black," of "noble" unless you understand that of "base," and so on. But the fact that two contrasting terms get their meaning by reciprocal definability, and in that sense "presuppose" each other, does nothing to cast doubt on their utility.[6] Nor would such doubt be cast by showing, as deconstructionists often do, that the "upper" term can be seen as a "special case" of the "lower" term. Practically anything can be seen, with a bit of imagination and contrivance, as a special case of practically anything else; dialectical and linguistic ingenuity will always suffice to recontextualize anything so as to cast doubt on its importance, or its previous role. But such ingenuity is in vain if it has no purpose more specific than "escaping from logocentrism."[7]

I am also baffled by Norris's (and Gasché's) invocation of the notion of "transcendental argument" as a description of what Derrida is up to. A transcendental argument is an argument to the effect that something is a condition of the *possibility* of something else—a *noncausal* condition. Kant's argument that a nonconscious synthesis of a manifold of intuition is a condition of the possibility of conscious experience should be viewed as a *reductio ad absurdum* of the very idea of such conditions. Taken at face value, arguments such as Kant's amount to positing an unverifiable I-know-not-what to explain a fact—a fact that only seems in need of explanation because one has previously posited that ordinary, scientific, causal explanations of it will not do.[8] The most charitable construal of such arguments is that they are misleading ways of making the point that a certain set of terms cannot be used by people who are incapable of using another set—as in Strawson's construal of the conclusion of Kant's "Transcendental Deduction of the Categories" as the claim that people who could not talk about things could not talk about sense impressions either.

Insofar as Derrida remains faithful to the nominalism he shares with Strawson, transcendental arguments will not permit him to infer the existence of such quasi entities as "différance," "trace" and "archi-writing." Insofar as he does not remain faithful to it, he is just one more metaphysician. A philosopher cannot, as Derrida does, set his face against totalization, insist that the possibilities of recontextualization are boundless, and nonetheless offer transcendental arguments. For how could he hope to grasp *the conditions of possibility of all possible contexts?* What context would he be putting the potential infinity of contexts in when he did so? How can Derrida's "trace," "différance," and the rest of what Gasché calls "infrastructures" be *more* than the vacuous nonexplanations characteristic of a negative theology?[9]

To sum up, I think it as important to insist that Derrida is *not* giving rigorous arguments against logocentrism, in the wide and vacuous sense of that term, as to say that he is indeed (like most other important twentieth-century philosophers) giving such arguments against what Norris calls "a quest for ultimate, self-validating truth." That these assumptions are pretty well moribund by now does not make Derrida's arguments less worthy, but it does mean that we have to seek elsewhere for an explanation of the attention he has received and the extent of his influence.

My own explanation of these phenomena goes like this. I think Derrida appeals to at least three different audiences. The first audience admires the way in which he continues a dialectical sequence that runs through Hegel, Nietzsche, and Heidegger. In his variations on the themes found in these writers—notably the theme of overcoming the tradition, of making a new beginning—he is splendidly original. His stature as a reader of Heidegger is on a level with Heidegger's as a reader of Nietzsche, and with Nietzsche's as a reader of Plato. A second audience admires him simply as a writer. However else Derrida may look to history, he will be viewed as one of the great French writers of his time—a writer who happened, like Sartre, to have started off as a philosophy professor, but who quickly transcended his humble origins. Apart from his incredible, almost Nabokovian, polylingual linguistic facility, he is a great *comic* writer—perhaps the funniest writer on philosophical topics since Kierkegaard.

I am an enthusiastic member of both of these first two audiences. But I see them as distinct from a third, and much larger, audience, to which I do not belong. This one contains most of the people who write deconstructive literary criticism. These people assimilate early Derrida to the thought of Paul de Man. They tend to accept de Man's explanation of what it is that readers of literature do: namely, continually rediscover, by close reading, the impossibility of reading. Even when they do not, they agree with de Man that philosophical reflection can teach literary critics something important, and useful in their work, about the nature of "language," "reading," or "literature." They think these words name distinctive natural kinds. For they believe, with Husserl, Dilthey, and de Man, that a great gulf separates "natural objects" and "intentional objects."[10] They accept de Man's claim that those who "resist theory," who do not read closely, assimilate texts to natural objects. They think philosophy can help us see why they are wrong to do so. This third audience, committed in advance to literary criticism as a pursuit, welcomes philosophical guarantees that their activity of close reading is indeed as important as critics take to to be.

De Man offered such guarantees much more explicitly than does Derrida. Far more than Derrida, de Man is responsible for the tone of the Anglo-American movement called "deconstruction"—a tone that mixes elegy with polemic. Consider such passages from de Man as the following:

The distinctive character of literature [is] an inability to escape from a condition that is felt to be unbearable. (*Blindness and Insight* 162)

Literature is fiction not because it somehow refuses to acknowledge "reality," but because it is not *a priori* certain that language functions according to principles which are those, or which are *like* those, of the phenomenal world. It is therefore not *a priori* certain that literature is a reliable source of information about anything but its own language. . . . Resistance to theory is in fact a resistance to reading.'' (*The Resistance to Theory* 11, 15)

Poetic language names this void [''the presence of a nothingness''] with ever-renewed understanding. . . . This persistent naming is what we call literature. (*Blindness and Insight* 18)

The systematic avoidance of reading, of the interpretive or hermeneutic moment, is a general symptom shared by all methods of literary analysis. (*Blindness and Insight* 282)

Reading or writing ''literary language'' or ''poetic language''—the sort of language that makes *evident* that ''language'' as such functions differently from ''the phenomenal world,'' the realm of ''natural objects'' whose ''meaning is equal to the totality of [their] sensory appearances'' (*Blindness and Insight* 24)— is, for de Man and his followers, a way of mourning a *Deus absconditus*, of participating in a divine absence. To have to do with poetic language in that special way in which those who do *not* ''systematically avoid reading'' have to do with it is an ascetic practice that confronts one ever and again with ''the presence of a nothingness.'' For de Manians, the analogue of bad, *positive* theology is attachment to a ''method of literary analysis'' and the analogue of good, negative theology is success in overcoming that ''resistance to reading'' that is also a ''resistance to theory.'' The positive theologians are the people who think literature *is* a ''reliable source of information about something other than its own language.'' The initiates, the negative theologians, the worshippers of the Dark God whose Voice is in the Literariness of Language, are those who no longer believe that ''language functions according to principles which are those, or which are *like* those, of the phenomenal world.''

Many readers of de Man, searching for reasons *why* poetic language—the most linguistic sort of language, as it were—names the presence of a nothingness, thought they had found the answer in such Derridean claims as the following:

The sign represents the present in its absence. . . . The sign, in this sense, is deferred presence. (*Margins of Philosophy* 9)

From the moment there is meaning there are nothing but signs. *We think only in signs.* Which amounts to ruining the notion of the sign at the very moment when, as in Nietzsche, its exigency is recognized in the absoluteness of its right. One could call *play*, the absence of the transcendental signified as limitlessness of play, that is to say as the destruction of ontotheology and the metaphysics of presence. (*Of Grammatology* 50)

But on my own nominalist and pragmatic reading of them, the only relevance of these Derridean claims to poetic language—with its familiar ''untranslatability'' and ''interpenetration of sound and sense''—is that such language is an especially good *example* of what is wrong with the Lockean idea that linguistic signs are sensible vehicles of intelligible meanings. This idea is equally wrong for flat-footed nonpoetic language. The right idea, according to us nominalists, is that "recognition of meaning" is simply ability to substitute sensible signs (i.e., marks and noises) for other signs, and still other signs for the latter, and so on indefinitely. This latter doctrine is found, for example, in Peirce, Wittgenstein, and Davidson as well as in Derrida. On this reading, Derrida is simply restating Peirce's attack on the idea that a regress of interpretation of a sign can be stopped by a self-validating Cartesian intuition—an attack he says "goes very far in the direction that I have called the deconstruction of the transcendental signified, which, at one time or another, would place a reassuring end to the reference from sign to sign" (*Of Grammatology* 49).[11]

The third audience I have described takes Derrida's revival of Peirce's anti-Cartesian point as the "philosophical basis" for de Manian readings of texts. The problem with putting de Man and Derrida together in this way, however, is that Derrida does *not* contrast the way language works with the way "the phenomenal world" works. He is not, as Michael Ryan has pointed out, "privileging language, rhetoric, or 'literary texts' " (24).[12] He does not distinguish between placid scientific or legal texts on the one hand and restless, self-deconstructing, literary texts on the other. The Diltheyan dualism that de Man takes for granted is not to be found in Derrida. Indeed, Derrida follows up his reference to Peirce by saying that "the thing itself is a sign"—*any* thing, a rock as much as a text.[13] For all the anti-Husserlian reasons given in Derrida's *Speech and Phenomenona* and all those given in Sellars's attack on "the Myth of the Given," we cannot preserve de Man's notion of "natural objects" as having a meaning exhausted by the "totality of their sensory appearances." Pace de Man, "the phenomenal world"—the world of nonlinguistic *things*—works just the way language does.

I take this difference between de Man and Derrida to be a mark of their divergent concerns, concerns that diverge more and more as one moves from earlier to later Derrida. To my mind, Derrida's best statement of his own project is the following:

> To make enigmatic what one thinks one understands by the words "proximity," "immediacy," "presence" (the proximate [*proche*], the own [*propre*], and the pre- of presence) is my final intention in this book. (*Of Grammatology* 70)[14]

Notice the difference between "making enigmatic what one means by" certain words and reacting to the absence of what one takes to be denoted by them. De Man is doing the latter. He *needs* the discourse of Cartesian philosophy—with its talk of immediate knowledge, self-validating intuitions, and all the rest of it—to remain intelligible and *non*enigmatic. He needs it to remain intelligible in order to contrast the way language works from the way "the phenomenal world" works (and, indeed, to make sense of the notion of "phenomenal"—what appears to the senses, what is present to consciousness, etc.) He needs "the discourse of philosophy" as a medium in which to write his elegiac readings of literature. He needs a clear vision of the dead, but luminous, God of Presence in order to display (by the contrast of darkness to light) his living but invisible God of Absence.

By contrast, as the passage about "making enigmatic" suggests, Derrida is torn between the negative theologian's urge to find a new pantheon—"trace," "différance," and the rest of what Gasché calls "infrastructures"—and the comic writer's urge to make something once held sacred look funny. In his later work, it seems to me, he is less torn. He is content simply to have fun rather than to feel haunted. De Man needs the "discourse of philosophy" in the way a negative theologian needs positive theology—as an exhibition of what we must forgo. De Man's analogue of negative theology is a way of "reading" that eschews "methods of literary analysis"—eschews the idea that structures of historical, scientific, psychoanalytic, or sociopolitical thought can be used to filter out what is essential from what is accidental in a literary text (in the way in which such structures *are* legitimately used in dealing with "the phenomenal world"). But, at his best, Derrida offers not a way of reading but a kind of writing—comic writing that does not presuppose "the discourse of philosophy" as anything more than a butt.

On my account, de Man (and the constructive and argumentative strain in early Derrida—the strain that produces notions like "trace") represents merely one more *inversion* of a traditional philosophical position—one more "transvaluation of all values" that nevertheless remains within the range of alternatives specified by "the discourse of philosophy." The great Greek logocentrists told us that reality is divided into two realms, one of which is the unwobbling pivot about which the other revolves. Their preferred realm is, as Derrida says, the one that gives a center to structures, which "limits what we might call the *play* of the structure" (*Writing and Difference* 278). If Derrida is read as confirming or explaining or arguing for the sort of thing de Man says about the difference between "language" and "the phenomenal world," he would have to be read as saying that the former is the realm of nonlimit, of play, of the unbearable absence of the present and fixed. He would have to say that whereas in "the phenomenal world" the flux is an epiphenomenon of the stable, in "language" the stable is an epiphenomenon of the flux, and that the latter realm is somehow more "basic" than the former.

If Derrida *were* saying that, he would indeed be just what he most fears to be—one more example of the inversion of traditional philosophical oppositions. Heidegger thought that Nietzsche's exaltation of Becoming over Being was an example of the fruitlessness of such an inversion—fruitless because it retained the overall form of ontotheological systems, merely changing God's name to that of the Devil, and conversely.[15] Derrida agrees with Heidegger that inverted logocentrism is still logocentrism, and that some movement more complex and powerful than inversion is needed. Furthermore, he thinks Heidegger himself did not succeed in becoming sufficiently different from what he was trying to evade.[16] I think he was on the right track when he suggested that the only strategy of evasion that is going to work will be to write in a way that makes the discourse of philosophy enigmatic rather than ubiquitous. At his best, Derrida realizes that one good way to make something look enigmatic is to treat it as a joke.

If Derrida does indeed want to make the discourse of philosophy enigmatic, then he should not try to do what Gasché and Norris say he tries to do: discover the conditions of possibility of language, and in particular of the discourse of philosophy. There must be something wrong with Gasché's claim that "Derrida's inquiry into the limits of philosophy is an investigation into the conditions of possibility and impossibility of a type of discourse and questioning which he recognizes as absolutely indispensable" (2). Specifically, there must be some sense in which Derrida regards this discourse not as "absolutely indispensable" but as the sort of thing we can make so enigmatic as to be no longer tempted to put it to argumentative use. There must also be something wrong with Norris's claim that Derrida's "rigorously argued case for the strict impossibility of conceiving language on the basis of an ideal speech-situation where words and meanings correspond in a perfect (self-present) reciprocity of sense" amounts to "a form of Kantian transcendental deduction." That case is, to be sure, rigorously argued, but it is just the familiar case every recent nominalist philosopher has made. It is a good case, but Derrida's importance does not lie in his having restated it.

Notes

1. See the chapter called "Changing Places" in Smith's *Contingencies of Value* (116–24). Smith goes on to note that "the cheapest way for any system to process an array of information is by binary classification, which is, of course, the minimal classification. Moreover, because, in an organic system, classification, like any other activity, is economically energized — energized, that is, by self-interest or, if you like, the profit-motive — any classification that is produced is likely to be an evaluative hierarchy.

2. I take this last phrase from Rodolphe Gasché, who says (*The Tain of the Mirror* 88) that "both Heidegger's and Derrida's approaches could . . . be viewed as inquiries, in a new sense, not principles of the ultimate foundation of all possible knowledge." Gasché agrees with Norris and with Jonathan Culler that praises of Derrida's writing as "free play" (by, e.g., Geoffrey Hartman and myself) are misleading. I criticize Gasché's reconstruction of Derrida as a quasi-foundationalist philosopher in a forthcoming article in *The Yale Critical Journal*.

3. See Samuel Wheeler, "The Extension of Deconstruction" and "Indeterminacy of French Translation." Wheeler draws parallels between Derrida's arguments and those of Quine and Davidson. The great difference between such writers and Derrida, of course, is that the former do not share Heidegger's sense of "Western metaphysics" as pervasive and all-encompassing. So their polemics lack the apocalyptic tone common to late Heidegger and early Derrida.

Notice, in particular, Wheeler's point that "the core-problem which drives the analyses of both Derrida and Davidson . . . is that allegedly non-Aristotelian and nonessentialist accounts of the world (e.g., Kantian and 'linguistic' ones) still seem to rest on essentialism about conceptual or linguistic items. . . . The radical break which both Davidson and Derrida make is to work out the consequences of denying essentialism and objective necessities across the board" ("Indeterminacy" 484). Whereas Davidson thinks these consequences can be worked out naturalistically, early Derrida and Gasché think that a nonnaturalistic theory involving notions such as "trace," "différance," etc., is required. My agreement with Davidson on this point amounts to saying that these latter notions are dispensable, and that there is no need for "transcendental deductions" in this area.

4. One consequence of getting rid of this picture is that it is no longer a criticism of philosophy to say, with Norris, that "its concepts most often come down to metaphors at root." In order to have a polemically useful contrast between "concept" and "metaphor" one would have to assume that concepts necessarily have literal meaning, and then construe such meaning as possible only by virtue of ostension (exhibiting a sensible or intelligible object to consciousness, bringing that which the concept signified before the mind and naming it). It would be hard to find an important twentieth-century philosopher (other than Husserl, Russell, and a few of their more ardent followers) who held any such view. Russell-bashing and Husserl-bashing remain good sport, but bashing their doctrines is not bashing anything central to recent philosophical thought. Husserl's "Philosophy as Strict Science" (which did indeed call for, in Norris's words, "the ultimate grounding of reason in a sense of those constitutive structures of knowledge and perception which *cannot be doubted*") proved to be a swan song, not a new beginning. The same fate has now overtaken Russell's "Logic as the Essence of Philosophy."

5. This pragmatic point is made by Derrida himself: "If words and concepts receive meaning only in sequences of differences, one can justify one's language, and one's choice of terms, only within a topic and an historical strategy. The justification can therefore never be absolute and definitive. It corresponds to a condition of forces and translates an historical calculation" (*Of Grammatology* 70). Dewey would have happily agreed, as would Wittgenstein.

6. It would cast such doubt only if one held that the "upper" term of an opposition must be definable by ostension—by direct confrontation with an object—whereas the "lower" can be defined only indirectly, parasitically, on the basis of an antecedent knowledge of the meaning of the "upper" term. But, as I have said earlier, it is getting pretty hard to find anybody who takes the notion of ostensive definition seriously. Aristotle, to be sure, can be interpreted as holding that we grasp some terms by *nous* and others by secondary and derivative means, but there are not many Aristotelians around anymore. Even Husserl and Russell, who do take ostension seriously, can hardly be saddled with this view of any and every binary opposition. Culler (*On Deconstruction* 160) says that in binary oppositions "the first term has been conceived as prior, a plentitude of which the second is a negation or complication." I think he would be hard-pressed to find recent philosophers who so conceive the matter.

7. Derrida's example has inspired a good deal of ingenious, and sometimes effective, recontextualization on behalf of less fuzzy purposes, e.g., overcoming patriarchy, and other forms of sociopolitical oppression. But such efforts are, I think, weakened rather than strengthened by attempts to associate such oppression with "logocentrism." In the narrow sense of that term, the association is hardly evident. In the wide sense, it is like associating something with Satan, or the Forces of Darkness. Like "capitalism" as used by some Marxists, "logocentrism" has become less and less useful as a scare-word as it has been stretched to cover more and more territory. It becomes vaguer and less scary with each stretch.

8. I have discussed transcendental arguments in "Verificationism and Transcendental Arguments" and in "Transcendental Arguments, Self-reference, and Pragmatism." I discuss Strawson's attempt to update, and make respectable, Kantian transcendental argumentation in "Strawson's Objectivity Argument."

9. Norris is quite right in saying that, on my view, early Derrida is "falling back into a kind of negative theology that merely replaces one set of absolutes (truth, meaning, clear and distinct ideas) with another (trace, *différance*, and other such deconstructive key-terms." But the main justification for distinguishing between an earlier and a later Derrida is that he *stops* doing this. Just as Heidegger stopped using terms like "phenomenological ontology," "Dasein" and "*existential*" about five years after *Being and Time*, so Derrida has pretty well given up using notions like "grammatology," "archi-writing," and the rest. This seems to me very sensible on his part. The Derrida of *The Post Card* is no longer warning us that the "discourse of philosophy" will get us if we don't watch out.

Instead, he alternately plays and struggles with concrete, particular, thinkers—e.g., Freud and Heidegger—rather than with a protean, putatively inescapable, quasi divinity called "the discourse of philosophy." As Michael Ryan says (xiv), Derrida's work since 1975 "has become increasingly difficult, self-referential and esoteric." It has also become much less easy to interpret as argumentative. I see this change as Derrida's attempt to avoid the sort of "falling back into a kind of negative theology" that I diagnose.

10. See de Man, *Blindness and Insight* 24.

11. On the analogies between Peirce's and Wittgenstein's insistence on the endlessness of interpretation, see my "Pragmatism, Categories and Language."

12. I am sympathetic to Ryan's point that "Derrida's emphasis on repetition and difference is lopsided. As Anglo-American literary critics prove, it can itself become a metaphysics." But I should prefer to say a "theology" rather than a "metaphysics"—the worship of a Dark God, the celebration of perpetual absence. A distinctively theological tone emerges in the chapter on de Man in J. Hillis Miller's recent *The Ethics of Reading*. Miller says that "the failure to read takes place inexorably within the text itself. The reader must reenact this failure in his or her own reading" (53)—an update of the Christian's duty continually to reenact the Passion. Miller sounds an eschatological note when he says, "I would even dare to promise that the millennium [of "universal peace and justice among men"] would come if all men and women became good readers in de Man's sense" (58).

13. On the general point that redescription can decompose anything—a piece of rock or a piece of writing—into a chain of relations to other things, see my "Texts and Lumps."

14. The passage continues as follows: "This deconstruction of presence accomplishes itself through the deconstruction of consciousness, and therefore through the irreducible notion of the trace [*Spur*] as it appears in both Nietzschean and Freudian discourse. And finally, in all scientific fields, notably in biology, this notion seems currently to be dominant and irreducible." For light on this last sentence, see *Of Grammatology* 9. There it is clear that Derrida has in mind the notion of a "genetic code" in biology and of "program" in computer science. I doubt that either notion is at all relevant to Derrida's project. But his *belief* that they are relevant does help confirm the claim that he is *not* saying that "Language is the realm of trace and difference; outside of language there is the realm of presence, phenomenality, structure, etc."

15. Such inversion was popular around the turn of the century. It is the least common denominator of Nietzsche, James, and Bergson. The later Heidegger tries desperately to distance himself from this exaltation of flux over permanence, an exaltation some readers had detected in *Being and Time*.

16. Referring to Heidegger, Derrida says "one risks ceaselessly confirming, consolidating, *relifting* (*relever* [Derrida's translation of *Aufhebung*]), at an always more certain depth, that which one allegedly deconstructs" ("The Ends of Man," *Margins of Philosophy* 135). In this same passage, and elsewhere, Derrida says that what is needed to avoid repeating Heidegger's failure is a "double" movement—one that "must speak several languages and produce several texts at once." This latter technique is, I think, what we find in later Derrida, in the writings that look less and less like one more "discourse of philosophy" and are less and less susceptible to the sort of reading Gasché offers.

Works Cited

Culler, Jonathan. *On Deconstruction: Theory and Practice after Structuralism*. Ithaca, N.Y.: Cornell UP, 1982.

De Man, Paul. *Blindness and Insight: Essays in the Rhetoric of Contemporary Criticism*. New York: Oxford UP, 1971.

_____. *The Resistance to Theory*. Minneapolis: U of Minnesota P, 1986.

Derrida, Jacques. *Margins of Philosophy*. Chicago: U of Chicago P, 1982.

_____. *Of Grammatology*. Baltimore: Johns Hopkins UP, 1976.

_____. *Writing and Difference*. Chicago: U of Chicago P, 1978.

Gasché, Rodolphe. *The Tain of the Mirror*. Cambridge: Harvard UP, 1986.

Miller, J. Hillis. *The Ethics of Reading*. New York: Columbia UP, 1987.

Rorty, Richard. *Contingency, Irony and Solidarity*. Cambridge: Cambridge UP, 1989.

_____. "Pragmatism, Categories and Language." *Philosophical Review* 70 (1961): 197–223.

_____. "Deconstruction and Circumvention." *Critical Inquiry* 11 (1984): 1–23.

_____. "Strawson's Objectivity Argument." *Review of Metaphysics* 24 (1970): 207–44.

_____. "Texts and Lumps." *New Literary History* 17 (1985): 1–15.

_____. "Transcendental Arguments, Self-reference, and Pragmatism." In *Transcendental Arguments and Science: Essays in Epistemology*. Ed. Peter Bieri et al. Dordrecht: Reidel, 1979. 77–103.

_____. "Verificationism and Transcendental Arguments." *Nous* 5 (1971): 3–14.

Ryan, Michael. *Marxism and Deconstruction*. Baltimore: Johns Hopkins UP, 1982.

Smith, Barbara Herrnstein. *Contingencies of Value*. Cambridge: Harvard UP, 1988.

Wheeler, Samuel. "The Extension of Deconstruction." *Monist* 69 (1986): 3–21.

_____. "Indeterminacy of French Translation." In *Truth and Interpretation: Perspectives on the Philosophy of Donald Davidson*. Ed. Ernest LePore. Oxford: Basil Blackwell, 1986. 477–94.

11

An Afterword:
The Lines Redrawn

Anthony J. Cascardi

The subject of the following remarks may be situated in the aftermath of the long and intricate debate in our culture between the divergent praxes or language games of history and theory. As the essays gathered in this volume make abundantly clear, both deconstruction and contemporary analytic philosophy have placed in doubt the possibility of ascribing normative force to historical paradigms while rejecting the possibility of a purely speculative discourse about such things as the ends of history, social relations, and the nature of the self. The attempt to find terms of discourse other than those history and theory provide has thus called into question the philosophical practice of justifying the specific modes of self-assertion in which we find ourselves engaged. Whether there exists a framework in which the various forms of expression available to us can serve as models for the creation and identification of the self remains to be seen, but it may in any case be said that the recourse to such concepts as "language game," "reading," and "metaphor" in the majority of these essays is a sign of the displacement of the established function of literature in this regard. If according to an older, humanistic ideal, literature served to mediate the categories of history and theory by universalizing the particular and by rendering the universal concrete, the attempt to pass beyond history and theory into the realm of language games has rendered the mediating function of literature in this regard all but obsolete. As has many times been shown, attempts to situate literature in historical and theoretical terms were intimately bound up with humanistic conceptions of the role of self-reflection and its place in the transmission of universal values and norms. But in the work of figures like Derrida, de Man, and Cavell, signal instances of "literature" (the texts of Shakespeare, Rousseau, Flaubert, and Mallarmé) have provided the means, or the terms, through which to question philosophy's powers of representation, its antiskeptical commitments to certainty, its confidence in the Idea, and its inevitable will to conclude. I take it as implicit in the effort to pass beyond history and theory that literature should challenge philosophy thus. What remains far less clear is whether this recourse to "literature" is not also an attempt to escape those projects that history and theory have left unfinished. Why is it, for instance, that the notion of a "general literature" (Lyotard's phrase) has come at the price of literature's increased marginalization within culture as a whole? Why has literature become for Paul de Man "the most rigorous and, consequently, the most unreliable language in terms of which man names and transforms himself" (*Allegories* 19)?

Insofar as the claims of history and theory are characteristically associated with "modern" discourse, I want to argue that the attempt to pass beyond or deconstruct the relationship between these terms represents a false interpretation of what postmodernism might be and projects an illusory conception of the possibilities that remain open for the self in the aftermath of the modern age. In so doing, contemporary critics like de Man and Hillis Miller, and contemporary philosopher-theorists like Lyotard, remain committed to ideas of human freedom that are implausibly empty, if not also abstract. In Hillis Miller's most recent work, and in deconstruction generally, the very idea of a moral self constituted in, and in relation to, an objective end is undermined by a nonteleological suspension of the ethical "must." For Lyotard, the notion of the "difference" operating between discourses or language games remains largely in the thrall of the imperative that discourse be constantly new (different). The claim to be made in reply to these positions is that there are enduring demands that both history and theory make on us, and that the need to fashion a mode of discourse in response to these demands in turn provides an image of what postmodernism might be. On the one hand, we are drawn to construct and live out ideals of freedom and significance that are not sheerly speculative or abstract; accordingly, history remains important in providing substantive images of what the self might be. Yet we must at the same time be able to imagine a world in which we might realize our best objective possibilities and self-ideals; hence history's claim to set the limits of speculative discourse cannot be absolute. As the concluding section of this essay suggests, I take literary writing as shaped by the tensions between these demands, hence as providing a compelling model for what the discourse of postmodernism might be.

I

Seen from the point of view of theory, the essays presented in this volume represent an attempt to resist any purely speculative reordering of the boundaries between analytic philosophy, deconstruction, and literary theory, in favor of a posttheoretical and sometimes heterogeneous conception of language: Derrida, Lyotard, and on some accounts Wittgenstein as well, are said to meet under the common umbrella of "language games," of a plural "reading," and of "literature"; in a similar fashion, the work of Donald Davidson and that of Paul de Man are seen as mutually illuminating insofar as each may be aligned with the tenets of a more general thesis concerning the nature of meaning and predication as metaphor, which allows us continuously to redescribe the world and refashion the self. Whatever one's judgment of analytic philosophy, deconstruction, or contemporary literary theory may be, the initial significance of this work must be measured against the purely conceptual framework of differences that once was thought to divide them, for it had long been held that no reconciliation at all would be possible between such disparate positions as analytic philosophy's adherence to the fantasy of a "magic language" of fixed essences on the one hand and deconstruction's insistence on the "free play of signifiers" on the other, or similarly between the analytic demand for an unambiguous conceptual notation and the poststructuralist insistence on the continual displacement or deferral of meaning. In one respect, it could be said that the essays gathered here have redrawn the lines between these fields by shifting the ground of their differences from the field of theory, which is that of the concept, to an understanding of language that replaces conceptualization in favor of the differentiating powers of discourse. Predication, which was once thought to be a conceptual act bound to essences, thus becomes a matter of "calling one thing by another's name" (see Wheeler); and judgment, according to Lyotard, becomes a matter of the analogous relationships that link the various language games.

Similarly, the encounter between analytic philosophy, deconstruction, and literary theory has taken place within what can only be called a "posthistorical" space. To be sure, even at this level of generality it may be possible to perceive the outlines of a prior, historically inflected set of beliefs whose presence has not altogether been erased from these essays. The project to redraw the boundaries between these fields cannot entirely avoid the invocation of such terms as "romanticism," "postmodernism," and "organic form," all of which must be understood against a historically charged background; and yet the more radical, historicist claims that these terms might ground have been consistently effaced. If history is not fully absent from these projects, but only held in suspension, or eclipsed, one must conclude that it is because "history" is believed no longer to exist—neither as the unreconciled antithesis of theory nor as that which both analytic philosophy and deconstruction necessarily had to exclude in order for their projects to be made complete. If history once challenged theory for possession of the ground on which the disparities of meaning or the pluralities of value judgments could be recuperated and made whole, it must at the same time be said that this was, in Hegel's assessment, a function of whatever claims to reason could be made by and through the process of history itself. The majority of the essays here may be read as "posthistorical," by contrast, to the extent that the historical implications of the terms they invoke neither serve as paradigms of value for the expression of divergent purposes nor generate teleological categories of judgment for the evaluation of conceptual differences. Similarly, Lyotard's insistence on the place of language games in philosophy, and Rorty's insistence on the role of philosophy "in the conversation of mankind," although historicist insofar as they assert the contingency of all discourse, constitute further refusals of the attempt by history to mediate and thereby recuperate the differences among divergent accounts of human nature or the world, for as the work of both Rorty and Lyotard records, those differences have mostly collapsed.[1] "History" may thus assert itself in these and other contemporary projects not as the court of the world's judgment but rather as the *fabula* or story line in terms of which its own extinction can be retold.

In the attempt to pass beyond history and theory and into the realm where the figurative powers of discourse allow us continuously to redescribe ourselves, contemporary analytic philosophy and deconstruction deepen a series of modernist commitments to the contextuality of truth and the revisability of all contexts; but neither has been successful in reshaping these commitments into a positive vision of society and the self.[2] With the exception of Charles Altieri's appeal to Rawls's political philosophy against the heterogeneity of Lyotard's postmodern language games—a case to which I shall return in somewhat greater detail later—and Richard Shusterman's call for a pragmatist mediation between analytic philosophy and deconstruction, I take these facts neither as signs that history has been avoided (in which case this Afterword would be written in the manner of a reproach) nor as evidence that the tensions between history and theory have finally been overcome (in which case these remarks might be taken as an expression of relief), but rather as an indication that the competing claims of these fields, and indeed the identity of each as shaped by and against the other, have for the most part been effaced. Some of the more important consequences of this effacement remain as yet to be seen, but I want at the outset to forestall the premature judgment that the contemporary recourse to language (to metaphor, reading, speech acts, and language games) conceives itself as providing a substitute or successor for theory, or similarly that analytic philosophy after Frege and Russell, or Continental philosophy after Heidegger, has each carried forward an incomplete, because unhistoricized, project.[3] To believe either of these things would commit us to a repetition of the totalizing critique of culture that Hegel undertook and, but for some of the more sophisticated versions of dialectical materialism, it remains unclear just how the Hegelian project might today be carried out;[4] as Reed Way Dasenbrock and Richard Shusterman rightly note, analytic philosophy and deconstruction both depend, albeit in vastly different ways, on the rejection of Hegelian thought.

Whether or not a posttheoretical account of language or a posthistorical concept of meaning will be able to provide the basis for a vision of the self that could offer positive characterizations of its actions and strong evaluations of the world—whether, in short, we can develop an *ethos* after history and theory have been eclipsed (some might say that this is where ethics leaves off and politics begins)[5]—remains also to be seen, but a look at almost any representative text of deconstruction, from Paul de Man's *Allegories of Reading* (1979) to J. Hillis Miller's *Ethics of Reading* (1987), would reveal that an effacement of the competing claims of history and theory yields an ethics of (nonteleological) "suspension," or displacement, which is to say an ethics in which the judgment of actions in relations to ends no longer holds a place. In claims for the priority of an "ethics of reading" over what he terms the "vague and speculative" politics of interpretation, Hillis Miller has proposed that storytelling generates an *ethos* that is bound to the principles of a moral law as to that which is at once abstract and subjective, imperative and free: "What happens when I read *must* happen, but I must acknowledge it as *my* act of reading, though just what the 'I' is or becomes in this transaction is another question" (43); yet his vision of storytelling posits a breach between cognition and performance that consistently casts doubts on the usefulness of reading as a process through which the self might evaluate the self-assertions it makes. Thus, in commenting on the work of de Man, Miller argues that "the category of the ethical or of 'ethicity' intervenes . . . where the act of reading bars access to an understanding of the act of reading. We can do it. We can read, but we cannot understand what it is we are doing. This means that what we do is always aberrant, since the only thing worth understanding is Reading itself" (48). Similarly, in Miller's discussion of Kant, ethical judgment is said to be exemplified in the alleged unreadability of the very example in which the principle of respect for the moral law (*Achtung*) is explained:

> On the one hand Kant asserts the rules whereby one can be certain to act ethically. He demonstrates the function of narrative as an essential part of that assertion, namely as the bridge between the law as such and any particular law applied in a specific familial, social, and historical situation. On the other hand, the story Kant tells, the story of the man who makes promises intending not to keep them, is undecidable in meaning. It therefore leaves the question open. The reader cannot decide whether the morality of promising is grounded in the law as such or whether it is an example of an ungrounded act which would define morality as a linguistic performative to be judged only by an internal temporal consistency which the example shows, as by a slip of the tongue, can never be attained. The unreadability of the text is to be defined as the text's inability to read itself, not as some failure on my part to read it. (38)

To say that the text is "unreadable" in this way is to suggest that it establishes a series of resistances to those very things it would seem to promise—knowledge, certainty, truth. This unreadability is, furthermore, said to be ethical, when it is seen as forcing us to question the very idea of an objective end. Hence "reading" replaces the ethics of Kantian idealism with a form of ethical delay: "The ethics of literature, in which much of its value consists, emerge most forcefully in this . . . delay, this coercion to inaction, this suspension between rhetoric's worldly persuasive power and philosophy's noncommittal abstraction" (Harpham 129). But to say that the reader is "commanded" by the (unreadability of the) text amounts to a demonstration of the purely formal nature of the "ethics" that this account of reading entails. Yet unlike Kant's understanding of the formalism of ethics, which was, however problematically, bound to the world of praxis, deconstruction remains the pallid reflection of an aestheticized view of ethical action; having ruled out the notion of action as having an objective end it remains imprisoned in a suspended state of reflection on the quasi-imaginative "free play" of signifiers.[6]

We shall see that for a thinker like Lyotard the aesthetic judgment may make powerful claims as the model for an ethics once history and theory have been eclipsed, but let us first consider some of the presuppositions of contemporary analytic philosophy, apparently so alien to the deconstructive fascination with "undecidability" and the aporias of reading and thought, for these reveal a vision of the ethical that is conceptually, if not historically, the predecessor of deconstruction's in many ways. In its characteristic preoccupation with the truth-conditions of propositional utterances, which are neither properly historical nor theoretical, as well as in what Iris Murdoch has described in *The Sovereignty of Good* as the constant will to trace "the continual flow of intention into act" (x), analytic philosophy reveals its commitment on the one hand to a series of empirical or "behavioristic" criteria and on the other hand to a vision of the will as the sovereign and inscrutable arbiter of values. Given prevailing assumptions concerning the nature of the will, and of its resistance to instruction by reason, it is no surprise to find that in the linguistic branch of analytic philosophy our performances are regarded as rational acts that are sufficiently defined insofar as they are open to public view. What remains troubling about this position is that in regarding actions as (propositional) "facts," the question of value is simultaneously ruled out of bounds. The beginnings of this dualism became strikingly clear in the attempt by G. E. Moore and the Oxford ordinary-language philosophers to turn all questions of value (e.g., "What is good?") into matters of fact that might be publicly verifiable in linguistic usage ("What does 'good' mean?").[7] But this leads to an understanding of value as something that no description of fact can possibly address; indeed, this is what Moore takes the ultimate value of value to be. A similar tension is visible in Wittgenstein's *Tractatus*. On the one hand Wittgenstein defines the world as "all that is the case," as being "determined by the facts, and by their being *all* the facts" (*Tractatus* 1, 1.1). And while he can say that propositions do not admit of value distinctions ("All propositions are of equal value"; 6.4), he goes on to speak of "things that cannot be put into words," like ethics, as both "transcendental" (6.421) and "mystical" (6.522).

In Wittgenstein's early work, the judging self remains speechless in a world of linguistic facts. By contrast, Wittgenstein's later philosophy may be regarded as his attempt to put into words those questions of value that, from the perspective of the *Tractatus*, stood outside the world of facts. Or, perhaps more accurately, Wittgenstein's method in texts like the *Philosophical Investigations* and the remarks on *Culture and Value* rests on the discovery that questions of value are themselves questions of discourse—that the "how" in terms of which values are expressed is constitutive of their nature as facts. As Stanley Cavell's work has made clear, the later Wittgenstein transforms those quintessential questions of fact provoked by skepticism ("Is it real?" "Does the world exist?") into questions of value, the answers to which can be provided only by looking at the ways in which the criteria for the determination of facts are expressed. The evaluative dimension of criteria in turn accounts for the importance Wittgenstein ascribes to the range of phenomena known as "practices" or "forms of life."[8] But in the work of most contemporary analytic philosophers, who stand in closer relation to the theories of reference worked out in, e.g., Quine's *Word and Object*[9] than to Wittgenstein, the relationship between value and expression in Wittgenstein's later work is often lost. In Davidson, for instance, observable behavior constitutes the preeminent criterion for the description of mental processes, attitudes, and states; in principle, these would provide a complete description of the human person:

> With the machine . . . as with the man, we would have to interpret *the total pattern of its observed (or predicted) behavior*. Our standards for accepting a system of interpretation would also have to be the same: we would have to make allowance for intelligible error; we would have to impute a large degree of consistency, on pain of not making sense of what was said or done; we would have to assume a pattern of beliefs and motives which agreed with our own to a degree sufficient to build a base for understanding and interpreting disagreements. ("The Material Mind" 258–59, my emphasis)[10]

In so saying, Davidson reveals himself as having been seduced by those purely epistemological ideals that Wittgenstein's later philosophy attempts to overcome.

We shall later see that Lyotard draws on Wittgenstein's notion of the language game in order to derive an interpretation of the *différend* and, consequently, of judgments as taking place without reference to fixed criteria; he argues that names are like hinges linking different registers of discourse and that the task of judging may be accomplished not by concepts but rather by a process of analogy that attempts to distinguish the modes of formation and the validation of phrases within different language games. Consider, for example, the effect of *différence* that Kant's notion of critique in general and the historical-political realm in particular have on one another:

> The one and the other have to judge without having any rule of judgment, which is different from the juridical-political (which has in principle the rule of law). In other words, just as a critique in Kant's sense cannot give rise to any doctrine (but to criticism), there must not be any doctrine of the historical-political. This relation is perhaps more than an affinity; it is an analogy; a critique (still in the Kantian sense) is perhaps the political in the universe of philosophical phrases, and the political perhaps a critique (in the Kantian sense) in the universe of sociohistorical phrases. (Lyotard, "Introduction a une étude du politique selon Kant" 91).

But let us first look further at Murdoch's complaint that the "behavioristic" assumptions of contemporary analytic philosophy support the fundamentally liberal and utilitarian views that valid judgments are positioned within a public space and that morality must address itself to objectively verifiable acts. According to John Rawls, the distinctive mark of a well-ordered state is its "publicity": "Everyone accepts and knows that the others accept the same principles of justice" (*Theory of Justice* 5).[11] Murdoch's would be an adequate description of certain aspects of liberal and utilitarian thought and of their alliance with a vaguely modernist epistemology, traceable to Hobbes, if it were not also the case that there exists a categorical difference between "public" actions that, as in the marketplace, may be open to full view, and "public" institutions (or practices) that play a role in determining what those actions might mean. And whereas an epistemology might well be powerful enough to address the former, a principle of interpretation drawing on the narrative and dramatistic contexts of action will virtually be required for the latter. Thus Rawls may well describe social institutions as public collections of rules and in so doing speak as if agents knew always and in advance on what grounds they stand, hence what ends they should choose: "In saying that an institution, and therefore the basic structure of society, is a public system of rules, I mean . . . that everyone engaged in it knows what he would know if these rules and his participation in the activity they define were the result of an agreement. A person taking part in an institution knows what the rules demand of him and of the others. He also knows that the others know this and that they know that he knows this, and so on" (*Theory of Justice*, 55–56). But whereas the strict contractarian interpretation of the "original position" of society attempts to legitimize the state of society and its actors as they stand, Rawls's invocation of a principle of neutrality and the guarantees of the fictional "veil of ignorance" are meant to provide agents with a framework in which their own self-characterizations, as revealed against a background of practices, could be conceived as conforming to the ideals of justice. Accordingly, Rawls has forcefully insisted that utilitarianism wrongly attempts to build a vision of society as a whole based on the principles of choice for one person.[12]

It would be instructive to contrast the epistemological constraints operative in the "veil of ignorance" behind which Rawls assumes the first social choices are made, and his understanding of the possibilities for (just) action that are ensured by the notion of institutions formed by contracts or "agreements," with the rhetoric of sublime nescience we find in the work of deconstructive critics like Hillis Miller and Paul de Man, and ask whether the deconstructive posture allows us to characterize actions or the practices they express with the richness, depth, or the view toward ends that would be required if they are to be characterized as just. But Stanley Cavell's critique of Rawls's earlier (1955) paper, "Two Concepts of Rules," provides the basis for a more direct assessment of the relationship between action and background practices and, I think, a compelling statement of the need to judge any interpretation of practices, and the institutions they inform, on the basis of the actions that they enable us to perform. To be sure, Cavell develops moments of anxious self-questioning in his later work—generally moments of sympathy with Freud and Lacan—in which the meaning of our actions seems to disintegrate first under the pressure of skepticism and then under the philosopher's postskeptical gaze; but on this earlier account he locates a certain legitimizing potential in the relationship between practice and action: "Where an action is (performed as?) an instance of a practice or social institution, then the *direct* justification or reason for performing it must be the one which refers the action to that practice. And in such cases, though a Utilitarian justification is relevant, . . . it is so only if it is meant to apply directly to the *practice*, not to the individual action itself" (*Claim of Reason* 292). If, as Cavell seems to suggest, actions have meaning only insofar as they are embedded in the narrative and dramatic structures that comprise our ongoing practices or forms of life, then no truly social practice (including justice, which must be first among these) can be modeled on the individual psyche or soul, for it would be equally accurate to say that the self is modeled *by* "public" practices, institutions, and rules.

In Cavell's interpretation, and in Michael Fischer's account of it here, the linguistic branch of modern philosophy that takes its bearings by Wittgenstein is thus not *just* behavioristic and empiricist in the way Murdoch suggests.[13] According to an interpretation that looks more to Austin than to Wittgenstein, ordinary-language philosophy is behavioristic, if at all, because of its failure to clear free of the philosophical discourse of modernity; this shows up in its inheritance of a series of problems rooted in skepticism, such as "mind-body dualism" and the "existence of the external world," which falsely idealize the claims of knowledge and mystify our relationship to the world. For Cavell, the hold of ordinary, prephilosophical consciousness on the world, like the meaning of ordinary words, begins to disintegrate as soon as it is faced with the skeptic's extraordinary doubts. This initiates a precipitous fall, in which our unexamined beliefs are eroded by the all-consuming power of doubt. In response to the skeptic's doubts, the philosopher continuously seeks to find traces, if only through his words, of the impressions that his actions leave on the world. But the ensuing quest for certainty, which may take temporary cover under a narrowly empiricist conception of the truth, results finally in a (post)philosophical anxiety that leaves the self torn between the sheer force of a will attempting to assert its claims on the world, and the burden of a knowledge (which the self might well like to repress) of its inevitable betrayal of, and by, the world. On Cavell's account, skepticism and analytic philosophy are two sides of the same coin, consisting in the will to knowledge and the denial of it; in skepticism, which denies the embeddedness of knowledge (and, indeed, of existence) in practices, we first "deprive words of their communal possession and then magically and fearfully attempt by ourselves to overcome this deprivation of ourselves by ourselves" ("In Quest of the Ordinary" 197). Hence it is not just the seeing of something, or the laying open of the human world to sight (as in Moore's "Here is one hand") but also, as Fischer explains, "the inability, or unwillingness, to notice something because it is before one's eyes and our wanting to *understand* something that is already in

plain view'' that (pre)occupy Cavell in his reading of Shakespeare and Wittgenstein. Accordingly, it is not enough to say that the work of ordinary-language
philosophy is to restore words to their normal or ''everyday'' use, as to health (a
claim that would provide no line of defense at all against Iris Murdoch's protest
and plea for theory—that "ordinary language is not a philosopher''; *Sovereignty
of Good* 57).[14]

On Cavell's account the philosopher may well find answers to skeptical
doubts, but these come at the price of the wholeness, or integrity, of the world.
The world that philosophy is able to buy back from skepticism is the world in
which history and theory, reason and desire, fact and interpretation, value and
rule, remain divided from within (Lukács would call these the antinomies of
bourgeois thought). At roughly this point, the stage is set for Hegel to recount the
birth of consciousness as the fall into knowledge, and for his subsequent attempt
to reunite history and theory under the aegis of the Whole:

> If the Fall is also to be read as an interpretation of this condition, it is no
> wonder that it seems a Romantic's birthright, not to say obligation, at some
> point to undertake an interpretation of the story of Eden. A dominant in-
> terpretation of it, as in Hegel, if I understand, is that the birth of knowledge
> is the origin of consciousness, hence self-consciousness, hence of guilt and
> shame, hence of human life as severed and estranged, from nature, from
> others, from itself. Hence the task of human life is of recovery, as of one's
> country, or health. I find myself winding up somewhat differently. The ex-
> plicit temptation of Eden is to knowledge, which above all means: to a
> denial that, as we stand, we know. (Cavell, "Genteel Responses" 60–61)

But since there is, on this account, no place in which knowledge is preserved
from skepticism's denials, the self becomes a battleground for the struggle between the claims of a knowledge that it seeks (out of shame or fear or guilt) to
"disown," and a history that it seeks to "disinherit." The result is a mode of
self-assertion that takes the form of self-repression or sacrifice:

> Founders generally sacrifice something (call this Isaac, or call this Dido),
> and teach us to sacrifice something or repress something. And they may
> themselves be victimized by what they originate. . . . As if to demonstrate
> their self-repression, hence their powers to undo this repression, were to
> educate us in self-liberation, and first of all to teach us that self-liberation
> is what we require of ourselves. That this is within our (American) grasp
> means that to achieve it we have above all to desire it sufficiently.
> ("Genteel Responses" 35–36)

On the one hand, the self attempts through these "foundational" efforts to
reclaim the value of existence from philosophical attempts to render it conceptual
and abstract (attempts, as in the case of Othello, to turn "the human condition,
the condition of humanity, into an intellectual difficulty, a riddle"; *Claim of
Reason* 493). Accordingly, it pursues a series of self-reliant stances modeled after

the Emersonian response to Descartes: "I am a being who to exist must say I exist, or must acknowledge my existence—claim it, stake it, enact it" (Cavell, "Being Odd" 282). On the other hand, the interests of history that are said to converge in the Emersonian inheritance of Continental philosophy virtually require this "saying" to become an ironic reenactment of an originally self-repressive act; this generates a (post)philosophical anxiety that is hard-pressed to say whence the ground of its inheritance comes, or where it now stands. The "achievement of the human" requires, on this view, not inhabitation or settlement but abandonment: "Everything depends on your realization of abandonment. For the significance of leaving lies in its discovery that you have settled something, that you have felt enthusiastically what there is to abandon yourself to, that you can treat the others there are as those to whom the inhabitation of the world can now be left" (Cavell, *Senses* 138). But if the self is best realized in departure, then how can it lay claims to public attention that will not be dismantled in the act?

Thus, for Cavell, the diagnosis of skepticism that asks the self to stake a claim beyond, if not against, history and theory, leads to a (post)philosophical anxiety that no longer knows whether it is philosophical or not. In this respect at least, the self-diagnosis of philosophy through the psychoanalysis of skepticism may be more closely aligned with de Man's rhetorical questioning—which, as we are told in *Allegories of Reading*, does not really know whether it is questioning at all—than with the more conservative interpretations of Wittgenstein that Fischer cites. It would not be inappropriate to say, as the essay of Jules David Law makes clear, that in deconstruction metaphor and indeed all modes of discourse are taken as forms or figures of expression built on unlocatable grounds. Metaphor is not so much the realization of intention in an act as it is a "pure performance," which is to say, an act without a ground. Seen in this context it may become clear why deconstruction has been taken by a thinker like Habermas as opposed to the transformative goals of the Enlightenment. For although deconstruction seems to preserve the freedom of self-revision that stands close to the heart of the progressive dimension of the Enlightenment dream (in *Allegories of Reading* de Man speaks of literature as the language through which man "transforms himself"), it seems at the same time to sacrifice "grounds," to lose hold of norms, and to count on the systematic misrepresentation of intentions in acts. Accordingly, it seems to demolish the hope that we might find an appropriate theoretical framework for the expression of our conceptual differences or locate a mode of historical association capable of accommodating our divergent purposes and ends. For de Man, the categories of truth and falsehood can never be reconciled with the rhetoric of persuasion to right and wrong, and yet both make unconditional demands on our attention. Hence in de Man's reading of Kleist, the process of "aesthetic education" into the polis is continuously undermined by the quasi-theatrical circumstances in which the process of instruction takes place, thus raising doubts about whether one might ever be prepared to enter Schiller's "Aesthetic State." And yet the attempt to legislate or read from the standpoint of the

Absolute results only in the defeat of the interpreter by the preexisting conditions of the text. De Man locates the image of one such "transcendental reader" in the figure of Kleist's fencing bear, whose ability is such that he is able to anticipate our moves and interpret each of them as in earnest or false:

> "The bear, as I in my surprise approached him, reared up on his hind legs, his back against the post to which he was chained, his right paw poised for the strike, and looked me in the eye: that was his fencing posture. I thought I must be dreaming to find myself faced with such an opponent, but Herr von G—called, 'Strike! Strike! And try to hit him!' Recovering from my surprise somewhat I made a lunge; the bear made a very short movement with his paw and parried my thrust. I tried fooling him with feints—the bear did not move. With spontaneous agility I lunged once more, and would surely have touched any human breast—the bear made a very short movement with his paw and parried my thrust. I was now almost in the same condition as the young Herr von G—had been. The earnestness of the bear was robbing me of my composure, thrusts and feints followed on one another, I was dripping with sweat: in vain! It was not merely that the bear, like the world's leading fencer, parried every one of my thrusts, but to my feints he reacted not at all (a feat that no fencer anywhere could match). Eye to eye, *as though he could read my very soul*, he stood with his paw poised for the strike, and if my thrusts were not in earnest he simply did not move." ("On the Marionette Theatre" 215-16)

In the context of the discussion surrounding this text, it becomes sufficiently clear that de Man takes this bear to represent Kant, and that deconstruction is de Man's alternative to reading in the face of the claims made by the transcendental principles of the understanding. The de Manian response to Kant avoids the totalizing search for a theory in which questions about any particular interpretation or action must be held in suspense until answers to all (logically) prior questions about interpretation or action can be found; at the same time, deconstruction recognizes our inability simply to circumvent the prior constraints of history and theory and their bearing on the institutional framework in which interpretation is carried out. Hence deconstruction has consistently sought to distinguish itself from the simple destruction of values and to defend itself against the charge that it is a belated form of nihilism. Whether or not deconstruction is at bottom nihilistic, it can nonetheless be said that the range of possible characterizations it has made available to us is so severely circumscribed by an awareness of the wastefulness of interpretation that it has not been able to assist in providing any positive terms for the refashioning of the social self.

For de Man, the process of reading (interpretation) is like fencing with Kleist's bear, "a battle of wits in which both parties are fighting over the reality or fictionality of their discourse, over the ability to decide whether the text is a fiction or an (auto)biography, narrative or history, playful or serious" ("Aesthetic Formalization" 282). Given the nearly systematic erosion of the universality claimed by the Kantian categories of judgment, this hermeneutic performance may have been bound to occur; but since we will inevitably want to evaluate our performances, whatever their grounds, and since our own self-regard will depend largely on whether those performances can lay claims to the attention of others, it may be necessary to pass beyond this groundlessness and ask which modes of discourse best allow for the creation of a self able to judge the performances in which we will inevitably be engaged. It is clear that in de Manian-style deconstruction, interpretation (and political action) must either be seen as trivial and superfluous ("we master the text and then we are able to but have no need to feint"; 282), or it must be regarded as necessary but impossible to achieve ("we don't [master the text] and then we are unable to know whether we feint or not"; 282). In either case, the enterprise is one that de Man himself characterizes as eminently wasteful, and which thus could never form the basis of a workable politics: "Why then indulge in reading (or writing) [or, I would add, in politics] at all since we are bound to end up looking foolish, like the fencer in the story, or to become the undoer of all pleasure and play, like the bear has become by the end of the story, when he has killed off all possibility for play by scoring whenever he designs to enter the fray — which he does only out of defensive necessity" (283).

II

It is within this posttheoretical and posthistorical and, perhaps, postliberal framework that I would situate Charles Altieri's discussion of Rawls and Lyotard. Let us consider Altieri's suggestion that Lyotard's vision of postmodernism and the politics of difference represents a version of "Derrida historicized." Since I have suggested that contemporary analytic philosophy and deconstruction are both posthistorical phenomena, I would dispute this claim[15] and argue that Lyotard represents something closer to Derrida "aestheticized," that *Just Gaming* is, or proposes to be, a "critique of (political) judgment" constructed along the lines of the counterfiction of the "postmodern sublime." But we may nonetheless start with a discussion of Lyotard's own historical description of modernity as that period during which the legitimation of practices was made by means of explicit appeal to the "grand narratives" of what I have called here history and theory. On Lyotard's account, the transition from modernity to postmodernism was brought about by forms of technical and scientific progress that produced a multiplicity of explanatory frameworks, with the corresponding displacement of the relative truth-claims of all of them. It is a story of the latest phase of post-Enlightenment culture as one of fragmentation, or dispersion, roughly akin to the one Flaubert foresaw in *Bouvard and Pécuchet*, in which the organizing centers of knowledge (the various "narratives" that comprise the whole) are successively splintered off from the totality of discourse. Yet whereas Flaubert's characters are left with the sublime emptiness of the Idea, the Lyotardian (postmodern) self is left with the pure heterogeneity of language games. This, rather than Flaubertian irony or decadence, provides Lyotard with the basis for a "pagan" conception of value that is meant to challenge our habitual modes of self-assertion:

> This is what paganism would be. The point is not that one keeps the games, but that, in each of the existing games, one effects new moves, one opens up the possibility of new efficacies in the games with their present rules. And, in addition, one changes the rules: one can play a given game with other rules, and when one changes the rules, one has changed the game, because a game is primarily defined by its rules. And here again it is a problem of inventiveness in language games. (*Just Gaming* 62)

Lyotard himself recognizes that the moves within language games are not wholly arbitrary (we cannot make just *any* moves) and that there must be a faculty or authority capable of determining the rules that constitute each game; thus he must at the same time posit a principle, ultimately one of justice, that would allow us to regulate the purity of the games. What will the principle of justice be? For Kant, the idea that is used to regulate decisions of justice is the totality: in morality this idea is constituted by the totality of reasonable beings; in politics, it is defined by the supersensible unity of humanity. For Emerson (and for Cavell insofar as his reading of Wittgenstein is colored by Emerson) the principle of justice is a reflection of the older notion of desert and rests on a form of self-regulation derived from a modernizing interpretation of Aristotle's concept of "virtue" (*aretai*) as "fate." When Emerson says in "Self Reliance," "Character teaches above our wills. Men imagine that they communicate their virtue or vice only by overt actions, and do not see that virtue or vice emit a breath every moment" (266), he posits character as determining what is due the self and what the self must in turn achieve. For Lyotard, the approach to any regulatory principle—and hence to the question of justice—is wholly bound up with the sublimity of postmodern self-invention. It must bypass the discourse of passivity (fate) as well as the discourse of autonomy (Christian modernity) in favor of the "pagan" discourse of novel self-creation, which in turn validates the principle of freedom as the supreme ethical idea of the (post)modern age:

> The relevant feature is not faithfulness: it is not because one has preserved the story well that one is a good narrator, at least as far as profane narratives are concerned. On the contrary, it is because one "hams" it up, because one invents, because one inserts novel episodes that stand out as motifs against the narrative plot line. . . .
>
> . . . There are even some [games] that are not invented yet that one could invent by instituting new rules; and that is quite interesting. It is in this way that something like the imagination, or the will, I don't know, could develop. . . .
>
> . . . ought . . . does not signal that a field of prescriptions is opening up; it marks a transit point from a descriptive game whose goal is knowledge of

the given, to a prescriptive game (by Ideas) of the exploration of the possible. (*Just Gaming* 33, 61, 59)

It must immediately be said that the tensions between history and theory — which are reproduced in the internal conflicts between reason and desire, fact and interpretation, value and rule, as well as in the various antinomies of judgment that Kant sought to resolve — would be swept magically away if we were to accept this view. In recent debates over the question of modernity, Rorty has tried to strike a bargain with Lyotard by attempting to "split the difference" between the politics of *différence* and Habermas's adherence to the modernist narrative of emancipation grounded in consensus, in favor of the smaller, metaphysically innocuous claims of postmodern bourgeois liberalism (Rorty's version of pragmatism); but in resolving (more accurately, in circumventing) the antinomies of modernist thought, Rorty has in effect effaced the terms involved. What remains after the distinctions between fact and interpretation, reason and desire, value and rule, and a host of other quasi-metaphysical categories have been dissolved is a posthistorical and posttheoretical form of talk that lacks the power of the *différend* and thus falls easily into step with the institutionalized values (largely those of technology) of the society in which it is set. Truth may then simply be described as "what works," and the good may be viewed as a function of innovation or novelty realized, as Rorty says, in the search for "new and more interesting descriptions" of ourselves: "The sense in which human beings alter themselves by redescribing themselves is no more metaphysically exciting or mysterious than the sense in which they alter themselves by changing their diet, their sexual partners, or their habitation. It is just the same sense: viz., new and more interesting sentences become true of them" (*Philosophy and the Mirror of Nature* 351).

If we were to take Rorty seriously here, it would be necessary to augment a discussion of these (post)theoretical language games with an examination of the aesthetic categories on which they rely. Lyotard is in this sense more ambitious than Rorty because he wants to accept "new" and "more interesting" as the categories of a critique of (political) judgment to be undertaken in the absence of transcendental grounds. In Lyotard's hands, the result is a politics of "difference" carried out in the interstices of the existing modes of discourse and that takes its bearings by the obligation to be different: "There is no politics if there is not . . . a questioning of existing institutions, a project to improve them, to make them more just. This means that all politics implies the prescription of doing something else than what is. But this prescription of doing something else than what is, is prescription itself: it is the essence of a prescription to be a statement such that it induces in its recipient an activity that will transform reality" (*Just Gaming* 23).

For Lyotard, the postmodern sublime provides a means to transform the aesthetics of innovation into a political vision and so to concretize the modern notion of freedom that was merely fictional, as in Kant's "other (transcendental) world" or in Schiller's "Aesthetic State." Thus, Lyotard's interest in a "postmodern sub-lime" (the terms are contradictory in some respects) begins as part of his attempt to reclaim the transformative power of desires from all efforts to contain them in the form of a metanarrative (historical) or representational (theoretical) frame-work and so to realize their virtues by overcoming the "otherworldly" (i.e., transcendental) basis on which they had previously been seen to rest. According to Lyotard, modern aesthetics and, presumably, the politics of liberalism as well, are constrained by an adherence to the "good forms" that reflect their nostalgia for the whole: "It allows the unrepresentable to be put forward only as the miss-ing contents; but the form, because of its recognizable consistency, continues to offer the reader or viewer matter for solace and pleasure" (*Postmodern Condition* 81). In his advancement of a postmodern project, Lyotard may be seen as carry-ing forward the modernist vision of a world and of selves that we might be free ever to recreate, but he wants to free these possibilities from their reliance on the purely "fictional" schema of Kant's "other world." Thus, Lyotard sees postmod-ernism as one way to liberate whatever was of value in the modernist vision of the self as open to continuous reinvention from the adherence to a politics of closure and containment, but not simply by invoking the possibility of self-revision within a framework of the totality of mankind or by initiating a search, through the sublime, for forms of expression in which the real is ceaselessly transcended and subsumed by the Ideal. These are all the pathways of modernity and are on his account all equally limited by their "nostalgia" for the (social, historical, theoretical, etc.) whole. Rather, Lyotard envisions postmodernism as the site, or multiple sites, that allow the "unpresentable" to be put forth not simply as the "missing contents" of some incomplete totality; instead, by denying itself the solace of the "good forms" of social, political, aesthetic, and philosophical ex-pression (consensus, harmony, taste), postmodernism challenges us to encounter a "stronger sense of the unpresentable": "The postmodern would be that which, in the modern, puts forward the unpresentable in presentation itself; that which denies itself the solace of good forms, the consensus of a taste which would make it possible to share collectively the nostalgia for the unattainable; that which searches for new presentations, not in order to enjoy them but in order to impart a stronger sense of the unpresentable" (81).

Seen in other terms, Lyotard attempts to liberate the concept of freedom as a form of progress seeking the knowledge of the true nature of man, as outlined for example in Rousseau's *Discourse* "On the Origins of Inequality Among Men," from the retrogressive lapses into history on the one hand and the speculative projections of theory on the other.[16] Rather, the self-creative potential of lan-guage games, as realized in the postmodern sublime, is seen as the posttheore-tical means by which we may make the future present and so render values con-crete. According to Lyotard, the postmodernist works "without rules in order to formulate the rules of what *will have been done.* . . . *Post modern* would have to be understood according to the paradox of the future (*post*) anterior (*modo*)" (81). But since the sublime in its modern (Kantian) mode is bound up with a psychology whose interlinked conditions of imagination and reason the Lyotardian self cannot possibly fulfill, it might be said that Lyotard's step into the "future anterior" results in a loss of values and a desublimation of the world. According to Kant, we experience the sublime when the imagination cannot find forms of representation adequate to its conceptions, or when we find ourselves confronting an idea for which we can find no example. These circumstances produce the ambiguity of a pleasure that derives from the apparently painful experience of reason when faced with its own insufficiency; and yet they generate a shudder of pain that is a source of elevation and an indication of human greatness. But as a posttheoretical thinker who wants to transform the painful pleasures of the sublime into a form of the "gay science," Lyotard must efface the difference between our ability to imagine new possibilities on the one hand and our ability to conceive them on the other. In this way, he seeks a form of self-creation unrestricted by the Kantian "fiction" of an "otherworldly" realm. As that which "puts forward the unpresentable in presentation itself," the postmodern sublime becomes a manifestation of the will attempting to realize the absolute novelty that is available to participants in and inventors of language games.

The aesthetic judgment in its modern (i.e., Kantian) mode is, furthermore, bound up with a series of antinomies that are reflected in the project to construct a social whole on the universalizable bases of judgment (e.g., Kant's "supersensible substrate of humanity"). Consider in this regard the "antinomy of taste" as described in the "Dialectic of Aesthetic Judgment" of the *Third Critique*. On the one hand, the diversity of judgments about taste, which reflect its "merely subjective" basis, have no power to command the assent of others: "The object is *for me* an object of satisfaction; by others it may be regarded quite differently—everyone has his own taste." On the other hand, judgments of taste admit of controversy and so must be based on concepts, which are universalizable; otherwise, Kant argues, we could not so much as quarrel about them. Kant resolves these apparent contradictions by showing that the concepts to which we refer the object are not to be taken in the same sense in both instances of aesthetic judgment. There is, Kant says, a "wider scope of reference" for the representation of both the object and the subject of the aesthetic judgment, in which these contradictions are resolved:

> All contradiction disappears if I say: the judgment of taste is based on a concept (viz., the concept of the general ground of the subjective purposiveness of nature for the judgment); from which, however, nothing can be known and proved in respect of the object, because it is in itself undeterminable and useless for knowledge. Yet at the same time and on that very account the judgment has validity for everyone . . . because its determining ground lies perhaps in the concept of that which may be regarded as the supersensible substrate of humanity. (185)

Some of the advantages of transforming Kant in such a way that the critique of (political) judgment is tied to a psychology of self-assertion free of transcendental assumptions are already apparent from Altieri's discussion of Rawls's theory of justice and Lyotard's heterogeneous language games. For the major portion of its modern history, which Altieri is loathe to forget, political theory has seen its task as one of synthesizing differences or regulating purposes through a series of abstract principles or rules. Throughout the modernist tradition, it has been thought that the theoretical commitments of modernity could be realized within history in the form of a society in which the differences among individuals could be mediated and their social purposes aligned. The notion of a society in which competing conceptions of the good could simultaneously be pursued thus stands at the heart of liberal modernity as a version of Schiller's "Aesthetic State," but not as a unified doctrine or a coherent program. Liberalism universalizes the ground of judgments (e.g., those of taste) but thereby radicalizes modernity's lack of any substantive conception of the good; accordingly, it easily shades off into the choice-ordering politics of utilitarianism. At the same time, modern political theory with roots in analytic philosophy tends to formalize the process of judgment as a mere procedure of choice in an effort to institutionalize a framework that will allow a diversity of goods to be ranked. In this dimension, the liberal vision reinforces the hold of the "iron cage" of bureaucracy (Max Weber) or the "Administered Society" of our day (Felix Rohatyn).

The political philosophy of Rawls, which Altieri invokes against Lyotard, may be situated both within and against this tradition. For whereas the majority of political thinkers, from Plato to Kant, have begun with a theoretical principle that would generate and ensure a hierarchy of competing value-claims, Rawls attempts to build an idea of justice based on the assumption that there is no higher, transcendental principle for synthesizing our diverse interests. Instead, he positions subjects behind a common "veil of ignorance" and asks them to assert their choices and then play out their differences in what Altieri calls a "public theater" of self-expressive action and discourse. In so doing Rawls remains faithful to the goals of the voluntarist line of modernist political theory: to supply a framework in which human subjects, exempt from prejudicial constraints, can be allowed to confirm their autonomy as social agents through the choices they make.

Whether Rawlsian-style liberalism, which leads in a fairly direct way to the politics of social democracy and the economics of the welfare state, is appropriate to the socioeconomic conditions of postmodernism, or whether those conditions have now outstripped the powers of liberal theory, remain important questions, and they are as yet unresolved. It is in any case clear that the Rawlsian political agenda encourages us to posit our differences in order to fashion a social whole rather than to find ways to articulate our differences *given* our preexisting situation within a series of all too pervasive (social, political, economic) wholes. But the initial attractiveness of Rawls's position may become clear if we contrast his account of the hypothetical "original position" of society with the assumptions at work in classical utilitarianism, for it is against the utilitarian analysis of the good that Rawls has made his most powerful claims. Utilitarianism may for

our purposes be described as the attempt to reconcile the two warring conceptions of totality with which any political theory must deal—that of the whole and
that of the all. Utilitarianism attempts to recognize a plurality of goods, interests,
and theories about their relative merits and appropriate distribution (the all),
while constructing society as an ordered state (the whole). In attempting to make
a virtue of these potentially conflicting demands, utilitarianism envisions the organization of society as following from the principles of choice for the
individual.[17] And yet these conflicts cannot entirely be resolved. In order to
ensure the coherence of a social body that permits rival conceptions of the good,
it must be assumed that this hypothetical "individual" occupies the position of
an impartial spectator (a theoretical position aligned with the whole) but is at the
same time ideally sympathetic with the members of the group (the all). According to Rawls,

> It is by the conception of the impartial spectator and the use of sympathetic
> identification in guiding our imagination that the principle for one man is
> applied to society. It is this spectator who is conceived as carrying out the
> required organization of the desires of all persons into one coherent system
> of desire; it is by this construction that many persons are fused into one.
> Endowed with ideal powers of sympathy and imagination, the impartial
> spectator is the perfectly rational individual who identifies with and expe-
> riences the desires of others as if these were his own. . . . This view of
> social cooperation is the consequence of extending to society the principle
> of choice for one man, and then, to make this extension work, conflating
> all persons into one through the imaginative acts of the impartial sympa-
> thetic spectator. (*Theory of Justice* 27)

According to one line of objections, all that utilitarianism gains in freeing us
from a fixed and rigid conception of the good is lost by its continued reliance on
the position of an ideal spectator with access to privileged claims of knowledge;
the vaunted neutrality of this position is thus seen to act as a cover for hidden
claims to power, and the values it generates can best be criticized on ideological
grounds.[18] On a view that has closer affinities with the one taken up by Rawls,
however, the failures of utilitarianism are registered more directly in its deficient
personal psychology. On Rawls's account, the presuppositions of utilitarianism
are such that it results in the conflation of all desires into a single system of
desire; rather than allow the individual to reproduce the many-sidedness of mankind, and thereby render the universal concrete, utilitarianism tends to efface the
difference between persons. Yet insofar as the "ideal spectator" is to resemble a
"person" at all, the position it describes must be fundamentally divided against
itself: for if the spectator's stance is to remain sufficiently detached, personal desires must be ignored; yet full self-interest must be assumed if the spectator is to
reflect the positions of others in the group and command their respect.[19]

In order to fashion a politics independent of the historical and theoretical assumptions of an "ideal spectator" and still preserve a place for the desiring self,

Rawls must invoke the radical fiction of an "original position" of society, free of any *specific* commitments concerning the nature of justice or the particular desires of the members of the social group. The "original position" captures in the form of a hypothesis concerning the access to knowledge of the parties to a contract the fundamentally modernist ideas that we should be free to redescribe ourselves through the choices we make and that our political institutions should impose no prior limitations concerning which version of the good life we may pursue. It is thus meant to secure our roles as social but autonomous value-seeking agents or, as Rawls says in another place, as "self-originating sources of valid claims" ("Kantian Constructivism" 543). The original position is more or less equal in power and scope to that occupied by the "ideal spectator" of classical utilitarianism; but it is not simply a principle of difference, since Rawls must specify equally what the contracting parties in this position *do* and *do not* *know*. What they *do not* know is what would distinguish any one of them from the others as the particular human beings they are;[20] it is in this sense a position of epistemological darkness that is meant to contain, rather than embrace, the difference that a knowledge of these differences would make. As Rawls says, "No one knows his place in society, his class position or social status, nor does any one know his fortune in the distribution of natural assets and abilities, his intelligence, strength and the like. I shall even assume that *the parties do not know their conceptions of the good*" (*Theory of Justice* 12; my emphasis).[21] Yet at the same time the parties to this position *do* know that they, like everyone else, are rational beings and therefore value certain primary goods, that is, "things which a rational man wants whatever else he wants": "Regardless of a person's values, plans, or ultimate aims, it is assumed there are certain things of which he would prefer more rather than less, on the grounds that they are likely to be useful in advancing all ends, whatever ends they happen to be" (Sandel, *Liberalism* 25).

Whether Rawls can coherently maintain these divergent positions—whether he can conceive of a desiring subject apart from any particular objects of desire, and whether his concept of distributive justice does not require a "thicker" self than the "original position" will allow—has already been the subject of much dispute. Bruce Ackerman, for instance, has argued that Rawls effectively establishes the set of the subject's possible choices as infinite while setting the chooser at zero; his inference is that when this Subject Zero confronts the Infinite Choice Set it will be unable to choose *any* principle of justice until *some* set of preferences is invoked (see *Social Justice* 339). Accordingly, Rawls must continuously specify what information will and will not be available to the parties to the social contract. But it is in any case clear that in marshaling Rawls, and by containing the problem of identification within the realm of the "hypothetical," Altieri hopes to appeal to a position that resists the political consequences of postmodernism by embracing its theoretical conclusions in advance, regardless of whether he can resolve the problem of indeterminate characterization in Rawls: "While human beings have probably never agreed on political ends, they have perhaps never had so many available ways to justify disagreement or even to find it impossible to understand what could possibly produce agreement.'' It may in this light become clear why Altieri sees Rawls's principal antagonist as Lyotard, for the heterogeneity of language games outlined in *Just Gaming* may be read as a radicalization of the ''emotivist'' stance described by Alasdair MacIntyre in *After Virtue* or of the voluntaristic ''behaviorism'' criticized by Iris Murdoch in *The Sovereignty of Good*. According to Altieri, ''There is no more pressing challenge to political philosophy than to establish normative models compatible with the diverse local positions that we must take as givens within the polity because there is no higher principle for combining interests or imposing shared criteria.'' This strikes me as an accurate, even admirable way to stake a claim for a politics of discourse that does not rest on ''foundational'' assumptions; but in order to accomplish this, Lyotard must be ''modernized'' and Rawls must be retrospectively transformed into a postmodern thinker who is said to have accomplished a virtually unprecedented feat: beginning from the ''primacy of difference,'' rather than from the principle of identity, this most rational of thinkers is seen to have constructed a ''reflective theater'' (Altieri's term) ''in which the differences can be negotiated and a complex model of hypothetical identifications elaborated.''

A conception of the subject as empty of substance would be the price to pay for the attempt to base a personal psychology, if not also a politics, on Rawls, whose indeterminate concept of identity is further constrained prior to the stage of self-reflection; as another recent critic of Rawlsian liberalism, Michael Sandel, has remarked, ''For a subject such as Rawls' the paradigmatic moral question is not 'Who am I?', for the answer to this question is regarded as self-evident [and, we might add, as given in advance by a prior process of individuation], but rather 'What ends shall I choose?', and this is a question addressed to the will. Rawls' subject would thus appear epistemologically impoverished where the self is concerned, conceptually ill-equipped to engage in the sort of self-reflection capable of going beyond an attention to its preferences and desires to contemplate, and so to re-describe, the subject that contains them'' (*Liberalism* 153). And while Rawls does indeed assert that the good most appropriate to an individual is the outcome of ''careful reflection,'' it remains clear that the objects of this reflection can only be either the various alternative plans and their consequences for the realization of the subject's desires, or the first-order wants and desires themselves.[22] The concept of ''difference'' thus has a primarily empirical and voluntaristic force for Rawls, as the plurality, or diversity, of choices that might go to make a rational life plan, and in none of these ways does reflection focus on the self *qua* subject of desires (see *Liberalism* 159).

Because of these and other limitations of *A Theory of Justice*, Altieri shrewdly supplements Rawls with a series of claims about the nature and plausibility of the ''dramatistic'' tests to which a self must submit in order so much as to fashion an identity or political role. What becomes essential to the operation of justice on this interpretation is not just the ''neutral'' framework of the original bargaining game or the force of competing wills within a competitive or ''agonistic'' arrangement, but the assumption that only agents who can provisionally character-

ize themselves within some interpretive context can also characterize themselves
as just or fair (cf. Rousseau: "The passage from the state of nature to the civil
state produces a truly remarkable change in the individual. It substitutes justice
for instinct in his behavior, and gives to his actions a moral basis which formerly
was lacking"; *Social Contract* I, viii, 185). We must, on this view, describe ourselves as agents of a particular kind (as characters), and these hypothetical identifications, "thick descriptions" of a provisional sort, must be able to meet the
tests of plausibility, if not also of objectivity, if they are to have any hope of commanding any general respect. And yet just as Rawls cannot coherently conceive
of a "general" subject of desire,[23] there is nothing to *guarantee* that the identifications thus adopted will remain provisional and not be torn apart into various
versions of the historically limited particular and the abstract universal. Accordingly, there seems no way to ensure that these "hypothetical" identifications will
be either substantive or transformable in any significant way: insofar as they
remain unrealized they quickly vaporize into wish-fulfillment dreams, yet insofar
as they are concretized they tend to become sedimented as permanent identifications or social structures.

In pointing toward identifications that are neither historical nor theoretical but
hypothetical, we leave off roughly where the problem of modernist politics
begins, namely, with Rousseau's willingness to confront the problem of justice
from a "provisional" point of view by "setting all the facts aside" (Rousseau:
"The researches which can be undertaken concerning [the origins and foundations of inequality among men] must not be taken for historical truths, but only
for *hypothetical and conditional reasonings, better used to clarify the nature of
things than to show their true origin*"; *Second Discourse* 103; my emphasis). In
considering the question of justice, Rousseau takes it as a matter of fact that there
exist a series of natural differences (more precisely, of inequalities) among individuals that cannot be made legitimate or justified. What he seeks specifically to
explain are moral or political inequalities and, on this basis, "by what sequence
of marvels the strong could resolve to serve the weak, and the people to buy
imaginary repose at the price of real felicity" (102), for these are the inequalities
that are reflected in the forms of political association that have been instituted
and agreed to by men ("The various forms of governments derive their origin
from the greater or lesser differences to be found among individuals at the
moment of institution"; *Second Discourse* 171). How can such inequalities be
justified or made legitimate? In the *Second Discourse*, Rousseau addresses these
questions in a two-stage process that forces us to consider the problem of difference as transcending the purely empirical plane: the one sets its sights toward the
"theoretical" problems of human beings, nature, and method, while the other
looks to the genealogy of society and avails itself largely of the language of historical critique. And yet it remains unclear from the *Second Discourse* just how
the differences between theory and history can be reconciled or their languages
linked. We have seen that for Lyotard, history and theory remain heterogeneous
"language games," neither of which has privileged access to the nature of truth;

he can thus regard the moral "ought" as a counterfiction of sorts, that is, as the demystified point of analogy or transition between descriptive and prescriptive language games; but we can also see that there is nothing save the will to regulate the purity of these different games, and that the only plausible imperative this vision can evoke is that statements be different: as a principle of political discourse, *différence* is faced with the implausible task of commanding the invention of rules for what "will have been done."

By contrast, the need to locate a form of discourse within the gap or *décalage* between history and theory is in de Man's reading assigned to literature, which on account of the "metaleptic" relationship between these terms is also "condemned" to being the "truly political mode of discourse" (*Allegories* 157): "The legislator has to invent a transcendent principle of signification called God in order to perform the metalepsis that reverses the temporal pattern of all promisory and legal statements. Since God is said to be, within this perspective, a subterfuge, it follows that the *Social Contract* has lost the right to promise anything. Yet it promises a great deal" (*Allegories* 276). Seen from one perspective, metalepsis reveals the temporal predicament of society and addresses the aporia of history and theory by uncovering the ruse involved in formulating rules to legitimize what "will have been done" (in Rousseau's somewhat less tendentious terms, that "effect should become cause, and the social spirit that the institutions are to produce should preside over their elaboration. Men should be, prior to the laws, what they are to become through them"; cited in *Allegories* 274). According to this view, political discourse derives neither from the need to reconcile the empirical differences between individuals, goods, or theories about their relative merits, nor from the discrepancy between the historical pressures of the real and the seductions of a speculative ideal, but rather from the fundamentally figural process by which some end state is projected or transposed under the name of something else.

Yet it is equally clear that in *The Social Contract* Rousseau has undertaken to explain the nature of political association within a framework of theoretical constraint similar to that which Rawls will later impose: "Since men can by no means engender new powers, but can only unite and control those of which they are already possessed, there is no way they can maintain themselves save by coming together and pooling their strength" (*Social Contract* I, vi, 179). As Althusser once argued, the entirety of *The Social Contract* may be defined by the limitations of the theoretical field in which the problem of justice is posed: "There is thus no transcendental solution, no recourse to a third party, be it God or Chance. The solution cannot be found outside the existing givens, a ruthless enumeration of which has just been established. The only solution possible inside the theoretical field constituted by men and the alienated relations whose authors and victims they are is for them to change their '*manner of existence*' " ("Rousseau" 123). In seeking to bring this social change about, Rousseau is forced to make a succession of "flights forward" into the projective ideal of a utopian state, which desperately needs transcendence but cannot, by his own theoretical lights, invoke it, and "flights backward" into history, which take the form of a regressive economic program that remains powerless to address the conditions of society as it stands. Since neither of these efforts can succeed within the scope of the languages at hand, Rousseau must move toward a new type of writing, a "fiction," whose success remains nonetheless clouded by its symptomatic placement beyond the limits of historical and theoretical discourse. Thus whereas deconstruction sees literature as ethical insofar as it resists desire's demands, literature is in this vision symptomatic of that desire that no ideology has so far been able to resist:

> Flight forward in ideology, regression in the economy, flight forward in ideology, etc. This time the Discrepancy is inscribed in the practice proposed by Rousseau. This practice concerns not concepts, but realities (moral and religious ideology which *exists*, economic property which *exists*). The discrepancy really is in so many words the Discrepancy of theory with respect to the real in its effect: a discrepancy between two equally impossible practices. As we are now in reality, and can only turn round and round in it (ideology-economy-ideology, etc.), there is no further flight possible in reality itself. End of the Discrepancy.
>
> If there is no possibility of further Discrepancies — since they would no longer be of any use in the theoretical order which has done nothing but live on these Discrepancies, chasing before it its problems and their solutions to the point where it reaches the real, insoluble problem, there is still one recourse, but one of a different kind: a *transfer*, this time, the transfer of the impossible theoretical solution into the alternative to theory [*l'autre de la théorie*], literature. The admirable "fictional triumph" of an unprecedented writing [*écriture*]. ("Rousseau" 159)

In this reading of Rousseau, the instability of what de Man calls the "figural" and Altieri the "hypothetical" nature of discourse is overcome, yet not without the significant risk that the gap between history and theory that fiction magically resolves may be taken as an incitement, alternately, to the naive idealism of wish-fulfillment dreams and the cynicism that breeds political despair. While the tensions between history and theory may thus be resolved, we are led to a new and more complex form of the problem of self-division, in which the antinomies of history and theory are reproduced in an unstable psyche that splinters the real into fragments of historical ascesis and projective desire.

In light of these divergent readings of Rousseau, it begins to become clear that any attempt to pass beyond or deconstruct the antinomy of history and theory by recourse to a "third term" of discourse ("literature," "language games," "metaphor") results in a reincorporation of that antinomy as a division within the social, political, or psychological self. In this final analysis of Rousseau the will to overcome these antinomies, hence to deny these desires, is projected onto "literature" itself: as the self seeks recourse in history for the theoretical programs that it cannot complete, literature takes shape as yet another object of desire and another form of denial; as one of Althusser's critics, Jerome McGann, says, literature at once "escapes a subjection to ideology and preserves itself as a weapon for exposing the existence, the precise character, and the domain of particular ideologies (and, sometimes, of ideology in general)" (*Romantic Ideology* 155).

Whereas deconstruction sees literature as "condemned" to a series of projects that it cannot possibly accomplish, and whereas Althusser locates literature as the solution to the work that history and theory could not complete, it would seem more accurate to see literature as a means of mediating between the historical and theoretical levels of all discourse. We may then consider the models of selfhood that literature generates not as the unfathomable origins but rather as the multiple effects of the competing claims made by each of these terms. Since early modern times it has been assumed that the purpose of theory was to defend the "autonomy" of literature—either by reference to social, political, and cultural patterns or practices, or in relation to a more general conception of the nature and coherence of the varieties of discourse; but once we begin to think of literature as shaped by the struggle between the historical and theoretical terms through which the self seeks to express itself and to evaluate the expressions it makes, then the provisional (one might as well say "fictional") identifications that literature provides can be seen not as the sites from which fixed identities might be invoked or an inflexible program of values pursued, but as products of the need to loosen the self-limiting constraints that bear on all such pursuits. Left to their own devices, it is clear that the language of history will lead us to interpret our differences as fate, while the lure of theory will tempt us to resolve those differences within the framework of purely speculative ideals. In light of postmodernism's continued commitment to an idealizing project that invokes no more substantive an image than that of a self open to revision and of a society open to transformation from within, literature begins to emerge as the ground on which the theoretical optimism of philosophy may be reshaped by an awareness of the historicity of every available mode of discourse. As such, literature may be taken as an exemplary site for the making and remaking of the self.[24]

Notes

1. I discuss Lyotard at some length later in this essay. For Rorty, see *Philosophy and the Mirror of Nature*.

2. See Unger, *Passion* and *Social Theory*.

3. Cf. Altieri's claim that Lyotard's understanding of the sublime in *The Postmodern Condition* is "Derrida historicized." This may well be the case, but only on the condition that it is understood that Lyotard supplies no historical principles for the "completion" of the Derridean project.

4. One might in addition mention Charles Taylor's efforts to salvage Hegel for modernity in *Hegel and Modern Society*.

5. Altieri's interpretation of Lyotard seems central in this respect: "The domain of politics exists because there are no universal imperatives and no means for deriving them by interpreting facts, since the facts must be construed within the narrative positions that are privileged by the various phrase regimes and genres of discourse."

6. Cf. Lyotard: "Can one engage in a politics without finality?" (*Just Gaming* 76). Cf. Samuel Weber's afterword to Lyotard's *Just Gaming*, cited by Altieri: "So perhaps there remains nothing for us to do but to judge, to play, to cut to the heart of the matter, to try to arrest the machine in motion, at least for a moment, for a twinkling of an eye, just long enough for a fitful start, judging as always . . . *de justesse*" (120).

7. See Iris Murdoch, *The Sovereignty of Good* 48.

8. Winspur's essay "Text Acts" provides ample discussion of "practice" and "action." Nonetheless we do well to distinguish between Wittgenstein's concept of practice and Aristotle's, as well as between Wittgensteinian therapy, through which we seek "happiness-through-living" (Winspur) and Aristotle's *eudaimonia*. The differences might be summarized by saying that Aristotelian practice makes reference to a concept of (human) nature that is independent of language, whereas Wittgenstein sees language as involved in the creation of human nature.

9. See also "The Ontogenesis of Reference" 80–124.

10. Rorty describes Davidson's "holistic" semantics as "an empirical theory of linguistic behavior, not as a successor subject to Kantian epistemology," in "Kripke versus Kant" 204.

11. Cf. Kenneth Arrow: "Social good, as in the determination of a just income distribution, is an abstraction of some kind from the individual members of the society. But this abstraction can only be based on interpersonally observed behavior, as in market purchases or voting, not in the full range of an individual's feelings" (*The Limits of Organization* 24).

12. See, for example, *Theory of Justice* 15–16.

13. I note in passing Cavell's gloss of Emerson's "far be from me the despair which prejudges the law by a paltry empiricism": "What is wrong with empiricism is not its reliance on experience but its paltry idea of experience" (*Senses of Walden* 126).

14. See also Rosen, *Nihilism*.

15. Thus Lyotard in *Just Gaming*: "There is no reason in history. . . . no one can place himself or herself in the position of an utterer on the course of things. And therefore there is no court in which one can adjudicate the reason of history" (73). But also: "There is no politics of reason, neither in the sense of a totalizing reason nor in that of the concept" (82).

16. Cf. Unger, *Knowledge and Politics*, passim, and also Paul de Man: "[Rousseau's] existential notion of freedom . . . accounts for the ambivalent valorization of all historical change, since any change will always have to put into question the value-system that made it possible: any positive valorization as progress always implies a regress, and Rousseau's text scrupulously maintains this balance. The impossibility of reaching a rationally enlightened anthropology also accounts for the necessary leap into fiction, since no past or present human action can coincide with or be under way towards the true nature of man" (*Allegories of Reading* 141).

17. On the purely theoretical difficulties in accomplishing this, see Arrow, *Social Choice*.

18. For a more serious and sustained discussion of neutrality, see Ackerman, *Social Justice*.

19. Rawls also says that "a rational and impartial sympathetic spectator is a person who takes up a general perspective: he assumes a position where his own interests are not at stake and he possesses all the requisite information and powers of reasoning. So situated he is equally responsive and sympathetic to the desires and satisfactions of everyone affected by the social system. . . . Thus he imagines himself in the place of each person in turn, and when he has done this for everyone, the strength of his approval is determined by the balance of satisfactions to which he has sympathetically responded" (186).

20. See Sandel, *Liberalism* 24.

21. Cf. Lyotard on the nature of justice in modernity: "Since Rousseau, the answer to the question of justice in relation to theoretical discourse, is displaced, because it has been thought that the just will be that which can be prescribed by the set of the utterers of the statements. The position is quite different from the Platonic one, because what the utterers state does not necessarily offer any guidance" (*Just Gaming* 29). Cf. also A. J. Cascardi, "Genealogies of Modernism."

22. Because the Rawlsian self is too thin to be capable of desert in the ordinary sense it must count on legitimate expectations or entitlements. Cf. Sandel: "Claims of desert presuppose thickly-

constituted selves, beings capable of possession in the constitutive sense, but the deontological self is wholly without possessions of this kind. Acknowledging this lack, Rawls would found entitlements on legitimate expectations instead. If we are incapable of desert, at least we are entitled that institutions honor the expectations to which they give rise'' (*Liberalism* 178).

23. This gap points to the obvious advantage of a notion like "social class," which to be useful in other than the strictly Marxist sense would have to be balanced with the liberal focus on individual preferences and rights.

24. I wish to thank Charles Altieri and Richard Eldridge for their comments on a draft of this essay.

Works Cited

Ackerman, Bruce. *Social Justice in the Liberal State*. New Haven, Conn.: Yale UP, 1980.

Althusser, Louis. "Rousseau: The Social Contract." In *Montesquieu, Rousseau, Marx*. Trans. Ben Brewster. London: Verso, 1982.

Arrow, Kenneth J. *The Limits of Organization*. New York: Norton, 1974.

_____. *Social Choice and Individual Values*. 2nd ed. New Haven, Conn.: Yale UP, 1963.

Carroll, David. *Paraesthetics: Foucault, Lyotard, Derrida*. New York: Methuen, 1987.

Cascardi, Anthony J. "Genealogies of Modernism." *Philosophy and Literature* 11 (1987): 207–25.

Cavell, Stanley. "Being Odd, Getting Even: Threats to Individuality." In Thomas C. Heller et al., eds., *Reconstructing Individualism*. Stanford, Calif.: Stanford UP, 1986. 278–312.

_____. *The Claim of Reason*. New York: Oxford UP, 1979.

_____. "Genteel Responses to Kant? In Emerson's 'Fate' and Coleridge's *Biographia Literaria*." *Raritan* 3 (1983): 34–61.

_____. "In Quest of the Ordinary: Themes of Recovery." In Morris Eaves and Michael Fischer, eds., *Romanticism and Contemporary Criticism*. Ithaca, N.Y.: Cornell UP, 1986. 183–240.

_____. *The Senses of Walden*. Expanded ed. San Francisco: North Point Press, 1981.

Davidson, Donald. "The Material Mind." In *Essays on Actions and Events*. Oxford: Clarendon Press, 1982. 245–59.

de Man, Paul. "Aesthetic Formalization in Kleist." In *The Rhetoric of Romanticism*. New York: Columbia UP, 1984.

_____. *Allegories of Reading*. New Haven, Conn.: Yale UP, 1979.

Emerson, Ralph Waldo. "Self Reliance." In *Essays and Lectures*. Ed. Joel Porte. New York: Library of America, 1983. 259–82.

Harpham, Geoffrey. "Language, History, and Ethics." *Raritan* 7 (1987): 128–46.

Ingram, David. "Legitimacy and the Postmodern Condition: The Political Thought of Jean-François Lyotard." *Praxis International* 7 (1987–88): 286–305.

Kant, Immanuel. *Critique of Judgment*. Trans. J. H. Bernard. New York: Hafner Press, 1951.

Kleist, Heinrich von. "On the Marionette Theatre." Trans. Philip B. Miller. In *An Abyss Deep Enough: Letters of Heinrich von Kleist with a Selection of Essays and Anecdotes*. New York: Dutton, 1982.

Kripke, Saul. *Naming and Necessity*. Cambridge, Mass.: Harvard UP, 1972.

Lyotard, Jean-François. "Introduction a une étude du politique selon Kant." In *Rejouer le politique*. Paris: Galilée, 1981. 91–134.

_____, and Jean-Loup Thébaud. *Just Gaming*. Trans. Wlad Godzich. Minneapolis: U of Minnesota P, 1985.

_____. *The Postmodern Condition*. Trans. Geoff Bennington and Brian Massumi. Minneapolis: U of Minnesota P, 1984.

McGann, Jerome. *The Romantic Ideology*. Chicago: U of Chicago P, 1983.

MacIntrye, Alasdair. *After Virtue: A Study in Moral Theory*. Notre Dame: U of Notre Dame P, 1981.

Miller, J. Hillis. *The Ethics of Reading*. New York: Columbia UP, 1987.

Murdoch, Iris. *The Sovereignty of Good*. London: Routledge & Kegan Paul, 1970.

Quine, Willard van Orman. *Word and Object*. Cambridge, Mass.: Technology Press of MIT, 1960.

Rawls, John. "Kantian Constructivism in Moral Theory." *Journal of Philosophy* 77 (1980): 515–72.

_____. *A Theory of Justice*. Cambridge, Mass.: Harvard UP, 1971.

_____. "Two Concepts of Rules." *Philosophical Review* 64 (1955): 3–32.

Rorty, Richard. "Kripke versus Kant." In *London Review of Books: Anthology One*. London: Junction Books, 1981. 198–204.

_____. *Philosophy and the Mirror of Nature*. Princeton, N.J.: Princeton UP, 1979.

Rosen, Stanley. *Nihilism*. New Haven, Conn.: Yale UP, 1969.

Rousseau, Jean-Jacques. *Discourse on the Origins and Foundations of Inequality among Men (Second Discourse)*. Trans. Roger and Judith Masters. New York: St. Martin's Press, 1964.

_____. *The Social Contract*. Ed. and trans. Sir Ernest Barker. New York: Oxford UP, 1962.

Sandel, Michael. *Liberalism and the Limits of Justice*. Cambridge: Cambridge UP, 1982.

Taylor, Charles. *Hegel and Modern Society*. Cambridge: Cambridge UP, 1979.

Unger, Roberto Mangabeira. *Knowledge and Politics*. New York: Free Press, 1975.

_____. *Passion: An Essay on Personality*. New York: Free Press, 1984.

_____. *Social Theory: Its Situation and Its Task*. Cambridge: Cambridge UP, 1987.

Weber, Samuel. "Literature—Just Making It." Afterword to Lyotard and Thébaud, *Just Gaming*. 101–20.

Wittgenstein, Ludwig. *Culture and Value*. Ed. G. H. von Wright. Trans. Peter Winch. Chicago: U of Chicago P, 1980.

_____. *Philosophical Investigations*. Trans. G. E. M. Anscombe. New York: Macmillan, 1953.

_____. *Tractatus Logico-Philosophicus*. Trans. D. F. Pears and B. F. McGuinness. London: Routledge & Kegan Paul, 1961.

Bibliography

Annotated Bibliography

Reed Way Dasenbrock

The purpose of this bibliography is to provide a thorough listing of works available in English that have contributed to the interaction between deconstruction and the analytic tradition, both in philosophy and in literary theory. Works within each tradition that do not engage the other have been omitted, as have applications of each philosophical tradition to issues in literary criticism, since any of these topics would by now be the subject of a book-length bibliography. I have not listed reviews, although some fairly substantial critiques of the books listed here are to be found in reviews; I have listed a few forthcoming publications when I have known of them, but these listings are necessarily extremely selective. The best two introductions to deconstruction in English are Christopher Norris's *Deconstruction: Theory and Practice* (London: Methuen, 1982) and Jonathan Culler's *On Deconstruction: Theory and Criticism after Structuralism* (Ithaca, N.Y.: Cornell UP, 1982); both have useful bibliographies.

For many good reasons, there is not a comparable introduction to the Anglo-American analytic tradition: it is, of course, a far more multifarious and longer-lasting chapter in the history of ideas and therefore much more difficult to summarize and encapsulate. G. J. Warnock's *English Philosophy since 1900* (London: Oxford UP, 1958) and J. O. Urmson's *Philosophical Analysis: Its Development between the Two World Wars* (Oxford: Oxford UP, 1956) offer a good account of the developments in England that gave birth to the analytic tradition. Coverage of the rather more disparate American philosophical scene is more problematic. Although now twenty years old, Richard Rorty's 1967 anthology, *The Linguistic Turn* (Chicago, U of Chicago P), offers a good summary of developments up to the date of its publication, and Rorty's *Philosophy and the Mirror of Nature*, though far from a history of analytic philosophy, offers in its own way an account of recent developments. What follows, therefore, is a fairly complete listing of the works in philosophy and literary theory in English that explicitly engage ideas from thinkers in both traditions, whether they see those traditions as essentially opposed or essentially similar. I have annotated the entries and asterisked what strike me as the essential works.

Abrams, M. H. "How to Do Things with Texts." *Partisan Review* 46, No. 4 (1979): 566–88.
    A criticism of Derrida, Fish, and Harold Bloom as "Newreaders" from a "commonsense" perspective. Briefly contrasts Derrida and Wittgenstein as philosophers of language dividing on whether language works or not.

*Altieri, Charles. *Act and Quality: A Theory of Literary Meaning and Humanistic Understanding*. Amherst: U of Massachusetts P, 1981.
    The most elaborate statement of the interpretation of Wittgenstein as essentially sharing with other

Anglo-American philosophers a commonsense view of meaning sharply opposed to deconstruction. This has been challenged by Staten, Norris, and others. But whether one accepts this view
of Wittgenstein or the theory of interpretation that comes out of it, Altieri is very informative on
the whole tradition of analytic philosophy as it comes to bear on literary questions, on the work
of Grice and Davidson as well as that of Austin and Wittgenstein.

———. "Wittgenstein on Consciousness and Language: A Challenge to Derridean Theory." *MLN*
91, No. 5 (December 1976): 1397–1423.
An early version of part of the argument of *Act and Quality*: Derrida and Wittgenstein are seen as
sharing a critique of traditional, "essentialist" philosophy, but Derrida is still caught in the categories of the philosophy he wants to criticize whereas Wittgenstein moves us firmly beyond
them.

Appiah, Anthony. "Deconstruction and the Philosophy of Language." *Diacritics* 16, No. 1 (Spring
1986): 49–64.
A critique of Christopher Norris's attempt to align deconstruction and analytic philosophy. He
perceptively notes an ambivalence in *The Deconstructive Turn* in that sometimes Norris deconstructs the analytic tradition and sometimes he wants to align the two. But Appiah is less convincing when he argues that the project of alignment is fundamentally misguided.

———. "Strictures on Structures: The Prospects for a Structuralist Poetics of African Fiction." In
Black Literature and Literary Theory. Ed. Henry Louis Gates. London: Methuen, 1984. 127–50.
An incisive criticism of the application of structuralism and poststructuralism to African literature
from a generally analytic standpoint.

Bouveresse, Jacques. "Why I Am So Very unFrench." In *Philosophy in France Today*. Ed. Alan
Montefiore. Cambridge: Cambridge UP, 1983. 9–33.
A delightful essay harshly critical of his French contemporaries by a French philosopher commit-
ted to an analytic standpoint.

Cascardi, A. J. "Skepticism and Deconstruction." *Philosophy and Literature* 8, No. 1 (1984): 1–14.
This essay sharply challenges the familiar notion of Derrida as essentially a skeptic.

Cavell, Stanley. "The Division of Talent." *Critical Inquiry* 11, No. 4 (June 1985): 519–38.
A discussion of the interaction of analytic philosophy and deconstructive literary criticism that is
considerably less sanguine about the current dialogue than most of the contributors to this
volume; discusses the work of de Man, Knapp, and Michaels, and other literary critics, presenting them as examples of "the antagonism between literary and philosophical studies."

———. "Politics as Opposed to What?" *Critical Inquiry* 9, No. 1 (September 1982): 157–78. Re-
printed in *The Politics of Interpretation*. Ed. W. J .T. Mitchell. Chicago: U of Chicago P, 1983.
181–202. And reprinted as "The Politics of Interpretation" in *Themes Out of School: Effects and
Causes*. San Francisco: North Point, 1984. 27–59.
This essay has a number of concerns, but is relevant here for its analysis and critique of the use
Paul de Man makes in *Allegories of Reading* of Austin's terms "performative" and "constative."

———. "In Quest of the Ordinary: Texts of Recovery." In *Romanticism and Contemporary Criticism*. Ed. Morris Eaves and Michael Fischer. Ithaca, N.Y.: Cornell UP, 1986. 183–225.
Although this essay is primarily about romanticism's response to skepticism, it also discusses Heidegger in a generally Wittgensteinian context.

Close, Anthony. "Centering the De-Centerers: Foucault and *Las Meninas*." *Philosophy and Literature* 11, No. 1 (April 1987): 21–36.
Close lines up Austin and Wittgenstein against Foucault and Derrida, arguing that the French critics hold on to the "Husserlian ghost in the machine" they attack, whereas the English philosophers move beyond the old metaphysical preoccupations in a way that enables a defense of traditional intentionalist interpretation. This concise and well-argued article is close to Altieri's and
Abrams's line of argument.

Culler, Jonathan. *On Deconstruction: Theory and Criticism after Structuralism*. Ithaca, N.Y.: Cornell
UP, 1982, particularly "Meaning and Iterability" (110–34).

In this chapter, Culler goes over the Searle-Derrida exchange in *Glyph* in some detail, arguing that Derrida's critique of Austin is completely correct and that any attempt to oppose Austin (and Wittgenstein) to Derrida is unsuccessful. There is some very clear exposition here; for a critique of Culler's arguments in this chapter, see Dasenbrock's "Coming to an Understanding of Understanding."

Dasenbrock, Reed Way. "Accounting for the Changing Certainties of Interpretive Communities." *MLN* 101, No. 5 (December 1986): 1022–41.
This essay is a critique of the explanations of change advanced by Stanley Fish and by deconstruction, arguing that a properly Wittgensteinian criticism gives us a better explanation of why textual meanings change across time.

_____. "Coming to an Understanding of Understanding: Deconstruction, Ordinary Language Philosophy, and Contemporary Critical Theory." *Missouri Review* 7, No. 3 (1984): 234–45.
Primarily an analysis of Culler's *On Deconstruction* that criticizes Culler's preference for Derrida over Austin and Wittgenstein.

_____. "Word-World Relations: The Work of Charles Altieri and Edward Said." *New Orleans Review* 12, No. 1 (1985): 92–96.
An exposition of Said's and Altieri's attempt to move beyond "textualism"; argues that the analytic tradition Altieri draws on is more useful in this regard than deconstruction.

de Man, Paul. *Allegories of Reading: Figural Language in Rousseau, Nietzsche, Rilke, and Proust.* New Haven, Conn.: Yale UP, 1979, especially "Semiology and Rhetoric" (3–19).
Relevant here for its use of Austin's terms "performative" and "constative," which de Man conflates with a series of other oppositions, including rhetoric and semiology and Frege's terms "sense" and "reference"; de Man's use of Austin is heavily criticized by Cavell in "Politics as Opposed to What?"

*Derrida, Jacques. "Limited Inc abc." Translated by Samuel Weber. *Glyph* 2 (1977): 162–254.
This is Derrida's response to Searle's response to "Signature Event Context." One of the key moments in the interaction of the two traditions, this piece has been extensively discussed by Culler, Norris, Staten, Spivak, Weber, and others. Depending upon one's point of view, this essay is either a brilliant deconstruction of Searle or very irritating.

*_____. "Signature événement contexte." In *Marges de la philosophie.* Paris: Editions de Minuit, 1972. Trans. Samuel Weber and Jeffrey Mehlman. "Signature Event Context," *Glyph* 1 (1977): 172–97. Also available in *Margins of Philosophy.* Trans. Alan Bass. Chicago: U of Chicago P, 1982. 309–30.
Far more "serious" in tone than "Limited Inc abc," this is a careful critique of Austin's "logocentrism" that links up with his critique of Plato, Saussure, Lévi-Strauss, and others in *Of Grammatology.* Discussed by Culler, Norris, Staten, Fish, Weber, and others.

*Felman, Shoshana. *Le Scandale du corps parlant.* Paris: Editions du Seuil, 1980. Trans. Catherine Porter. *The Literary Speech Act: Don Juan with J. L. Austin, or Seduction in Two Languages.* Ithaca, N.Y.: Cornell UP, 1983.
A marvelous study of Austin that sharply distinguishes him from more systematic speech-act theorists such as Benveniste or Searle. Criticized by Culler for attributing to Austin everything she learned from Derrida's critique of Austin, Felman more than anyone else has allowed us to see Austin as a mediating figure between Derrida and Searle, which was a crucial step in opening a dialogue between the two traditions.

Fischer, Michael. "Speech and Writing in *The Senses of Walden.*" *Soundings* 68, No. 3 (Fall 1985): 388–403.
Argues that Cavell in *The Senses of Walden* adumbrates a more constructive response to the skepticism of deconstruction than the commonsense approach of M. H. Abrams.

Fish, Stanley E. "With the Compliments of the Author: Reflections on Austin and Derrida." *Critical Inquiry* 8, No. 4 (Summer 1982): 693–721.
A discussion of "Signature Event Context" and Austin's *How to Do Things with Words* that more

carefully (or with less dash) comes to much the same conclusion as Felman, namely, that Austin and Derrida are in many respects closer to each other than Austin is to Searle.

Fuller, Steven. "Is There a Language-Game That Even the Deconstructionist Can Play?" *Philosophy and Literature* 9, No. 1 (1985): 104–7.
A response to Cascardi's essay that restates the customary view of Derrida as a skeptic.

Garver, Newton. Preface to Jacques Derrida, *Speech and Phenomena and Other Essays on Husserl's Theory of Signs*. Evanston, Ill.: Northwestern UP, 1973. ix–xxix.
Garver argues that "Derrida's critique of Husserl is a first-class piece of analytic work in the philosophy of language," and he relates it to Wittgenstein's critique in his later philosophy of his own earlier work.

Grene, Marjorie. *Philosophy in and out of Europe*. Berkeley: U of California P, 1976, especially "Life, Death, and Language: Some Thoughts on Wittgenstein and Derrida" (142–54).
A comparison of Wittgenstein and Derrida that establishes both similarities and contrasts; part of a larger argument that Anglo-American philosophers should not ignore Continental philosophy or forget the Continental roots of much analytic philosophy.

Guetti, James. "Wittgenstein and Literary Theory I." *Raritan* 4, No. 2 (1984): 67–84.
Like Abrams and Altieri, sees Wittgenstein as an antiskeptical philosopher who has a "disruptive force" on deconstruction; also uses Wittgenstein to contest the claims of literary theory in general.

———. "Wittgenstein and Literary Theory II." *Raritan* 4, No. 3 (1985): 66–84.
Continues the use of Wittgenstein to criticize literary theory. Some good discussion of Wittgenstein's criticism of systematic philosophizing, but his application of this to literary theory is weakened by his failure to define literary theory. What distinguishes his own critique of theory from theory?

Johnson, Barbara. *The Critical Difference: Essays in the Contemporary Rhetoric of Reading*. Baltimore: Johns Hopkins UP, 1980, especially "Poetry and Performative Language: Mallarmé and Austin" (52–66).
This is a critique of Austin's work directly based on Derrida's "Signature Event Context."

Llewelyn, John. *Derrida on the Threshold of Sense*. New York: St. Martin's Press, 1986.
One of a number of recent studies placing Derrida in the context of Continental philosophy. Points out similarities between the work of Derrida and Wittgenstein, but does not engage in any systematic exposition of these similarities.

Mitchell, Sollace. "Post-structuralism, Empiricism and Interpretation." In *The Need for Interpretation: Contemporary Conceptions of the Philosopher's Task*. Ed. Sollace Mitchell and Michael Rosen. London: Athlone Press, 1983. 54–89.
An examination of Derrida's theory of meaning from an analytic perspective that criticizes "the idealist semantic theory found in post-structuralism [for failing] to give us any clues as to why our words are meaningful, either in terms of a referential relation holding between sign or thing or in terms of what a speaker must know if he is to understand the language." The volume from which this essay comes is of interest; it is a collection of pieces by analytic philosophers dissatisfied with analytic philosophy but not fully embracing any of the alternatives either.

Mulligan, Kevin. "Inscriptions and Speaking's Place: Wittgenstein and Derrida." *Oxford Literary Review* 3, No. 2 (1978): 62–69.
Assimilates Derrida to Wittgenstein's "deconstructions of metaphysical positions"; focuses on the problematic implications of taking speech—not writing—as the norm for constructing a theory of meaning.

*Norris, Christopher. *The Contest of Faculties: Philosophy and Theory after Deconstruction*. London: Methuen, 1985, especially "Sense, Reference and Logic: A Critique of Post-Structuralism" (47–65), "Philosophy as a Kind of Narrative: Rorty on Post-Modern Liberal Culture" (139–66), and "On Not Going Relativist (where it counts): Deconstruction and Convention T" (193–217).

This collection of essays explores a number of interconnections among analytic philosophy, deconstruction, and issues in literary theory. "Sense, reference and logic" summarizes Frege's distinction between sense and reference and argues that Frege's work does not support a theory of reference that could be used against poststructuralism. "Philosophy as a Kind of Narrative" begins a critique of Rorty continued in this volume. "On Not Going Relativist" summarizes the work of Donald Davidson, arguing—in contrast to Wheeler—that Davidson's work offers the "only alternative to the sceptical rigours of deconstruction."

_____. *The Deconstructive Turn*. London: Methuen, 1983, especially "Deconstruction and 'Ordinary Language': Speech versus Writing in the Text of Philosophy" (13–37), "The Insistence of the Letter: Textuality and Metaphor in Wittgenstein's Later Philosophy" (34–58), " 'That the Truest Philosphy Is the Most Feigning': Austin on the Margins of Literature" (59–84), and "Deconstruction, Naming and Necessity: Some Logical Options" (144–62).
The first three essays on Ryle, Wittgenstein, and Austin argue both that in some respects their positions are close to deconstruction and also that where they are not, they are vulnerable to a deconstructionist critique. This book is mainly a deconstructive analysis of the analytic tradition; in the later *Contest of Faculties*, Norris instead urges an assimilation of two equally valuable traditions. "Deconstruction, Naming and Necessity" marks the shift in positions, as it argues that Kripkean semantics may be capable of meeting the challenge of deconstruction. See Appiah for a critique of Norris's project.

_____. "Home Thoughts from Abroad: Derrida, Austin, and the Oxford Connection." *Philosophy and Literature* 10, No. 1 (1986): 1–25.
Like Felman's book and Fish's essay, a treatment of the relation between Derrida and Austin that positions Austin as closer to Derrida than one might think; interesting for the ways it also positions Derrida as close to the traditions of Oxford philosophy.

Novitz, David. "Metaphor, Derrida, and Davidson." *Journal of Aesthetics and Art Criticism* 44, No. 2 (Winter 1985): 101–14.
Novitz finds Derrida's and Davidson's views on metaphor, although they initially seem completely opposite, to be essentially similar and fundamentally in error.

*Petrey, Sandy. "Castration, Speech Acts, and the Realist Difference: *S/Z* versus *Sarrasine*." *PMLA* 102, No. 2 (March 1987): 153–65.
An extremely interesting essay that deconstructs along Austinian lines Roland Barthes's deconstruction of Balzacian realism in *S/Z*. Petrey's argument is that "speech-act theory furnishes a way to defend realism's classic definition as the literature of social specificity," once the language of extratextual, objectively valid reference is replaced by that of constative utterance, true relativized to a social scheme or language.

Pradhan, Shekhar. "Minimalist Semantics: Davidson and Derrida on Meaning, Use, and Convention." *Diacritics* 16, No. 1 (Spring 1986): 66–77.
Relates Davidson and Derrida in their denial of a conventional theory of meaning and their contention that "signs are born semantically free."

Putnam, Hilary. "A Comparison of Something with Something Else." *New Literary History* 17, No. 1 (Autumn 1985): 61–79.
Primarily a comparison of Quine and Rorty that also compares Quine's views on truth and reference to Derrida's and criticizes all three for their "transcendental Skinnerianism," their inconsistent talk of some views being better than others, despite their (pretending to) abandon talk of "truth."

_____. *Reason, Truth and History*. Cambridge: Cambridge UP, 1981, especially "Reason and History" (150–73).
Putnam criticizes the work of Michel Foucault in the context of a general and penetrating attack on relativist notions of truth.

*Rorty, Richard. *Consequences of Pragmatism: Essays 1972–1980*. Minneapolis: U of Minnesota P, 1982, especially "Philosophy as a Kind of Writing: An Essay on Derrida" (90–109) and "Nine-

teenth-Century Idealism and Twentieth-Century Textualism'' (139–59).
A collection of essays that continues the project of *Philosophy and the Mirror of Nature*, extending it to philosophers and critics not focused on in that book.

————. "Deconstruction and Circumvention." *Critical Inquiry* 11, No. 1 (September 1984): 1–23.
Argues that the influence of Derrida and deconstruction may have oversold us on the importance of philosophy and the "ontotheological tradition" within it. Some shrewd criticism of Derrida's betrayal of his own project by producing a "new metalinguistic jargon." Putnam's "A Comparison" argues that Rorty's own position has the same weakness; also see Staten's response.

————. "The Higher Nominalism in a Nutshell: A Reply to Henry Staten." *Critical Inquiry* 12, No. 2 (Winter 1986): 461–66.
A friendly reply to Staten's critique of Rorty's "Deconstruction and Circumvention" that sees Staten—not himself—as the one still operating within a traditionally philosophical framework.

*————. *Philosophy and the Mirror of Nature*. Princeton, N.J.: Princeton UP, 1979.
An extremely important and influential book that lines up Wittgenstein, Heidegger, and Dewey as the three great "antifoundationalist" philosophers who have abandoned the claims of philosophy to provide a systematic ground for our ways of knowing. Important in this context for the way it perceives the work of Wittgenstein and American pragmatism as parallel to that of Heidegger in ways that break down a rigid distinction between the Continental and Anglo-American philosophical traditions. Also extremely informative on the analytic tradition it criticizes from within.

————. "Philosophy without Principles." *Critical Inquiry* 11, No. 3 (March 1985): 459–65. Reprinted in *Against Theory: Literary Studies and the New Pragmatism*. Ed. W. J. T. Mitchell. Chicago: U of Chicago P, 1985. 132–38.
A response to Knapp and Michaels's "Against Theory."

*Searle, John R. "Reiterating the Differences: A Reply to Derrida." *Glyph* 1 (1977): 198–208.
A widely discussed response to Derrida's critique of Austin in which Searle takes on the role of representative for the Anglo-American tradition. See Derrida's response in turn and discussions by Staten, Norris, Culler, and others.

Shusterman, Richard. "Analytic Aesthetics, Literary Theory, and Deconstruction." *Monist* 69, No. 1 (January 1986): 22–38.
A discussion of how the traditions of analytic aesthetics and deconstruction have ignored each other; argues that deconstruction avoids the confrontation with analytic aesthetics because of deconstruction's origins in Crocean aesthetics, sharply challenged by analytic aesthetics a generation ago.

————. "Deconstruction and Analysis: Confrontation and Convergence." *British Journal of Aesthetics* 26, No. 4 (Autumn 1986): 311–27.
Shares the starting point of "Analytic Aesthetics" that analytic aesthetics and deconstruction have ignored each other; influenced by Rorty, sketches some possible ways analytic aesthetics can respond more positively and fruitfully to deconstruction.

Spivak, Gayatri Chakravorty. "Revolutions That as yet Have No Model: Derrida's *Limited Inc*." *Diacritics* 10, No. 4 (December 1980): 29–49.
A discussion of Derrida's response to Searle that is unqualified Searle-bashing: "Derrida exposes Searle's critique to be off the mark in every way."

Staten, Henry. "Rorty's Circumvention of Derrida." *Critical Inquiry* 12, No. 2 (Winter 1986): 453–61.
Criticizes Rorty's "Deconstruction and Circumvention" for reading Derrida "as a philosopher reads," disregarding "most of what is involved in Derrida's *writing*."

*————. *Wittgenstein and Derrida*. Lincoln: U of Nebraska P, 1984.
An extremely important study that lines up Wittgenstein and Derrida as parallel in their deconstruction of traditional metaphysics and sharply challenges the presentation of Wittgenstein by Altieri, Abrams, and others as offering a contrast to Derrida. Perhaps goes too far in assimilating the two figures, but valuable—like Felman—in the way it makes Wittgenstein out to be a medi-

ating figure and suggests "an Anglo-American context within which deconstruction makes philosophic sense." Also contains a discussion of the Derrida-Searle exchange.

————. "Wittgenstein's Boundaries: A Reply to John Ellis." *New Literary History* 18, No. 2 (Winter 1988): 309–18.

————. "Wittgenstein and the Intricate Evasions of 'Is.' " *New Literary History* 18, No. 2 (Winter 1988): 281–300.

Weber, Samuel. "It." *Glyph* 4 (1978): 1–31.
More Searle-bashing by the editor of *Glyph* and translator of "Signature Event Context" and "Limited Inc abc" who initiated the Derrida-Searle exchange in the first place.

Wheeler, Samuel C. III. "The Extension of Deconstruction." *Monist* 69, No. 1 (January 1986): 3–21.
An exposition of deconstruction in the terms of analytic philosophy that sees Derrida's notion of deconstruction as closely compatible with Quine's work on indeterminacy of translation and his denial (or deconstruction) of the analytic-synthetic distinction.

————. "Indeterminacy of French Interpretation: Derrida and Davidson." In *Truth and Interpretation: Perspectives on the Philosophy of Donald Davidson.* Ed. Ernest LePore. Oxford: Basil Blackwell, 1986. 477–94.
Continues the project of "The Extension of Deconstruction" of translating Derrida's ideas into analytic language. Compares Derrida's notion of the indeterminacy of intepretation to Davidson's notion of radical interpretation.

————. "Wittgenstein as Conservative Deconstructor." *New Literary History* 18, No. 2 (Winter 1988): 239–58.
Compares Wittgenstein's attempt to guard against theorizing to deconstruction's attempt to deconstruct all systematic hierarchies; a sensitive comparison alert to resemblances and differences.

Winspur, Steven. "Wittgenstein's Semiotic *Investigations.*" *American Journal of Semiotics* 3, No. 2 (1984): 33–57.
An insightful close reading of the *Investigations* that relates it to the discipline of semiotics.

Wright, Edmond. "Derrida, Searle, Contexts, Games, Riddles." *New Literary History* 13, No. 3 (Spring 1982): 463–77.
Criticizes Altieri, Searle, and others for arguing that we can stabilize textual meanings by referring to shared conventions and rules: "Constitutive rules can specify the coincidence of agreement, but they can never specify what responsible agents individually understand by that agreement."

Wyschogrod, Edith. "Time and Non-Being in Derrida and Quine." *Journal of the British Society for Phenomenology* 14 (1983): 112–26.
Sees a convergence between Derrida and Quine in their moves "against the epistemic difficulties of classical empiricism, an effort to fashion 'an empiricism without dogmas.' " Focuses particularly on their attention to the temporality of language.

Notes on Contributors

Charles Altieri is Professor of English at the University of Washington. He is the author of *Enlarging the Temple* (Bucknell University Press, 1979); *Act and Quality* (University of Massachusetts Press, 1981), the most thorough application of the work of Wittgenstein and Anglo-American philosophy of language to issues in literary theory; *Self and Sensibility in Contemporary American Poetry* (Cambridge University Press, 1984); and the forthcoming *Thinking through Literature: Essays in the Pragmatics of Aesthetic Idealism.*

Anthony J. Cascardi is Associate Professor of Comparative Literature at the University of California, Berkeley. He is the author of *The Bounds of Reason: Cervantes, Dostoyevsky, Flaubert* (Columbia University Press, 1986) and the editor of *Literature and the Question of Philosophy* (Johns Hopkins University Press, 1987).

Reed Way Dasenbrock is Associate Professor of English at New Mexico State University. He is the author of *The Literary Vorticism of Ezra Pound and Wyndham Lewis* (Johns Hopkins University Press, 1985) and the editor of a critical edition of Wyndham Lewis's *The Art of Being Ruled* (Black Sparrow, 1989).

Michael Fischer is Associate Professor of English at the University of New Mexico and is the author of *Does Deconstruction Make Any Difference?* (Indiana University Press, 1985) and coeditor of *Romanticism and Contemporary Criticism* (Cornell University Press, 1986).

Jules David Law is Assistant Professor of English at Northwestern University. In addition to his essay "Uncertain Grounds: Wittgenstein's *On Certainty* and the New Literary Pragmatism," he has a book-length manuscript nearing completion on Dickens, Conrad, and Joyce.

Christopher Norris teaches English at the University of Wales and has been a visiting professor at a number of universities, including the University of California at Berkeley and CUNY Graduate Center. He is the author of *William*

Empson (1978), *Deconstruction: Theory and Practice* (1982), *The Deconstructive Turn* (1983), *The Contest of Faculties: Deconstruction, Philosophy and Theory* (1985) (all published by Methuen), and, most recently, *Jacques Derrida* (Fontana Modern Masters, 1987) and *Paul de Man and the Critique of Aesthetic Ideology* (Methuen, 1988).

Richard Rorty, one of the most distinguished of contemporary analytic philosophers, is Kenan Professor of Humanities at the University of Virginia and the author of *Philosophy and the Mirror of Nature* (Princeton University Press, 1979) and *Consequences of Pragmatism: Essays, 1972–1980* (University of Minnesota Press, 1982).

Richard Shusterman is Associate Professor of Philosophy at Temple University. He is the author of *The Object of Literary Criticism* (Rodopi, 1984) and *T. S. Eliot and the Philosophy of Literary Criticism* (Columbia University Press, 1988), and the editor of *Analytic Aesthetics* (forthcoming from Basil Blackwell).

Henry Staten is Professor of English and Philosophy at the University of Utah and is the author of *Wittgenstein and Derrida* (University of Nebraska Press, 1984).

Samuel Wheeler is Professor of Philosophy at the University of Connecticut and the author of a number of studies relating deconstruction to analytic philosophy.

Steven Winspur is Associate Professor of French at Columbia University; in addition to a number of articles on Wittgenstein, semiotics, and literary theory, he is the author of *St. John Perse and the Imaginary Reader* (Druz, 1988). He is currently writing a book on the way texts change their readers' worlds, entitled *Literary Pragmatics*.

Index

Abrams, M. H., 8, 13, 49-54, 56-57, 58n; "Construing and Deconstruction," 50, 52, 59n; "The Deconstructive Angel," 52; "How to Do Things with Texts," 50-53
Ackerman, Bruce: *Social Justice*, 236, 242n
Adorno, Theodor W., 186n
Alexander the Great, 30
Althusser, Louis, 23, 239-41; "Rousseau: The Social Contract," 239-40
Altieri, Charles, 8, 13, 23, 49-54, 56-57, 144, 171, 187n, 220, 229, 234, 237, 240, 241n, 242n, 243n; *Act and Quality*, 6, 51-52, 54, 59n, 89n; "From Expressivist Aesthetics to Expressivist Ethics," 89n; *Thinking through Literature*, 87n; "Wittgenstein on Consciousness and Language: A Challenge to Derridean Literary Theory," 49, 51, 53, 164n
Analytic philosophy, 4-5, 9-20, 27-28, 37-40, 62, 76, 94, 96, 106-7, 110, 116-17, 122-23, 135, 163, 191, 217-20, 222-25, 234
Anscombe, Elizabeth, 5
Aphrodite, 33
Appiah, Anthony, 15-16
Aristotle, 3, 29-31, 93, 102, 106, 111n, 128-29, 135, 173, 177-78, 213n, 214n, 230, 242n; *Nicomachean Ethics*, 186n; *Poetics*, 143-44, 148
Arrow, Kenneth J.: *The Limits of Organization*, 242n; *Social Choice and Individual Values*, 242n
Augustine, Saint, 148
Austin, J. L., 6-12, 14, 50, 53-54, 58n, 137n, 164n, 169-73, 177, 184, 186n, 195, 207, 225; *How to Do Things with Words*, 6, 24n, 169-72, 185n; "Other Minds," 53

Barthes, Roland, 104
Bataille, Georges, 196
Baudrillard, Jean, 74, 86, 87-88n, 89n; *Simulacres et simulation*, 88n; *Les Stratégies fatales*, 88n
Beardsley, Monroe C., 3, 92, 111n
Bennington, Geoff, 89n, 202n; "August: Double Justice," 75n, 88n
Benziger, James, 99
Bergson, Henri, 24n, 64, 106, 215n
Berkeley, George, 8, 117, 128, 140-41, 158; *Three Dialogues between Hylas and Philonous*, 140
Blackmur, R. P., 3
Blocker, Gene, 90n
Bloom, Harold, 205
Bohr, Niels, 32-33

257